Extraordinary Anthropology

Extraordinary Anthropology

Transformations in the Field

EDITED BY Jean-Guy A. Goulet
AND Bruce Granville Miller

WITH A PREFACE BY Johannes Fabian

UNIVERSITY OF NEBRASKA PRESS
LINCOLN & LONDON

Portions of "On Puzzling Wavelengths"
originally appeared in *Journeys to
the Edge: In the Footsteps of an
Anthropologist* by Peter M. Gardner, by
permission of the University of Missouri
Press. © 2006 by the Curators of the
University of Missouri.

"Moving Beyond Culturally Bound Ethical
Guidelines" was first published in 2004
as "Une question éthique venue de l'autre
monde: Au-delà du grand partage entre
nous et les autres," in *Anthropologie et
Sociétés* 28 (1): 109–26.

Library of Congress Cataloging-
in-Publication Data

Extraordinary anthropology :
transformations in the field / edited by
Jean-Guy A. Goulet and Bruce Granville
Miller ; with a preface by Johannes Fabian.
p.   cm.
Includes bibliographical references
and index.
ISBN-13: 978-0-8032-5992-8
(pbk. : alk. paper)
ISBN-10: 0-8032-5992-1
(pbk. : alk. paper)
1. Ethnopsychology. 2. Dreams.
3. Ecstasy. 4. Ethnology—Field work.
I. Goulet, Jean-Guy. II. Miller, Bruce G., 1951–
GN502.E98 2007
305.8—dc22
2006036210

To Victor Turner and Edith Turner,
who have inspired so many within
anthropology and beyond

Contents

Contents

Preface

Anthropological field research is a means toward an end: ethnographic knowledge. Being a practice in the service of a discipline, it must rely on tried and tested habits, techniques, and strategies. It must serve a scientific, hence public, purpose rather than the needs and desires of a person; it must pursue theory rather than a private quest. This has been the conventional and reasonable view of the matter. But it is hardly a secret anymore—at a time when ethnography has become a matter of concern and a subject of debate among philosophers, students of culture (if that is an appropriate label for those engaged in "cultural studies"), other social scientists, including historians, and even among artists—that our conventional certainties are no longer what they used to be.

This is not the place to tell the story of our certainties getting shattered; it is too long and complicated. Instead, it occurred to me that it may be of interest to recall just one intriguing episode. When I received my training at the University of Chicago, in a department that was hardly a marginal contributor to establishing anthropology as a modern, empirical, and scientific endeavor, separate courses on field methods were not part of the curriculum. Why? Other things were more important. Our critical energies were channeled toward discussion of theory. Debating theory rather than worrying about practice was a luxury we enjoyed, but not for long. Momentous changes brought about in our "fields" by incipient de-colonization abroad and social upheavals at home forced us to rethink the premises of our projects and to say what had gone without saying for a long time. Critical anthropology emerged, inspired by Marxism, European phenomenology, American pragmatist philosophy, and (Batesonian) ecology, and when we almost believed (falsely, of course) that the critical work had been done, there came Hayden White, Michel Foucauld, Edward Said, and others. Perhaps they seduced some of us to new kinds of grand theorizing and wallowing in post-modernism, but there is no doubt that they also moved us to new levels of critical reflection on what anthropologists actually do when they work in the field and at home.

Where does this collection of essays fit in the current anthropological landscape? When we want to characterize publications as being important, we often call them seminal; they were, or are likely to become, seeds. We have no corresponding term to designate work that brings in an exceptional harvest. In the historical perspective in which I read this volume, I cannot help but see it as reaping the fruits of critical labors that anthropology undertook, or had forced upon itself, during the last four decades. Most exciting for me has been to find, in chapter after chapter, evidence that distinctions and oppositions that once were thought essential to maintain—subjective versus objective, science versus politics, being agnostic versus being a believer, control versus abandon, to name but a few—appear to have been re-cast as what they should have been all along: quandaries that generate tension, and creative efforts producing knowledge that would have been impossible to attain (or to present) had anthropology persisted in the paradigms that were dominant a generation ago.

Moreover, as the editors make it clear in their introduction, theirs is by no means an idiosyncratic enterprise. They join a growing "literature." I use this term advertently because it seems obvious to me that the writing represented here has matured into a genre expressive, as is the case of all genres that are alive, of a shared communicative praxis. It is a genre in which involved narration rather than monographic representation predominates but manifestly not to the detriment of scholarship and critical discussion. No matter what their orientation in anthropology may be, and taking into account that a certain boldness displayed in these essays may cause anxieties or aversion, reasonable readers—all of us, we assume—will not be justified in dismissing what is offered here as gratuitous navel-gazing, hypertrophic reflexivity, exhibitionist confessionalism, or whatever the invectives may have been in recent years.

Lest I get carried away with praise, I should add a few critical remarks. Gratifying as the positive response to my observations on ecstatic moments, not as impediments but as integral parts of field research, may be, the prescription, if it is one, should be treated with caution. The ecstatic in our work is not limited to "the field," a point made by the editors and one of the contributors, Guy Lanoue. He warns us against the dangers of a new kind of spatialization-cum-reification of the "field" that may have the effect of forgetting time—the time it takes to make and represent ethnographic knowledge after having left the field. Another point is perhaps of a more personal nature. The position I reached with the essay subtitled "From Rigor to Vigor," and later in *Out of Our Minds*, had a history, one part of which seems to have gone unnoticed: the inspiration my generation of critical anthropologists took from Dell Hymes and his "ethnography of communication." Neither he nor some other important contributors to that particular turn in the recent history of our discipline are mentioned in this volume.

I am not suggesting that this is an omission that should be remedied. Such seeming absence may, as is often the case, be proof of effective presence. Nevertheless, we should keep the memory of where "we come from" alive. Finally, I must confess that reports of ethnographers embracing either the religion of those they study or some other religious faith (particularly Catholicism; see the repeated references to Victor and Edie Turner who became Catholics following their experience of rituals, both of healing and of initiation, among the Ndembu, in Africa) make me uneasy. As a certified Catholic agnostic I would not for a moment deny the importance of religious knowledge, especially of the kind of bodily experience that comes from participating in ritual, in ethnographic inquiries of religion—as long as this does not make us ignore the fact that the discipline that got us to where we are now had its beginnings during the Enlightenment as part of a movement of emancipation from religion. Arguably, that movement has not ended with success, but it should not be abandoned either.

Does this not also hold, analogously or homologously, for anthropology itself? Crossing boundaries between faith and science, dream and reality, reason and madness is fine, but, for the time being at least, I expect society will let us earn a living as explorers rather than crossers of boundaries. Of course, it is an achievement, demonstrated here, that we no longer have to act as guardians and defenders of boundaries.

I wish this volume the success it deserves. Novices and seasoned practitioners both will learn much just from reading the introduction. But I am sure they will not be able to stop there; I wasn't.

Acknowledgments

The idea for this collection of papers first came to mind in the course of a conversation we had at the annual meeting of CASCA (Canadian Anthropological Society/Société canadienne d'anthropologie), in Montreal, in 1994. Bruce and I were meeting for the first time, soon after the publication of *Being Changed by Cross-cultural Encounters: The Anthropology of Extraordinary Experiences*. As we talked, we shared the conviction that experiences such as those presented in *Being Changed* and those described by Bruce in his chapter in this book deserved more attention since they challenged widely held assumptions about how fieldwork actually unfolds when one is deeply involved in the lives and environments of one's hosts.

This initial conversation led to the organization of a symposium on this topic at the 2000 CASCA annual meeting in Calgary, Canada. As a title for this event we chose *Ethnographic Objectivity Revisited: From Rigor to Vigor*. The description of the symposium read as follow:

> The title of this symposium is borrowed from a paper by J. Fabian published in 1991. In this paper, Fabian wrote that "much of our ethnographic research is carried out best when we are 'out of our minds,' that is, while we relax our inner controls, forget our purposes, let ourselves go. In short, there is an ecstatic side to fieldwork which should be counted among the conditions of knowledge production, hence of objectivity." Contributions to the symposium will explore the contents, preconditions, and ethnographic relevance of ecstatic experience—including experiences of

personally and socially significant visions and dreams in the context of fieldwork.

Since then, many more conversations on this topic with colleagues in other national and international conferences led to the decision in December 2003 to engage in the preparation of this book. It contains the expanded and revised versions of the four papers presented at the CASCA symposium, along with the contributions of twelve other colleagues. Many among them are well-established authors in their own right, with numerous significant publications to their names; others are at the early stage of their teaching and academic careers, coming after most creative fieldwork as manifest in each of their chapters. The quality of their contributions led one reviewer to write that "there are several junior authors within the collection whose work I would advise [the University of Nebraska Press] to seek out for future book-length publication."

Each chapter makes original contributions to sociocultural anthropology and makes obvious our indebtedness to the men and women, old and young, who have been our teachers and mentors in the field. Through patient association with us, they showed us how to be attentive to *their* lives and to *ours* as they unfolded, in *their* environment, *as they feel and know it*. Throughout the book, readers will become familiar with some of these mentors. In three chapters, contributors chose not to identify by name individuals with whom they interacted and from whom they learned so much. This is the case for Peter Gardner with the Dene of Canada's Northwest Territories, Anahí Viladrich with the Argentine tango dancers in the city of New York, and Millie Creighton in Japan. In all other chapters, we know who the key mentors were: Shura Chechulina and Nina Uvarova among the Kuriak in the northern tundra of the Kamchatka Peninsula; Gloria, Marvin, and Morris among the Kainai in southern Alberta; Jessie Wirrpa in Yarralin, in the Northern Territory of Australia; Michel and Sylvie among Spiritualists in Montreal; Mary Ellen Thomas, Udlu Pisuktie, and their children in the Canadian Arctic; Alhadj Touré among the Mandinga of Guinea-Bissau; Alexis Seniantha among the Dene Tha of northern Alberta; Marie and her dog among the Sekani of northern British Columbia; Don Antonio and Don Patricio among the Mazatec in Mexico; Vera—a young Maya weaver, and Alyssa in California; Don Tun Kaían and Manuel among the Maya in Guatemala; Ustar Zahir Hussain and Zakirji in New Delhi and California; Roberto Mendez Mendez, the Jaguar Twins, and Bishop Luis in the region of San Andrés, Chiapas, Mexico. The circumstances in which these individuals encountered us over extended periods of time in their homelands or in their places of adoption vary. In all cases, these mentors prompted us, as professionals and fellow human beings, to strive with greater determination to "reach the highest goal of our work," which consists in "fashioning representations of other cultures [and of other people] that do not erase their immediacy and presence" (Fabian 2000, 120).

We are most grateful to Johannes Fabian for the preface to this book. We thank the two anonymous reviewers whose judicious comments and supportive recommendations enabled us to improve upon our work. We are grateful to Mélanie Simoneau from the Faculty of Human Sciences at Saint Paul University (Ottawa) for the preparation of the electronic version of the manuscript and to Alexis Goulet-Hanssens for checking all references included in the chapters against the entries in the general bibliography at the end of the book. Thanks also to the staff at the University of Nebraska Press for their enthusiastic support for this project. Finally, but not the least, this book has benefited greatly from the skills of copy editor Jackie Doyle. As is the case with all publications, in this book there are undoubtedly points of views and facts that we, or others, will later want to modify or correct. The shortcomings, whatever they may be, although unintended, remain our responsibility.

Extraordinary Anthropology

Communities Discussed in Volume

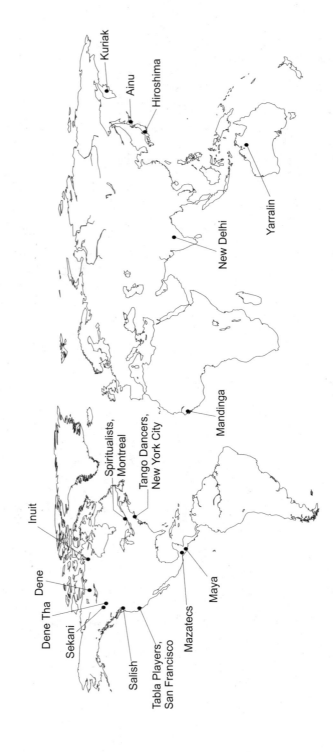

Introduction

Embodied Knowledge: Steps toward a Radical Anthropology of Cross-cultural Encounters

JEAN-GUY A. GOULET & BRUCE GRANVILLE MILLER

In "Ethnographic Objectivity Revisited: From Rigor to Vigor," the opening chapter of *Anthropology with an Attitude: Critical Essays*, Fabian maintains that "much of our ethnographic research is carried out best when we are 'out of our minds,' that is, while we relax our inner controls, forget our purposes, let ourselves go. In short, there is an ecstatic side to fieldwork which should be counted among the conditions of knowledge production, hence of objectivity" (2001, 31).[1] We are in basic agreement with this view. We know firsthand that in our own research activities we gained significant insights and knowledge precisely when we found ourselves, inadvertently, beyond the boundaries of our initial research intentions and proposals. The ecstatic side of our fieldwork was experienced when the single-minded pursuit of data within a clearly defined research agenda was momentarily set aside, and the opportunity to enter deeply into the world of our hosts was embraced. To our surprise, this led to insights and knowledge that redefined the relationships with our hosts, deepened our ability to interact with them in more meaningful ways, and opened the door to epistemological and ontological issues that begged to be addressed.

We believe in the importance of reporting and reflecting upon these crucial transformative moments experienced in the field. We know that to stick "with ethnography through thick and thin" is to also participate in efforts by many other anthropologists "to write one's way out of a tradition that one wants both to preserve and change" (Marcus 1998, 231, 234). In this book, the aspect of the tradition to preserve is that of intensive and extensive fieldwork, at home or abroad, as a condition of ethnographically based knowledge; the aspect of the tradition to change is that of the systematic exclusion of oneself out of one's ethnography, especially when it problematically concerns the setting aside of events or of experiences that challenge our own epistemological, ontological, and ethical assumptions. This change, heralded by contributors (Fernandez, Breidenbach, Samarin, Janzen, and Wagner) to the special issue of *Social Research* on charismatic movements, edited by Fabian in 1979, is well under way, as obvious in the recent work of numerous colleagues.[2]

The main objective of this book is to deepen our knowledge of the ethnographic self in interaction with others, and within the field. Field refers here to both the home environment of our hosts and to the discipline that defines our intellectual horizon in our pursuit of knowledge. This quest is at the heart of all disciplines, including anthropology. The research methods, qualitative or quantitative, that we draw upon in our investigations are the means to discipline and sustain the generation of reliable knowledge about a wide range of social institutions and practices. Systematic comparisons between cultures and across historical periods enable us to identify differences and similarities between and within various human populations. In this manner, we seek to understand the impact of constraints, physical and institutional, on social behavior, and to grasp more fully the creative, intersubjective, social dimension of all human lives. This has been the case since the beginnings of the discipline, when, in eighteenth-century Germany, "a sense of the environmental context of human experience led to a fascination with non-Western cultures and the full-blown pursuit of *ethnography*—a term coined for Germany by August Ludwig von Shlözer" (Zammito 2002, 236).

Given this book's focus on the interaction between ethnographers and their hosts as a condition of ethnographic knowledge, all contributors describe and discuss the work that they, as professional anthropologists, and their local mentors, interpreters, and momentary life-companions actually engage in as they interact in situ to "create their indeterminate realities, and act in them" (Barth 1992, 66). To be involved or implicated with others in their world is to become both a relatively incompetent and competent actor in coactivity with those who are local. These local actors, in turn, are also, to some degree, in the dark about various aspects of their home environment. In such circumstances, as ethnographers we come to acknowledge "the fact that interaction promoted through long-term participation produces not only 'observations' but also conceptualizations and insights that are clearly a joint creation of the anthropologists and his/her local partners in interaction" (Barth 1992, 65).

In *The Ethnographic Self*, Amanda Coffey comments favorably on "instances where researchers have reported extraordinary experiences that have occurred to them during fieldwork," noting that "these experiences are extraordinary in the sense that conventional fieldwork wisdom would dismiss or be unduly pessimistic about them" (Coffey 1999, 33). She mentions *Being Changed by Cross-Cultural Encounters: The Anthropology of Extraordinary Experiences*, co-edited by Young and Goulet (1998), which contains examples of such "accounts by social anthropologists who have seen or experienced the unusual or unexpected during fieldwork. These include seeing a spirit (E. Turner, 1994a); acquiring the powers associated with a shaman (Guédon 1994); and witnessing the reappearance of the dead (Goulet 1994a)" (Coffey 1999, 33). In Coffey's view, since "these accounts are based on the 'real' experiences of the researchers, and echo the experiences of other social actors (or members) in the field," they should not "be conceptualized (and indeed criticized) as 'going native' types of story" for "they are presented in a somewhat different light: as evidence of knowledge gained that would otherwise have remained partial and opaque" (Coffey 1999, 33). In other words, Coffey argues that the exclusion from one's ethnography of the insights gained through the ecstatic side of fieldwork is unwarranted and detrimental to the development of the discipline. This is why we welcome Fabian's "call for more attention to ecstasies" in the production of ethnographic knowledge (2001, 31).

From this epistemological perspective, Amanda Coffey's "concern is not so much with the 'truth' of such accounts, as with the ways in which they challenge the harsh rationality of the distinction between observer and observed in the conduct of fieldwork and reconstruction of culture" (Coffey 1999, 33, our emphasis). It is in this vein that we explore the contents, preconditions, and ethnographic relevance of the "ecstatic side of fieldwork" —including, but not exclusively, experiences of personally and socially significant visions or dreams in the context of fieldwork. From this vantage point, "ecstasis, like empathy, communication, and dialogue, as well as age, gender, social class, and relations of power, belongs to concepts that impose themselves when we reflect critically about what makes us succeed or fail in our efforts to produce knowledge about Others" as we interact with them in their worlds (Fabian 2000, 280).

While fieldwork remains the hallmark of anthropology as a discipline, contemporary anthropologists no longer subscribe to the eighteenth-century European assumption that "traveling in space also meant traveling in time," the Others encountered being "earlier versions of themselves" (Fox 1995, 16). Following the pioneering work of Said (1978), Wolf (1982), and Fabian (1983), it is now generally accepted that others should be seen not "as ontologically given but as historically constituted" (Said 1989, 225). "The representation of others and of ourselves is always, and necessarily so, a derivative of social positions and interpretive assumptions, those of the anthropologist and /or of the other" (Goulet 1998, 251). Experiential ethnographers accept this. They reflect upon the processes whereby they enter the field, associate with others who become their hosts and mentors in their world, and endeavor as best as they can to become "one with them, but not one of them" (Obeyesekere 1990, 11).

As experiential ethnographers, we know that once engaged with our hosts in their lifeworld, we could not simply exit the field at a convenient time and declare the experience over and done with.[3] Instead, we found out that the field was co-extensive with our homes, our minds, and our dreams, and involved even the bodies of our own family members and friends who were themselves sometimes affected and transformed by our ethnographic practice. To our surprise, we realized that they too could end up being directly engaged in our extraordinary experiences. For many researchers, fieldwork involved a sort of non-linear, non-Newtonian, quantum physical world in which related, connected events unfolded simultaneously in various locations. Various examples are provided in the subsequent chapters. While some of these examples evoke a road-trip, travelogue sensibility, they are not one-way trips in space and time. They do share something with the literary genre created by Kerouac and Kesey in which travel through space into unexpected cognitive domains supplements other modes of knowing.

In this book, as in Fabian's work, "the current meaning of ecstasy as nonrational, erratic, escapist, enthusiastic behavior (such as that described in, say studies of cult and movements)" is rejected (Fabian 2000, 8). Ecstasis is not one among many other possible research methods, "something to pursue in the practice of ethnography—getting drunk or high, losing one's mind from fatigue, pain and fever-induced delirium, or working oneself into a frenzy" (Fabian 2000, 181). In other words, ecstasy is not "a kind of behavior" one engages in, but a "quality of human action and interaction—one that creates a common ground for the encounter" with the Other, in his home-land (Fabian 2000, 8). The ecstatic side of fieldwork is understood here at this potential to step outside one's taken-for-granted body of knowledge (academic and worldly) and truly enter the realm of the Other's lifeworld. Stated differently, and most importantly, "Ecstasis, in a nontrivial understanding of the term, is (much like subjectivity) a prerequisite for, rather than an impediment to, the production of ethnographic knowledge" (Fabian 2000, 8). Ecstasis is the condition that enables us to embark on an ethnographic journey that takes us into uncharted territories.

In essence, this is what all contributors to this book endeavored to do. If we argue against a positivist view of anthropology, we hold strongly to a disciplined effort to produce valid and valuable ethnographic knowledge. If we recognize the necessity of being out of our minds part of the time while in the field or in our usual home and academic environments, we also insist on being in control of our aims and of standard ethnographic skills such as learning local conventions and abiding by them when communicating and learning with our hosts. Ecstasis as a pre-condition of ethnographic knowledge is evident throughout this book, not only when we report how we experienced lack of control and were unable to follow well-articulated research agendas.

The epistemological value of ecstasis is truly grasped when we discover that, while letting go, we were also able to draw upon unanticipated abilities to experience the real. In this sense, ecstasis "is not the theoretical, logical opposite of control but becomes its pragmatic and existential negation." In brief,

> Ecstasis, like empathy, communication, and dialogue, as well as age, gender, social class, and relations of power, belongs to concepts that impose themselves when we reflect critically about what makes us succeed or fail in our efforts to produce knowledge about Others. (Fabian 2000, 280)

We may add that this knowledge is also about Ourselves interacting with Other subjects in their world (Fabian 2000, 279). This is why experiential ethnographers strive to write accounts of personal experiences in the field without falling victim to the accusation of being narcissistic, and thus invite the native's reprimand: "That's enough talking about you, let's talk about me!" (This joke, attributed to Marshall Sahlins, is reported by George Marcus [1994, 569] and reproduced by John Van Maanen 1995, 29.)

In many collections of similar papers, experiential ethnographers do not write about themselves out of self-indulgence. Rather, they acknowledge the significance of transformative moments in the field, ones that changed them in a manner that definitely modified how they viewed, reacted to, or understood events lived with others in the field (Kisliuk 1997, 39). To include such moments in one's ethnographic account is to present not only knowledge obtained but also the processes through which such knowledge was gained and the circumstances in which such processes became operative.

The papers included in this book tend to differ significantly from the ones published in *Being Changed by Cross-Cultural Encounters* (Young and Goulet 1994). Essays in this book pay much closer attention to the impact on the researcher and on one's research project of the social, economic, and political contexts of the lives of the people with whom the ethnographer lives and works. This book focuses on the "ecstatic" side of fieldwork more than does *The World Observed: Reflections on the Fieldwork Process* (Jackson and Ives,

1996a) and other similar collections of fine essays, such as *Construct-ing the Field: Ethnographic Fieldwork in the Contemporary World* (Amit 2000). In common with contributors to such books, we chal-lenge the notion of a "field" that exists prior to and independently of the ethnographer actively interacting with others in their home envi-ronment. Moreover, in a very practical way, we demonstrate how to creatively engage the intellectual, ethical, and practical dimensions of the challenge described in *Figured Worlds: Ontological Obstacles in Intercultural Relations*, namely to elucidate the "ontological con-ceptions upon which culture is ultimately based, and in the friction between which, in a pluralistic world, conflict is generated" (Clam-mer, Poirier, and Schwimmer 2004, 1). In continuity with *Fieldwork Revisited: Changing Contexts of Ethnographic Practice in the Era of Globalization* (Robbins and Bamford 1997), of *Auto-Ethnographies: The Anthropology of Academic Practices* (Meneley and Young 2005), and of *Critical Ethnography: Method, Ethics, and Performance* (Mad-ison 2005), we extend the range of contexts in which to consider is-sues of professional accountability and ethical decision making in co-activity with others in their worlds.

In our field experience, transformative events lived with others in their world cannot be wished away. Our hosts know this and we do too. They expect us to take seriously what we have lived with them and have learned from them. In other words, the expectation is that we rise to the challenge of effective and respectful cross-cultural com-munication. We are called to transcend our own ethnocentrism and to explore forms of knowledge production and knowledge dissemina-tion that serve the best interests of our hosts and our profession. This is why the following chapters are all about ethnographically based experiential knowledge and depict others and oneself in interaction. These papers demonstrate the value of shifting "from participation observation to observation of participation" (B. Tedlock 1991) and of recognizing that "critically understood, autobiography is a *condi-tion* of ethnographic objectivity" (Fabian 2001, 13).

The significance of this recognition is best understood if we com-pare and contrast the positions taken by Geertz and V. Turner in re-spect to anthropological approaches to the study of religion and/or rituals and also to the study of other aspects of people's lives in their home environment. They take a very different stance as to what is the appropriate distance or standpoint from which to gain significant knowledge about the realities we intend to investigate. In *Islam Observed*, Geertz contended that in the study of religion, we anthropologists wait for the propitious moment to interview individuals "in a setting about as far removed from the properly religious as it is possible to get. We talk to them in their homes, or the morning after some ceremony, or at best while they are passively watching a ritual" (1971, 108). Geertz reasserts this point in a recent essay when he writes that "one doesn't, after all, so much 'examine' religion, 'investigate' it, as 'circumambulate' it. Skulking about at the edge of the grove, one watches as it happens" (Geertz 2005, 13–14).

The association of moving among others in a stealthy manner to avoid detection with scientific objectivity or interpretive clarity calls for forms of control of self and of other. I look, always, from the outside. At best, I interview the Other as he walks home away from the ritual in which he participated. Doing so, I preclude any possibility of sharing with him the experiences that would have been mine had I engaged with him in singing or dancing, making offerings, or calling on the assistance of spirits. Conversely, he knows that he is speaking to an outsider, someone who cannot speak from experience. What will he tell me? What will I be able to understand from his account of his experiences?

Circumambulating religion, or for that matter any social phenomenon, removing oneself from ritual settings as much as possible, is to preclude the possibility of discovering what one would sense and know from within that setting. This possibility is precisely what experiential anthropologists seek to gain. Contributors to this book gain this experience not as an end in itself, but as a means to learn firsthand what people talk about when they describe their lived experience. This is particularly called for when, among people, "the attitude of 'do it and see if it works' is widespread" (Kawano 2005, 1). Learning how it works in the "real world" of our hosts is definitely transformative as illustrated again and again in the following chapters.

Geertz maintains that since "we cannot live other people's lives, and it is a piece of bad faith to try," it follows that as ethnographers interested in the meaningful lives of others "we can but listen to what, in words, in images, in actions, they [others] say about their lives" (1986, 373). Notwithstanding his stated interest "in the meaningful lives of others," to which most anthropologists would subscribe, Geertz exemplifies a commonly shared methodological assumption: that it is possible "to understand [a] native religion and yet remain outside of it" (D. Tedlock 1995, 269). In a similar vein, Fabian argues that if early explorers, and after them ethnographers who espoused a positive view of their activity, "seldom ever sang, danced or played along" with their companions and hosts, it is because "their ideas of science and their rules of hygiene made them reject singing, dancing, and playing as source of ethnographic knowledge" (Fabian 2000, 127). This rejection leads to impoverished understanding of human lives and social institutions. Perhaps the widespread reticence among anthropologists to sing, dance, play, and pray with their hosts stems from the recognition that "performing rituals might eventually lead to personal commitment to religious ideas and doctrines" (Kawano 2005, 1–2).

To subscribe to the sort of anthropological investigation advocated by Geertz is to ignore native views on epistemology and to privilege limited Eurocentric canons of investigations (Goulet 1998, 253). This is fundamentally why Victor Turner differed so profoundly from Geertz on these matters. He does not claim that we can live other people's lives, nor do we. He knows however, as we do, that we can do more than interview people outside or after their involvement in a given activity, ritual or other. As demonstrated in our papers, we know firsthand the merits and benefits of learning rituals "on their pulses," "in coactivity with their enactors," making ourselves "vulnerable to the total impact not just of the other culture but of the intricate human existences" of others with whom we come to share time and interaction (V. Turner 1985, 205). Implicit in this approach is the notion of the body as becoming mindful through interaction with others, the idea of the body that literally embodies thoughts and ideas (Lock and Scheper-Hughes 1987).

It is in the context of "joining in," of being in the midst of social activities enacted "in co-activity" with our hosts, that we suspend our social conditioning. Doing so, we distance ourselves from an interpretivist "conception of ethnography as *observation*" (Fabian 1979b, 26, emphasis in original). We also move beyond the "notion of ethnography as *listening* and *speaking* (rather than observing)" (Fabian 1979b, 27, emphasis in original).[4] To "move" with others, in association with them, in the context of their activities is to engage in radical participation in their world. Under such conditions, as demonstrated again and again by contributors to this book, ethnographers do have "sensory and mental knowledge of what is really happening around and to them" (V. Turner 1985, 205, in Goulet 1994a, 26).

In *Religion and Modernity: Some Revisionary Views*, Geertz appears to open the door to the kind of radical participation discussed here as a mode of gaining entry into the world of our hosts whose religious views we wish to appreciate and understand.[5] In this recent paper, Geertz notes that social scientists turned their attention away from religion over the past decades because they assumed—wrongly they now recognize—that religion was a waning social force. Since religion is here to stay, a permanent feature of the world stage, Geertz maintains that we must revise some of our assumptions and set guiding principles to direct us in its study. Chief among these principles is that of proceeding from the "Native point of view."[6] To do so, he argues, "we need a combination of phenomenological analyses, that enable us to connect with the human subjectivities at play, with what believers really think and feel" (Geertz 2006b, 6).[7] Each and every chapter in this book does this, demonstrating time after time that it is possible to connect with our hosts in their world. How do contributors do so? By adopting indigenous epistemological and ethical perspectives. By parting with some deeply ingrained academic habits of thought to engage in radical embodied participation in a wide range of social settings, in co-activity with their hosts. The outcome of this approach is seen in the fine phenomenological descriptions of their experiences of transformation in the field. In the end, we recognize with Geertz (1971, vi) that "an anthropologist's work tends, no matter what its ostensible subject, to be but an expression of his research experience, or, more accurately, of what his research experience has done to him."

In this book, as in publications mentioned earlier, readers are often startled by accounts of this sort of knowledge gained through radical participation in the world of others. In this experiential perspective, reliable ethnographic knowledge is generated through radical participation and vulnerability, not distance and detachment. How else are we to grasp a "people's point of view, *their* relation to life, to realize *their* vision of *their* world (Malinowski 1953, 25; emphasis in original). In brief, ethnographers "use 'participation' much more radically as a method than most interpretivists have imagined" (Barth 1992, 66). The recourse to radical participation as a method enables us, "if only for a moment, to reach the highest goal of our work, fashioning representations of other cultures that do not erase their immediacy and presence" (Fabian 2000, 120).

Together, all the essays in this book argue that "the triumph of logic and rationality, the clever architecture of theoretical artifices, and the cunning methods devised for novice researchers do not make science" (Fabian 2000, xii). What, then, do these procedures do? According to Fabian, "What they do promote is ascetic withdrawal from the world as we experience it with our senses. In the end, science conceived, taught, and institutionalized in such a manner is sense-less" (2000, xii). Against such a conception, we can choose to come back to our senses. We write, then, in a manner that captures meaningfully the immediacy of the experiences that challenged us to think beyond our taken-for-granted notions of the real and of true knowledge.

Radical participation as a process becomes intrinsic to our search for knowledge and understanding of the human experience. Through radical participation or experience of the ecstatic side of fieldwork, we discover new forms of engagement with others in the everyday world. We are then confronted with the realization that we often can't find the line to know if we have passed it, that we have transcended the academically defined boundaries of the knowable and are therefore in relatively new territory. We are then confronted with an alternative: either repress the experience, or express it in an intelligible form for colleagues and the public at large to grasp.

At the heart of this transformation in the field lies hospitality: that of our hosts (human or otherwise), who introduce us to their social world in all its complexities; that of ourselves, who learn from personal experiences important dimensions of the human potential for meaningful interaction with others; that, finally, of the discipline that seeks to understand as best as possible how human beings shape their experiences of themselves, individually and collectively, in the context of shifting circumstances and convictions.

The sixteen contributors to this book convey to readers a sense of the deep humanity of those who have been mentors. This was so among Aboriginal peoples in Australia for Deborah Rose; in Mexico for Edward Abse, Duncan Earle, and Jeanne Simonelli; in the United States for Janferie Stone and Bruce Miller; in Canada for Peter Gardner, Barbara Wilkes, Edmund Searles, Guy Lanoue, Bruce Miller, and Jean-Guy Goulet; and in Siberia for Petra Rethmann. Other contributors write from contemporary urban settings in which they were transformed through their interaction with individuals and groups who in their environment are considered marginal. For Deirdre Meintel, these were Spiritualists in Montreal; for Anahì Viladrich, Argentinean immigrant tango dancers in New York City; for Denise Nuttall, tabla drummers in New Delhi and San Francisco; and for Millie Creighton, members of various minority groups in Japan. If there is one notion that stands out from these essays, it is that "just as mind and body are not separate entities, so person and place are characterized by their interactive connectedness" (Kawano 2005, 129).[8] (See map of peoples and places mentioned in each chapter.) This book thus demonstrates that consent to be touched by lived experiences and letting go of predetermined agendas lead to significant contributions to an anthropology of cross-cultural encounters.

Notes

1. In Calgary in May 2000, at the annual meeting of the Canadian Anthropological Society, we (Jean-Guy Goulet and Bruce Miller) drew on Fabian's work to organize a symposium entitled *Ethnographic Objectivity Revisited: From Rigor to Vigor*. Four of the papers presented at this symposium were revised and expanded to become part of this book

(Creighton, Goulet, Miller, and Wilkes). Twelve other like-minded colleagues have graciously agreed to contribute their own original work to this book.

2. In this respect, beyond Fabian's reminder that "autobiography is a *condition* of ethnographic objectivity" (2001, 12), the titles and contents of recent publications is revealing. See the works listed in the bibliography by Amit (2000), Behar (1996), Coffey (1999), De Vita (2000), Dewalt and Dewalt (2002), Jackson and Ives (1996a), Okely and Callaway (1992), Reed-Danahay (1997), Smith and Kornblum (1996), and Wernitznig (2003). This constant stream of papers that transcend the "false dichotomy" between the personal and the professional self (Bruner 1993) demonstrate that contemporary anthropologists are more likely than their predecessors to report their dreams in their work, as noted by B. Tedlock (1991) and Goulet and Young (1994). Nonetheless, E. Turner and colleagues' observation (1992) that ethnographers are generally embarrassed to use their own dreams and visions in their work is apparently as accurate today as it was thirteen years ago.

3. In this introduction, as in chapter 8, the expression lifeworld is used as defined by Schutz and Luckmann (1973, 3) as "that province of reality [as opposed, for instance to the province of reality of art, science, or religion] which the wide-awake and normal adult simply takes for granted in the attitude of common sense [as opposed, for instance, to the attitude of the artist, of the scientist, or of the mystic]." See Rogers (1983, 47–66) for a comprehensive examination of this concept central to phenomenology.

4. This is the view espoused by Fabian in 1979, in the context of a series of papers organized around "the ideal of anthropology as interpretive discourse" (Fabian 1979b, 27). The choice of this key concept to organize a collection of essays is built upon Foucault's view of discourse as a type of event about which one may ask "how is it that one particular statement appeared rather than another?" (Fabian 1979b, 28). This theoretical view, which avoided equating culture and linguistic expression (or speech acts), also carried "connotations of activity in space and time, of unfolding in a process of internal differentiation, and of openness to response and argument from audience" (Fabian 1979b, 29). Discourse is not even listed in the index of *Anthropology with an Attitude* (2001). Fabian's recent collection of critical essays continues nonetheless to deal with praxis, openness, and transformation. The index includes many entries that are central to the sixteen essays presented in this book: authenticity, autobiography and ethnography, body, embodiment, confrontation and communication, ecstasis/ecstatic, ethnography and authority, intersubjectivity, memory work, narration and narrativity, recognition and alterity, understanding and misunderstanding.

5. This paper was presented at the international and pluridisciplinary colloquium *Social Sciences in Mutation*, held in Paris in May 2006 and organized by the Center for Sociological Analysis and Intervention (CADIS). See www.ehess.fr/cadis/english/index.html for the program of the conference.

6. My translation from the French version of this paper, Geertz 2006b, 5. "L'étude de la religion . . . devrait s'opérer a partir, comme on dit, du 'point de vue de l'indigène'" (Geertz 2006, 6).

7. My translation from the French version of Geertz 2006b, 6. "Et pour cela nous avons besoin . . . d'une combinaison d'analyses phénoménologiques, à même de nous mettre en contact avec les subjectivités humaines en jeu, avec ce que les croyants pensent et ressentent vraiment."

8. For examples of this kind of ethnotheory, see De Boeck 1998, Feld and Basso 1996, Lovell 1998, and Kawano 2005.

Part One

Beyond Our Known Worlds

We begin with three descriptive accounts of unanticipated participation in events that directly confronted ethnographers with dimensions of life that drew them beyond the parameters of their immediate research agenda and taken-for-granted epistemological assumptions. In the process, we discover how anthropologists transcended their initial predilection for this or that theoretical perspective and came to work and to learn beyond the vantage point from which they thought they would carry out all their research. They learn that the substance of their fieldwork brings them to participate in events that are beyond their "capacity to understand and to control" (Toelken 1996, 1).

In the opening chapter, "On Puzzling Wavelengths," Peter Gardner shows how even seasoned anthropologists run headlong into experiences they deem paradoxical, extraordinary, shocking, or baffling. He found himself confronted with a series of these in the course of studying "Northern Dene" during the 1970s in the Canadian Northwest Territories. He shares four of these experiences, leading the reader closer and closer to the paradoxical and puzzling: recourse to the state of drunkenness to solve problems of communication; cases of extraordinary communication with dogs to perform unprecedented and totally untended tasks in medical emergencies; manipulation of what the Dene call "power" to alter the course of events; and his getting into trouble after he, himself, stumbled upon a wholly new way of seeing—thereby perceiving things that he *knew* had to be impossible for him to see.

Petra Rethmann's chapter, which follows Gardner's, is entitled "On

Presence." She explores what constitute two supposedly contrasting sides of fieldwork: intimacy and alienation. While intimacy suggests a sense of profound togetherness and state of oneness, alienation points to a darker side of fieldwork, suggesting isolation, disconnection, and separation. These two states, far from being mutually exclusive, are almost always at the heart of what we do in the field. Rethmann works through senses of intimacy and alienation by closely examining states of "being out of one's mind" and "being in one's mind" during an intense fieldwork period from 1992 to 1994 in the northern Kamchatka Peninsula in the Russian Far East. Learning how to drum became an intrinsic part of learning how to be with herself in the world, in the same way those around her had learned to be at home with themselves, often in eloquent silence, in their environment. Throughout the analysis of these states, she brings into dialogue a phenomenological approach with political ethnographic material.

In her own chapter, Barbara Wilkes asks basic questions: reveal or conceal? What is the place of ecstasis in one's ethnography? In answer to these questions, she argues that the adoption of a somewhat dispassionate or scientific stance in research does not mean that we must be passion-less in the field. Rather, as suggested by Fabian, passion—understood as both drive and suffering—can be seen as a condition of knowledge. In this perspective, ethnographic objectivity is the outcome of passionate personal experience that mediates between the I and the Other in the production of ethnographic knowledge. Telling the story of how she came to participate in and appreciate Kainai ways of learning about one's place in a web of significant relationships, Wilkes offers a new kind of scholarship, one that fully accepts the challenges of decolonizing methodology and writing. This new scholarship that has yet to emerge fully in its own right is "based on Aboriginal cognitive and spiritual maps"; it "adheres to Aboriginal protocols at all stages of its enactment," and it uses "Aboriginal methodologies, as appropriate to local traditions and the subject matter being addressed" (McNaughton and Rock 2004, 52).

1. On Puzzling Wavelengths

PETER M. GARDNER

Even seasoned anthropologists run headlong into things they find paradoxical, extraordinary, shocking, or baffling when they are engaged in fieldwork.[1] I had several experiences like this in the course of a study during the 1970s, and they all had to do with communication. They entailed surprising interaction between humans; almost unbelievable understandings between dogs and their masters; people dealing with forces they called power, with extraordinary consequences; and, finally, my perception of things that I knew were impossible for me to see. All these experiences beg to be shared. I was living and working at the time in a Northern Dene settlement, in a richly forested part of Canada's Northwest Territories, about an hour's flight from the nearest road. But, before I broach what it was the Dene had in store for me, you surely need a bit of background on what the community was like, what sort of a person is reporting all this, and what it was that took a colleague and me into the Subarctic to undertake the research.[2]

Background

The Dene Settlement

Like many communities in the north, the settlement we worked in had grown up around an early nineteenth-century trading post on the bank of a large river; the Catholic Church had also been there almost from the start. Because our project proved to be quite intense for everyone, and because the people were wonderful about it, I think they have earned a bit of privacy; it seems appropriate to leave the place nameless to help ensure this. The number of people actually in residence peaked seasonally at slightly more than a hundred Dene adults. There were just over a dozen Euro-Canadians as well, including a government-appointed settlement manager, two RCMP officers, a nurse, forestry staff, two teachers, a store manager, a Catholic priest, a Protestant minister, and a few of their family members. Depending on the time of year, a trickle of travelers came and went by boat, by sled, on foot with pack dogs, or by bush plane.

It was a serene place, so far from the bustle of twentieth-century Canada that, unless the radio was on or the mail had just arrived, we gave the outside world scant thought. After all, the Northwest Territories in those days had thirty-one square miles per person. This hideaway of ours was green with spruce, pine, tamarack, birch, aspen, and balsam poplar as far as we could see. Our settlement lay just below the confluence of two large rivers.

The smaller of the two flowed in lazily, between high bluffs, from swampy lands to the east; the other was a wide, swift, cold, and turbulent river that rose at the Continental Divide and drained a sizable area in the northeastern Rockies. Low mountains were visible across the big river, to the west. Behind us, forested lowlands dotted with uncountable fishing lakes and scattered patches of muskeg stretched on and on for hundreds of miles.

The community looked surprisingly dispersed to me. It was a mile-and-a-half long, made up of several loose clusters of log cabins and canvas tents broken up and spaced by groves of trees.

A couple of the most distant cabins were located in forest on the far side of the river. I was unprepared to see tents in use right through the winter, both in town and out on traplines. Eventually, I was to learn myself what it felt like to sleep in tents and cabins at −30 to −35 degrees Fahrenheit while accompanying several men on their traplines in midwinter. And, to my astonishment, the shelters were left unheated except at mealtimes. Tough people!

The community had a small nucleus of public buildings that included a Hudson Bay store, a school, police and nursing stations, forestry buildings, a log-built community hall, the settlement manager's office, and several government houses. Inland from the river, beyond a dense stand of young trees, there was a grassy firebreak that served in both dry summer weather and in snow as our landing strip.

Most families spent two to nine months of the year away in the bush, meaning that the segment of the population actually present in the settlement was usually well below its theoretical peak. Whole families went to fishing lakes for the summer; many more spent the winter months in trapline cabins and tents. Their comings and goings were timed in accordance with weather conditions: snow, ice, or dry ground being needed for easy movement on land and open water for travel by river.

Dene appreciated the rewards of living in both settings. The town had its social and technological richness, and the bush offered personal freedom. People gave clear signs of anticipating eagerly each move from town to bush and bush to town. Anyone having a vacation retreat should be able to understand this; it feels good to get away from congestion and equally rewarding to return to the usual amenities and bustle. I accompanied the young chief to his trapline on his first trip of the winter, setting out on the very day that ice on our smaller river was deemed safe to cross. A scant five miles from the settlement, he stopped, built a fire to heat a frying pan of snow for making tea, grinned at me, and summed up his feelings in two words: "No boss!"

Despite their involvement in the world fur market, the people had certainly not given up hunting and fishing for their sustenance. Fresh or dried moose meat could be found in 90 percent of the households on any given day, every month of the year, with caribou, bear, and beaver to supplement it, or perhaps rabbit meat in a pinch. Fishing for whitefish, lake trout, northern pike, burbot, and sucker was also an activity that went on all year, except in late winter, both for human consumption and as food for sled dogs. There were also game birds, plus berries in season. And people from the elderly down to the most modern youngsters still went through meticulous ritual disposal of moose heads, fish innards, and so on, when butchering, doing so out of respect for the creatures that they had been obliged to kill in order to sustain themselves. A youth might playfully have stood up in a moving boat and put a .22 long bullet through a moose knee to bring it down, but the killing itself remained a serious activity.

Before they had guns, steel traps, and snare wire, Dene used a variety of dead falls and nooses to procure game, enormous ones being needed for moose. Knowledge of how to construct this traditional equipment persisted, even among young adults who eagerly built and demonstrated it for me.

The Writer

I have been a rambler most of my life, growing up in various parts of England, western Canada, an isolated Maori community in New Zealand, and the United States of America. And, by the 1970s, my research in anthropology had already taken me to the jungles and cities of India and to Japan as well. Personal and professional experience had taught me that the options for human living are many and diverse. This surely contributes to the relaxed, open stance I take in life. And it seems to have fed my appetite for enquiry and for yet more encounters with new peoples and places.

But, there is an equally strong and altogether different side of me. From early boyhood, I was certain my life was going to be that of a scientist. The rigor of science had a profound appeal to me. I was a physics major at the outset, then veered off after two years into scientific study of a yet more intriguing subject—people. Given what you are about to read, it is important to know from the outset that I not only have a deep trust of my senses in professional matters but am a committed empiricist in private matters, too. Bear this in mind.

Our Study

What had taken a colleague (Jane Christian), me, and our two families to the Subarctic was a problem having to do with thought, individualized thought. Toward the end of an earlier project, among hunters and gatherers in south India's dry, forested hills, I saw strong hints throughout my notebooks that those individuals I knew best differed even from other family members in the way they categorized and labeled essential items, such as food species and the woods from which they made their basic tools for subsistence. But, was that really so, or had I been sloppy in my research? If I was right about the interpersonal diversity, how marked were their differences? Were they greater in some subject areas than in others and, if so, what might account for that? Unfortunately, I began thinking about all this toward the end of the study. By then, I did not think I had either the professional tools or the time to test all my hunches before I left the field; only further formal study could reveal the nature, extent, and causes of such variation. But, I must confess that I had a growing curiosity as to whether there were differences across the world's societies in the extent to which people exhibited individualized concepts and beliefs. Perhaps it could even be quite marked (see, especially, Gardner 1966, 2000).

Émile Durkheim told us almost a century ago, in *Les Formes Élémentaires de la Vie Religieuse* (1912), that the sharing of concepts was necessary in a human society, and most of my fellows in anthropology had no apparent disagreement with him. They spoke comfortably about Navajo beliefs, or about Ainu concepts, as if these were standardized from one human head to another within each society. The general public did this too. Yet, only four years after Durkheim's theoretical pronouncement, the young Bronislaw Malinowski, a fact-oriented fieldworker, painted a wholly different portrait of people in his paper *Baloma: The Spirits of the Dead in the Trobriand Islands* (1916). He reported that personal opinion varied from person to person within communities in the New Guinea area, and it was only public belief, as expressed in formalized myth and ritual, that was standardized. Some early-twentieth-century pioneer scholars in sociology and folklore talked in the same vein.

It you stop to think about it, the nervous systems in which we take care of all our perceiving and thinking are inherently private. We also have entirely different histories and experiences from one another even within a small community. A lot of our knowledge simply has to be idiosyncratic. Let me turn the picture around: how could one ever explain any of us having knowledge, concepts, or beliefs that are identical or closely similar to those of our neighbors?

As a result of discussion I had with the late June Helm, we had chosen Northern Dene as a people with whom we could take up these questions. My interest in the north began when June heard me describe my data from the Indian jungle at a conference at the National Museums of Canada in 1965. She told me right away that my huntergatherers in India sounded similar in their values and their individualistic behavior to a hunting band she had done research with in Canada.

Studying people in the way we planned involved interviewing large numbers of bush- and town-oriented men and women of all ages and backgrounds. It also meant working with them as much as possible in their own tongue, a Dene (or Athapaskan) language that was distantly related to Navajo and Apache. Our Canadian field site was far from the mainstream, so only a third of the adults who lived there had developed much facility with English. This may have been precisely the situation we sought, but actually conducting the interviews in their language was a daunting prospect, for Athapaskan languages were notoriously difficult to learn. Remember the "Wind Talkers" in World War II. More than the first half of our time would have to be spent acquiring the ability to undertake what we had set out to do. If that was what it was going to take, however, that was what we would have to do. And the study did bear fruit (Gardner 1976; Christian and Gardner 1977).

Being Drunk to Communicate

The most readily explained of the surprises I faced was the practice of pairs of individuals becoming stone drunk together, ritually and in certain circumstances, as a means of solving communication problems in their relationship. It was not at all obvious to me, initially, that heavy drinking had a positive contribution to make to communication; surely, we all realize that alcohol consumed in excess can only impair understanding. To appreciate how their practice works we need to look, first, at the general values of Dene and at the relationships among adults in their society.

I described the settlement as having loose clusters of log cabins and canvas tents. These tended to belong to sets of families that were not only closely related to one another but also associated with given hunting and trapping areas lying upstream, for instance, or downstream, or toward the mountains. The loosest cluster of all, the cabins across the river, belonged to two amiable brothers who dwelt more than half a mile from one another. But then half a mile is only a few minutes' walk. People liked to live near relatives and spend time with them, but they exhibited an exaggerated need for space.

Within limits, Dene households ought to be independent and self-sufficient, they believed. Nonetheless, because their main sources of food were enormous, it made sense to share any large animal kill with close relatives and with whomever else in the community dropped by for a share. This was absolutely routine with moose or caribou; I saw it done, too, when a trapper brought in the carcasses of ten beavers at one time, a substantial amount of meat. It was quite clear to us that a couple of men who never hunted were given shares of meat hesitantly and reluctantly. We heard them scorned for living such that they and their dependents always turned out to be receivers of food.

Pairs or small groups of people worked as teams in brief tasks, such as hunting, butchering, hide scraping, and building cabins or sleds, but they did so as well in season-long trapping arrangements. These long-term partnerships had to be especially stressful for the individualistic Dene. If trapline partners happened to be grandfather and grandson, or uncle and nephew, this might not happen, but it seemed inevitable that unrelated partners would experience difficulty in coping with disagreements and differences of opinion when coordinated work was called for.

I learned about this from direct experience. The first person who took me out to his trapline for a few days found me puzzling at times. For reasons I did not really understand, he would look at me now and then with a searching, troubled expression. I sought to participate as much as possible and be helpful, but my suggestions and actions weren't always received as I had hoped. Perhaps I was not comporting myself as a learner should. Perhaps I made too many suggestions, or made them too eagerly, or it could be that some of my ideas struck him as being off the wall. He also behaved as if he thought I was annoyed over his losing his rifle shells along the trail as a result of storing them too casually. In truth, I was. By and large, it was a good trip, however, and these were subtle little matters. While they all passed without discussion, they remained undealt with.

In my mind, the biggest problem of all came when he asked me to stay at his house right after we returned, in order to have several rounds of drink. To his great dismay, I declined. I did so on the grounds of my own culture-bound ideas: that our outing was now over, that it happened to be my customary meal time, and that I owed it to my family to let them know I had returned from the bush in one piece. I had no idea why my companion appeared injured by my insistence on going home right away. Fortunately, he seemed to have strong commitment to our association, and I believe he wrote off my walking out on him as a simple function of my ignorance and innocence.

What I eventually came to see was that it was usual for partners to hold their tongues over differences of opinion while at work, then get intoxicated together when they came back to the settlement for a break. I stumbled slowly into my appreciation of this technique. Alcohol relaxed them enough to overcome the restraint they had grown up with, freeing them to express all that had been bothering them while working together. Loud arguments and fights were a routine aspect of these post-teamwork drinking bouts; injuries sometimes resulted. But the sweet part of using intoxication in this way was that, the next day, one was permitted to claim amnesia for all that had been said and done. After they got disagreements and irritations off their chests, the partners could, and did, walk off together once more with a smile. Co-operating with other members of society, when one has been trained from childhood to be a quiet and undemanding person, an independent decision maker, and a self-reliant worker, calls for a high level of restraint on everyone's part. Suppressing one's discontent for days at a time has to be stressful. I came to see the practice of workmates drinking alcohol together as allowing them important and licensed moments of cathartic irresponsibility in a society that otherwise called for an almost unbearable level of responsibility.

I watched one courting couple use the same technique. They put aside everything else and staggered around in a totally drunken state together for two days while they opened up toward each other and began to negotiate formation of their relationship. I kept an eye on them. They came to blows at one point and, because he was considerably larger and stronger than she was, when she came to our door for refuge, we let her sit down for a few minutes in our kitchen. When her fiancé arrived at our place, close on her heels, we lied through our teeth and denied having seen her. After a few minutes, she thanked us and slipped back out with a smile to get the process of their mutual opening restarted. Then he stopped by next day and told us sheepishly, "Yesterday, [pause] you done right."

My understanding of all this came slowly. What a wonderful drinking bout we had after three of us worked for several days to make a new (toboggan-style) sled of birch we had cut ourselves! Although we did not accumulate much that needed to be resolved during this project, there were a couple of minor peeves, and I did have a sense that it would be good for us all to air them. When a grumble or two did come at the height of the party, I experienced an epiphany: I at last appreciated the fact that we were doing something far more serious than taking a celebratory drink.

I learned to play the game. Later in the project, an elderly man asked me to come over in the evening to share his home brew. I did, but I was welcomed with more than a constantly refilled mug. As we slowly fell into intoxication, he began to attack me bitterly for having included only one member of his family in my sample, his daughter-in-law. What a sharp tongue he had! He knew nothing, of course, about our rigorous stratified sampling techniques or about the set of criteria by which we selected people to work with us. Realizing full well this time what was happening, instead of subjecting him to a defensive discourse on scientific method, I let him get all his resentment off his chest. The next day, he sidled up to me hesitantly in the Hudson Bay store, wearing a tense, sheepish smile. "My wife tells me I didn't talk good to you last night," he said. "I don't remember," I replied, in the requisite, singsong voice. As it dawned on him that I was offering a culturally appropriate response, his smile changed character. It grew into a relaxed grin. And the two of us walked off as buddies with other matters to talk about.

Communicating with Dogs

Some years ago, a priest's sled arrived in midwinter at the isolated trapline cabin of a family I worked with during my pilot project in the north. The priest's dogs were starved and scrappy, their harnesses were tangled, and the priest, himself, was delirious with pneumonia.

The trapper faced a difficult situation. The weather was nasty, food was short, his wife was in the hospital at that time, and, as he was caring alone for several young children, he could not simply ask his children to look after themselves while he did the 120-mile round trip to transport the priest to Fort Simpson hospital. And there were too many in the family to consider all going in a single sled. So he covered the ill man up with the blankets he could spare, hitched his own dogs to the priest's sled, and knelt down to talk with his lead dog. He told it to take a wooded route around the shoulder of the low mountain they lived on, then follow the Mackenzie River to Fort Simpson and its hospital. We are not talking about following a clear, simple, much-used path. There are branching trails, the route around the mountain was a brushy one, and the river ice was perilously rough. There were innumerable places for untended sled dogs to get into difficulties. How the lead dog kept to the right trail, how it managed to head off dog fights, how the team avoided getting their traces tangled in the underbrush, and how they kept to their task for sixty miles without further human assistance will never be known. But Fort Simpson inhabitants can give us the end of the tale: a sled with no driver, carrying a bundled up and now unconscious priest, ascended the steep riverbank and came to an orderly stop on the main street of the town. I learned about this feat years after the fact from two of the daughters who witnessed the start of the trip and from residents of Fort Simpson who were able to tell me about the priest's arrival and survival. The real story for me, though, has to do with communication between a man and his lead dog.

I have a companion tale about a much-admired man I interviewed and know personally. One winter night, he rolled into a fire in his open-air trapline camp. His face and one arm were terribly burned. Despite excruciating pain, he readied his sled, harnessed all his dogs to it, and instructed his lead dog to take him twenty miles up river to the community's nursing station. Then he simply collapsed into the sled. As in the previous account, underbrush and rough ice made it a treacherous and difficult route for dogs that had to make their way on their own. And, again, we have the story that everyone in the community knows, of the man's dogs arriving untended and coming to a halt directly in front of the nursing station with their unconscious load.

Both the lead dogs were asked by their masters to do a novel task—to travel to a distant but known place, without any further guidance—and both are attested to have accomplished precisely what they were instructed to do. If I did not know the people and the places involved, and if the two stories were not so similar in their details, I would have to admit to quite a measure of skepticism.

Coping with Power

Dene dealt with what they called "power," and did so with what I viewed as unexpected consequences, including consequences for me. Power was a preoccupation. Although I did not intend to study the subject, I kept encountering evidence that the Dene thought of power as abounding in nature. Some attempted to share what power they had themselves obtained; others attempted to manipulate it. I noted four aspects to it. First, there were creatures in the forest that seemed to be ordinary birds and mammals but were, in actuality, spirit beings able to protect particular individuals. Second, there were truly frightening creatures such as frogs and huge underground beings that, although alive, were incapable of consciousness. Third, people sought spiritual knowledge through dreams or altered states of consciousness. What they learned thus might be shared with the community. Finally, there were people who manipulated power ritually for personal benefit. These several aspects of power are more closely linked than they may sound, as you will see.

Protecting Beings

One day, while a sixty-six-year-old Dene man and I were leafing through a bird book, he launched into a tale about a strange happening in a quiet bush camp, years before. A lone American coot had waddled into the camp, right up to his tent and cooking fire. Everyone knows that coots are shy waterfowl, yet his little intruder showed not one trace of fear. His explanation for its boldness was that the bird he ever after called "my visitor" was in fact a personal protecting spirit.

A young man also talked about birds. He was a huge, heavy fellow, built like a defensive lineman for a professional football team.

Some years ago, in midwinter, he had been running across the ice on a fishing lake some twelve miles from town. His leg suddenly dropped into a crevice in the ice that he had not seen on account of the glare. Because of the massive bulk of his upper body, he fell forward with enough force to snap both bones in his lower leg. Going back to his isolated cabin made no sense. Abandoning whatever he had been doing, he started crawling toward town on his hands and knees, on into the night, dragging his limp leg behind him. The pain and cold were awful. There were times when he simply had to halt for a rest and times when he probably collapsed unconscious. Although this was hardly the time of year to be seeing them, he soon realized that geese were flying along with him, giving him protection. As he tells the tale, the details of his hours and hours of painful crawling are trivial; what he really wants to tell is the tale of his geese. He takes for granted that their protection saved his life.

One old man I knew well, who was ridiculed behind his back for making birch bark containers (he does "women's work," they said of him), once intimated that he never went out to hunt because he had no protecting spirit. He was savvy about power, though. Indeed, he asked if he could give lessons to my eleven-year-old son whom he thought had a promising, pattern-finding mind. But he was candid with me about his personal dread of going too deeply into the forest.

Creatures beneath the Earth

People regarded it as empirically attested that creatures resembling dinosaurs lived beneath the earth. For one thing, a man from our community had worked at the wellhead, on a gas-drilling crew, at the time the well was due to blow in. He told his fellows afterward about the strange moaning he had heard in the pipe when the well finally struck gas. He didn't mean "moaning" in a figurative sense; for him the wail came from something disturbed by the drilling. These great subterranean creatures were even nearby. Who didn't realize that beavers could not possibly survive in such a cold place? The mere presence of beavers in the ponds around us testified that something dwelt below each pond, warming the water sufficiently for beavers to live there. In midwinter, one occasionally sees yellow water overflowing the ice in forest streams. People became excited when they saw my aerial photo of one such overflow quite near us. The yellow liquid was, of course, monster urine.

There was understandable fear of small relatives of the huge beasts as well; even bold teenagers would not touch or approach frogs, which their classificatory verb stems told me they regarded as living but unconscious beings. They would look at one, shiver, and retreat. For our neighbors, then, there was ample evidence of the creatures of a lower realm, and it was all around us.

Dreams

Dreams are a means for getting knowledge, and this, in turn, can be a source of power. It is understandable, then, that dreams are valued and sought. Although dreams often come to us at night, we may also be visited by them when unconscious, a valued state. Unconsciousness was achieved in a variety of ways in the past. Since the 19th century there has been the easy path of alcohol intoxication. I once watched a playful twelve-year-old with a Pepsi bottle in his hand staggering realistically down our street and telling a buddy in a slurred voice, "Maybe I pass out tonight." A game? Certainly so. But it reflected the goals of the adults around him. People who drank to achieve unconsciousness were labeled "alcoholics" by two welfare staff with whom I discussed this, a diagnosis that makes no sense medically if intoxication occurs only a few times a year. One has to bear in mind the value of trance states for many Native North Americans. I acknowledge that inebriation can be a source of problems, but we are talking here about religion, not problematic recreation.

The settlement had two wells. Authorities wondered why Dene used well water for washing clothes but went down to the river's edge for drinking water, regardless of whether it ran clear or thick with silt. But we noticed our neighbors going to the wells when they fetched water for making home brew. The explanation was simple. The subterranean world, including its water, is dangerous because of the power found down there. Remember the monsters. Yet, how attractive that power becomes when one is pursuing the world of important dreams.

Except for the New Year's Eve dance—a drunken, but Western-style function that was held in the community hall—dances generally took place on grassy banks on long, golden summer evenings. All that was called for were an open space, a fire, a couple of drummers, some dancers, and people who have "songs" to share.

The spirit of sharing was what struck me. Earlier I described the individualism of the Dene; this is the point at which I can give you a glimpse of an activity that brought out the coherence of the community as an organic whole. Drummers provided a loud, hypnotic beat as a singer led a line of male and female dances in a slow circle. They locked arms, swaying in a simple step together as they followed along. What I have called "songs" might be better called chants. They are strictly in the Dene tongue, and each is the personal property of a singer, for it is a text that has been received by that person in a dream. Everything I learned about the songs is consistent with what Robin Ridington has told us so eloquently in his *Trail to Heaven* (1988) and *Little Bit Know Something* (1990), about comparable song among the adjacent Dunne-za peoples. In sharing them, the singer offers to others spiritual knowledge that he or she had been given about the trail we all must follow after death. It was a precious offering that shortened the path. And what a gift for the anthropologist to have two smiling grannies step out of an ongoing dance, take him firmly by the elbows, and insert him into the dance line between them.

Sorcery and Kindred Phenomena

Medical and other researchers can tell us a great deal about the actual effectiveness of certain rituals. There appear to be several physiological means by which belief one is under a magical attack can have fatal consequences. Let me give one example. An endocrinologist, Curt Ritcher, has examined autopsy reports of people in the city of Baltimore who died believing they had consumed a lethal dose of some poison—when, in fact, it was proven later they had taken a far smaller dose than would have been fatal (1957). These Baltimore cases, medically studied deaths from magic attack in the Australian desert, and experiments with comparable reactions in lab rats, show that being resigned to the inevitability of death can have a prompt and fatal effect. It leads to a major production of an adrenal hormone that precipitates a rapid, well-understood syndrome called vagus death. It usually takes a human about seventy-two hours to succumb.

And Barbara Lex has hypothesized yet another physiological explanation for vagus death. She holds that it could be brought on by what the medical world calls "tuning" in the automatic nervous system. Reciprocal relationships between the sympathetic and parasympathetic systems can fail, such that "stimuli which usually elicit response in the non-sensitized system instead evoke a response in the sensitized system" (Lex 1974, 820). The body of the victim can precipitate its own demise in more than one way. We have a variety of scientific reasons to take magical death seriously.

Some evenings during the summer, elders could be heard drumming and chanting in the woods. People simply said they sought power. Although this subject was well outside the scope of what I chose to study, I kept tripping over it. A male neighbor of ours believed himself to be the target of someone's sorcery. His wife, however, was descended from a line of ancestors who had been famous for manipulating power. I have heard her say, in all earnestness, that her grandfather controlled the great, feared subterranean creatures. She, apparently, was using every means she had to counter the attack on her husband and save him. It was an ongoing aspect of their life.

But, look at the following case, which involves injury rather than death. Early during our study, a youth accidentally gave a companion a broken leg. The victim's mother came storming out of her house, wagging her finger at the one who caused the accident, shouting, "My son will not be the only one to break his leg!" In the next several months, young men in the community suffered six broken legs. These seesawed back and forth between the two families originally involved. One was actually self-inflicted: a youth had recently come out of hospital where doctors had repaired his badly smashed leg and, in the course of demonstrating a karate chop to a friend, he accidentally re-broke his own limb. Another case in the series was yet more bizarre. At our New Year's Eve dance, an intoxicated youth from one of the two families sped off on a snowmobile with his brother's fiancée astride the machine behind him. They hit a tree at high speed. Both were thrown clear and the only serious injury was a broken leg for the driver.

Enough is enough, the two families thought. A powerful Cree medicine man was flown in at great expense from southern Alberta to try to bring the whole business to a halt. He was pale and huge, standing a head taller than most people in the community. And everyone looked at him anxiously. After all, the Dene term for Cree translates as "enemy." Once the visitor had completed his rites in private, the jubilant chief attempted to get a dance going. We had the requisite drums and people. The Cree medicine man himself even started to play a drum. The chief, however, totally failed to entice anyone to follow him in the circle he trod. At least the broken legs came to an abrupt end.

I made mistakes in the field, especially toward the end. Hearing a fight, I looked out my window to see a middle-aged woman on the doorstep of her cabin, two doors away, arguing with two men. This is the neighbor I described earlier who was heavily involved with power. While it is my usual practice to avoid all surreptitious photography in the field on ethical grounds, I picked up the camera and shot the scene. There was a strange noise as I pressed the shutter release. For some reason, the camera stopped working. I borrowed a replacement camera and mailed my own to a repair shop in Chicago. In due course, the shop wrote back asking what I had done to the camera. Its entire shutter mechanism lay in a puddle at the bottom of the instrument, every single piece undone. When my film came back from processing, I got another shock. The picture of the fight had come out, but over the powerful woman's head there was a black vortex. This I report as a skeptical scientist, for whatever it is worth. None of it was ever explained.

Seeing with One's Eyes Closed

Summer is a season for socializing, with dances, stick games, and children playing on into the seemingly endless evenings. That is when the fewest people are tied up with work. It is also the time of the year when the community reaches its peak size and when there are several great changes in the usual character of interpersonal relations.

The stick game was a wholly different matter from dance. It didn't unite, it divided; it didn't bring the two sexes together, it was just for men. Yet, there was a comparable spirit of intense excitement and involvement. The stick games were always played in a big tent near the riverbank, to several loudly beating drums. While, technically, the men gambled, the short willow sticks they stood to lose took only a couple of minutes to make. Two teams of about four men each knelt facing each other across a central blanket. Each member of one team hid an object in one hand behind his back. It could be a penny or a pebble. Then, in unison, they put both clenched hands in front of them, under the edge of the blanket. The captain of the opposing team taunted them and, by suddenly using one out of a large set of hand signals to indicate the hand in which each opponent held his hidden object, he flashed his signal to them. All the opposing team members then opened their hands to show whether they had won or lost. The point was not accruing profit; it appeared to be a specially licensed way of competing in a society that otherwise discourages headlong competition.

During some of my last evenings in the field, men were playing stick games near the riverbank in the usual way. After watching for two or three hours one night, I was permitted to join the chief's team. Later, when the chief announced his need for a bathroom break, I asked him whether I could serve in his place as an interim captain. This was a serious matter for him. He looked pained, hesitated for ages, then awkwardly agreed to it. Knowing only a few of the signals, all I could do was make my best effort. I knelt, head down, wondering how to second-guess all my opponents. I even closed my eyes to concentrate. When I closed them, I had a strange sensation. It was as if there were a dark blob to the right or left of each opponent who faced me. For some reason, I chose my signals as best I could to match them. And my clumsy signals had a strange effect. I was actually devastating the other team. Following several rounds of this, someone in a back corner of the tent suddenly called out, "You are cheating. You closed your eyes, so you can see." Embarrassed, unable to deny the charge, I had to terminate the game. Thirty-one years later, I still wonder about this one.

Opening Up

I told you in my introduction that our project bore fruit. Jane and I determined that the Dene varied considerably from one another in their terms, concepts, and broad frameworks for thinking about things that were familiar and important to them. This was evident from their terminology for birds, fish, moose anatomy, trap parts, and so on; it was also clear from the ways they oriented their traps and from their sense of how, where, and when to fish (Gardner 1976, Christian and Gardner 1977).

Variations in their moose anatomy terms were representative. Recall that moose was every family's foremost source of meat, and it was the creature whose killing was marked by the most-elaborate rituals of respect. Just as everyone ate moose, every adult butchered it. Parties of male hunters did butchering as a group; so did husbands and wives, if they felled one while traveling or while working on their trapline.

When I interviewed thirty-two people about moose anatomy with a picture of a moose skeleton before us, my subjects proved able to name even the minor bones. In one extended family, during a trial run, three of the adults systematically divided a moose leg into two named parts and showed me the boundary; the other three divided it clearly and elegantly into three named parts. They came to know about this variation in casual conversation with one another afterward, then brought me in on their discussion. Their two approaches could not be reconciled. It was not as if they had provided me with general and specific versions of the same thing, or with the classification of meat versus one of bone. They were surprised—and amused as well—to realize that their bush-oriented family was host to two contrasting ways of conceptualizing a valued part of their precious moose. The spine of the moose and its main sections were labeled even more variably across the community. There were three main terms for the spine as a whole, and diverse, divergent approaches to naming its four recognized parts. Everyone characterized the spine and its lumbar segment in particular as "connectors," but there was more than one way to express this in their tongue. How divergent were they? Starting with the most prevalent term for the spine as a whole and each of its four segments, it would seem possible to come up with a "most representative" set of terms for the spine. Are you surprised to learn that only one of my thirty-two consultants, an elderly woman, gave me that precise set of terms?

Because you were probably not ready for them, you may well consider these findings on variation from person to person to be almost as baffling or extraordinary as things that I've described to be strange to me. I suspect you do, because your experience is different from mine. By virtue of my background, I have come to anticipate that each new culture I study will be uniquely systematized and a new approach to reality. If we are lucky in the field, we anthropologists not only get glimpses of these differing realities but sometimes also achieve explanations of them that we can accept scientifically. That is one of the supreme pleasures of life in the field.

Every once in a while, however, the glimpses we get are the kind that only tease or baffle us. The dog tales, the totally disassembled camera shutter, and the persistent "visions" I had in the course of captaining the stick game, belong to the latter kind of experience. The last two, especially, have left me absolutely stumped. While the empirical facts of these cases are as clear to me as can be, and while my mind continues to ask for a rational explanation of them, I am obliged to conclude for now that reality is more complex than the scientific side of me has been able to accept. But, then, I have never been one to ask that my experiences be simple or predictable. If I had asked that, I would surely never have ventured out into far corners of our rich planet. And, surely, life without puzzles would be life bereft of all flavor.

Notes

1. This chapter draws on and elaborates material from five chapters of *Journeys to the Edge: In the Footsteps of an Anthropologist*, Columbia: University of Missouri Press, 2006. I thank the curators of the University of Missouri for permission to use material published in that book.

2. Research on the Northern Dene was supported by NSF grant GS 43057 and an Urgent Ethnology Programme contract from the National Museums of Canada. Preparatory and pilot projects were supported by University of Missouri Research Council grants URC NSF 1201 and 1209. Because our project was collaborative, Jane Christian and I fed each other information and theories all year. While she contributed to my understanding of the community, our perspectives were often quite different. She is not in any way responsible for the thoughts I am offering here.

2. On Presence

PETRA RETHMANN

This article of three parts deals with the paradox of being out of one's mind, while simultaneously being in "the present." Taking its cue from the title of this book, it asks about two kinds of being "out of one's mind." The first kind refers to the kind of anxiety, fear, and desperation that scholars, including students, teachers, and researchers, frequently experience in relation to their work. It is the kind of being out of one's mind that makes one wonder if one's work is good, robust, or vigorous enough. If it is appreciated by one's peers. If it will be published. If it can garner funding. These are questions full of anxiety, worry, and fear. When they are experienced as overwhelming, unbearable, or strong, they can truly drive one out of one's mind.

I believe that these are questions that trouble more academics than those people usually let on. They are also questions that relate directly to the second kind of "out of one's mind" that I want to explore here. This is the kind of out of one's mind that, paradoxically, leads one back to one's mind, to a state of wholesomeness and peace, instead of leaving one stranded in states of anxiety and desperation. It is the kind of being out of one's mind in which one does not exist in the grip of emotions but in a state of mindful-ness and awareness. I first experienced inklings of this kind of being out of one's mind in the summer of 1992 when I lived with a reindeer-herding brigade in the northern tundra of the Kamchatka Peninsula. In the beginning, I truly thought I would go out of my mind. In the tundra, there were no longer any points of reference or knowledge to which I could adhere. There was a great deal of uncertainty and irritation. The boundaries between the spheres of what I thought then were reality and fiction began not only to blur but to collide. Feelings of anxiety, helplessness, and desperation set in. They shaped a great deal of what I then experienced. Shura Chechulina was the woman I, like so many other people in Tymlat, the village in which I lived, called grandmother. It was only through her teachings that the first kind of being out of one's mind became more clear to me, and venues into the second kind of being out of one's mind opened up. It is the second kind that interests me here.

Many of the insights offered in this article derive from the almost five years I spent in the northern Kamchatka and Chukotka peninsulas in the Russian Far East between 1992 and 2000, in periods varying from one month to two years. These were formidable years that, from the beginning to the end, set me on a path that returned me to some of the issues and themes by which I had always been intrigued, whose pursuit inspired me to embark on an academic career, and that I had begun to forget in the course of my graduate education. But the insights offered here also emerge out of the wisdom offered by Buddhist teachings, in particular the Zen teachings of the Soto schools. I have encountered these teachings only recently, but much of what I have gathered from them relates to a kind of inner patience and peace in which life is no longer controlled by the fear and anxieties of the mind. It is not necessarily the case that these teachings are exclusively related to Eastern philosophies. Within the context of Western spiritual traditions, Francis of Assisi and Teresa of Avila, for example, developed certain meditations, peaceful and compassionate practices and writings. I have found these teachings inspiring in a variety of contexts, for a variety of reasons. They also inspire me here.

From an academic point of view, the problem with the teachings and names of those identified above is that they do not possess many intellectual credentials. For the most part, these teachings and teachers are the objects, and not subjects, of critical inquiry. In fact, information about their philosophies and wisdom is more easily found in the curricula of religious studies departments than in the seminars and courses of cultural anthropology. Buddhist, spiritual, mystical, and other kinds of teachings provide the sites (for example, Obeyesekere 1984) but not frameworks for inquiry. Looking for literature concerning this article, I have come across only Michael Jackson's (1998)

Minima Ethnographica, which builds on Buddhist teachings to some extent. These teachings, indeed, are often slated into prefabricated rubrics concerning such esoteric-sounding phenomena as shamanistic, supernatural, and mystic. That's why, at least in university contexts, they are often regarded with great suspicion, ridicule, or trepidation. Again, at best they are the objects but not subjects of study. For example, I have a friend who is currently writing on South Africa's Truth and Reconciliation Committee and would love to use the writings of Pema Chödrön, a Tibetan Buddhist nun, for her explications. Alas, she feels that in the academy these writings might be, yet are not, part of the accepted interpretative record. More often, they are part of that New Age science and religion that academics, myself included, love to criticize. Self-respecting academics rarely like to think of themselves as spiritually too far out.

In this essay, I want to turn some of these academic conventions on their head. I am asking what it means to be out of one's mind, second kind, not only for academic research and practice but, perhaps more generally, for one's life. The guiding metaphor for this exploration is the notion of the presence. *Presence* is a term with which I became familiar in the context of the Zen teachings that I mentioned before. It is a notion that does not dwell on the future or the past but reveals what is (this is it!) in the presence, the moment, the now. I have found this notion both inspiring and useful for examining more closely what keeps me often out of my mind, first kind. These are worries, anxieties, and fears, often emerging out of a (personal) past and translating into my interpretation of the present, or anticipations of the future in which my mind paints frightful scenarios and images, scenarios in which I fail, always falling short of one thing or other. It is the present, the kind that keeps one in one's mind without letting it run the show, that I seek. And I am asking why, in this case related to a few research issues, this seems often so hard to do.

This essay is divided into three parts. Part I tells the story of an article that I published a few years ago and whose afterlife continues to engage me. The article was generally well received, but also considered, at least by some, as *too* romantic. I am asking how and why this was the case. Romanticism may be everything: a well-worn feature, indictment, and allegation in anthropological circles, but it can also be part of a self-imposed denial of what I have called elsewhere (Rethmann 2000) the "poesis of life." Essentially, I ask what we miss when we fail to recognize our own analytical conventions and limitations. Part II elaborates on the presence of silence. There is a great deal of silence in the northern Kamchatka Peninsula and Chukotka (as almost everywhere in the North, as I've been told), but ethnographies themselves have evinced a great deal of silence about the notion of silence. Why is this the case? And what can silence teach us about the presence? Part III brings aspects of these questions together. It does not rehearse or summarize the arguments and thoughts I have provided in parts I and II but rather asks what we can learn from them. It does this in a somewhat roundabout way. It works through what I think of now as the lessons of Shura Chechulina. When I use the word lesson here I do not mean self-conscious teachings delivered in the style of a talk or lecture. Neither do I mean the passing on of fixed knowledges and wisdom. What I mean are openings, forays into (at least for me) new forms of being that are more audacious, centered, and connected than the ones I knew so far. Trying to be present to what is, with all its multitudes, challenges, and facets, is perhaps one of the greatest challenges there is.

In 1995, when I was first writing up the materials of my fieldwork into a dissertation, I looked at it as a journey. Instead of including a chapter entitled "Introduction," I began with a section entitled "Departure." The purpose of this move was to keep a sense of travel, movement, and openness—after all, I was writing about people who moved with their reindeer herds often across the land—alive. For the same reason, the dissertation did not offer a conventional conclusion that summarized its findings but instead a chapter entitled "Arrival." Again, I wanted to keep the flux and flow of life alive. In this piece, too, the underlying idea is to get at something one might call "life." Not just in its existential but also its experiential sense.

Romanticism

In the year 2000, I published an article in *American Ethnologist* entitled, "Skins of Desire: Poetry and Identity in Koriak Women's Gift Exchange." The article, from what I projected as the Koriak point of view, dealt with such mundane and everyday affairs as the sewing and tanning of animal skins and hides, in particular, those of reindeer, but with the aesthetics and exchange practices. The theme of this article had emerged out of two particular experiences. First, since my arrival in Tymlat, I had worked in the local *masterskaia*, a small workshop that was part of Tymlat's collective farm where women skinned, tanned, and sewed the hides that brigade workers in reindeer-herding camps in the tundra sent to the village. Second, I had spent a great deal of time in those camps and the tundra and wanted to find a way to articulate the love and care with which people referred to animals, and the ways in which they articulated that love to refer to themselves. By and large, the argument was set against the rather functionalist frameworks that, at that time, were still prevalent in Russia-centered anthropology to explain the architecture, clothing, and foods of northern Russian reindeer herders. I wanted to give expression to the feel, sense, and smell of fur and hides, to their palpability. I also wanted to give expression to the experience of their touch. To the symmetrical, carefully thought-out, and outrageously beautiful patterns with which people, in particular women, arranged and sewed fur. In this sense, "Skins of Desire" was as much the outcome of Koriak desires, as perhaps it was the outcome of my own desires.

In, and beyond, the intellectual circles in which I then moved, the article was well received. But a funny thing happened. It was, some said, *too* romantic. The idea of romance was rarely elaborated, but I think what people meant was that it was too loving, too extraordinary and idealistic. "Skins of Desire" built on my visceral sense of living in the tundra but also on the experiences, feelings, and words of Koriak women and men who clearly loved the animals with and by which they lived. This was new territory in northern Russian research. It flew in the face of a historical materialism that posited evolutionary stages and organizational features as the ultimate in explanatory logics. It forced analysts to think about animals as more than vehicles for food, clothing, shelter, and transportation, and instead as both subjects and objects of aesthetics, art, and desire. It provided, I thought, a more encompassing view of both animal and human lives in the northern Kamchatka tundra.

A caveat is here in order: In the Tymlat of the 1990s, Koriak ideas and animals, and associated life in the tundra, went beyond ancestral traditions. Moreover, there were deep generational differences. In those years, Tymlat was a ruined place. As a result of the increasing presence of Russian merchants and traders at the northeastern shore, Tymlat emerged in the mid-nineteenth century as a small settlement (Vdovin 1973, 54) in which Koriak women and men began to live permanently. Originally populated by *Nymylany*, a self-designation used by the groups usually described as Maritime Koriak, in the mid-1950s it was transformed into a *sovkhoz* (state-run collective farm). But in the mid-1990s, Tymlat displayed all the historic signs of the Soviet dream of progress and modernization, the ruin of that dream, and the sense of a life run down. Many Koriak women and men I knew, indeed, considered leaving the village for the tundra, a consideration in which material factors played an important role. The bureaucracy and institutions of the Soviet Union had fallen almost completely apart, and life in northern Kamchatka villages was marked by increasing social competition, anger, hostility, and jealousy. There were severe shortages in money and food, and, really, people asked, how much money would they need in the tundra, and would there not be enough food to eat? But beyond these material advantages that people hoped life in the tundra would bring, there was also a sense of longing for its calmness and peace or, at least, that was what people hoped to find there. In Tymlat, these dreams were often contrasted with the metaphors with which people described life in the village (*voniaet*; literally, "it stinks"). "Stink" can have many meanings; for example, it can describe the terrible material conditions resulting from economic collapse, unemployment, drinking, and the high-blood pressure (*davlenie*) that kills women and men before they reach their mid-forties. People resort to stealing, marriages do not last, and people envy (*zavistiat*) each other the little they have. There is an increasing sense that people have become selfish and think "only about themselves" (*toliko dlia sebia*).

So, in my interpretation there may have been a certain romanticism at work. Perhaps some of my own, for I clearly enjoyed living on the land (projecting romanticism on other places, projects, peoples, and so on, has become every anthropologist's nightmare), and perhaps even some generated by Koriak women and men. But what is this romanticism we are speaking of? Is it just part of the exoticism with which Western anthropology and thought has for so long forced others, Natives, mystics, "the mad," and so forth, into offensive slots? Or is it part of the naive notion that the natural world can save us from the pressures of modern life, the onslaught of the capital economy, information technology, and industrialization? I do not think so. If the article contained any traces of romanticism, it was a romanticism born out of the sources of pleasure and joy of living on the land, and the hard realities of life in the village, and also the knowledge, pleasure, stories, and wholesomeness (at least for the most part) of Tymlat's elders. I do not mean to sound dreamy or simplistic. But neither do I think that romanticism, if that's what we mean, should be reduced to almost always a point of accusation. For what we easily convict as *too* romantic may also provide openings into new realms of knowledge, comprehension, insight, and awareness.

For all the rightful-ness of the comments mentioned above, I suspected that something else was at work here also. For the next question is: To whom, and for what reason, did the article appear to be too loving and affect-laden? The question is not aimed at individuals, but rather asks about scholarly sentiments and conventions. I suspect that the article was deemed too romantic also because it worked against analytical trajectories that were then still dominant in post-Soviet cultural anthropology, and certainly with regard to analyses concerning the Russian North. Socialist realism's doctrine of *partijnost* (or "Party-mindedness," that is, the stipulation that many scientific and literary works be infused with the party's point of view (see also Clark 1981), had also left its mark on anthropological analytical trajectories and led to the production of ethnographic texts that were largely set in evolutionary frameworks, with little diversion from the social progress-embracing story line that marked Soviet anthropology to a large extent.

This is not to say that the Soviet Union's ethnographic record is entirely homogenous, but there is an argument to be made for an underlying formulaic prose that generated highly conventionalized texts

(Rethmann 2001, Sorin-Chaikov 2003). These texts have performed different functions, ranging from analyses of historical change in indigenous regions to supporting official myths about the progress of the Soviet Union. What they did not do, and were not destined to do, was to convey a sense, a feel, of living. But that was what I then saw as my task. To do precisely this: to put into words not only what animals, fur, and all the other things might mean but how all of this was experienced, what life in northern Kamchatka was like. That was what I had set out to do.

Although, among other things, "Skins of Desire" was meant to challenge conventional Soviet-centered analytical trajectories and interpretations, it was not meant to be heretical. It truly emerged out of a kind of viscerality that marks living on the land. It was not meant to provide yet another functional analysis of reindeer husbandry and herding but rather to convey a sense of presence, of just "being with" and "being there" (Taussig 1987). This, it seems to me, is one of the hardest things to convey, although this difficulty should not prevent us from trying. Perhaps it is so difficult because, so far, nobody seems to have worked out what, really, that notion of "being" is. Some sort of nothingness, Zen teachers might say. And those most frequently evoked—Heidegger, Sartre—might agree. For most anthropologists it goes without saying that "being" is culturally and historically contingent, never simply a given that is always already there. And yet, in a way, "being" *is* always already there—perhaps in infinite ways, but there.

SilenceSilenceSilenceSilenceSilence

In late January 1992, I arrived for the first time in Tymlat. We, a local reindeer herder, Tymlat's veterinarian, and I, had embarked on this journey by dog sled because at that time helicopters were no longer flying, and fuel for snow mobiles was expensive and rare. The night was freezing, and the journey arduous and long. The snow was almost too soft for travel, and our sled continued to sink deeply into it. The veterinarian loosened the reigns of the dogs and, snow to our hips, we began to push. Halfway on our way to Tymlat, we stopped for a couple hours at a place people in the region call *piannoe ozero*,

"Drunken Lake." On the journey from Ossora to Tymlat, or on the way back—Drunken Lake is where people usually stop to drink. The reindeer herder went off. The veterinarian and I sat on the sled, staring into the starry night, waiting for our guide to return. In those hours, we did not say much, but there was no uncomfortable silence. The night was cold but beautiful, and there was simply not much to say. The silence was full and perfect; words would have marked it as empty and unfulfilling.

In the tundras of northern Kamchatka and Chukotka, I encountered this sort of silence frequently. It did not matter if I found myself drinking tea for hours with Koriak friends in silence, whether in the village or the tundra. If broken at all, the silence was interrupted only by the word *eshche*, whose intonation in those situations simply meant "more tea?" Or sometimes I found myself in the camp, watching reindeer with others for hours on end. And sometimes we just sat outside in front of the tent, tanning. At other times, we stood for a long time, observing the direction of the wind, trying to tell if tomorrow the snow would be heavy enough to let us embark on sustained travel. There were many moments like this, all of them marked by silence. As for me, I frequently experienced these moments as peaceful and whole, because nothing mattered then except the company of people, motions of the body and hands, tea, or the feel of the weather and the wind.

How does one begin to think about silence? And, even more difficult, how does one speak about it, about that which, almost by its very nature, is unspeakable. Silence is hardly the sort of thing, if thing it be, that makes for good ethnography. Not much, except perhaps for the boredom that Michael Taussig (2004, 59) mentions—could be less the stuff of exciting ethnographies or more resistant to representation. Ethnographies rest on the written word, and everybody wants to know what people said. But why do people remain silent? Especially when there is nothing in particular to hide? I do not think that the reason is the lethargy to which, at least in northern Kamchatka and Chukotka, some fairly high-ranking administrators, indigenous and otherwise, sometimes refer. As if silence, like the lethargy (so they say), were innate. Perhaps it is just the sense of the land, the presence of the tundra that calms people. In it one can feel one-self more clearly. No wonder, then, that Native bands in Labrador, Canada, for example, have introduced retreats on the land to tackle issues, such as those related to drinking, that are to be found in villages and communities.

There is a great deal of silence in the North and, as I have said, it is hard to put that silence into words. Silence is never quite empty, and much learning can transpire in quiet moments. So, this is perhaps the misunderstanding, the trap into which ethnographers tend to fall: The only thing worth attending to are worlds of sounds: the barking of dogs, the chatter of people, the noise of the city, and so forth. In the tundra, it is not so much the words of humans but the sound of the breaking ice, footfalls on the hardened snow, the gush of rivers, the cries of wild swans, the crackling of grass, the puddles of waters that grow into ponds, the yelping dogs, the rustling of feathers in the snow, and so on, that fills the silence. This is not noise. These are the barely audible sounds that get lost when one's focus is on either the absence of talk or the obsession with verbal communication, the discomfort that can arise when one is not comfortable with silence. How to describe this silence? And how to make sense of it not only in an ethnographic but in an existential way (however unpopular this may be)?

I have thought for a long time that anthropological writings on the North are underrated. There is perhaps not an immediate lushness of landscape that grabs one's attention, and there are even perhaps not the kinds of theoretical explications that have been attributed to a former anthropology, a regionally based anthropology (Melanesia comes to mind). But notwithstanding some of the terrible political and economic conditions of Native living in the North, there is also a great deal of calmness and peace. That is perhaps the reason it is so challenging.

For all the time I spent in the Russian tundra, the silence has never bothered me. I often relished and enjoyed it. But I also recollect times of discomfort, and the sense of being out of my mind. Even after all the time that has passed, I remember the panic I felt when I thought about the necessity, the impending task, to render that silence into an ethnography, a dissertation. The thought that at some point in the not-so-distant future I would need to return to Canada (where I went to graduate school for my dissertation), would need to return to supervisor, university, or department, and somehow would have to transform this silence into a dissertation, articles, and eventually a book kept piercing my enjoyment. I grew desperate at the thought of not having enough "data." Writing and silence seemed a contradiction in terms. I felt I was being asked to come up with interesting ethnographic details, or to explain cultural functions and patterns. But how could silence be interesting, and how could it be explained?

A great deal of my dissatisfaction with writings on the North, including my own, is that these writings never seemed able to capture the essence of things. I am aware that this is a rather out-of-date statement, destined to garner criticism in some of the academic quarters to which I belong. And I am even not quite sure what I mean by essence here. I certainly do not mean that there is some sort of overarching, metaphysical, or universal spirit that lurks in the north and that one could unravel, but when I think back to those moments of silence, in houses, camps, and in the tundra, it seems as if there was something going on that related to an intrinsic sense of being. It is this sense that I have found most challenging and intriguing. Perhaps the expression "the feel of life" jives better here, certainly in the sense that it is more palatable to most social scientists. And here I am not interested in fighting over expressions. What continues to fascinate me is the being-ness of being. And it is from this that I continue to learn.

As for the Koriak women and men I knew, silence is almost a natural component of time. And to me, this silence has always felt like a moment of presence. So, instead of allowing the silence to melt into language, a device to propel a plot, it should be perhaps left as what it is: a connection with something larger than the self.

Presence (November 3, 2004)

I have reworked this article several times, but I have reworked this section most. I still find it difficult to speak about the presence. It is as if it were something awkward. I am somewhat uncomfortable with advancing such a notion in a book with academic credentials, that is.

46

Anxieties related to the first kind of being out of one's mind kick in. Aren't the points I make overworked and clichéd? It is a worn-out truism to point out that fieldwork can be accomplished only in the presence. Isn't it too self-reflexive? Knowing that my current project is more steeped in the history of political imaginations, why do I want to talk about the presence? And do I, in a certain way, have the guts to talk about it only now? These are some of the questions that have troubled me in the context of this writing.

As I said in the beginning, I have learned about the notion of the presence only recently. And this is strange because it is essentially what I teach my students, but I have a harder time doing it myself. For the message is: Do not do only what is doable, but do also what you are passionate about. Follow your heart. As one eminent scholar said to me recently, "That's great that you follow your heart." "Doesn't he?" I wondered.

Let me make one more point—albeit in a roundabout way, via a detour through experience and writing. Take, for example, the cover of *Writing Culture*, a book of profound influence in the discipline, and one with far-reaching implications for our anthropology's own professional self-understanding. Ethnography is not simply a form of the real but is also fabricated and fictitious, the message says. You see Stephen Tyler sitting on the steps of the veranda, writing, amid people quite aware of him. And although writing, using language, is a large part of what we do, it also struggles to convey what I have been calling here "presence." Perhaps that kind of mindfulness and awareness, if you want to think about it that way, is better conveyed through experience, to be then followed up by its reflection (for example, via writing).

Shura Shishkin, the woman I called grandmother, was not at all convinced by the anthropological project. It was she who demanded a different kind of presence. Writing, even taking photographs as a hard-nosed form of cultural documentation, made sense to her. After all, she saw language and knowledge around her, to speak with the words of Koriak elders—dying (*vymiranie*). Her concerns were the concerns of many elders, not only in the peninsulas of the Russian Far East, but beyond. People forgot their language, their stories,

47

their ancestral teachings, their myths. Forgot the rituals. Forgot giving thanks to the spirits. Began to forget to protect themselves from the evil ones. Began to forget, and had already forgotten much. In Tymlat, elders of her kind rarely condemned the government, or as people called it, "the power" (*vlast'*), but seemed to imply that the safeguarding of particular ways of life was their responsibility. As Nina Uvarova, an elder and a friend of Shura Shishkin, said so poignantly: "Today it makes me sad that I cannot talk with some of my children and grandchildren. They don't understand our language anymore, and they tell me things I don't understand. Today people say it's the government's fault, but I am not sure. I believe it is up to the parents, my daughters, to tell their children about our way of life."

To whomever it was who should convey the myths, practices, and stories, and there were and are many discussions around this in Tymlat and beyond—Shura Shishkin was a person of high spiritual standing. This was made most clear by the way people visited her. Most of the time, Shura Shishkin simply sat on the floor in the one room that she shared with her granddaughter and three great-grandchildren, ranging in age from nine months to six years. When her granddaughter had to leave the house, Shura Shishkin took care of the children, in particular the youngest. She did not speak Russian, and like so many other elders in northern Kamchatka was almost blind. This was because of the reflections of the sunrays on the snow, people said. At her house, the door was always open, and people would drop in just to sit with her for a while. It made them feel better, they said. And it was true. I, too, used to sit with her. It made me feel better as well.

Shura Shishkin was often called when somebody had died. She was in charge of the proper process of rituals. Koriak spirituality involves the existence of "another world" (*drugoi svet*). In essence, that world is a replica of the world that can and is directly experienced, and it exists in the here and now. When people—or animals—die, the living have to make sure that the dead person reaches the other world. Reaching the other world involves a ten-day-long hike along a treacherous path. Animals and other kinds of beings can attack, and one needs at least a stick and a drum to make it to the other world. Men also often take spears with them, and women are given needles and threads so that they can immediately set themselves up in the other world. Shura Shishkin had to make sure that all of this happened. On those occasions, she insisted on my presence. She held up objects given to the dead person so that I could better photograph them. She also taught me something about the proper dealings with (what we call) magic mushrooms (*mukhamory*) and spirits. The day I left to live in a reindeer camp in the tundra, she gave me little parcels filled with *lauteng*, a sort of sacred grass, reindeer flesh, beads, and tobacco. They were for me to drop on the way to the camp, to ensure my protection and safety.

Shura Shishkin's idea of learning, I believe, was steeped in experience. And what that meant was that one had to be present. Not just "there," but fully aware of the moment, of the now. To be fully open to what was happening in the moment. And nothing evinced this better than her insistence that I needed to play the drum. There were two old drums hanging over her bedstead, and one of her grandchildren had scribbled little pictures on one of them. While Shura Shishkin appeared unconcerned, in the beginning I was troubled by this. For, to my mind, initially at least, the drums were part of Koriak artifacts, ritual objects, sacred, through which one could communicate with the spirits. Or so it had been written in the books on Siberian anthropology. In fact, I had written an MA thesis on the concept of ecstasy in Siberian shamanism around the area of Lake Baikal and thought I knew something about it. For Shura Shishkin, it turned out, the drum was living and not dead. To me the drum was interesting but, in a way, also dead: I had never used it. Shura Shishkin saw things quite differently. Who cared if there were a few scribbles on it? Perhaps her grandchild had had fun drawing those pictures, and perhaps it made him quiet. The drum could still be used to quiet oneself and others, and to call on other beings.

And this was what Shura Shishkin set out to teach me. To play the drum. Let's be clear: I was never very good at it. Moreover, most of the time I felt embarrassed. I had read so much about anthropological criticisms of fieldwork, research, and "going native" that I entirely refused to play. I was, after all, a person with a critical mind—and mostly only allowed myself to experience things through the mind, not the body. I was somebody who liked, and still likes, theory and intellectual thought. But that these were strengths as well as limitations only slowly occurred to me.

So, every morning I found myself sitting on the ground, playing the drum and producing strange sounds. This, I continued to feel, was a truly absurd position. People moved in and out of the room, looking for Shura Shishkin's granddaughter, looking for their children, wondering if there was some bread and tea (these were the days when shortages were all-pervasive in Russia). Nobody seemed particularly perturbed at the sight of me sitting on Shura Shishkin's bed and singing, but I also received a few knowing smiles, as if people knew, and they probably did, what grandmother was up to. So, I was sitting there and trying to sing. And, damn it, it rarely worked. Sometimes I thought I managed, but Shura Shishkin remained dissatisfied. She suggested I sing from within (from the heart?) because it was there where proper singing was produced. In my mind, this translated into "deeper." It did not work, and I went almost out of my mind.

Resistance was rising. Resistance against Shura Shishkin's lessons, fieldwork in general, and people in Tymlat. I was so much in my mind that I could not even appreciate Shura Shishkin's teachings as teachings. Teaching, to me, meant involving arguments, sentences, and words, not practice, listening to one's self, and silence. In retrospect, these kinds of teaching seem almost zen. (I have a colleague who spent a great deal of his life working with a Native group in the Canadian North and who, too, says that the closest equivalent that comes to his mind when he thinks about them or their teachings is zen. But, just like me, my colleague has never talked publicly about it.) There was a serenity, quietness, and peace connected with the teachings that I find hard to describe.

Now, in hindsight, I think that all Shura Shishkin was asking of me was to be present. And to do that, I had to let go. Let go of the anxiety and desperation. Of my discomfiture. Of my shame. Of the stories I was telling myself about myself. This was what it meant to be in the present.

There were many moments when I hated fieldwork. Where I thought I wasn't cut out for it. When a sense of fear and desperation was so overwhelming that it submerged everything that I truly enjoyed and liked. There were many difficult moments, and I associated most of them with failure. But the difficulties lay within me. Not simply in the form of partiality and bias but also in what I had brought to the situation. Anxiety and fear, not ease. And I realized a few things. I had a hard time being the kind of anthropologist that I thought I needed to be: Shouldn't I be busy running around with pencil and paper, asking important questions that would secure my anthropological fame? Shouldn't I come up with some marvelous descriptions of some ritual, tragedy, or important event? Ethnographies were full of myriad descriptions of interesting rituals, incidents, and myths. Most of the time, however, fear, alarm, and panic set in. Panic at not asking enough questions, not being inquisitive enough, not getting enough data, not being sociable enough, being an ethnographic fiasco. Until, at some point, it dawned on me that this was simply not what I liked to do. I loved listening to people's stories, but I did not like to be inquisitive about them, in particular when I did not know people well enough. I loved being in northern Kamchatka, but at that time, I saw little sense in statistical, numerical, and other kinds of positivistically driven research when everything seemed so chockfull with experience. I just really liked "being there." And when I could reach that stage, things went more smoothly.

But somehow I thought this was not what my discipline asked me to do. This is perhaps one of the most important things I learned: to stay with myself. Connectedness. Perhaps it is this that easily creates a certain kind of romantic image. Who knows? But this connectedness is also part of the silence that can and does translate into openness and awareness.

In a way, I felt out of my mind during the entire time I spent in northern Kamchatka. Halfway through my first stay, somebody gave me a sticker, one of those badges that were ubiquitous in the Soviet Union and usually displayed Lenin, Stalin, or some other functionary or hero of labor in some aggrandizing pose. The one given to me was slightly different. It did not flaunt somebody's stature but outlined the physical shape of the Kamchatka Peninsula. There was, too, an inscription: *Kamchatka, eto strannoe mesto*, "Kamchatka is a strange place."

There was laughter from my friends when I realized what was written on the badge, perhaps because those closest to me had an idea that the wording mirrored quite well how I felt while I was there. And with every return, that sense of wonder and strangeness that I experienced the first time in the Russian Far East would come back. Now, I have not been in the Kamchatka Peninsula for a long time, but I still have that badge. It is a constant but also well-hidden reminder of the extraordinary sense of self I experienced in the peninsula. Of presence. I say well hidden because, as you might realize by now, in many places silence is key, and these things are rarely talked about.

3. Reveal or Conceal?

BARBARA WILKES

The paper consists of an accounting of a series of ecstatic experiences that arose from and informed my work among the Kainai (or the Blood Tribe), members of the Blackfoot Confederacy in southern Alberta. On the basis of personal experiences and experiences reported by colleagues in publications and conversations, it is clear that the transformation of the researcher by virtue of immersion in a fieldwork culture is not merely inevitable but desirable, as transformations contribute to the production of meaningful, valid ethnographic knowledge. Accordingly, this paper argues that in the end, "who I am," as transformed through ecstatic experience, contributes not only to personal and professional development but, more importantly, to the production of valid local knowledge.

I begin with a reflexive narrative of my journey, starting in 1996, on the path toward the Sundance. This account is modeled after Kainai epistemological principles to clarify the meaning of the narrative and is presented in a format consistent with Kainai storytelling traditions as four steps to the Sundance. I follow with a review of some of the principles that govern the production of knowledge among the Kainai, to argue that ecstatic experiences contribute to the production of valid ethnographic knowledge and that the failure to share such stories of ecstasis does a great disservice to the discipline and its practitioners and especially to our fieldwork cultures.

A Circuitous Path to the Sundance

The First Step

Serendipity marks my personal experience with the Sundance. In the spring of 1995, I was a third-year undergraduate at the University of British Columbia satellite campus at Kelowna (now the University of British Columbia–Okanagan). During the Easter holiday, my parents arrived from Calgary for an extended visit with myself and my spouse at our home in Oyama (about midway between Vernon and Kelowna). We had recently acquired a twenty-foot motorboat with a sleeping compartment, a fridge, a stove, and other amenities to spend weekends on the lake. We decided it would be a lovely way to spend an Easter Sunday with my parents.

When we arrived at the marina, a golden eagle, sitting high in a nearby tree, drew my attention. I perceived it to be very distressed and was convinced it would not survive. As I watched, I was overcome by an intuition we ought not go out on the lake. There was not a single rational reason that this should be the case, as the sun was shining and the lake was calm. I hesitated to mention it to my husband, who is generally inclined to go along with such intuitions because of their relative accuracy. Finally, I drew him away from my parents and directed his gaze toward the eagle. We stood for a few minutes discussing its condition, and I expressed my apprehension that we should not go out on the lake. My husband wondered if it would be fair to my parents, as this would be their only opportunity to see the lake. In the end, we agreed to take the boat out, and I tried to rationalize my feelings about the eagle by telling myself it was likely old and, perhaps, starving.

A few minutes later, my mother and I were sitting at the front of the boat, gazing at the hill, when we spotted a group walking along the edge at the top of a cliff about seventy-five feet above the level of the lake. We noticed a young girl walking some distance apart from the others. I had barely said, "Oh, my God, she's going to slip" when, sadly, she did. She landed on the rocks at the water's edge, and we sped toward her. We called 911 to provide directions to the accident site. By the time we reached the rocks, others had climbed down the cliff and were attempting to assist the girl. We offered blankets to try to prevent shock and to keep her as comfortable as possible until the paramedics arrived.

Nearly half an hour later, the paramedics had still not reached the area, as there were no roads leading to her location. Ultimately, one paramedic made his way through the bush to a position nearby and called out to us. He requested we go back to a cove to pick up the others and their equipment. He continued overland, scaling the rock-strewn cliff walls to try to reach the girl. We picked up the other paramedics and returned to the accident site to drop them off. The conditions made it exceptionally difficult for the paramedics to maneuver and administer care. After a few minutes, they asked to load the girl, now fixed to a stretcher, aboard. We agreed. The stretcher was loaded across the bow of the boat, where I sat to hold it steady.

As we slowly made our way back to the cove, where the ambulance awaited, I held the stretcher in one hand and the girl's hand in the other. She appeared to be no more than eleven or twelve years of age. She was momentarily semiconscious and cried out for her mother. I soothed her as best I could and tried to ensure she remained calm, as I feared any sudden movement might cause the stretcher to slide across the fiberglass bow. At one point, she appeared to look directly at me and cried, "Mom." "It's alright," I said. "You're OK. You've been in an accident, and we're taking you to the ambulance. It's alright. Your mom loves you, and she'll be here soon." It was all I could think of and was what I hoped another mother would say, were my own child in similar circumstances. Yet it was woefully inadequate, and I admit I was relieved when she again lost consciousness. Sadly, when we arrived at the cove, the paramedics pronounced her "dead on arrival." They nonetheless administered CPR as they transferred her from the boat to the ambulance. Remarkably, as we prepared to pull away, we heard them shout that they had re-established a heartbeat.

The next day the newspapers published her name. Elena had a thirteen-year-old twin brother who had, mercifully, not been present at the scene of the accident. She had gone out for a walk with some friends and their parents, but the soft moss on the edge of cliff had caused her to lose her footing. Elena spent several days on life support in the hospital, where she underwent surgeries to reduce and contain the swelling of her brain. Ultimately, the damage proved too extensive. Tragically, Elena passed quietly a few weeks after Easter Sunday.

Why do I tell this story? Oddly, it represents my first step on the path toward the Sundance. My family was terribly shaken by the incident, and we all attended victim counseling, though for different lengths of time. After the initial visit, I refused to return, reasoning that I had had a moment with Elena, and, consequently, had a sense of closure the others lacked. I was determined to deal with the situation in my own way. Weeks later, however, I was still very distressed. Should I contact Elena's parents to express my condolences? I felt I should tell them she had called for her mother. However, I vacillated too long, missed the funeral, and then felt that to contact them would only intrude on their grief and increase their pain. For weeks I thought of little else. Other than brief attendances at classes, I remained at home most of the time.

Several weeks later, believing it would do me some good to get out of the house, my husband encouraged me to attend an archaeological field trip that I had previously scheduled. The purpose of the tour was to view a number of ancient Native pictographs, either carved or drawn on the rock walls of the hills above Kelowna. The highlight of the tour was to be a visit to a promontory overlooking Okanagan Lake, which local Native legends maintained had been a former sacred site used for vision quests and healing rituals. More than anything else, that is what appealed to me. On the morning of the tour, not yet prepared to be social, I decided to walk alone. As I did so, I noticed a Native woman who was slowly falling behind the group. She appeared to be struggling to breathe, held one hand over her chest, and stopped frequently to rest. I slowed my pace, hoping she would catch up and, when she did, we introduced ourselves. Her name was Gloria. A little embarrassed, Gloria indicated she had been watching me (much to my chagrin!) and believed that I was "troubled" or "suffering." I explained how impressed I was that she had perceived anything at all, as I thought I had done a good job of concealing it.

Despite the fact we had just met, I relayed Elena's story. When I finished speaking, Gloria shared her own story, giving the details about how she had lost her eldest son in a motor vehicle accident on Easter Sunday. I commented on the coincidence that we had had similar experiences on Easter Sunday. Gloria emphatically replied, "There are no coincidences. Everything happens for a reason." By way of proof, she cited the fact that we had both been "tuned in to each other" *before* we had known we shared similar experiences, and that each of us had been so accurate in our perceptions of the other. Gloria explained that, "In the Blackfoot way," (she is a member of the Blood Tribe) our meeting had been "intended." We had both been "brought" or "led" to the same place, and at the same time, so that we *would* meet. Gloria believed we were intended to share our mutual grief and build a strong friendship.

As we made our way up the mountain, Gloria spoke at some length about the Sundance, a ceremony I knew relatively little about. She indicated she was engaged in "preparations" to dance at the Eagle Society Sundance in mid-June. This intertribal Sundance society was not affiliated with a particular band or tribe and was not drawn from a single cultural tradition. Several times, she stressed that she was going to dance for her son. I noted she did not mention him by name but consistently referred to him as "my boy." When I inquired, she indicated it was not proper, in "her way," to speak the name of a deceased until the first anniversary of the death. At that time, she would sponsor a "give-away" and distribute all his belongings to his family and friends. Anything left over, she would burn, and the smoke would release him back to the Creator. In so doing, she explained, she would let him go. Only then would it be acceptable to speak his name. Eventually, we reached the promontory where the group had stopped to rest and eat lunch. We located a nice spot quite close to the edge where we sat by ourselves. Suggesting that we were, perhaps, too close to the edge, Gloria reassured me: "It's OK. This is a holy place. Nothing will happen here."

As we sat, a golden eagle swooped up the side of the ridge, startling us both. Neither of us had seen or heard him coming. We watched intently as he circled over our heads several times and, then, just as quickly, quietly disappeared. Though I had told Gloria about Elena's story, I had not mentioned my intuition about the eagle, and I was surprised when she proclaimed it "a sign" that *Pi'ita* "Eagle" had taken an interest in me. Gloria suggested that *Pi'ita*'s flight signified to her that I should attend the Sundance, albeit as a supporter not a dancer. "Not yet anyway," she laughed. "That won't happen until Creator wants it to." Gloria explained that a "purpose" had been set in motion "to help you and me in some way." As politely as I could, I indicated I knew very little about the tradition of the Sundance, or Native spirituality, for that matter. In response, Gloria spent the better part of the day explaining the particulars of the pictograph and vision quest sites. She patiently answered my questions to ensure, she said, that I would have what I needed. I indicated I would like to learn more, and Gloria suggested I should attend my first sweat lodge ceremony the following Saturday, at a Sundance Lodge maintained by her friend and fellow dancer. I accepted the invitation, and the following weekend, while in the lodge, I brooded over Gloria's notion that some "purpose" had been "set in motion." Following the sweat, I committed myself to attend regular "preparation" sweats with Gloria, at Merritt. Within a week or two, I had also agreed to attend the Sundance. As Gloria had suggested, I would attend as a supporter; though I still had little idea what that meant or what it entailed.

The Second Step

Most of what I learned at that first Sundance I gleaned from working with the elderly "aunties," "grammas," and others (both men and women), either in the open-air kitchen, or in the makeshift day-care center used for the dancers' children. For four days, I cooked and gathered firewood, served Elders, cleared and washed dishes—often until 2:00 or 3:00 a.m., despite the fact that the entire camp was awakened each morning before sunrise, and I was "dancing" the first round of the day before the first light over the mountaintops. This, perhaps, sounds deceptively simple. Let me assure you it was not. In some ways, the experience defies description and certainly exceeds anything I had ever experienced. Dancers are focused on two things: their prayers and the dance. In contrast, supporters do virtually everything else required to be done, and it is physically exhausting work. Nevertheless, the camp's remarkable warmth, collegiality, mutual support, generosity, affection, and humor were irresistible. The anthropological training I had received served me quite well. I kept a detailed journal of each day's experiences; recorded names, addresses, and kinship relations; detailed family genealogies, tribal, and individual myths and stories; and wrote down numerous personal reflections. The entry that stands out most clearly is the ecstatic experience that represents the second step on my path to the Sundance.

As the dance progressed daily, it became increasingly evident that the quality and intensity of the dancers' suffering had expanded and deepened. Some fell to the ground exhausted, dehydrated and shaking weakly. To my surprise, the others ignored them entirely, maintaining a sharp focus at all times on their own "purpose" and reluctant to interfere in the "gift" of the "dream" that was perhaps being offered to those who fell.[1] The temperature soared and often exceeded 40 degrees Celsius. The humidity was all but visible. There were no clouds or breezes to offer temporary relief. Nonetheless, the dancers appeared joyful, compassionate, and humble, at times even radiant as they fell and rose, cried and prayed. As the final moments of the dance wound toward their ultimate release, the dancers engaged themselves ever more fully, drawing on even deeper reserves of strength that many had not known they possessed, to "push" to the finish, to fulfill their commitment. Shortly before noon, and with a total absence of fanfare, they danced out of the circle for the last time as the drums ceased the all but ubiquitous steady beat that had prevailed from sunrise to sunset for the four days.

I watched with the others through the now-shriveled and dusty leaves of the arbor enclosure, as their "helpers" brought them tiny cups of berry juice. Though their need was obviously great (having had no food or water for four days), each took a moment to gesticulate a prayer of silent gratitude for the "gift" they cradled between their hands. They sipped slowly, and with obvious relish, and the immediacy of their revival was evident. Smiles broke across their faces, their eyes twinkled, and they laughed and joked with one another.

Parents sought out their children and gathered them into their arms momentarily. Their intense pride was unmistakable to all who were watching.

After a short time, the dancers rose as if a single being and formed yet another single line, the men leading the women, as was customary. With measured steps, really hurting now after a brief rest, they made their way back into the Sundance circle and formed a long, crescent-shaped line facing the eastern gate. The supporters drifted into the circle, where they formed a receiving line that brought the dancers face to face with grandparents, parents, spouses, siblings, children, nieces, nephews, and friends. As the spectators filed past, the dancers solemnly shook hands with strangers, and caressed friends and families with near abandon. Tears flowed freely and without shame in both the men and the women.

There was little sense of urgency in this final performance. In fact, it appeared as if no one was anxious to have the ceremony come to an end. As had the others, I made my way up the line and eventually reached my friends Gloria and Edna. We laughed and cried as we held each other, and I exclaimed how proud I was of them and how incredibly strong I thought they were. Surprisingly, they both indicated they were also proud of me. They exclaimed that I had made it through my first Sundance and they were now certain that when the time was right, I would dance. Having witnessed the inconceivable hardship and suffering they had just experienced, I was not at all convinced that I had what it takes to fulfill such a prophecy.

As the lines continued to move past each other, I shook hands and hugged other dancers. Over and over again, as I thanked these virtual strangers, I was caught off guard as each, in turn, also thanked me: "For pulling me through!"; "For giving me strength!"; "For helping me maintain my focus!"; "For being strong!"; "For having strong prayers!" they said. More confused at each stop, I reached the end of the line and shook hands with Calvin, the Sundance leader, or sponsor, whose words were equally shocking as he congratulated *me* and said, "See *you* next year." As I moved away, I reasoned he was simply being polite, or had perhaps confused me with another supporter.

The very last person in the line was Marvin, known as the "Medicine Man." Over the course of the Sundance, I had learned that many of the women had "a crush" on Marvin and were also in great fear of him, believing, they said, that he had "certain" powers about which they rarely elaborated but often joked. In fact, the women thought I was very brave to have spent some time alone with him in the kitchen on the first evening of the dance, when he had arrived in the kitchen shortly after midnight at the conclusion of the first public sweat, and he came in looking for something to eat. All the food had been packed away for some time, so I offered him a steak I had in my cooler, cooked it for him, and sat with him as he ate. While he certainly radiated a strong presence and gave the impression of having experienced unfathomable depths of suffering, I was left with an overall impression of wisdom. Beneath his somewhat inscrutable facade, he appeared, to me, at least, to be a very "gentle" man. As I came face to face with him on the final day of the Sundance, I put out my hand, but he did not take it. I hesitated, becoming confused and somewhat embarrassed.

A moment or two passed as I stood in front of him before I looked up at his face. He was smiling slightly, and when he caught my eye, he actually laughed! I did not know what to do, but the stories the women had told about Marvin's "strange powers" ran through my mind. My impulse was simply to walk away. An awkward moment passed before he softly said: "You know, I've been watching you. What Calvin said is right. We will see you again—as a dancer." I stuttered and mumbled as I tried to explain that while I was honored at the suggestion, and grateful for having been given an opportunity to learn about the Sundance, I thought it unlikely I would dance. Again, he simply smiled, giving the impression he knew something I did not. Finally, he put out his hand, but as I reached for it, he once again withdrew it. I believe I audibly gasped that time, and was even more humiliated. But as I turned to walk away, not knowing what else to do, he reached out and embraced me (something I was later told, by those who had noticed it, was quite unusual) and wished me luck in *my* "preparations." Having finished paying my respects, I walked away from the line to seek Gloria and Edna.

As I approached, Gloria smiled and reached for my hand. We stood together, not speaking but making contact and listening to the talk all around us. One of the eldest aunties standing in the group next to us passed her granddaughter into my arms. This was no common infant but the Sundance child, who had been born the previous year, following the ceremony. I stood stunned, closely cradling and looking at the sickly baby. Though I knew relatively little about her condition, the rumor was that there had been "bad" dancers the previous year who were, perhaps, "on drugs" and who had *caused* the child to be born "sickly." In fact, she had been born prematurely and had never taken well to breastfeeding because of some form of stomach malformation that required she be bottle fed a mere two ounces of milk, at two-hour intervals. I also knew the family was planning a naming ceremony immediately following the Sundance. While it had not been said outright, I had been left with the impression the child might not survive. The parents were thus anxious to conduct the ceremony.

All at once, Gloria, Edna, and I became aware that an excited whisper had begun to make its way through the crowd. We sought its source, as did the others. We noted people pointing animatedly toward the sky. We looked up and, flying above our heads, making a pass directly across the circle from the eastern to the western gates, was *Pi'ita*, a golden eagle! The crowd erupted in unrestrained excitement, waving their arms in the air, trying to catch the eye of a friend or a dancer to share their exhilaration. "A blessing," someone whispered; a "great power," another said. I glanced at Gloria and Edna, who had tears streaming down their faces, and realized that I, too, had begun to cry. It was all the more remarkable as the eagle did not simply make a pass and continue on its way. Rather, as I stood, cradling the Sundance child in my arms, it circled over our heads (some said four times—though I was too distracted to notice). While others ran about the circle tracing its path, Gloria, Edna, and I stood rooted in place—literally awestruck. I could feel the heart of the Sundance child blending with the beating of my own. As I gazed at the child who lay so quietly oblivious in my arms, I experienced the most powerful and compelling impression of warmth and completion that can, I think, only be described as sheer joy.

When the eagle finally left the circle, Gloria looked at me intently but spoke quite softly, asking, "Did you feel that?" "Yes! It was amazing. It must have been the eagle whistles! I've never seen an eagle circle a crowd like that before!" I babbled. She smiled. "No, it wasn't the whistles," she said. "No coincidences, remember?" She continued. "No. Who's the one holding that Sundance baby?" she said, looking at me intently. "We *all* prayed for that one [the baby] at that tree, and some of us prayed for you." Firmly, she insisted, "This was meant for *you*. I told you before *Pi'ita* has taken an interest in *you*. And that's a *good* thing. I just *know* you're gonna dance—and soon!" I was nearly staggering as I passed the child back to her auntie. All I wanted was to get away from there, to put the circle behind me as quickly as possible. I could neither comprehend nor rationalize in any meaningful way what had just happened, despite having witnessed it myself. I desperately wanted to retreat, to be alone, away from all the eyes that had, *apparently*, so resolutely followed my every move for four days. I needed to quietly "reason" out what I had experienced.

I walked away from Gloria and made my way through the crowd. As I approached the exit at the eastern gate, Marvin stood in my path. I stopped several yards away, not wanting to engage in conversation, and he momentarily but intensely scrutinized my face. Having apparently satisfied himself as to some aspect of my condition, he gave a short, sharp nod, smiled enigmatically, turned, and walked away. Based on his manner and the intensity of his visual inquiry, I was convinced he had overheard what Gloria had said. However, at that distance it seemed impossible that he could have, and the more I tried to reason it all out and grapple with the accuracy of my perceptions, the more assured I became that Marvin, indeed, had uncanny powers.

That was the summer of 1995, and, although these events represent the second step on my path to the Sundance, I did not dance with my friends at Merritt. Instead, I moved to Calgary the following spring to undertake a master's degree, and later entered a PhD program, to examine the social construction of disability among the Kainai. I did not realize that my research would represent the third step on my path to the Sundance.

The Third Step

In 1996 I engaged in a great deal of rapport work among the Kainai, sat on several boards and societies, and met with the members of a variety of local agencies. My fieldwork formally began on the reserve in the summer of 1997. I was invited to attend a teaching circle sponsored by the members of the Blood Tribe Disabilities Society. The society's plan was to teach a third-grade class on the reserve everything they needed to know about disability. Essentially, their purpose was to humanize the disabled by debunking popular stereotypes the students may have inherited from others. Each speaker (two male quadriplegics, a male paraplegic, and a female amputee) explained the cause of their disability and assured them they could approach a Native disabled person to give them a hug, or simply speak to them directly without apprehension, if they chose to. They wanted to convey the fact that they experienced the same joy, sorrow, pain, fear, suffering, and laughter, and failed and succeeded in their lives in the same manner, and to the same extent, as the non-disabled or able-bodied did.

When joining them, my friend Butch introduced me to Carolla, one of his relations, who was, he pointed out, the women's Sundance leader on the "north end" of the reserve. She was (and is) as engaging and intelligent a woman as I have ever met, and following the meeting I drove her home and stayed for tea. Carolla asked how I had come to the reserve, how I knew Butch, and why I wanted to work with the disabled. In addition to "caring for the women" at the Sundance, Carolla explained she was also involved with the Blood Tribe Disabilities Society. Within a period of five years, she had had a limb amputated as a result of a motor vehicle accident, had undergone breast-removal surgery for cancer, and had been diagnosed with diabetes, but remained strong, vibrant, engaged, and dedicated to the Sundance and the disabled. In turn, I explained the connections between my family and the disabled, having originally met Butch through my husband's former employer, the Canadian Paraplegic Association. I also told Carolla of my recent move from the Okanagan and some of my experiences with the Eagle Sundance Society.

I was curious about any differences between the Eagle Society Sundance and the Sundance on the reserve. Carolla explained that

Butch's having introduced her as the "leader" of the women's Sundance was somewhat misleading, her role was simply to "look after" the women. The leader was her elder brother, Maurice Crow Spreading Wings. I explained how I had been invited to dance several times but had always refused (though I did not give a reason). I said I missed my friends and the weekly sweat-lodge ceremonies. Carolla indicated she had a sweat lodge in the backyard, which had "come to her" through an elder brother who had passed a few years earlier. She generally held a sweat each Saturday afternoon. In addition, Carolla explained she was holding the first Sundance fast of the year the following weekend. She added further details about the event, by way of invitation in the "Blood Way," stating when it would begin, what the women needed to bring: their sleeping bags, a dress for the lodge, something in which to sleep, their pipes, and some sage and tobacco. I explained, somewhat disappointed, that I was not a pipe carrier. Carolla assured me it was unnecessary to hold a pipe to participate in a fast. In fact, the only way to earn such a pipe was to make and fulfill a Sundance commitment, which many of the women had done, or would do, following the fast.

As I left Carolla's home that evening, I contemplated the possibility of attending a fast and reflected on the "coincidence" that it would be held on Easter weekend. My thoughts returned to the events on the lake in the summer of 1995. Perhaps Carolla, Maurice, and the Sundance were part of the "purpose" Gloria had foretold? I mused at the statistical probability of Carolla's being the first person I met socially among the more than 9,200 members of the community. Adopting a purely pragmatic and somewhat expedient attitude, I reasoned it might not be such a bad idea to spend the Easter weekend at a fast. Accordingly, I arrived the following week early in the evening, unannounced, at Carolla's home.

Carolla had been expecting me to "turn up" and had prepared a place for me. As we worked together fixing the food for the feast before the midnight commencement of the fast, I began to doubt. What had I committed myself to? I knew I would comport myself well enough in a sweat lodge but had grave reservations about the prospect of a full fast without food or water for four days. It was not until much later in the evening that I realized the rules of the fast also precluded touching water—no washing or tooth brushing—for the duration! At that point, I nearly panicked and had to work diligently to subdue a sudden desire to make an excuse and leave.

That Saturday evening, it rained, which in the Blackfoot "way" signifies that the Creator has "taken pity" on the fasters and shown compassion. Accordingly, we were allowed to take a small amount of water. The catch was that it had to be rainwater collected from the "natural" environment. Carolla advised us there was a hole in the eaves trough at the front of the house. Myself and the others, barefoot and in our pajamas, were soon scrambling desperately in the dark through the thick, clay mud, trying to catch a drop of rainwater in a jar as it leaked through a hole in the gutter.

On the final evening of the fast, after the feast had been cleared—some given away to friends and relatives, and the remainder packed away—the women gathered around the kitchen table to sit and talk, and I sat across the table from Yvonne, a quiet young woman who appeared to be about thirty-five years of age. I indicated to Yvonne that I had recently moved from the Okanagan Valley to Calgary. Yvonne replied that she had a sister who lived there and who was also a Sundancer. Yvonne knew about the Eagle Sundance Society, the satellite college in Kelowna, and the sweat lodge at Duck Lake. Incredibly, I found myself was face to face with a sister I did not know Gloria had.

As it was late and most of the women had to work the following morning (and I had yet to drive the more than 180 kilometers back to Calgary), we began to pack our things and bid each other goodnight. Invariably, as I said goodnight, each woman offered a similar comment, "I'll see you at the Sundance." When I returned to the table, Yvonne asked, "Why don't you come? You don't have to dance if you don't want to. That's OK. But why not come as a supporter?" When I did not answer right away, Carolla added, "You don't have to make a decision right now. Just pray about it. Pray about it and ask for guidance." Without making any commitment, I left and once again mused, as I drove away from the house, about the sheer number of "coincidences" I had encountered since I had first met Gloria only fourteen months earlier. In that light, I had more or less decided

I would attend the Sundance as a supporter, but the farther away I drove, the more my thoughts shifted back to the concerns of family and work. As June approached, I wavered for several days undecided. Could I spare the time? Did my desire to see the women again constitute a valid reason to attend? Would I go?

The Fourth Step

So it was that in June 1997 I determined to follow the directions I had been given and drove off the highway into what appeared to be an unkempt field. After driving for nearly two miles, I reached the anticipated turn in a dirt road, which brought me alongside a steep coulee, several hundred feet high above a wide oxtail turn in the Oldman River. As I had been told, I could see a house, a campground, some tents, camper trailers, a Sundance arbor, all sheltered within a grove of massive old cottonwood trees, I was overcome by a powerful impression that somehow I had "been here before." What prevailed was a sense that somehow I "was home," and I could not shake the feeling. I began to tremble and had to remain in the truck for several minutes to collect myself and explain myself—to my husband and grandson who had accompanied me.

As I struggled to regain some control, it began to grow dark and the wind picked up in the kind of gale that is typical of the prairies at sunset; it also felt as if it might rain. Seeing my grandson's face in the rearview mirror, I realized we had to quickly set up camp and drove down the coulee and chose a site under a large cottonwood overlooking the riverbank. We struggled to wrap a large tarp around the tent to ensure that my grandson would not get cold or wet during the night. The wind and the darkness worked in tandem against our efforts, and suddenly, the rain pelted down so hard it was painful. The tarp became tangled around my legs. I was standing in one place, spinning around, trying to unwrap myself, when a man stepped out of the semi-darkness and asked if he could help. We quickly regained control of the tarp and secured it for the night. We shook his hand and he asked if there was anything else we needed. We assured him we were fine and thanked him for his assistance. He indicated to us that if our son was cold or wet in the night, we could come up to the house and help ourselves. We thanked him again, and he walked away, quickly disappearing in the darkness. I liked him immediately, as did my husband.

It was not until the next morning as the dancers entered the arbor that I realized it had been Maurice, Carolla's elder brother and the Sundance leader. I was impressed again by his humility and by the gentle but quietly self-assured manner in which he maneuvered the dancers into their places. As it happened, the spot in the arbor where we set up our chairs and my grandson's playthings was next to the drummers' enclosure by the western gate. Over the next four days, I scrutinized Maurice carefully, as he alternately sang at the drum and danced. I grew increasingly comfortable and familiar with his kind demeanor and mischievous sense of humor. Maurice would periodically catch my eye and make a face, tell a joke, sing a "goofy" song such as "They Call Me Billie Jack," or deliberately throw off the rhythm of the other drummers by modifying his beat. He was a natural comedian and had a way of putting everyone around him at ease. At the same time, it was evident he was highly respected by all in attendance, and there was little doubt about who was "in charge."

As I had done in Merritt, I listened, watched, and participated in the Sundance as a supporter, helping my friends meet their commitments in any way I could. Intermittently, Maurice sought us out to "check in," he said, to ensure there was "nothing we needed," and I began to feel that *if* I were ever to dance, I might do it there. In fact, everything seemed to be moving me in that direction. On the final day, however, following the ceremony when they called the "pledgers" to the tree to make their commitments for the next year, I did not join them.

Several weeks later, I visited Carolla; and while we sat drinking tea and chatting, the subject of the Sundance came up. I was, I told her, "apparently" incapable of making a decision about whether to take part in the Sundance. After I spoke, we sat for several moments in silence before Carolla said, "You need to pray about it. Just pray about it and you'll know. Pray about it and start your preparations. So, if you'll decide to do it, then you'll be ready. Just pray about it and ask for guidance." For several months thereafter, I drove to the reserve every Sunday morning to participate in the preparations and sweat-lodge ceremonies. I acted "as if" I were going to dance and learned the songs and the protocols, the stories and the history of this Sundance and participated in the semiannual fasts. I got to know the women and men who had already pledged. I actually began to feel fairly comfortable about my potential participation.

As Carolla had suggested, I spent my time in the sweat lodge praying and waiting patiently for an answer. I had no idea what form such an answer might take, nor, indeed, whether I had missed my answer not knowing what form to expect it in. Despite Carolla's assurances that an answer "would come," I was beginning to doubt that would be the case. It seemed that no matter what activity I engaged in, the single question, whether to dance or not, remained foremost in my thoughts. Then, one night, I had the following dream.

It was a lucid dream, one in which the dreamer is aware she or he is dreaming. It was as if I were standing outside of myself at the bedside and watching myself sleep. At the same time, I felt as if I were fully conscious of my thoughts inside and outside the dream. As I slept, I heard a voice, sharp and insistent. I could not grasp the words, or comprehend their meaning, but recognized they were spoken in Blackfoot, which I could not comprehend at the time. The voice was calling *me*. Whether it was calling me by a "name" or simply "calling" to attract my attention I could not tell. I mumbled, "Leave me alone. Go away. I'm tired. Just leave me." But the voice pressed me to acknowledge it. I made up my mind to ignore it, and so continued to say as earnestly as I could, "I am too tired to bother." Ultimately, it became clear the voice would not leave me alone. So I rolled over in my sleep toward the sound, and there, at the edge of my bed, to my astonishment (even in my sleep), stood a golden eagle. It spoke to me then in English and simply said: "Come with me."

I was frightened and tried to roll away, vehemently explaining that while "I would like to go" it was impossible. I was too weak and too tired to follow. In the dream I remember thinking, "This is really crazy." It is simply not possible that I am lying here in my own bed, with my husband lying beside me (I could see him in the dream but do not know why I did not try to wake him), and speaking Blackfoot! English! To a golden eagle! Its presence was inescapable, and though I was completely unnerved, I finally indicated: "*Okí, Pi'ita!* I would follow you but I cannot fly." The eagle respectfully but firmly commanded, "Just grab my tail feathers." I did, and we were immediately airborne.

Flying at a considerable height over the prairies, we found the wind coming directly at us from the south, becoming increasingly stronger until *Pi'ita* was struggling, and I could barely maintain my grip on his tail feathers. I called out to him that I could not hold on anymore; it was too difficult, and I was very cold. I wanted to go home, I said. I listened carefully, but there was no audible response. The eagle then shifted direction radically westward, toward the very edge of the foothills. As we approached the mountains, he turned slightly south again. We were now tucked up close to the mountains, and the wind became a gentle, though still quite cold, breeze. I felt I had a good sense of where we were, over a country road I frequently used to avoid traffic on my Sunday trips to the reserve. I was, at one and the same time, fully enjoying the trip (it was beautiful) and terribly frightened, as I had no idea what he wanted from me or, ultimately, what was going to happen.

Now that the eagle was flying south, the trip became much easier, and I relaxed the hand that had originally seized his tail feathers in a fist, until I barely had a fingertip on a single feather. I marveled (in the dream) that he could support our combined weight and drag, and that just the slightest contact between us, just the pad of one fingertip, was sufficient to keep us connected and airborne. Though still anxious, I began to relax and surrender to his direction. For some time, I simply watched as the landscape transformed below. I realized that I was in pajamas, actually a long cotton gown—not something I ordinarily wore, and that my feet were bare. I was almost too relaxed now. I tried to lean over a bit to look over the eagle's left shoulder so I could see his face and speak to him. Then, suddenly, my fingertip lost contact with his tail feathers. I held my breath for a moment, anticipating a fall. Instead of falling, the journey abruptly ended. We did not land, nor even attempt to land. We were simply on the ground standing by a Sundance tree in the midst of an abandoned arbor.

The place was familiar. In the dream I remember thinking it was

Maurice's. We were close to a river; I could hear it in the dream. For some reason, it seemed inappropriate to speak aloud. Accordingly, I queried him with a look asking why he had brought me here. He responded by silently reaching for my right hand and placing something in its palm, he closed my fingers tightly around four small sticks. I did not know what the sticks were for, but I did know that they were what he had brought me there to retrieve. I remember thinking maybe they were piercing pegs, but simultaneous with that thought, I was instantly awake and sitting bolt upright in my bed.

Without thinking about what I was doing, I peered over the edge of the bed, fully expecting to see the eagle still sitting there. Somewhat disappointed, I sat back up and actually opened my hand, which was still clenched tightly into a fist, anticipating the four sticks he had placed in my palm. While I could not see them (it was dark in the bedroom), I could sense their weight and feel their texture against my skin. I could even smell the scent of freshly cut or broken branches. But there was nothing there, and again, I experienced a profound sense of disappointment. As I slowly regained full consciousness, I began to shiver and became so disturbed by the contents of the dream that I woke my husband. It was 3:03 a.m. and I relayed the entire dream to him. For some time, we laughed and traded potential explanations for the dream. I felt relieved and, after talking for about a half an hour, we rolled over, and I immediately fell back into a deep and dreamless sleep.

The next morning, however, the dream was still very much with me. While it had seemed somewhat entertaining the night before, the whole experience was too tangible to be made fun of in broad daylight. As the affect stayed with me for several days, I began to seek out a number of the Sundancers, believing one of them would be able to clarify the dream. However, no one I spoke to was able to recognize a specific message, and each, in turn, suggested I seek out Maurice.

The following weekend, while driving to Maurice's to attend the sweat lodge, I decided I would ask him to interpret the dream for me. I was familiar with the protocol and so began to stop along the way to purchase the items I needed: print (cloth), two pouches of tobacco, a large flank steak (a perennial favorite among the Bloods), and some hard tack candy, which I knew he liked. I wrapped the whole thing up in a bundle with some spare red cotton cloth and, at the last minute, included a fifty-dollar bill. With these gifts, the request for an interpretation could be properly made.

As was customary at the conclusion of the sweat lodge, everyone returned to Maurice's house for a feast, which often lasted for several hours, as people ate, relaxed, talked, and accepted teachings from the male and female leaders who were present. I stayed later than usual, waiting for an opportunity to speak with Maurice alone. Finally, after nearly three hours, I sat with Maurice at his kitchen table and asked if he would be willing to interpret a dream I had recently had but could not comprehend. Maurice agreed to do so, and I offered him the gifts according to local protocols, which he accepted with a suggestion that I follow him into a back room where we could speak privately.

Sitting together on a small couch in the back room, I suddenly felt timid, ridiculous, a little unsure of myself, and even less certain of my purpose. Maurice, perhaps, sensed my hesitation and began to speak first. He asked about my family (which he invariably did) and spoke for a few moments about his most recent "bad" luck at bingo. Once he had me laughing, it was clear the floor was mine. I told the dream exactly as I have written it, and included the story of Elena's death, my experience at the Eagle Society Sundance, the fast at Carolla's, and the Sundance preparations I had engaged in, and briefly described some of the other dreams I had had.

I spoke for nearly half an hour, and Maurice had said not a word nor asked a single question. Even after I finished, he remained very still and said and did nothing for a full ten minutes. When he began to speak, I could barely hear his words, for his head was down and he was speaking directly into his chest. I had to listen carefully. He began with an abridged version of his life story in the form of a verbal genealogy, starting with his grandparents, moving on to his parents, and then to his brothers and sisters. He made a self-deprecating joke about his third "marriage" and finally spoke about his children and his grandchildren. Maurice, then, offered several vignettes about dreams he had had as a young man. In addition, he spoke about his career as a former award-winning powwow dancer. The stories included the details of a number of events that had occurred while he was on the "circuit" and that had irrevocably changed his life, including the fact that he had spent some time in jail (which I had known before). Maurice stressed the fact that he had known "full well" what he had been doing at the time of his offense and made no excuses for his behavior; rather, he felt he had done so for good reasons (as that is his story, I will not repeat it here). Finally, he made it clear to me that he had accepted full responsibility for his actions in the Blackfoot "way" (where the acknowledgment of personal responsibility is critical, as no absolution is possible; and, where, ultimately, failing such acknowledgment, he would have been separated from his ancestors in Cypress Hills, forever). However, he appeared completely at ease about his past and the contributions he had made to it. I had *no* idea what any of it had to do with my dream.

At this point, he began to tell a story about a small group of Blackfoot warriors in pursuit of enemies across the prairies in the dead of winter. In great detail, he spoke of how the group became lost in a blizzard and somehow ended up on the wrong side of a river not solid enough to cross safely on horseback. One of the group volunteered to risk his life to break the ice, swim across the river, climb out on the far bank, locate some dry wood, and build a roaring fire before the rest of the group could cross. His voice was filled with obvious admiration for the bravery of the young man's actions. Maurice spoke at length of the qualities of sacrifice, bravery, and caring for the needs of others, as opposed to fulfilling your own wants. The young man, he explained, was a distant ancestor who had counted many coups during his warrior days, and thus, lived "many winters," a Blackfoot euphemism for a long and fulfilling life. In the Blackfoot way, such genealogies serve as the speaker's bona fides, and Maurice was telling me his history and justifying his leadership at the Sundance.

Maurice was a natural storyteller, and it was easy to be swept along as he told a tale. As he shifted his narrative to yet another subject, I was seized by dread. The longer he spoke, and he had been speaking for nearly an hour, the less and less confident I was following him, or that I had grasped the meaning of what it was he was trying to tell me. I became confused and despondent and stopped trying to record his words. Perhaps, alerted by the discontinuation of my scribbling, Maurice looked up for the first time since he had begun speaking, and made direct eye contact. His look was mild and gentle though he appeared to be far away "as if" he did not see me clearly. Although he continued to speak in a soft voice, his tone changed and his words became increasingly forceful. This new posture served to increase my distress and confirm my growing conviction that I had entirely missed his meaning and would be unable to answer the inevitable series of questions I felt he would ask to check the quality of my perception. I became conscious I had lost the direction of the narrative, and scrambled to write down his every word as he continued speaking. I "tuned" back in just in time to record the following interpretation of the dream:

> . . . and so my Blackfoot name is Naatsohsowaatsis, Last Tail Feathers. I think the dream was good. Pi'ita (Eagle) brought you to the circle. He wants you to find your place in that circle. Everyone has a place there that belongs to him. And you'll find what belongs to you. And so Pi'ita put you in that circle. Maybe it's for your husband? I always pray for your husband. Every day at that tree, I'll pray for him. And for all those cripples (disabled). Pi'ita is telling that you could call on him. That he'll help. If you get into a trouble you could call and he could help you out. And protect you. Ah, he'll watch over you like ah...ah guard. Like an angel, you know? Like a guardian? But you need to honor him. You'll honor him. You'll have to know that eagle song. Do you know that song? [Yes. But I'm not sure I know it very well]. Then, first thing is . . . then you learn that song. And learn it good. 'Cause you'll honor him with that song. Pi'ita is giving you that song so you can use it. And so you're brought to this place and to me. Those tail feathers? That's me! That's my Indian name, Naatsohsowaatsis, Last Tail Feathers. In that dream, that's me. And Pi'ita is telling that it's gonna be better if you'll be in one place. That wind? It's gonna be hard if you'll jump all around. Listening to this one and that one [various Leaders]. If you'll do it that way, then it's gonna be no good. It's gonna be hard and maybe too hard [like the wind in the dream until Pi'ita shifts his course]. And maybe you'll pay too

much [suffer]. You understand? [Stay on one path?] Yeah, just in one place. They're all gonna want you to go with them [to other Sundances]. But just stay in one place and learn what you need to learn. If you'll go, after you do your four years, then it's gonna be OK [if I teach you]. But if you'll go in one year or two years it will be hard. I can teach you that. Pi'ita is saying that it's OK [that you are worthy to be taught]. In that dream he's telling me it's OK. And I know you. I know how you are inside. I've seen you for a long time now. I've watched you. I know who you are [I am Ni'itsitapi, a real person. A Blackfoot compliment, a way of indicating I have few pretensions and am one of them]. And so I'm gonna tell you how it happened [how he became Sundance leader]. I'm gonna talk about all those choices that I made. And then you'll see how it [the Sundance] came here. How it came to me. How I brought that Sundance here because of all my decisions. Because of all the things I've done. And my family's done. And so that's it. I think it's pretty clear. It's a good message. It's good you're here. This is where you should be. It's where He [Creator] wants you to be. And so that's it. And it's an answer. It's a good answer. And so it's up to you. Pi'ita is telling you that you need to make a choice. You need to make that decision. That's all I have to say. (Fieldnotes, April 26, 1998)

Kainai Conception of "True" Knowledge

Cycles. Circles. Ages. Stages. Relations. Interdependence. Balance. Harmony. Flux. Change. Growth. Knowledge. Concentric circles and interrelations. These are the preconditions of knowledge production among the Kainai. Although I understood that at an intellectual level before the Sundance, only having lived these principles in conjunction with the ecstatic experiences that led me to them, made them real, a part of who I am and, thus, made them available to me as tools in the production of knowledge and ethnography.

Fabian's "out of mind" is neither a flight of pure fantasy nor a work of fiction. Ecstasis is akin to a Sundance, a ceremony, a vision quest, or a dream in the Kainai world. To be "out of mind," in this way, is not to be mad, unscientific, or non-objective (in fact, for the Kainai it is so ordinary it does not bear mention). Nor does it signify that one has "gone native." Instead, it is an opportunity to glimpse the moral, emotional, physical, intuitive, and spiritual realities and experiences of others firsthand as we take part in the transformations our hosts experience. Thereafter, we have an obligation to determine what such experiences may add to our perceptual and conceptual understanding not only of our fieldwork cultures but of all human phenomena, including ourselves. It is possible to vitalize our ethnographies concerning "others" by including our own ecstatic experiences, which in any event indirectly acts to validate our host's ecstatic accounts. To ignore such experiences, either because they do not meet the requirements of our own epistemology or because we fear we will expose too much of ourselves, is indicative of a fundamental disrespect for the very people we write about, as it continues to set them apart as "others" who are fundamentally irreconcilable with our "ways of knowing." In the end, we owe it to ourselves and to those we try to represent, to produce an ethnography that makes "sense" not only to us but to *them*. If ecstasis provides a tool that facilitates greater veracity in our attempts at "sense making," we owe it to ourselves and to those we represent to make use of that which is available to us. To me, that is the best measure of the quality of a good ethnography—it should open one's mind, heart, and behavior to a given lifeworld, in this instance that of the Kainai.

The traditional Kainai universe is populated with animate, sentient, and spirit beings existing in a relational order with human beings. All beings are governed by a constant state of "flux" (Little Bear in Battiste 2002, 78) understood as the potential for growth or adaptation essential for the continuity and well-being of all. This relational principle is of utmost importance not merely because all beings exist "in relation" to one another, but because all beings are inherently interdependent. Hence, the Blackfoot phrase *Okí Ni'itsokowa* "all my relations!" is less a colloquialism than a literal rendering of Kainai "first principles."

The Kainaiwa orient to reality based on the principles of "relations," "space," and "place," as opposed to the more familiar time and context of the Western world (Little Bear 2002, 82; Crow, personal communication, 1998). Space refers to a specific physical location in an environmental context. Place denotes an inherently reciprocal position in the relational order of family, community, and the larger global village (Crow, personal communication, 1998). Each human being is unique among all others and is at liberty to interpret the collective cultural code based on his or her experiences (Little Bear in Battiste 2002, 84; Crow, personal communication, 1998; and Calf Robe, personal communication, 1999). Each person is, therefore, capable of making a "contribution" to society through innovation or adaptation of that collective code. The value of wholeness (flux, place, space, relations) ensures that if all do their part, social order, harmony, and balance will be the result (Little Bear, in Battiste 2002, 84).

In the Kainai worldview, knowledge *is* stories, as each story contains both ideas (subjective theories) and actions (objective methods). The potentialities within stories are vitalized by experience. As a process, experience mediates between ideas and actions, and the transformation that occurs is a result of human creativity and innovation and reflects the ongoing flux of the universe, understood as a natural tendency toward change through growth and adaptation. Thus, as the essential element of the universe, flux acts upon both the environment and human beings. Humans experience flux as birth, the developmental stages of life, death, and reincarnation. In an endless and self-sustaining cycle, flux takes the form of the self-sustaining generative, degenerative, and regenerative cycles that produce regular patterns or occurrences, such as the seasons; annual animal migrations; the spiritual ceremonies of individual and communal renewal, such as the Sundance; and the songs and stories of the people and the aesthetics and conventions by which they are formed and performed (Little Bear, in Battiste 2002, 78). In this manner, the ceremonies, songs, and stories of the Kainai are the repository of the full corpus of cultural knowledge.

Accordingly, the goal and the product of *all* knowledge is the introduction of change into the world. Understood as the potential for growth, adaptation, and transformation, knowledge is essential for the perpetual renewal and continuity of all creation. Similarly, stories are both the vehicle through which knowledge (ideas, actions, and experience) enters and affects the world, and the medium that records and represents that knowledge to others as a potential for learning (growth and transformation).

The concept of *Kxa'khom* or Mother Earth is, perhaps, the best conceptual example of relations, space, and place as the primary precondition of Kainai knowledge production. *Kxa'khom* exists in a literal, not metaphoric, sense as the Mother or generatrix of all life. This includes the Kainai, who, as an autochthonous people, were born of her womb. The cultural symbol of that womb is found in the dome-shaped sweat lodges used by the Kainai for prayer and purification. The sweat-lodge ritual use is a symbolic act of spiritual rebirth. As all Kainai are born of the same Mother (the Earth), classificatory terms, such as *niitsistowahsin*, "brother," are not simply rhetorical. Rather, they express the nature of this primary kinship relation. Thus, an individual becomes fixed in "space," "place," and the reciprocal relational order of Kainai society, governed by the principles of mutual respect, trust, and the fulfillment of kinship roles and obligations.

Being born of *Kxa'khom*, the Kainai participate in the sacred substances and actions of creation. At death, the spirit leaves *akáa'tsis*, the body—a temporary "robe"—protection afforded to the spirit—and returns to *Kxa'khom* to contribute to and participate in the renewal and regeneration of new life (Crow, personal communication, 1998; Calf Robe, personal communication, 1999). Ceremonial events such as the Sundance, understood as individual and communal acts of purification, thanksgiving, and renewal, are both symbolic of and productive of that continuity. The notions of "relations," "place," and "space" as repetitive motifs not only affect internal individual behaviors but manifest themselves in the social behavior of the Kainaiwa, such as in the social and spatial organization of the community (Little Bear in Battiste 2002, 81). On an individual basis, "space" refers to the specific area of reserve lands that extended families originally occupied and have continued to occupy for generations (Little Bear, in Battiste 2002, 81).

As do all animate and sentient beings in the Kainai universe, *Kxa'khom* wishes to exist in the normative state of wellness intended for all beings at the time of Creation. Wellness is conceptualized as balance and harmony. The potential for harmony (or fulfillment) exists only when all forces and beings in the universe (the individual, the family, and the tribe) are in balance. In addition to existing within the relational order, *Kxa'khom* also exists in the Kainai spatial and social orders. In terms of "space," this relationship is exemplified in the strong connection between the Kainai and *Kainaissksááhko*, the land, or, literally, "Kainai land." Traditionally, it included the territory from the North Saskatchewan River through to and including Yellowstone Park. The Blood Reserve is now understood as their tribal "home."

For the Kainai, a moral breach or a failure of reciprocal obligations calls for the repair of damaged relations. At death, the spirit of a Kainai who had maintained and fulfilled its reciprocal obligations during life and, thus, had not broken faith with the local moral order, was admitted to the Cypress Hills, and there resumed life in all its particulars, with ancestors who had gone before (Calf Robe, personal communication, 1999). In contrast, a Kainai who committed a serious and unremediated offense (understood as the failure to accept personal responsibility for one's actions) would be refused entry and, thus, risked becoming separated for eternity from earthly and spiritual kin relations. To break with the precepts of the local, moral order was to risk everything and represented the most severe form of retribution a Kainai could experience.

The Kainai worldview privileges process as opposed to product, or actions as opposed to goals (Little Bear, in Battiste 2002, 78). Every thought or action, from its inception to its fulfillment, is valued equally. For example, in intuiting the design of a drum, gathering the materials and fashioning a finished product, each step is equally satisfying and fulfilling. All things happen when the time is right, when each of the necessary preconditions for an occurrence have been satisfied. There is nothing to be gained by rushing or taking shortcuts. The preference is always to let the process play out "on its own" or in the "the right" time. Pleasure is consequently understood as a feature of the process as a whole, rather than as a reward deferred until a goal has been realized. Thus, time cannot slip away, be wasted, or be lost. Time is without direction (lineality) and cannot impose itself on an individual being or the world. Time exists and unfolds in natural cycles as part of the essential perpetual flux of the universe. Time just is (Little Bear, in Battiste 2002, 78).

The process orientation and relational order of the Kainai universe is reflected in the Blackfoot language, which is verb-oriented rather than nominal. There are no distinctions between genders, nor is the language precisely inflected as to animate and inanimate, though it appears to be. Everything is more or less animated (Little Bear, in Battiste 2002, 78). The importance of a given act of speech is the action, "what is happening," as opposed to the nominal, the being, the object or place toward which an action is directed. In this universe "trees" speak, "rocks" become grandparents, and "buffalo" or "coyote" take an interest in human beings and offer guidance, protection, knowledge, and power (Little Bear, in Battiste 2002, 78). Accordingly, human beings may transform themselves into another being and display the primary characteristics associated with such a being, whether animal or spirit. A "bear dancer" does not merely mimic the actions of a bear, he *is* a bear, dancing.

The Kainai worldview has important implications as regards the inclusion of ecstasis within ethnography. First, since ideas are subjective, it is not possible to know what ideas exist within the mind of another. Access to the knowledge of another is made possible only through actions, or story. A story transfers knowledge when a listener who wishes to learn applies "active" listening skills and, having heard the story, "acts" upon that knowledge. Second, each Kainai experiences the world differently (as, indeed, all human beings do). The Kainai therefore insist there are many local, contingent, experiential, temporal, flexible, contextual, and gendered subjectivities, or truths. Thus, when an individual shares a story, and, in so doing, potentially engages in a knowledge transfer, the listener can assume the storyteller has, to the best of his or her ability, faithfully recreated the experiences upon which that knowledge depends (Little Bear, in Battiste 2002, 80).

In short, the Kainai are an embodied people. The Earth is, literally, their Mother, and all beings, human, animal, spirit, and other are brothers and sisters in Creation. All exist within a highly moralized, cyclical, and spiritual environment within which each is charged with the well-being and continuity of the community through participation in the natural flux of the universe. Stories of their experiences effect individual and communal transformations and result in the production of knowledge necessary to ensure the balance and harmony of all. Being fixed within the spatial and relational web of the Kainaiwa, having "found my place" in the Sundance circle, according to Maurice's directions, was instrumental in the development of my knowledge and understanding of the Kainai and essential to the production of ethnography. Only through ecstasis and the visceral experiences of the Sundance was I able to embody these "first principles" and move beyond the realm of an objective, intellectual exercise to a full appreciation of Kainai truths.

Conclusion

Beginning in 1998, I did dance at Maurice's Sundance. To date, I have completed three years of a four-year commitment. I will not say more about why I dance other than that I do so for my family. I will say, however, that the ecstatic experiences noted in this piece were instrumental, ultimately, in my reaching a decision to dance. Suffice it to say that my ecstatic experiences and my participation in the Sundance shook the very foundation of my perceptions and conceptions of the Kainai and of their identity as a people. Looking back on my journals, they conjure a virtual reproduction of that time. What cements each event in my mind is the congruency that exists between my notes and my recollections of my own experiences. As I reread the diary, each experience is revitalized and produces a visceral reaction so authentic that I can smell and taste the food (and especially the "camp" coffee); see the children in bare feet with runny noses and burr-filled socks; hear their shrieking and hysterical, raucous laughter; and feel the warmth of their hands in mine. I can conjure the smells of the kitchen and the camp, including the sweetgrass mixed with the blood, sweat, and tears of the dancers and myself; and smell the body odors of the "old ladies" cooking three meals a day for a crowd of more than one hundred people; and that of the men who worked day and night chopping wood and throwing it into the fire pit. Looking back upon my own experiences, I can see, feel, taste, touch, and hear the Sundances I attended and those in which I participated. The beating of a drum or the smell of burning sweetgrass or sweet pine immediately conjures the experience of enduring days without food or water: the relentless prairie sun burning my skin, the physical pain of long hours dancing, singing, and sweating under those conditions. The social pleasures of friendship and shared suffering combined with the intense spiritual joy of prayer and thanksgiving. The "gift" of simple respite and rest at the end of the day and the delight of reuniting with family members embedded in my marrow. A chance meeting with another Sundancer automatically unites us in joy, pain, and suffering. I *know* these people and they know me with an uncommon intensity. Without this firsthand experience of a new way of being (new for me, not for the Kainai), I could not have contemplated the potential contributions of ecstasis as an epistemological tool.

Ecstasis moved my conception of the Kainai and the Sundance to a more widely inclusive plane, a holistic or unified level that encompasses all aspects of myself and of the people (the Kainai and others), including our joint and several histories, our mutual and individual experiences, and our expedient and common needs, desires, and goals. There is no loss of "self" or "objectivity" in this, but rather an enrichment of self *and* other. I now have a deep appreciation of the spiritual, emotional, psychological, and physical similarities and differences between us that, rather than obscure, actually clarify and explicate a common humanity. As a result, I appreciate and carry with me, always, the social and emotional weight of such a commitment to myself, my family, my Sundance brothers and sisters, the leaders, and the community (especially the elderly, the sick, and the disabled). I fully appreciate at an embodied level what it means to suffer and to give fully of oneself on behalf of others.

Similarly, I have a firsthand appreciation of the true measure of such a pledge, including both its gifts and the heavy cost of suffering it demands. I can access, utilize, interpret, and apply meanings to intuitive and aesthetic materials, which I could not comprehend before, and am able to dream in a familiar and culturally authorized idiom, supported by and reflective of community standards, morals, and values. I have realized firsthand the process and the state of constant flux in the universe and have developed an appreciation of its value as a source of change, growth, and transformation, and as a precondition for knowledge production. I now recognize that stories *are* knowledge and have the potential through process and transformation to actualize both theory and practice. I am sensitive to and aware of the constant movement between the positive and negative forces of the universe and ourselves, which constantly seek their own level and thus produce balance and harmony in the world. And I now know with certainty that everything in the Kainai world is *literally*, not figuratively, charged with the positive value of spirituality and relations.

Likewise, I now know that there are no simple oppositions in the world, no obvious demarcations between those who are good and those who are evil, and I realize that both are necessary and coexist in us all in equal measure. I now know that the choices we make in life and the steps we take (both conscious and unconscious) define our moral position in the universe, as there is no natural justice or absolution, only responsibility and the full recognition that it is not possible to save or change another. Each one must access the flux and seek transformation for him or herself. I have learned that the world's full measure of justice is found in the sum of what we each put into it and that we each carry the weight of our own culpability for suffering throughout our lives. I now know that only relationships add positive value to life (this one or the next) and that material pleasures are fleeting indeed.

In truth, we need very little to survive in life, some water, a little food, and good relations. Thus, I know that reciprocity and sharing is always a gift to the self. I also know that death is not the irrevocable loss I always believed it to be; rather, it is a part of the process of natural flux and continuous regeneration, a momentary loss that accompanies a transformation of form, as the energies of the universe readjust to our passing. Finally, I now know that there is grace in aging and in learning life's lessons well and that there are pleasures and penalties associated with each age.

As Gloria knew all along, and as I learned through ecstatic experiences, the teachings I received from Carolla, Naatsohsowaatsis, and many other Elders and dancers, and my subsequent participation in the Sundance, flux or change is always transformative; even the tragic death of a child or the acquisition of a major disability, whether one's own or that of another. That such transformative events may be positive (moral) or negative (immoral) depends entirely upon the individual agent experiencing that flux or change. Attending to my own physical, emotional, intellectual, moral, spiritual, *and* ecstatic experiences since Elena's death has enhanced my perceptions and conceptions of the Kainai, and their spirituality, soteriology, and worldview. Thus, *my* story, and my own transformations, both as individual and as ethnographer, reflect the fact that ecstasis is both an acceptable form of knowledge production and transfer among the Kainai, and a useful research tool for the production of ethnographic knowledge in a manner that is accessible to and reflective of the worldviews and experiences of those we represent.

Notes

1. This behavior varies by tradition and is not indicative of all Sundances.

Part Two

Entanglements and Faithfulness to Experience

Anthropological research involves a process called recursion. Defined as conditions under which "events continually enter into, become entangled with, and then re-enter the universe they describe" (Harries-Jones 1995, 3) recursion leads to deutero-learning that presses one to exceed the boundaries of not only disciplines and categories but also a normative or rational self, and to accept particular kinds of faithfulness to experience and to ethics. To exceed boundaries is to access hitherto-unknown territory. From that point on, "apprehending the world is not a matter of construction but of engagement, not of building but of dwelling, not of making a view *of* the world but of taking up a view *in* it" (Ingold 1996, 121; Poirier 2004, 61; emphasis in original).

In "Recursive Epistemologies and an Ethics of Attention," Deborah Bird Rose draws upon her rich research experience with Australian Aborigines to demonstrate how, step by fateful step, an anthropological practice located in the real here and now of encounter takes us into the heart of an Aboriginal homeland and the people intimately associated with it. Rose argues convincingly that her own connectivities or entanglements with Debbie, a true Aboriginal mentor, became constitutive of her own personhood, and, as such, entered into her research in unexpected ways. She notes that having crossed an epistemological threshold, the process of discovering the spiritual dimensions of Aboriginal lives called her into fidelity, into change, into question. To understand the transformation lived in the field, she finds Bateson's concept of recursive epistemology useful because it speaks to our connectivities with our research partners and teachers. Recursive epistemology expresses the dynamics of the ethical and epistemological process that concerns her.

In "Ethnographic Rendez-vous: Field Accounts of Unexpected Vulnerabilities and Constructed Differences," Anahí Viladrich conducted the first study on Argentines living in New York City (NYC), where she entered tango-dancing halls (tango *milongas*), in which Argentines (tango artists and customers) exchange valuable social resources on the basis of social solidarity, common interests, and friendship. Viladrich demonstrates how ethnographic data emerges from dialogues. Study participants, it is shown, reinvent themselves by telling, retelling, creating, and weaving more than one story from which to make sense of their unthreaded migratory paths. From there, they assemble (and imagine) promising migratory trajectories. Within the delicate balance of structure of opportunity, social conditions, and serendipity, Viladrich illustrates the games of social identification and divergences between the ethnographer and her study participants as two sides of the same coin bringing esthetic moments of mutual understanding, even when these are also the source of elusive resentments, inconclusive demands, and somehow-painful acted-out expressions of indifference.

"When the Extraordinary Hits Home: Experiencing Spiritualism," the book's sixth chapter, consists of an account by Deirdre Meintel of her extended field-based research among Spiritualists in Montreal where she discovered that her own experience was crucial for even knowing what questions to ask about matters such as clairvoyance and healing. She is an intellectual originally from France, and they are mainly francophone Québécois of working-class origin. Yet, in the course of her research, she finds no radical distinction between home and field, "us" and "them," her experience and theirs. Meintel initially expected to *receive* clairvoyance and healing as part of the research; to her surprise, she was invited early on to learn how to *do* them. She describes how being the subject of clairvoyance and healing and also becoming a clairvoyant and healer involves a great deal of learning through nonverbal means, notably via bodily experiences or mental ones that involve bodily metaphors (e.g., "hearing" and "seeing" things). Meintel examines the "events" (in the sense given to this term by Augé) that have shaped her study of Spiritualists and shows how they have proved integral to the research itself.

Like many previous fieldworkers trained in the tradition of ecological and cognitive anthropology, Edmund Searles was perplexed by the tales of sorcery, reincarnation, and prophecy that he encountered while doing fieldwork in the Canadian Arctic in the 1990s. The more Searles pondered these tales, the more he realized that his initial reluctance to engage with them was a symptom of his insecurities as a scholar rather than a reflection of the realities of Inuit social life and experience. In chapter seven, "Prophecy, Sorcery, and Reincarnation: Inuit Spirituality in the Age of Skepticism," Searles examines these stories in light of his recent encounters with the mystical and the sacred in his professional and personal life. From this vantage point, he demonstrates how Inuit accounts of sorcery, reincarnation, and prophecy are part of a concrete and complex world of religion and spirituality that includes both Christian and pre-Christian beliefs and practices.

4. Recursive Epistemologies and an Ethics of Attention

DEBORAH BIRD ROSE

Step by fateful step, an anthropological practice located in the real here and now of encounter takes us beyond our previously known worlds. One crosses these epistemological thresholds, and still the process continues to call us: into fidelity, into change, into question. My aim here is to explore some entanglements of friendship and epistemology across the threshold of life and death. My exploration causes me further to reflect upon silences, ethics, and connectivities.

I was privileged to do my graduate studies in anthropology at Bryn Mawr College and to study under Professor Jane Goodale. Her work with Australian Aboriginal people inspired my own research (Goodale 1971 [1994]), and her field methods course guided it. Goodale taught us a full range of anthropological methods. The emphasis, however, was on participant observation, and this method was set within the broader epistemological frame of deutero-learning, or learning to learn. Drawing on the work of Gregory Bateson, Goodale taught us that in our learning from others in the field, a central method was learning to learn. Our task as anthropologists, it seemed, did not allow us simply to transfer our epistemologies into another context. Rather, it required that we learn how other people learn, that we open our minds and our bodies to other people's epistemologies. For this reason, and as a result of her own extensive field experience, Goodale taught that good field learning is a whole-person experience. Our most important research tool, we were taught, was our own self; self-observation and self-awareness were not to be suppressed in the work of observing and gaining an understanding of others.

The implications of deutero-learning take us into an anthropology that is wonderfully open. Jean-Guy Goulet, for example, writes of his work with the Dene Tha: "Dene informants are firm in their conviction that individuals, including ethnographers, who have not directly experienced the reality of revelation or instruction through dreams and visions do not and cannot understand a crucial dimension of the Dene knowledge system" (Goulet 1998, xxix). His narrative ethnography seeks to communicate this and other aspects of his deutero-learning over many years with these people.

As the work of Goulet, among others, makes clear, the issue is not only epistemological in the methodological sense but also leads into a rich metaphysical domain concerning the human condition and the condition of life more generally. This openness leads to an anthropology that is dialogical, reflexive, and attentive to process, and that extends beyond the human and into the lives of plants, animals, and all manner of extraordinary beings and modes of communication. The ethics and methods Goodale's students learned in the classroom already predisposed us to work outside the constraining structures, analyzed so eloquently by Johannes Fabian (1983), that produce representations of distanced others. The co-eval chronotope of ethical ethnography is founded in attention to the actual here and now of the encounter. In my view, the ethical encounter demands that anthropologists engage attentively *both* with our research partners and teachers *and* with that which engages their attention. Such attention is demanding. As the years went by, I began to realize that I needed to improve my skills in history and geography. Then it was botany and ecology, and, later, environmental philosophy and ethics. Holism or hubris? Bradd Shore (1999) asks in an essay on anthropology's engagement with a holistic approach to humanity. Perhaps some of both, it seems to me, but, in any case, a legitimate demand on a whole-person research scholar.

Deutero-learning presses one to exceed the boundaries not only of disciplines and categories but also of a normative or rational self. Fabian (1991, 399–400) expresses the view that a lot of our research "is carried out best while we are 'out of our minds,' that is . . . when we let ourselves go." He notes that "ecstatic" experiences are rarely reported, and he calls for more analysis of the "epistemic content" produced in this manner. As is the case with many others, the willingness to follow, to try to learn what my teachers were trying to teach, and to act on that knowledge in responsive and responsible ways has led me outside many norms. This paper tracks one such excursion. Rather than pursuing Fabian's call for epistemic content, however, I examine the ethics of experience.

The story I offer here primarily involves my relations with people in the communities of Yarralin and Lingara, in the Northern Territory of Australia, where I began my research in 1980. In particular, it concerns my friend and teacher Jessie Wirrpa. She took me into her care not long after I arrived in Yarralin in 1980, and kept me under her wing until her death in 1995. I have already written about one aspect of what I think is important to say about Jessie in an essay called "Taking Notice" (Rose 1999). A brief summary follows.

When Jessie and I took a walkabout, she called out to her ancestors. She told them who we were and what we were doing, and she told them to help us. "Give us fish," she would call out, "the kids are hungry." Jessie's country included the dead and also the living, and when she called out, she addressed the dead.

Her brother Allan Young explained it this way: "At night, camping out, we talk and those [dead] people listen. . . . When we're walking, we're together. We got dead body there behind to help. . . . Even if you're far away in a different country, you still call out to mother and father, and they can help you for dangerous place. And for tucker [bush food (Australian term); food gathered in nature] they can help you" (Rose 2002, 73).

As Jessie and I walked, we took notice of other living things. When the cockatoos squawked and flew away, Jessie laughed because they were making a fuss about nothing. When the march flies bit us, we knew the crocs were laying their eggs, and Jessie began to think about taking walks to those places. When the *jangarla* tree (*Sesbania formosa*) started to flower, we knew, or Jessie knew, that the barramundi would be biting. The world was always communicating, and Jessie was a skilled listener and observer.

In "Taking Notice," I wrote about paying attention to the world:

about how the world is in communication and how a person like Jessie understands that and becomes part of it. One of the points I made was that I came to know that Jessie's country gave her life because I walked with her and observed the process, and I knew it experientially because it gave me life too. She was a presence in her country, a known and responsible person who belonged there. I came to understand that Jessie lived an ethic of intersubjective attention in a sentient world where life happens because living things take notice. Tagging along behind her, I did my best to take notice too.

Whole-person deutero-learning required me to learn types of observation and communication that had formerly been unknown to me. I had to develop an awareness of several root principles: that the living world is filled with both human and non-human forms of sentience; that the world is filled with patterns and communications; that living responsibly requires one to take notice and to take care. This was threshold learning for me; once across those leaps, it was neither reasonable nor possible to go back. Having learned to experience the vivid and expressive presence of other living things, there was, for me, no good reason, and probably no way, to return to a duller world.

My experience may constitute more than what is implied by the term deutero-learning. Bateson developed the term "recursive epistemology" later in life, according to his intellectual biographer Peter Harries-Jones (1995, 9). This term expresses more fully the dynamics of the ethical and epistemological process that concerns me here. Recursion is defined as conditions under which "events continually enter into, become entangled with, and then re-enter the universe they describe" (Harries-Jones 1995, 3). Recursions are iterations and entanglements; they are "rampant" in ecological systems (Harries-Jones 1995, 183) within which human societies are embedded. The concept of a recursive epistemology connotes the ways of knowing and the kinds of knowledge that arise in contexts in which self and other are both knower and known, and to the same degree, and are mutually embedded in encounter, exchange, mutual influences, and collaboration. In the context of anthropological research, a recursive epistemology connotes the situated connectivities within which knowledge comes into being. The anthropologist's thought is shaped by her teachers as her life shifts more deeply into relationships with people, places, and concepts that become increasingly constitutive of her own thought and being. While fostering porous proximities, a recursive epistemology does not lead toward homogeneity. Rather, it works productively with difference, change, and exchange. In addition, it demands a re-thinking of ethics. I return to this latter point shortly.

Recursive epistemology helps me account for the ongoing entan-glement of my own learning. Jessie's teachings were not just in my notebooks but were becoming formative of my own experience of the world. They were shaping my life, my questions, my perceptions, my hypotheses, and much that I would later write.

Jessie was a great hunter—the Ngarinman term is *Mularij*. Every-body wanted to go with her all the time because they knew they would get a feed. Her forte was fish. She never missed. Jessie and I went to just about every junction, every permanent waterhole, and most creeks and billabongs within her sections of the Victoria and Wickham riv-ers. Sometimes we went on foot, more often by motorcar; sometimes we went with a large group, occasionally she and I would take a cou-ple of kids and strike out on our own. Some of those days were so glorious that they remain among the most beautiful times of my life. Others, of course, were dreadful. If I never again sit on a steamy riv-erbank in forty-five-degree heat with my head about to explode from the reverberations of the screaming cicadas, and with blood running down my legs from the march flies, that will be OK with me. Jessie almost always seemed happy, but sometimes there were too many kids, too much nuisance, and everybody wanting to borrow her gear, messing it up, and then sitting around waiting for her to catch fish so that they could have dinner. We hunted together in good times and tough times.

Jessie died in 1995, leaving me desolate and also worried. Was our friendship over, or would something remain in addition to the notes, tapes, photos, and memories? This question brings me to the next phase of the story I am pursuing. In that same year, I had reason to take a group of indigenous people from North America to Litchfield National Park (just south of Darwin) for a day. I had been working with a group of the traditional owners of that area for a few years, and my plan was to take the visitors to the park and then stop by the little bush town of Batchelor on the way home to introduce them to Nancy Daiyi, the senior woman for the country. I rang her first, to ask if this was OK. She said yes, and I asked if I could take them into an area where the water is free of tourists and where the mermaid custodians of the country are said to live peacefully (Rose 2002). She agreed to that too. Late in the day, we got to Batchelor, and I told her what we'd done and said that I'd made sure to splash water on the visitors. She asked if I had called out, and I said no. In her grumpy and imperious way, she said I should have called out to the old people. I was not aware that I was authorized to do that, and I had to tell her that I didn't know how. She told her daughter Linda to show me, and Linda did.

I should state that Nancy's pedagogy works like this. Her default position is that the people around her are intelligent and competent and have observed what to do and know how to do it. She doesn't praise people for getting things right; she just growls at them for getting them wrong. I knew why she was saying what she was saying, and I could appreciate why she was annoyed. However, the following year, I made the same trip with my young niece, and although I knew I was supposed to call out, I could not bring myself to do it. I just couldn't. What I remember is that my throat wouldn't work.

I now jump to the year 2001, when my sister Mary visited me in Canberra. We drove to Darwin by way of the Birdsville track, the Victoria River District, and Kakadu National Park. We went out to the Vic River, and when we got to one of the main crossings, we stopped. I took Mary down to the riverside, got a cup of water and splashed her, and called out loud and clear. I addressed Jessie, and my voice was absolutely right.

A question I ask myself retrospectively is: why was I able to call out in one area and not in another? The quick answer is that in one area I had spent years of my life fishing with Jessie; we were there together all up and down this river. On top of that, Jessie, my friend, was dead, and thus when I called out I could address someone I had known and been close to. These are good personal and social reasons for the difference, but they actually are not experientially what the difference is. The experiential difference is this: in one place, I could hear; and in the other, I could not.

Along the Victoria River, on that day, I could hear something I had experienced often with Jessie but hadn't quite realized and hadn't quite thought to try to articulate. I could hear a listening presence. The world at that time was not just a place, it was a presence. I could hear awareness, and so I could call out.

The temptation, when using the written word in academic contexts, is to find reasons and explanations that fit the existing discourse. And yet, what happened was embodied responsiveness. It did not matter exactly what I knew or thought I knew. It mattered that here I heard something around me and here I had a voice. Here it seemed that that which was beyond me called forth my voice. All I had to do was let it move. The call seemed to be invited from beyond me, but, as Goulet (2004, personal communication) points out, consent came from within. Entanglements brought my voice into Jessie's world.

I am not saying that these two places are qualitatively different; I am saying only that my experience of them was qualitatively different. For me, the difference is that my ability to hear gave me a voice. In contrast, at Makanba, where I had every good reason to call out, having been specifically instructed to do so, I was able to voice nothing.

This experience seems to lie outside the general domain of what is sayable in normative anthropology. Povinelli (1995), for example, contends that such matters fall well outside the normative modernity in which anthropology and other social sciences ground their legitimacy. So the experience of finding my voice had a paradoxical effect: when I returned to the academy, I started to feel voiceless. The finding of a voice in one context rendered me nearly voiceless in another. My silence in the academy is built up from my knowledge and experience of boundaries and censure, but perhaps it is also influenced by the silences that pervade the place. These boundaries, these limits to what is sayable, are made evident primarily by being breached, and that rarely happens, so usually it may not be apparent that in an academic context that is founded in seminars, lectures, letters, articles, books, and coffee breaks, there are actually some terrible silences. They are overcome from time to time by works of passion and daring that leave one longing for more such riches.

Colin Turnbull wrote just such an article, published in 1990, in which he contends that anthropological methods and boundaries, linked with a constrictive ideal of objectivity, have limited us and incapacitated us in our fundamental endeavor of understanding. He notes the criticism, leveled by "third world scholars and laymen alike," that we fail "to be fully human and [thus fail] to use our full human potential." This failure leads us to treat others "as though they were indeed not full human beings themselves but things that could be satisfactorily examined and explained through the artifice of reason alone" (Turnbull 1990, 51). He goes on to describe our superficiality as a major weakness of anthropology.

Anthropology and its silences: thinking about theories of absence in the context of my own silences demonstrates to me the limits of a strictly discursive approach. To put it abrasively, normative anthropology's silences are not so much signs of repression as they are signs of amputation. These silences do not produce an excess of meaning and desire; rather, they diminish meaning while producing complacency. They dumb down toward instrumental modes of explanation, and they excise vast amounts of experience, including the encounter with mystery and the experience of joy.

But my own silences can also be understood as part of a much broader set of processes that are amplifying silence in both ecological and social spheres. In contrast to a recursive epistemology that adds depth and richness to life through entanglements, another set of processes is reducing, debilitating, and silencing life. I can approach this reductionist process through the concept of double death (Rose 2004), drawing on Bateson's insights concerning entropy and the disorganization that starts to ramify with the loss of meta-patterns (Harries-Jones 1995, 169, 210). Long before Jessie's death, I had written about death, life, and what becomes of human beings after death, according to Vic River people. I will return briefly to some of this earlier discussion in order to look at the twisting together of life and time, so that death is bent back to affirm and contribute to the life of the country.

As I discuss in *Dingo Makes Us Human* (Rose 2000), Vic River people talked about the components of the human person in ways that suggested at least two animating spirits (I expressed caution about

95

the use of the term "spirit"). One of them keeps returning from life to life, so that death becomes an interval leading into transformation into new life. Often, the genealogy of "spirit" includes animals as well as humans—this life force moves through life forms and continues to bind death and life into the ongoing and emerging life of the place. Another "spirit" returns to the country to become a nurturing presence. These are the "dead bodies" mentioned earlier—the dead countrymen who continue to live in the country and to whom people appeal when they go hunting. This ecology of emerging life sets up a recursive looping between life and death; the country holds both, needs both, and most importantly, keeps returning death into life. The return is what holds motion in place, and in the dynamics of life and death, life is held in place because death is returned into place to emerge as more life.

Double death breaks up this dynamic, place-based recursivity. The first death is ordinary death; the second death is destruction of life's capacity to transform death into more life. In the context of colonization, double death involves both the death that was so wantonly inflicted upon people, and the further obliterations from which it may not be possible for death to be transformed. Languages obliterated and clans or tribes eradicated are examples of double death.

Ecological violence performs much the same forms of obliteration. Thus, species are rendered locally or everywhere extinct, billabongs and springs are emptied of water, and soils are turned into scald areas. This violence produces vast expanses where life founders. It amplifies death not only by killing pieces of living systems but by diminishing the capacity of living systems to repair themselves, to return death back into life. What can a living system do if huge parts of it are exterminated? Where are the thresholds beyond which death takes over from life? Have we exceeded those thresholds violently and massively in the conjoined process of conquest and development? These double-death processes are not always irreversible, but in many areas the answer is yes.

In Jessie's way of life and death, she has joined the other dead bodies in her country, and, like them, is becoming part of the nourishing ecology of the place. In life she was a great hunter, in death she joins the ancestral providers. Double death puts her in double jeopardy. The rivers are rapidly deteriorating from erosion and, even more severely at this time, from the invasion of noxious weeds. It is probable that in the near future riverine ecologies will collapse, and with that collapse the possibility for living people to go fishing and feed their families will be radically impaired, if not completely obliterated. For Jessie, then, there is a doubling up: first her own death as a living person, and subsequently, her obliteration as a nurturer within a flourishing country.

I can imagine that there could be yet another form of obliteration— a triple death, perhaps, with anthropology as a contributor. As scholars, we are vulnerable to being colonized by reductionisms and to reinscribing their legitimacy by refusing to name and challenge their power. Our boundaries around what is sayable, and our elisions that treat as real only that which can be subject to constricted modes of social analysis, have the potential either to excise a great range of experience and knowledge, or to drag it back into the familiar, thus depriving it of its own real power.

The concept of multiple death requires us to think about what is happening in the world. Death is overpowering life, and some of our practices may facilitate this violent thrust of entropy. Normative modernity's progressive emptying of the human capacity to imagine non-human life in subjectively vibrant forms of self-realization, self-repair, and self-organization is matched by practices outside and beyond anthropology that progressively are emptying the living world of its subjectively vibrant life forms. Social and ecological entropy go hand in hand. Anthropology's silences have the potential to reduce or obliterate much of what people have to say about the process and to excise from the record much of the human evidence concerning violence. Fabian (1991) demonstrates that anthropology has consistently allowed itself to be deflected from the challenges of epistemology and enabled itself to find a zone of security.

In contrast to security, Fabian contends that ethnographic knowledge is an open process. His passionate and perhaps risky protest in favor of a processually engaged anthropology returns me to a basic question: who or what was I addressing when I called out to Jessie

Wirrpa on the banks of the Victoria River a few years ago? The short, pithy answer is "I don't know"; in Aussie vernacular, "I wouldn't have a bloody clue, mate." That is factual, but I can also say that I was not indulging in clueless behavior.

A significant point that Fabian did not discuss, and that I believe follows directly from a recursive epistemology, is faith. I would say that when I called to Jessie, I acted in faith, and I mean the term in several senses. The first is that of faithfulness or holding fast, such as is implied in the idea that I acted in good faith. My action was faithful to Jessie's teaching, and in good faith it continued the mutuality we shared in life. I claimed an enduring bond of connection, implicitly asserting that just because one of us was dead it did not follow that the relationship was finished. And indeed it is not. As this paper shows, Jessie's gifts continue to shape my life, and clearly I intend my work to analyze and make publicly explicit some of the perils she and her country now face.

Another meaning goes to the question of the non-secular. A number of scholars today pursue a distinction between faith and belief. Turnbull, for example, describes belief as a domain of mere reason and rational forms of religious experience (1990, 70). Similarly, Debjani Ganguly (2002), one of the new wave of postcolonial Indian subaltern scholars, insists that although belief can be reduced to political-cultural calculation, the force of *non*-secular language and experience challenges, and may fracture, the apparent hegemony of modernity. With these and other scholars, I suggest that faith is not defined solely by cognition; it can be located throughout the body, and it may often erupt mysteriously, being called into existence by that which is outside us or precedes us. Faith, in my view, is action toward intersubjectivity. It is called forth by that which is beyond the self and thus equally is action arising from intersubjectivity.

Jessie taught me about a communicative world by taking my hand and walking me in it. Through her own listening, she taught me to listen. Having held her hand and followed in her footsteps, I know that my life takes a twist into life-affirming action when I ground my life's work in her intersubjectivity of place. I call out as a gesture of faith: that country matters; that life has its own vibrancy, intensity, and modes of attention; and that my voice has a place in this world.

In calling out, I take a stand, and I now clarify this position. I noted that recursive epistemology leads one directly into ethics. This is so for several reasons; for me the most interesting point is the convergence between biological theory (see, for example, Maturana and Varela 1998), and late- twentieth-century philosophy's turn toward ethics. Emmanuel Levinas, a major twentieth-century philosopher of ethical alterity, moves away from the insular totalizing self and toward relationships. "Self is not a substance but a relation," Levinas (1996, 20) writes. Recursivity between subjects posits a similar mode of becoming and thus requires "abandoning the ontologies of our time," as Levinas (1996, 24) so forcefully puts it. Thus, the anthropologist, too, becomes embedded in intersubjective encounters and engagements. It must, therefore, give primacy to ethics. Ethics involve relations between self and other and thus actively abjure homogenization, appropriation, objectification, and amputation. Both self and other matter in their difference: in their capacity for relationships and for mutual influences.

Methods for intersubjective encounter depend, I believe, on a radical theory of dialogue. Although Fabian (1991, 394) objects to the term *dialogue* because he thinks it sounds soppy—"anodyne, apolitical, conciliatory," I think that the term has a good history and an excellent future. Granted that the term *dialogue* is often used loosely; I mean it quite precisely. Dialogue is a form of ethical practice among subjects (not a subject–object relationship, but a subject–subject relationship). Dialogue seeks connection with others and need not be restricted to human others. The philosopher Emil Fackenheim (1994, 129) draws on the work of Rosenzweig to articulate two main precepts for structuring the ground for ethical dialogue. The first is that dialogue begins where one is, and thus is always situated; the second is that dialogue is open, and thus the outcome is not known in advance.

The situatedness of dialogue is context-specific. It includes the here and now of the encounter—its place and its time. It includes the history of the place and the personal and social histories of the parties to the encounter. The situatedness of dialogue means that our histories precede us, and that the grounds of encounter are never abstract or empty. In the Victoria River valley, for example, the ground between myself and my Aboriginal teachers was already occupied in the first instance by Captain Cook. A history of conquest, white rule, dispossession, and cruel decades of colonization stood between indigenous people and any outsider, particularly a white person, in the first instance. That was the situatedness of our encounter. Other possibilities were open to us, and Aboriginal people's efforts to assert the existence of, and to specify, moral others (in Burridge's 1960 sense of the term) offered generous paths toward alternative grounds of encounter. But such developments depended on the process of the relationships through time, as we revealed ourselves to each other through our actions. Other contexts, in Australia and elsewhere, have their own unique situatedness. Situated dialogue is never abstract.

The concept of openness may sound obvious, but it is equally challenging. Openness is risky because you do not know where you are going to get to. You cannot have a mission statement, a set of goals, targets, charters, and performance indicators. You would have to be clever in your proposal writing if you hoped for funding. To be open is to hold one's self available to others: you take risks and make yourself vulnerable. But this is also a fertile stance: your own ground, indeed your own self, can become destabilized. In open dialogue, one holds one's self available to be surprised, to be challenged, and to be changed. This ground of openness to change is the place where knowledge arises; it is an essential basis to a recursive epistemology. It seems important, therefore, also to assert that openness depends on an underlying faith in pattern, connection, and communication. That is, while the outcome is not determined in advance, one works with an expectation that random or chaotic outcomes will be the exceptions rather than the rule.

From an anthropological perspective, this theory of dialogue is a position of situated availability. One is situated in one's own history, training, desires, and self and is available to be called into change through the teachings of others. One holds one's self open to recursive epistemology both by knowing and learning one's own situatedness and by being available to become enmeshed in the teachings one has struggled to encounter.

Situated availability poses a further challenge. One of my favorite philosophers, Lev Shestov, says that for us moderns, faith is audacity: it is a refusal to regard anything as impossible (1970, 33). One can read Shestov's audacity as a theological claim, which is certainly part of his project, but one can also read it today as an ecological claim. From this point of view, as long as the living world is fully alive, it will be self-organizing and self-repairing, and thus it is a dynamic system in which the whole is greater than the sum of its parts. It is not knowable as a whole by any of its constituent parts. Faith in both social and ecological terms is audacious because it rests on consent. It requires submission to, and thereby enables a flourishing participation in, pattern, process, and mystery.

Shestov's (1982, 105) view is that the desire to be able to encompass and explain everything constitutes a forfeiture of "the capacity to come into contact with the mysterious." This view holds special significance for anthropologists, as our work brings us into contact not only with that which is mysterious to us but also with that which is mysterious to our teachers. Impossibility, in an ecological context, defines the paradoxical knowledge that life exceeds our capacity to understand it. In the context of anthropology, audacity can be read as faith in three conjoined propositions:

- That differences within the human family are real (see Hornborg 2001),

- That understanding is possible across differences, and

- That understanding never exhausts itself; there are always possibilities for more questions and more understandings.

My commitment to a recursive epistemology urges me to resist conclusions, but I shall offer a few words in the mode of summary. Bateson's concept of a recursive epistemology speaks to our connectivities with our research partners and teachers, and these entanglements become constitutive of our own personhood. The practice thus requires particular kinds of faithfulness to experience and to ethics. When we become entangled in an ethics of dialogue and fidelity, we are called upon also to bring those entanglements into our academic lives and work. Anthropology thus has the potential to contribute to the leading edge of major paradigm shifts within the natural and social sciences and also the humanities, dynamically working to overcome the subject–object paradigm that we now know to be so damaging to people and to the world. Our challenge, as Turnbull put it to us, well over a decade ago, is to open our humanity to the full, and thus to further connectivities and entanglements in all the contexts of our lives.

5. Ethnographic Rendez-vous

Field Accounts of Unexpected Vulnerabilities and Constructed Differences

ANAHÍ VILADRICH

This chapter presents a reflexive invitation to examine the subtle ways through which the field experience labels us through social categories that shape our beings in terms of identity markers, which not only allow us to play diverse roles in our everyday dramas but also make us vulnerable during our (often) unexpected social encounters in the ethnographic field.[1] My interest in tango as a research topic emerged almost as a fieldwork accident, one of the countless providential serendipities that make ethnography a unique field among the social sciences.

A few years ago, in 1999 to be exact, I decided to conduct the first anthropological study on Argentines in New York City (NYC), as the basis for my PhD dissertation thesis at Columbia University. My research project explored the social careers of Argentine immigrants in NYC, and the diverse health systems they gain access to through their informal networks and the exchange of social capital, defined as access to resources via social relationships. As an Argentine immigrant myself, I began asking my Argentine friends and acquaintances for assistance identifying the maze of Argentine immigrants' 80 social networks in the city, which are not concentrated in a particular geographical area as is the case with other ethnic minorities. Therefore, a great deal of my initial time in the field was spent on drawing the geographical and social map of Argentines in NYC.

While trying to find Argentine enclaves, I ended up discovering the world of nomadic *milongas* (tango-dancing halls), which, in recent years, have been supported by an eclectic community of tango fans who gather weekly in different entertainment venues. Tango gatherings play a powerful role in attracting Argentines on the one hand, and publicizing Argentine events to the wider public on the other. Little by little, my incursions in the tango field led me to an awareness of its importance in supporting the careers (and everyday lives) of an increasing number of Argentine artists and entrepreneurs who have made tango their purposive drive in New York City.

Over time, my research also underscored the magnitude of the Manhattan tango world as an exemplary *multiplexial* (rich and diverse) social network, which encourages the circulation of social resources (including health information and medical referrals) not only among Argentines but also within an international community of tango fans from different socioeconomic strata, professions, and generations. By participating in diverse tango activities, I was finally able to examine the visible facade of the Argentine minority that, until recently, had remained a hidden immigrant group in NYC.

Fieldwork consisted of visiting tango milongas, mostly in Manhattan, where I met tango regulars and artists of varied sorts, some of whom became my key informants and led me to other Argentine settings. What almost started as an unplanned turn of events soon became central not only to my project but also to the inconspicuous search for my own ethnic roots in NYC. Through my tango cruises, I was finally able to find traces of my Porteño (referring to people born in the city of Buenos Aires) urbanite spirit.

Contrary to what I had initially anticipated, some of the most conflicting episodes during fieldwork emerged from what seemed to be the easiest: my becoming a participant–observer in tango milongas, where Argentines and an international crowd of *tangueros* (tango dancers) congregate to dance and exchange valuable resources, from visa information to free prescription drugs, in exchange for tango lessons. If, on the one hand, milongas constituted ideal fields from where I was able to explore the ways through which social capital is shared; on the other, I was confronted with social dynamics as in no other place during fieldwork, as recorded in the following notes:

> I need these pieces of my own identity that had been borrowed
> from my ethnographic encounters; I need the familiar faces of

people I have hardly known, and I should not trust, but who greet meet me as a distant cousin that has finally got back home after having lost her path. I give myself to them, knowing about their desperate need to transcend with the help of my compulsive tape recording of their words, while being also aware that the intensity of our encounters is as powerful as fragile and volatile. They can love me and hate me all at once. They may promise to keep in touch but it is always me the one to blame for our distance. I accept their patronizing attitude, their taken-for-granted assumption that it is my fault if they have lost contact with me; their indifference when I tell them that I wish I could be there more often. They don't care, or they don't care much, but it is this overwhelming feeling of being in Buenos Aires even for a few hours, while surrounded by desperate beauties and forgetful souls, the powerful force that brings me back to them, over and over again. (Tango notes, October 10, 2001)

The above notes are among the ones that suffered from my own censorship and never saw the light in my doctoral dissertation. Now that the rite of passage is over, I have begun to reclaim the genealogic layers of knowledge, to paraphrase Foucault (1984), and to bring up their hidden construction of meaning. From my role of vulnerable insider in my own ethnic minority, I moved to the one of a vulnerable observer (see Behar 1996) as part of my ethnographic coming of age. The contradictory feelings of sudden euphoria, enchanting relationships, and frustrating misunderstandings I encountered during fieldwork are by no means unique. They are shared by most ethnographers who, after hours of listening and recording a seemingly endless progression of words, often feel disappointed and taken for granted.

In the following pages, I describe my personal discoveries in the field, from the original tensions that my position as a tango voyeur brought along, to my becoming an accepted non-dancing *tanguera*, a role that somehow enabled me to mingle with the cosmopolitan tango scene. I begin by briefly examining the tango renaissance in the last fifteen years as a global phenomenon that has become a unique passport for Argentine tango artists eager to join the international entertainment economy. Next, I analyze the role of tango as an identity marker for Argentines living abroad and as a metonymic expression of our lost urban environment. Finally, I examine my personal experience as a tango ethnographer, from my initial problematic representation as a non-dancing observer to my successful personification of a trusted conversation partner.

Tango Milongas and the Argentine Tango Trade

The tango, a centennial musical and dancing form born in the Rio de la Plata region (Buenos Aires and Uruguay) has achieved an unusual degree of international attention in recent years as a result of the globalization of entertainment industries, the transnationalization of ethnic trends, the increasing demand for ethnic tourism, and the renaissance of Buenos Aires as the "Tango Capital." For the past fifteen years, Argentine tango has become a traded icon of for-export artistic spirit ready to be consumed by varied audiences around the world (Pelinski 2000, Viladrich 2004b).

Tango became most visible in Manhattan in the mid-1990s, when it left its hidden place in the inventory of the ballroom dances and attained a social identity of its own, partly as a result of the talent of local entrepreneurs who foresaw its potential amid an international New York clientele. Thereafter, middle-class Argentine immigrants and international entrepreneurs made tango a centerpiece of Manhattan dancing salons, cafés, and restaurants. The booming tango fever (*tangomanía*) has been accompanied by the arrival of a new generation of Argentine immigrants and amateur artists encouraged by promising job prospects in New York City.

In recent years, Manhattan has become milongas' ultimate hub to bring together Argentines from different professions, generations, and interests with an international community of tango aficionados (Viladrich 2003). It is only natural for Argentines to become tango fans when they are away from their country for a considerable time (see Savigliano 1995).[2] Argentines from middle-class backgrounds dream of home when listening to tango tunes, since most of these songs refer to a "missing other" in the urban world: the old neighborhood, the lost friendship, the abandoned lover. Even if passionate, tango never portrays a superficial happiness, a joyful cheerfulness in which everybody dares to celebrate carelessly. Many Argentines I met during fieldwork freely acknowledged having become tango fans after joining the loosely organized group of Argentine émigrés. Not only did they learn to listen and sing tango tunes in New York City, but they also became fond of other Argentine cultural trademarks. In some cases, their entrance into the tango world implied their acquisition of some Argentine habits and preferences that they lacked at home, including learning to drink maté (an herbal infusion), watching soccer games, and participating in national festivities.

The tango has a history and a unique nostalgic philosophy, which has been kept alive by those who combine melancholic sagas of a cherished past with the expressionism of the ballroom floor (see Viladrich 2004a). Argentines in New York City, Barcelona, and Milan are drawn to tango venues for reasons that escape conventional wisdom and relate to their need to connect with those bonded by national iconographies of place, taste, and urban tales. That I was no exception is reflected in the following journal entry:

> It is like nothing has changed, being here and there is like the same.
> . . . Here I am as at *Milonga X* that reminds me of *El Café de los Angelitos* (a well-known tango café in Buenos Aires), like if Buenos Aires was only a subway ride from my NYC home. Today, I felt a little bit uneasy coming here with my American friends. They seemed not to understand the codes beyond the etiquette. Even if everybody spoke English, it is like we (Argentines) have a way to recognize each other's gestures, a certain sarcasm in the way we speak that is often missed by others. I wonder if the whole thing about tango is for me a way to recover something that I feel has been lost. What is it? Do I also need to be understood? Am I feeling lonelier than I think? (Tango notes, October 5, 1999)

Many of my Argentine acquaintances and I have nurtured the recreation of a far away land, through allegoric social iconographies of an urbanite Argentine neighborhood that we have left behind, simulacra that protect us from the amorphous sense of vulnerability nurtured by our new multiethnic milieu. Our homesickness for Buenos Aires let us perform in tango sites "as if" we were still there, in a theatrical mise-en-scène of vernacular emotional spaces. Given the scarcity of distinct Argentine social enclaves in New York City, nomadic milongas have become unique reservoirs for Argentines in their search for familiar vocabulary, flavors, and music. Unsurprisingly, my increasing interest in tango also paralleled the acquisition of my migratory habitus (Bourdieu 1984) that translated into my craving for Argentine sounds, smells, voices, and places, even at the cost of idealizing what I had left behind.

Entering the Field: A Non-dancing Tanguera

Very early in my ethnotango incursions (fieldwork at the milongas), I had decided to do what my colleagues in the tango field would probably consider a profanity: I decided not to dance tango. Far from being a well-designed strategy, this decision resulted from an intuitive assessment of the social dynamics I had witnessed in the tango milieu, where multiple layers of social hierarchies are intertwined in the tango savoir-faire. As an insider–outsider (insider as an Argentine immigrant; outsider as one who does not enter the tango floor), my position as an ethnographer in the tango world has often been scrutinized not only by colleagues, who actually are tango ethnographers, but also by some of my tango interviewees.

While discussing tango with peers (Argentines and non-Argentines) I have often felt like an agnostic attending a ritualized ceremony, which can be intellectually understood but not sensitively experienced. What is the authoritative standpoint on tango from which I am able to digress, if I have not yet submitted myself to the tango's embrace? What is the source of my legitimized knowledge if all I know is intelligible rhetoric, which has not been triangulated (confirmed, validated) by my bodily experience? Needless to say, tango, in its recent globalized construction as Latino passion, is the ultimate oxymoron that has increasingly attracted the interest of an eclectic international clientele, which has often become frustrated when realizing that this author (the tango lady) does not exercise the talents that interest her ethnographic endeavors.

In various conferences and seminars, almost every time I present my research on tango immigrants, I am either invited to demonstrate my tango skills, or asked to teach a tango workshop afterward. My answer has always been, and still is, that what distinguishes my work from that of others is that I focus on tango as a distinctive epiphenomenon of the entertainment field, or as the stargate that leads into the realm of unique social relationships built upon tango dancing. My work on tango has become a metaphor to represent the social relationships concealed behind dancing, which reveals the exchange of social resources and the construction (and reaffirmation) of identity through the recreation of unique tango personas.

By being a non-dancing observer, I have allowed myself to experience a certain emotional detachment from the feverish intensity of the tango coupling, what some people in the tango world call the addiction to the tango's embrace. This is defined as a sort of tango obsession that takes on those who are being initiated into the tango as a powerful communicator of passion. Many of the Argentines I interviewed call it an obsession, a fever, a high, which may last from a few days to weeks or even years. In some cases, it never reaches its illusory target; in others, it turns into a nirvana of unearthly feelings. For many, it is characterized by a sort of intoxicating urge to hold (and be held) while keeping the magic embrace for as long as possible. This ecstasy is also supported by the need to be out there showing off, rehearsing steps, figures, kicks, movements, touches, while sharing subtle caresses with a tango partner for a brief period.

Savigliano (1995, 2003), the female tango anthropologist par excellence (who has extensively written about tango and the global political economy), describes the addiction to the tango embrace as a passion, referring to the endless search for it rather than its consummation. Like other anthropologists who have researched tango, Savigliano has merged with her object of study not only intellectually but also sensitively, enabling her to establish meaningful liaisons between the emotional and the sociopolitical aspects of the genre. For example, speaking from her own experience as a researcher–dancer, she challenges conventional wisdom regarding the tango's gender relationships by suggesting that women have subtle roles as leaders of the dancing duet and are not merely passive followers of their male partners' dance routines.

From my position as a non-dancing observer, I mostly intellectually apprehended the effect of tango on those committed to its practice. Not only did I never experience the psychosocial and emotional effect that the tango embrace imprints on its dancing carriers, but I actually feared those effects as potential threats that would haunt me for as long as my research kept me on the tango floor. I had seen some of my Argentine friends lost forever in *tangomanía*, spending countless hours of precious sleep-time practicing feverish steps in shady tango venues. Worried about losing control over my sensorial persona and also over the social routine that excruciatingly discriminates harshly between masters and apprentices, I decided early on to become a non-dancing player in the tango hall. This resolution led me to bypass some of the tango conventions. In the end, my role as a marginal presence at the milongas not only provided me with a unique perspective from where to examine the tango world but also vested me with a unique aura of removed self-exclusion that opened the door to unexplored sides of gender relationships, which will be examined next.

Unspoken Gender Rules

Typically, in the traditional tango scenery of Buenos Aires, men ask women to dance with only a gesture or a wink, which can be easily ignored by their prospective belles without the men's risking the painful humiliation of an open rejection. Subtle invitations to joining the dance involve a delicate bodily code through which *tangueros* read gazes and gestures from potential partners. Women, for their part, also stare at men and convey bodily messages inviting them to the winking game. Things are less subtle in New York City, partially because the international democratization of gender codes is here supported by transgender dancing practices, such as the all-female tango practices and gay tango salons. As a cosmopolitan hub where nobody knows exactly what planet the person sitting next to them belongs to, the New York City tango field allows many stringent Argentinean rules to be broken, forgotten, ignored, and forgiven. Therefore, men in New York City frequently ask women to dance either verbally or by approaching them, thus making their invitation so obvious that the wink often becomes an accessory, the sort of: "Hey, you cannot miss my wink, so I am asking you to dance with me, whether you like it or not."

Nevertheless, anywhere, in Tokyo, London, New York, or Buenos Aires, the mainstream (and heterosexual) tango etiquette stipulates that women will behave as spectators of the male gaze and therefore will patiently wait to be asked to step out onto the dance floor. This passive role, which is shared by women in most ballroom scenes, not only places women at a disadvantage, as they are the ones being sought and chosen, but also makes them noticeable and exposed to social scrutiny and judgment, particularly if they remain seated for a long time. This is especially so if they are asked to dance mostly by inexperienced men. In addition, women's reputation as good *milongueras* is at stake not only when dancing but even more so when "wallflowering" (which literally means to stand by the wall waiting to be chosen), thus secretly testing their appeal to be desired by potential tango partners (see Savigliano 2003).[3]

During the initial period when I was still trying to negotiate with myself on what role to undertake, I secretly experienced conflicting feelings: Would I reluctantly submit to the unwritten consensual battle of the sexes for gaining entry onto the dance floor, and eventually overcome the potential threat of remaining a wallflower for good? Would I risk my neutral perspective and leave my protective role as an outsider to turn into one of them? Would I be sucked into "draculizing" myself to live at night? Would I use the days as a passing activity until the next tango evening finally arrived, as I knew other anthropologists did? My answer to these questions was to differentiate myself from the dancing crowd (rather than identifying myself with it), as revealed in the following notes:

> I need this physical, emotional and symbolic distance from them. No hands embracing me, no risk of falling into the tango fever that becomes enacted via the neurotic repetition of tango figures and steps. Being away from the tango floor has been my way of differentiating myself from them, of making clearer to them (and

to myself) the purpose of my being there. (Tango notes, May 25, 1999)

Needless to say, during my first ethnotango incursions I was secretly terrified at the prospect of becoming one of them, a want-to-be-chosen tango practitioner committed to dancing well enough to be invited to join the tango race. While stoically enduring the social pressure to dance with my tango pals, I could have foreseen myself as a suffering wallflower enduring the anticipated sense of rejection (for not being asked to dance or for not being asked often), afraid of forgetting that I was there to accomplish something else. As much as I had been hypnotized by the ritualized sensual embraces that I had witnessed in so many tango salons, I finally kept my itch to dance to myself and got ready to assume my role as a chaperone.

In the end, rather than being marginalized in the ballroom by remaining on the sidelines, like the protagonist in Jane Austen's *Pride and Prejudice* (1999), I cautiously reversed the passive role of the anxious waiting gal that would be eventually stigmatized if not chosen by the male gaze. Instead of expecting to be asked to dance, I hoped to be chosen to talk, a seeming oddity in a place where "conversing" is often seen as nothing more than a failure to dance. Nevertheless, both Austen's waiting flowers and I shared this need to be accepted within social milieus where women, more than men, are subjected to subtle rules of inclusion and exclusion.

In addition, I often felt awkward when trying to identify potential informants willing to share with me their everyday issues, including details about their health problems. An uncomfortable task for me was indeed to move from the spontaneous exchange of information with my occasional companions to the arrangements for a longer interview at a later time, as summarized in one of my journal's entries:

> Again today I found myself faced with blurred frontiers between "real" life an fieldwork and felt unclear about my role. When I was still feeling remorse for having tried to pull out information from her too soon [referring to a potential informant], here she was suddenly bursting things for which I wish I had had a tape recorder ready. She just got into telling me about her troubles, about how

tough it is for her to meet the right guy here, about her foot problems and her lack of health insurance; and about all the extra help
she gives and receives from her tango comrades in spite of all the
gossiping going on. . . . She kept talking and talking about all the
things I wanted to ask her, but I somehow felt that this was not the
right time. . . . I am still impressed about the easiness with which
some people will digress about intimate details of their lives, even
if they hardly know me. This is the kind of serendipity that I am
still getting used to. (Tango notes, June 30, 2000)

Ironically, it was often easier to obtain meaningful details about
the lives of my tango pals when engaging in informal chatting, without the obtrusive barrier of a tape recorder or the fierce solemnity of
a guided interview.

Only Two to Tango?

The problems did not end with my deciding to remain off the dance
floor, as I did not initially realize that my presence as a non-dancer
tango voyeur could somehow challenge the tango's ritualized gender
hierarchies. Unspoken gender rules not only elicited power asymmetries with Argentine males but also brought up additional difficulties
to my accepted representation in the field. What to the untrained eye
appear to be subtle codes, among *tangueros* reveal discreet conventions that work as both inclusive and exclusionary practices, through
which some are allowed to play femme fatales and others seductive
men. Tango-dancing halls are sites for the ritualistic reproduction of
seeing and being seen, along with the recreation of tango characters.
Above all, tango salons are panoptical sites where actors are being
watched by everyone else, while pretending to be glancing at nobody
in particular. Dancing then becomes the foundation of their ritualized social exchanges.

The commitment of tango aficionados to their practice was one of
the topics that typically emerged during my spontaneous conversations with tango friends. In addition, my periodic observations of the
social (and bodily) exchanges taking place in the tango world provided me with some clues to understand the range of motivations
leading international New Yorkers into tango dancing, beyond the

obvious exchange of passionate embraces. These motivations include a mix of curiosity and time to spare, along with the inner challenge of learning a sophisticated dance in the company of others. Feelings of solitude, and the potential to meet interesting men and women for romantic purposes, constitutes another subtle motivation that leads spirited urbanites into the tango hall. Unequal expectations are also the backdrop of interpersonal tensions, as some men (and women) actually find in the milongas opportunities to engage in romantic relationships. Sexual claims are a sort of latent drive that may (or may not) be expressed in the tango encounter. In any case, for those expecting to meet either sexual or romantic partners, the tango room provides a permissive environment, where social embraces constitute the backdrop for sensual intentions to be sought in slow motion without awakening suspicion or loss of face.

In these contexts, the production of my social persona called for the creation of a tango character that would represent me as a potential subject for collective identification (see Kulik and Wilson 1995). I remember my first incursions into the tango hall, timidly sitting there trying to engage in small talk with my occasional companions, for the sole purpose of finding out more about their social worlds that I was not really ready to join. In spite of my efforts to portray myself as an ethnographer, I often wrongly gave the impression that I was there wallflowering, waiting for the right partner to lure me from the safety of my seat on the side. Although I did not look as flamboyant as a tango dancer, I did try to camouflage myself by dressing like one of them, to resemble an unassuming target. For some (men) this somehow "confirmed" their suspicion that I was actually concealing my real motives (waiting for a dance) under the guise of an ethnographer. Therefore, I often encountered problems convincing some Argentine males that I was there not to get free tango lessons or to pick up guys but to conduct research. Why would a woman without a tango partner be hanging out in a tango venue, often until very late at night, if tango dancing were not her basic motivation? This question was mostly on the mind of some older men, who somehow felt entitled to display macho traits in the form of verbal aggression and impropriety, while feeling protected by the cultural backdrop of the

Argentine-tango environment. The following note illustrates my encounter with Mr. B, a well-known Argentine *tanguero*, famous not only for his unique tango steps but for his discourteous demeanor when approaching women:

> Today was a tough one, and at some point I thought it would become ugly. Mr. C had already noticed that Mr. B was drunk and had already annoyed other women in the place. But as with Murphy's Law (if something can go wrong, it will) I ended up standing face-to-face to him. Mr. B asked me who I was, and I began with my rehearsed soliloquy to describe my research project. He was neither impressed with my academic credentials nor with the purpose of my research. The fact that he considered me an Argentine was enough to cause him drop any pretense of courtesy, and he almost shouted at me in Spanish: "*De dónde sos, flaca?*" (Where are you from, woman?) "*A mi no me mientas, vos sos de las nuestras mamita,*" and "*andá con ese verso de la investigación para otro lado.*" (Don't lie to me, you are one of ours, little mother, get out with that story of the research somewhere else). (Tango notes, August 30, 2001)

Paradoxically, the tensions I experienced with some men (of course, not all as rude as Mr. B) did not require my becoming culturally competent or savvy, for they were familiar with my Argentine idiosyncratic background.

Whether men or women, we Argentines are trained in a sort of verbal convention that relies on a socialized vocabulary that often becomes a weapon to unlock the doors of potential emotional encounters.[4] My familiarity with this sort of gendered dynamics did not help ease the tension. Because I was as an insider, or one of them (an Argentine woman after all, so unworthy of political correctness), some men eventually assumed the implicit right of making me the object of dirty jokes, subtle provocations, and misguided interests in my research agenda.

Curiously, women took my removal from the tango floor with a more welcoming attitude than I had initially anticipated. By excluding myself from dancing, I assured my gender alliances with them while avoiding the often understated competition for male partners. In addition, my female tango pals taught me more than anyone else did about how to deflect and manipulate the aggression and subtle sexual insinuations of men. How? By reacting as a typical tanguera would, through direct and abrasive verbal (and even physical) gestures to convey a single and forceful message: "Leave me alone and go bother someone else."

Tango Capital: Overcoming Voyeurism

To dance tango and dance it well requires discipline, patience, practice, and more practice, and as in the professional-sport philosophy, the more responsible the practitioner, the more respect he or she will command.[5] As I witnessed the dancers, I often thought to myself: "Watching them, you might think they are getting ready for a doctoral comprehensive examination, but they are not: they are just very concentrated collapsing into each other's arms, while sweating like hell. . . . And still they look so engaged in what they are doing. . . . Are they enjoying it?" (Tango notes, April 25, 2001). As this reflection suggests, tango amateurs, serious about their enterprise, will fall prey to the tango métier. They will endure the cumbersomeness of rehearsing the same steps over and over again not only as a painstaking effort to achieve perfection but also as a means to develop a genuine *tangoesque* style that will make them stand out within the tango crowd. For the sake of mastering the tango, the apprentice will devote countless hours of unpaid work to rehearse steps that will be carefully choreographed and syncopated with (and against) a partner, and therefore subject to surprises, improvisations, unforgettable mistakes, and bodily misunderstandings.

No matter how different tango techniques may be, one rule of thumb prevails: the more *milongueros* join the dancing floor, the more experienced their bodies will become to the spontaneous reflexes of their partners' movements, and to the timing of other couples that religiously follow the clockwise rotation of the tango etiquette. This embodied social knowledge, which I refer to as *tango capital* (an indirect product of social capital as is learned and shared with others), is only possible through the tango embrace to which want-to-be *tangueros* have to surrender if they wish to succeed. Consequently, it is not enough to intellectually learn the steps, or even to practice the coordination of figures and routines. The body must develop its own tempo to achieve mastery because tango dancing (more than any other ballroom style), depends on the partner's embrace to inscribe the harmonized knowledge into a sensorial schedule of ritualized bodily motions.

I have always secretly admired tango dancers who surrender themselves, with almost an irrational zeal and draconian commitment, to a cause that seems to lead to an aimless routine that repeats itself night after night. With the exception of summertime milongas, which take place in the day in eclectic and spontaneous places, such as Central Park (by the Shakespeare statue) or at the seaport, tango dancing is a nocturnal event that occurs in a "different dimension" on the "dark side" of life (see Savigliano 2003). Committed tango practitioners (Argentines and non-Argentines alike) spend countless evening and early-morning hours dancing and practicing, as evidenced by the all-night practices periodically run in New York City.

I have also been surprised by the ways through which an informational economy is widely reproduced and shared in the tango field, including the knowledge (and cognizance) of different dancing styles according to distinctive Argentine tango orchestras. A complex philosophical lingo also characterizes the tango capital, through a language that often tends to mystify (rather than clarify) what tango dancing is or is supposed to be. *Tangueros* speak of making enlightening, inner discoveries through the tango embrace, unique experiences of metaphysical selves, raptures of emotional involvement that come to life within the collective tango conscience (in Durkheim's terms), as a supra-entity that gets turned on at the culmination of the milongas. It is not surprising therefore to find poets, writers, bohemians of all sorts, want-to-be journalists of passion, and tango dancers who try to be all the above in the tango crowd.

Nevertheless, time spent at the milongas has many more meanings beyond practicing the tango and achieving higher states of consciousness. Above all, milongas are camouflaged social fields that allow distinctive social worlds to be intersected, shared, and even created. As I have argued elsewhere (Viladrich 2003), people from different social geographies and educational and professional backgrounds who would not dare to gather in the light of the day will bump into each other at the milongas to chat, hug, share breath mints, and sweat together. They do so on the basis of belonging to one social field and sharing one passion: tango. Transgressions are here not only permitted but are transposed onto the real (productive) world. The time and energy spent at *milongas* also mean social capital (e.g., contacts, relationships, referrals) that becomes meaningful leads during the daytime. What happens at night will continue the following day, particularly among those for whom milongas are not just social resorts of volatile passion but nurturing social hubs that protect lonely souls from the hostile democratic anonymity of their cosmopolitan North American milieu.

Daylight also transforms the social personas of tango dancers into different selves. Many of them endure less flamboyant lives than their images on the tango floor as want-to-be femme fatales and seductive Valentinos (polished, elegant, and refined) would suggest. This is the case with many struggling tango artists and other immigrants embedded in the informal economy. Even among the lucky ones who have become the stars of fancy tango shows, many endure exploitative relationships and unstable or low-paid jobs that do not provide them with either health or social benefits (see Viladrich 2004b). And for me, an anthropologist, after all, the more fascinating (and frequently painful) thing to do during my nocturnal incursions into the tango field was to discover who these *tangueros* were outside the dance hall, after they hung their dance clothes in the closet until the next evening.

With the curiosity of a surgeon, and the compassion of an (albeit agnostic) missionary, I have unwrapped wounded souls to reveal tango dancers' bruises and scars, their dramatic migratory tales and unsolved family dramas. Almost always during my ethnotango incursions, I have discovered how everyone has the potential to become someone else, with a drama, big or small, to share with a soul who conveys the necessary (com)passion for and interest in to their *petite histoires*. Behind the most seductive womanizer I found an Italian pizzeria's busboy, begging for emotional attention; underneath a model-like prima donna I met a former abused woman surviving in a trashy Latino restaurant where he made *empanadas* (Argentine turnovers);

and behind a young-looking blond tango amateur (whom I baptized the "Little Prince") I found, and protected, an undocumented teenager who was working as an apprentice in the tough construction world of Queens.

> Today I returned to *Milonga X* after a while of being away from this world, so close and estranged to me. To them (my tango pals) I am a confidante, an ally, a witness to their attempts to succeed, an equal. But we are different, of course. I am the anthropologist, as everybody is proud of introducing me, as if I bring a token of academia into the tango floor. Fortunately, I have been careful enough to build up my reputation as someone who keeps people's information confidential. I ask about their lives; I listen; I guide them through their own dilemmas and experiences. Above all, I am another Argentine they can relate to and trust. (Tango notes, November 30, 2001)

Like the lone lemonade maker under the hot desert sun, I secretly profited from the emotional needs of my tango friends. I took advantage of their eagerness to be listened to and taken care of, while serving as the emotional reservoir of their unsolved troubled lives. After all, almost everybody at the *milonga* is there to dance, to be seen, to show off, to grip the stage and make the world a dance floor for their own fancy square of rehearsed steps. There I was a patient voyeur, waiting for my captive informants to return to their seats, hoping to turn their confusing storytelling into logically framed life narratives. After many years of being involved with ethnographic studies, more than learning how to improve my research skills, I have learned the craft of listening (something that clinical psychologists take for granted) and the techniques of indirect questioning. No matter how difficult or embarrassing a topic might be, people will openly talk about any delicate issues, following a syncopated structure (a spontaneous plot that follows a logic) of life events (see Denzin 1989, 1999), as long as they feel comfortable and safe. I have often sat and stood in the hazy corners of the tango salon, indiscernible and visible at the same time, mysterious and familiar, needed and ignored, subject to the contradictory roles that have become my unique tango persona.

Over time, by being purely a spectator in the Manhattan tango field, I became a conversation partner ready to offer my time to tired dancers who would join me around the tango table between dances, and who would find in me an unconditional and confidential listener. Occasionally, at the beginning of my tango incursions, and more regularly later, many would sit at my table throughout the evening to talk about a variety of personal matters: from their temporary visa status and broken relationships to their everyday disappointments. In some cases, my informants' demands for support exceeded the stipulated rationality of the field encounter, which, although camouflaged under the rubric of emphatic rendezvous, always has a temporal limit whenever the data had been saturated or when new hypotheses (and projects) led us to new research queries.

In the end, becoming a familiar figure (what most books on ethnographic research teach) in the tango field was no longer an issue. My anthropological costume became meaningless in a space within which the simple fact of being there led me to engage in conversation with others, who finally acknowledged me as *la antropóloga*, "the anthropologist," who were ready to share their stories with me. Our interviews became a sort of therapeutic catharsis, through which the private would turn into meaningful public social experiences, worth being reproduced and translated into the words of the ethnographer (see Behar 1993, Eunshil 1998, Spivak 1988).

Epilogue: Tangoified Relationships

By entering the tango world, I had initially attempted to examine the social relationships through which Argentines (tango artists and customers) exchange valuable social resources on the basis of social solidarity, common interests, and friendship. Later on, tango-dancing halls became an ideal niche from which to explore the tensions of gender dynamics that characterized my participation in the field. I have been there, at the milongas (as I often still am) eager to examine how tango (or even better, its tangoified relationships) has become a socialized metaphor for something else: for relationships to be established, for social and economic transactions to take place, and for reciprocity to be instituted. Through time, I found in the tango field my own niche of ritualized performance from where the meta-language of Argentines' social solidarities and conflicts are exposed, dramatized, shared, and occasionally solved.

As shown in this chapter, a generous part of my ethnotango incursions were spent trying to figure out how to represent myself (and how to be represented by others), which in the end led me to create my own version of a non-tanguera who likes tango, or even better, who likes hanging out with tango dancers of all sorts. Initially, my incursions into the tango world had provided me with a unique opportunity to place myself within a transient state in which I parsimoniously moved from being just an observer of the tango scene to becoming an active anthropologist doing her job. Following a symbolic pilgrimage from my identity as an Argentine to that of an anthropologist I was finally able to connect with others on the basis of these dual social identities. This transition between roles nurtured my unexpected encounters in the field in which a sense of "communitas" was built (V. Turner and E. Turner 1978). Neither a dancer nor a tango fan, my lack of ascription to any of the social roles typically attached to most tango habitués provided me with a safety net that nurtured countless opportunities for dialogue and endearing confessions on the part of my informants. As occurs with others in contexts of rituals of pilgrimage, we (so-called anthropologists and tango dancers) could engage in spontaneous social liaisons because we left aside the social markers that would have created barriers between us in other circumstances. Relieved of the pressure of being who were supposed to be, my tango friends and I recreated a temporary space in which our interactions were supported by the certainty that our paths would miss each other in the mainstream world.

Over time, the tango field played a greater emotional role in my personal life than my professional persona would suggest. I often found myself longing for the time I had spent with some of my tango pals, chatting over the ordinary and uneventful details of the vernacular tango scenery. Occasionally, I was faced with the puzzle of wanting to remain in the tango milieu above and beyond my corseted costume as an anthropologist. If, on the one hand, studying ethnic nationals had been a source of confusion in other venues, in the tango world, I was ultimately welcomed as a familiar figure where my intellectual endeavors no longer surprised anyone. In the end it became the social space in which my gendered invisibility achieved its maximum expression. Curiously, in a social field where flamboyant characters are the norm, I became the opposite sort of character. Within the cosmopolitan tango sociography, a concoction of multiple nationalities and professions (including anthropologists who do dance tango), my presence at the tango salons was not only finally understood but often expected and, almost always, welcomed. By becoming a non-dancing tanguera, my own place in the tango world was finally created.

Nevertheless, my journey from my own country to my peripheral role in the U.S.-centered intellectual geography left me, at the close of my ethnographic adventure, with a variety of unsolved conundrums: Who am I in multicultural America? How have my own social networks, including the ones I developed in the tango field, led me to achieve my own share of social capital that has helped draw my path to the American dream? In the end, the Argentine tango scene has allowed me to be among my own for just enough time to travel back across the virtual bridge to my amorphous New Yorker persona, a transition that has mingled my dual cultural identities (Anzaldua 1999, Maher 1998).[6]

Being among my tango friends, like being in Buenos Aires, has fostered my longing for familiar voices, assumed attitudes, self-explanatory silences. I can be an anthropologist among them but, above all, I am another Argentine looking for recognizable features in the faceless Manhattan crowd. Far from being a means to uncover my bodily experiences through dance steps, the tango world has become my gateway to escape from my often oppressive alien self, a purposive drive that has rescued me from the chaotic endless resistance to anonymous representation that is a feature of social life in New York City.

Notes

1. An earlier version of part of this article was presented at the 2003 American Anthropological Association Annual Meeting in Chicago. I thank Vincent Crapanzano for his insightful comments on my paper during the session. I am also grateful to Sherry Ortner,

Ana Abraído-Lanza, Robert Fullilove, Kathy McCarthy, Peter Messeri, Richard Parker, and Terry Williams for our conversations on placing the intricacies of the tango world into my broader research agenda on social networks. As usual, Stephen Pekar provided invaluable comments and generous assistance in editing this manuscript. This research was partially supported by a grant from the Center for the Active Life for Minority Elders at Columbia University.

2. As Marta Savigliano (1995, xiii, xiv) argues, "Tango and exile (in the sense of 'being away from home,' for whatever reason) are intimately associated." She continues, "It is more than common for any Argentine living abroad to connect the experience of longing and nostalgia to the tango. It is a recurrent pattern, even for those of us who do not consider ourselves connoisseurs or fans of the tango, to be affected by the tango syndrome after being deprived for a while of our *argentino* 'environment.'" Certainly, the novelty of the tango's revival relies on its role as an emblem of Argentines' cultural nationalism (term used by Castells 1997), which, in the midst of globalization, is being nurtured through local religious forms, ethnic foods, and patriotic celebrations. As Castells (1997, 53) suggests: ethnicity is being specified as a source of meaning and identity, to be melted not with other ethnicities, but under the broader principles of cultural self-definition, such as religion, nation, or gender.

3. Milongas follow a carefully orchestrated tango-hierarchy, where the skills and reputation of practitioners are definitely ranked above looks. Savigliano (2003) argues that the roles of women as wallflowers allow them to gamble their own femininity (as femme fatales) on the tango floor.

4. There is a rich literature on gender issues and fieldwork that deals with diverse issues: from the existential nature of gender relationships to practical solutions women can use to protect themselves and conform to local gender ascriptions without jeopardizing fieldwork (see Whitehead and Conaway 1986; Golde 1970).

5. These practices rely on commodified bodies (see Scheper-Hughes 2002), which demand ritualistic training and practice that is only showed off in a stage drama.

6. The need for a categorical cessation of time through departure is within the very nature of fieldwork, which, sooner or later, will bring the ethnographic encounters to a close (Crapanzano 1986). "The ethnographic encounter, like any encounter, however distorted in its immediacy or through time, never ends. It continually demands interpretation and accommodation" (Crapanzano 1980). "The sadness, the guilt, the feelings of solitude, and the love that come with departure and death will not, cannot, end" (Crapanzano 1980, 140) Ortner (1995, 173) notes that the ethnographic stance (as we may call it) is as much an intellectual (and moral) positional, a constructive and interpretive mode, as it is a bodily process in space and time.

6. When the Extraordinary Hits Home

Experiencing Spiritualism

DEIRDRE MEINTEL

We are seventeen in number, sitting in a circle in a darkened room on a Friday night in winter. We are in a church; actually, it is a rented space on the second floor above a used book and video shop in a slightly seedy street in central Montreal. Among the Middle Eastern grocery stores, used bookstores, and other small businesses, restaurants, and cafés, one also finds a sex shop with life-size mannequins in the window, and a strip club. For us, though, the lights and sounds of downtown, just outside the window, seem far away.

Michel sees a man standing behind Daniel, describes him as "big, like a Viking." When it is Sylvie's turn to talk, a woman in her early sixties, she talks about the same entity, invisible to the rest of us: "The one with the mustache, right?" she asks. "Yes, that's him," Michel answers (Fieldnotes, January 26, 2001).[1]

This incident, part of my ongoing fieldwork on Spiritualists in Montreal, allowed me to glimpse intersubjectivity of a very different kind from what is usually presented in methodology handbooks. I hope to show here that participating in extraordinary experiences such as the one just described has shaped my interpretations about what I observe and has allowed me to better understand the extraordinary, sometimes ecstatic, experiences of those I study.

Fieldwork in the Cape Verde Islands in 1972 (Meintel 1984) allowed me to observe ecstasy in others for the first time, and, in a small way, to experience it myself.[2] In the celebrations for the patron saint of Brava, the island where I lived longest, the saint's banner is of great significance. In the concluding event of the feast, which has been going on for more than a week, the banner is borne by a mounted horseman into the house of the sponsor (the one paying most of the expenses of the celebration). Amid the overwhelming noise of drums, call-and-response singing, and fireworks going off, I was struck by the transported, beatific expressions on the faces of participants when the banner was passed. Malinowski's notion of "phatic communion" came to mind, and I could see the resonance between this event and V. Turner's "communitas" (1968). I envied those I was observing. How could they be so deeply part of something beyond themselves as to lose their usual preoccupations with quotidian individuality, if only for one glorious, evanescent moment? The closest I came to such a state myself was during my last weeks in Cape Verde, after formal interviews and systematic observations were finished. By then it seemed that my mind, my dreams, even my daydreams, were taken over by the lives of others, their worries and hopes and dramas, small and large, giving way to a heady sense of "losing myself."

In the fieldwork that I present here, regularly letting go of the conventional researcher role has allowed me to experience the meditative and trance states that are part of Spiritualist religious practice. "Losing oneself" becomes an integral part of the research process, however paradoxical this might seem. In terms of classical notions of objectivity, where intellectual rigor is predicated on the externality and emotional distance of the observer from the object of inquiry, the emphasis on the visualist is open to criticism, as noted by Fabian (1983, 107) and Clifford (1988, 31). Moreover, a number of ethnographers working on religion, spirituality, witchcraft, and so on have, by their research *practice* and styles of written representation, challenged modernist notions of objectivity (e.g., Goulet 1998, E. Turner et al. 1992, E. Turner 1996, Favret-Saada 1977, Cohen 2002).

I hope to show that taking a highly participatory role in certain Spiritualist activities has shaped and benefited the research. I cannot fully discuss here questions related to intersubjectivity, religious community, and the role of the body in perception. Here I seek to share what it is like for a researcher to enter into such trancelike experiences and convey something of how they transform one's sense of self, one's notions of what is real, indeed, one's view of the world. After a brief presentation of Spiritualism and the church that is the principal site of this study, I explain the research process in greater detail.[3]

The Spiritual Church of Healing

The Spiritual Church of Healing (SCH), where my research is focused, was founded in Montreal in 1967 by a married couple from England, both Spiritualist ministers.[4] The religious movement that came to be known as Spiritualism dates back to 1847, when Margaret and Kate Fox, two sisters living on a farm in Hydesville, New York, heard strange noises. The girls managed to establish contact with their source, which they eventually determined to be the spirit of a peddler who had been murdered in the house. His skeleton was later found in the basement (Aubrée and Laplantine 1990, Goodman 1988). The religious movement that developed around the two girls spread across the United States in a climate influenced by Emerson's transcendentalism, and soon spread to England. In France, it influenced the development of French Spiritism, also known as Kardecism, after its leading figure, Alain Kardec. Spiritualism enjoyed great influence in the United States over the latter part of the nineteenth century and was especially popular among feminists and other progressive thinkers (Braude 1989). Some estimates of the time found its adherents numbering in the millions. The lack of institutional centralization that even now characterizes Spiritualism makes such numbers difficult to verify (Braude 1989, 25).

The Spiritual Church, as its members often call it, developed in the middle of the Quiet Revolution, a period of rapid secularization for Quebec in the 1960s, when religious institutions changed greatly. While most Franco-Québécois remained nominally Catholic, clergy declined drastically in number as did religious practice among the Catholic laity (Linteau et al. 1989, 648–649; Bibby 1990, 135). At the same time, many new religious groups, notably Pentecostal churches, challenged the position of classic Protestant churches, such as the Anglican and Presbyterian, and continue to do so (Polo 2001).

When the founders of the Spiritual Church of Healing left Canada in 1975, a young Québécois, Michel, replaced them, and gradually the congregation became primarily francophone in its clientele and activities. At least five other Spiritualist groups function in Montreal at present, four of them seem to be primarily English-speaking; one mainly anglophone congregation was founded at around the same time as the Spiritual Church; another is a prayer group that has split off from an established Spiritualist church and meets in a member's home. Unlike the Spiritual Church, not all of the older congregations have the legal status as churches that would allow their ministers to perform marriages and hold funerals.[5] Spiritualist ministers in the Montreal area collaborate informally on occasion, and from time to time officiate as guests in congregations other than their own. As I have discussed elsewhere (Meintel 2003), members of one congregation may sometimes go to services at other Spiritualist churches (or to Catholic services or those of other denominations, for that matter).

In general, churches that call themselves Spiritualist share the seven basic principles of Spiritualism, albeit worded a bit differently from one church to another. These include the existence of God (sometimes called Universal Intelligence), the fraternity of mankind, the responsibility of individuals for their own actions, the consequences, good or bad, of these actions in the afterlife, the eternal spiritual progress possible for every individual, the continued existence of the human soul (many believe that animals have souls and an afterlife as well), and the communion of spirits. The latter implies the possibility of communication between the living and spirits of the dead, especially those considered spirit guides.[6]

The SCH has some 175 members at present, and like most of the other Spiritualist groups in Montreal, is located in the city center, making it easy for the many members who depend on public transportation to get to it.[7] None of its five ministers (who include two women), are paid for their services, nor are healers or mediums; expenses such as heating, rent, repairs, and the recently installed air-conditioning are paid for by collections during the services or personal offerings by members.[8] Most Spiritualist churches have limited means (see Zaretsky 1974, 177). Indeed, the church is modestly furnished with paintings of angels, spirits, Jesus, and usually a few flowers or seasonal decorations. In front, on a low platform, stand a podium and several chairs with a small organ beside them. A large Bible, the King James version, sits in front of the podium. In the large room upstairs, there is a Spiritualist library from which members may borrow.

Like several other Spiritualist congregations in Montreal, the SCH is loosely identified with a particular family and is often referred to as the Guérins' church. Michel and his younger brother are both ministers and have important roles in the church, as do their parents (who came to Spiritualism through Michel). The SCH is governed by an administrative council of twelve, including the president (Michel), who is responsible for practical matters such as finances; the pastor, or spiritual head of the group; and the five ministers (who include two women), and also a number of mediums and other members. The congregation comes from all over Montreal, with many living in francophone working-class neighborhoods, and others in nearby suburbs.[9]

Most newcomers discover the Spiritual Church of Healing through a friend or family member. When several generations of adults are present, it is usually the children who have influenced their parents to come. Inevitably, other family members are not interested in or are even hostile to Spiritualism. Proselytizing is strongly discouraged, and the church itself is nearly invisible, in its urban setting. There is no telephone, and only a discreet cardboard sign in the doorway marks the entry to the church. I myself had passed by hundreds of times without noticing it. Significantly, there are no special activities or facilities for children.

Two public services are held at the Spiritual Church on Sunday, with a healing service in between. Another service is held on Thursday evening. All services begin with opening prayers, including the Protestant version of Our Father.[10] Regular services include several hymns; these are taken from the hymnbook provided some years ago by an Anglican minister whose wife, a member of the SCH, translated the hymns into French. The latter include familiar Protestant classics, such as "Nearer My God to Thee" and "The Battle Hymn of the Republic." Services often include a guided meditation, with imagery suggested by a medium or apprentice accompanied by instrumental, New Age music. This is sometimes replaced by a sermon (a dissertation, in Spiritualist parlance). This is followed by the collection, the blessing of the

offerings, and clairvoyance, when messages, as clairvoyant pronounce-
ments are called, are given by one or several mediums to individuals
present.[11] A prayer and hymn conclude the service.

Messages given by mediums at church services may concern, for example, health, work, or relationship issues; the spiritual development
of the individual addressed; or several such themes. Usually the medium does not know about the personal life of those receiving clairvoyance. Discretion is generally used when talking about personal issues ("I don't know if you have anyone in your life right now, but if
you don't, you will soon!"). In messages about health problems, mediums are supposed to present any advice as suggestions, mainly to
avoid violating laws against practicing medicine without a license
(e.g., "I see green vegetables all around you, you need to eat more
green vegetables; just a suggestion, we're not doctors here."). Messages may refer to spirits the medium sees, for example, a spirit guide
("your native guide") or a deceased relative ("I see a mother figure,
she could be your mother or your grandmother"). Occasionally, a
trance service is offered where a medium goes into a deep trance and
channels a spirit guide.

Interestingly, glossalalia (Goodman 1972, Csordas 2001) is not
found in the mediums or among members of the congregation. Moreover, spiritual gifts for different kinds of clairvoyance or healing are
not considered signs of spiritual merit, as among Pentecostals (Goodman 1972). One rarely hears proscriptions of any kind in the SCH;
however, Michel often warns against esoterism (exploitation of such
gifts for non-spiritual, egotistical ends).

At the healing service, a minister and several healers transmit healing through the laying on of hands in an area arranged for this in the
front of the church. A guided meditation, with New Age music in the
background, occupies those present until their turn is called. In fact,
the healers normally do not touch the body of the person seated in
front of them but rather pass their hands over the area around the individual, considered to be their energy field. The healers' way of working somewhat resembles that of the *magnétiseurs* (literally, "mag-
netizers") described by Acedo (2000). As in other kinds of services,
there is a collection, a blessing of the offerings, and opening and closing prayers.

Health services are generally in French, though a monthly bilingual service has been introduced recently to accommodate English-speaking visitors from other Spiritualist congregations. Most of the mediums are bilingual and give messages in English when the individual addressed does not understand French well. Attendance is variable, ranging from fifty or more at the principal Sunday service to barely a dozen on some Thursday evenings. Men make up about a fifth to a quarter of the group on most occasions, though the number of male and female healers and mediums is roughly equal. From 2002 through 2004, the congregation became somewhat younger, losing a number of members over sixty and attracting newcomers in the thirty-to-fifty age group.

This is the cohort that predominates in the closed groups, sometimes called closed circles; that is, groups not open to the public. Closed groups focus more on clairvoyance than on healing, but healers (who may also be mediums) are generally drawn from the closed groups. At the Spiritual Church, closed groups are also known as courses in spiritual development. Most meet twice a month under the direction of a minister or medium. The closed groups give members an opportunity to discover for themselves the experience of clairvoyance; a few members go on to become recognized mediums by the church and are allowed to give messages at services. While it is usual to speak of giving clairvoyance in the Spiritual Church, those who do so are called "mediums" rather than clairvoyants. From Michel's point of view, a clairvoyant may be a mere fortuneteller, whereas a medium is in contact with the spirit world and seeks not only to give information about the future but to put it in a wider spiritual context.

Michel sees training in clairvoyance as a means to deepen spirituality, and also as a practical tool for everyday living, in that the exercises done in class (i.e., in the closed group) tend to sharpen the participants' intuitive powers in their daily lives. In fact, most long-term participants experience not only heightened intuitions but revelatory dreams, premonitions, flashes of clairvoyance, and sometimes, visions, outside the group context. Everyone I have interviewed has developed personal spiritual practices and rituals in their daily lives, even though no instructions in this regard are ever given in the church. At most, a medium might give someone a message such as, "Your guides would like you to meditate now and then." A few read the Bible, while most read inspirational books from various spiritual traditions, at least occasionally. Most pray at odd times during the day for help with the difficulties of daily life (a stressful coworker, a child taking drugs, marital problems, unemployment), and many have a period of prayer or meditation that is part of their daily routine.

The Research Process

This study was born of a series of fortuitous events. One of my doctoral students, Louis-Robert Frigault, began doing work on spirit possession in Brazilian *umbanda* in a southern Brazilian city that I found fascinating (Frigault 1999). Around the same time, I was invited to teach at the University of Lyon2, where I became familiar with the work of François Laplantine. His approach to religious phenomena, and the book he wrote on a clairvoyant medium in Lyon (Laplantine 1985), helped me see the anthropological relevance of clairvoyance and healing in the modern, urban context. Moreover, teaching the anthropology of religion at Lyon2 made me realize that what were once exotic religious phenomena are now much less so. My own religious background in a devoutly Catholic family (daily Mass, Benediction on Sunday, observance of Lent and Advent, novenas, rosaries, etc.) was probably more exotic and remote to my students than were the religious phenomena typically considered the province of anthropologists. Few had been brought up to practice their ancestral religion as I had, but most had heard of visualization, Wicca, white and black magic, and reincarnation.

It was in this general context that I met Michel through a friend. Said to be a gifted medium and healer, Michel, in his late forties at the time, was personable, dynamic, and youthful in appearance. As I later learned, he grew up in a working-class neighborhood in Montreal but was sent to an English-language school run by the Jesuits, his father's hope for upward mobility for his five sons. After studies at a local university, Michel worked for many years in finance for a large corporation and now does accounting half-time. Widowed and later divorced, Michel now shares his life with Elisabeth, a Spiritualist medium who is active in the Spiritual Church.

At our first meeting, Michel's ability to capture the important elements of my past and present, while giving very precise predictions for the future (later borne out), impressed me. Beyond what he had to say, I was deeply affected by the experience of being with him as he went into a trancelike state. Although unable to verbalize it, I felt the experience itself to be just as important as the content of what was said. We spoke in English, Michel being fully bilingual. Most of the time, Michel had his eyes closed; he explained that he received clairvoyance from his guides, spirits who help him. Then he thanked them, opened his eyes and told me what he had seen, a sequence that would be repeated many times over the course of an hour. At the end, he said, "We have a church here, you are welcome to come see it."

Very curious to see what kind of church could harbor such an individual, I began to go to services at the SCH, where, over the next few months, I witnessed a series of mediums give messages to a middle-aged-and-older, predominantly female congregation that looked to be mostly working-class. Occasionally, one or another medium would channel for a spirit guide. I was a bit ill at ease in the vaguely Protestant, somewhat threadbare (at the time) decor of the church. I had rarely entered a church in many years and my experience of Protestant congregations was mostly limited to a few observations in Cape Verde. Yet I sensed the sincerity of those present and felt a familiar energy around me, one I knew from experiences of deep meditation in an ashram where I had spent a few weekends some years earlier. The sense of sociological distance from, and yet inner proximity to, what was happening in this church turned my visits into fieldwork without my thinking about it, and I soon found myself taking notes after services.

Feeling a bit uneasy about the ethics of all this, I called Michel for another appointment, to talk about my involvement in his church. On this second occasion, I asked Michel if he wanted to do clairvoyance before we talked, whereupon he began to see books all around me, research activities, writing. He asked, "I see you writing a book, is that possible?" When I explained that my interest in the Spiritual

Church of Healing was also professional, and that I was an anthropologist, he immediately invited me to join a closed group (the first time I had heard of such groups), on the condition I be discreet (i.e., not disturbing the religious atmosphere of the gathering) and participate like other members. I accepted these conditions enthusiastically, since what interested me most was the Spiritualist experience, what it was like to see clairvoyantly, to give healing, and to know how everything fit in with the daily lives of the participants. At the time, I was unaware of the privilege such an invitation represented; later I would find that there are fewer places than there are would-be members for the groups Michel directs. (These are limited to twenty or fewer individuals.) I expected that the group would be a way of meeting members of the church and perhaps even for getting to know a clairvoyant or two. It would prove to be much more.

Inspired by Favret-Saada's study (1977) of modern witchcraft in Normandy, my own research, from 1999 to 2001, was based exclusively on participant observation, with note taking reserved for later, outside the church context. I went on this way for about two years, except for three interviews with Michel the summer after I joined the closed group. It was clear that in order to study the experience of Spiritualists, I would have to, paraphrasing Favret-Saada, agree to become a participant in the situations where it is manifested and in the discourse in which it is expressed (1977, 43).[12]

By 2001 I knew a number of members of Michel's group informally, meeting some outside for coffee, a meal, or a leisure activity such as roller-blading, and moreover, I had a sense of them as Spiritualists, that is, a sense of their commitment to spiritual development and their particular gifts as mediums or healers. I began to interview ten key informants, later enlarging the study group to sixteen, evenly divided between men and women, mostly between thirty-five and fifty years of age, who had been going to the Spiritual Church for at least three years. Interviews cover topics such as the individual's life history, religious trajectory, and beliefs and experiences around healing and clairvoyance. This ongoing fieldwork continues part-time, since the closed group meets twice a month for nine months a year, and, like me, most participants in the study work full-time. Some of the Spiritualists I interview work in the lower echelons of the health care system (e.g., as home caregivers or massage therapists), in service jobs (e.g., sales clerk), or in skilled occupations (e.g., mechanics). Most have been divorced at least once, and most are in a stable couple relationship.

The present study marks a departure from my previous work in several ways. First, it concerns religion, whereas all my previous work was focused on migration and ethnicity; second, unlike my other projects, it does not involve a team and several assistants. Rather, it has been primarily an individual project, with minimal funding so far. This has made it feasible to carry out the study in real time, rather than in the artificially compressed time frame in which most research must be done, with no pressure to produce results prematurely. Thus, I have been able to let relationships with participants in the study evolve naturally and to allow myself the time needed (impossible to program) to become acquainted with Spiritualism in a direct, personal way.

Until this project, my research had always been defined in terms of institutions (clinics, for example), or bounded groups (Cape Verdeans, Portuguese), however hypothetical such frontiers may be in the case of ethnic groups. Early on, it became clear that the Spiritual Church of Healing was made up of several networks, each centered around a minister–medium. The core of the networks comprises individuals who frequented the groups directed by that minister and went to his services. It soon became clear that some of these networks overlapped, but others did not. A few people go to several of Michel's groups, but church rules prohibit going to more than one minister's closed circle at a time, as each teacher works in her or his own way. It can happen that a minister leaves one church to go to another, or to form his own church, in which case the network tends to follow. At one point, I realized that if Michel ever changed churches, his network, and my project, would move with him.[13] Moreover, the SCH itself moved (although not far), because of a fire some years ago and could do so again. Spiritualist churches like this one are not the permanent site of a bounded group but rather the spatial focus, often temporary, for several networks (Meintel 2003).

Following Fonseca (1991), I wanted to see how the religious practice and beliefs of my interlocutors wove into their daily life, so that, insofar as possible, it became my practice to meet study participants outside the church, in cafés, or at my home or theirs. The first interview done with the sixteen key informants concerns their life history (religious background, employment, family and couple relationships) and how Spiritualism, the SCH, and their connection to Michel fit into their personal trajectory. Other interviews focus on experiences of spiritual gifts (e.g., trance, healing, clairvoyance) and other extraordinary occurrences, such as astral projection, attacks by negative spirits (*mauvaises entités*), premonitory dreams, and so on.

Interviews with Michel and sixteen members of the SCH who have been in Michel's closed groups are conducted in tandem with ongoing participant observation. At the beginning of the study, I expected that I would be the recipient of others' healing efforts and that Spiritualists might, as they put it, give me clairvoyance. Indeed, I welcomed these possibilities. From the Spiritualist point of view, everyone has spiritual gifts of some kind. I was nonetheless taken aback when I realized that joining the closed group meant actually *doing* clairvoyance myself. Later I was invited to learn to heal and to heal others at the church's healing service. These were unexpected roles, ones that did not correspond to my self-image; though I believed myself to be a fairly intuitive person, I certainly did not see myself as a clairvoyant or healer. Assuming these roles and accepting all the experiences they have brought was not initially part of my research plans. Rather, the research project evolved organically for the first several years and has gradually grown into its present form. Being the subject and not just the object of healing and clairvoyance has enriched the research immeasurably.

I am often asked why I would study something so different from my usual interests. Part of the answer is simply that I cannot fully take on a Cape Verdean perspective nor fully enter into the experience of a Portuguese immigrant to Canada. However, I can enter into the Spiritualist experience as far as my personal capacities and inclinations allow. This research project has led me to a broader interest in the anthropology of religion in the modern world. Originally, my interest was less about religion than about epistemological issues: how can we study things that do not make sense in terms of conventional notions of reality and that are yet part of the experience of many people in our own and other societies? And how to describe such experiences as a researcher without doing violence to those experiences? One novel aspect of this endeavor is that whenever I present this research, the question of how I situate myself (my own beliefs) arises, something that is rarely brought up when one is studying, say, class, ethnicity, or race, though perhaps it should be. When the subject is religion, as Hervieu-Léger (1993, 22) has noted, there is no high scientific ground from which to speak: whether one is religious, without religion, or worse, has left religion (*défroqué*), one can be accused of having a built-in bias. After working in a field where abstractions such as ethnic group are often discussed by researchers as if they exist as objects in nature, I now find myself working in an area where what actors (including researchers) may experience as real is assumed to be unreal by many in the academic world (cf. Stoller 1989b).

A few final words on the methodology of the study: to paraphrase Favret-Saada, ethnographers who distance themselves see their object slip through their fingers; at the same time, participation obliges them to take on the risks of subjectivity.[14] While adopting a largely subjectivist, "experience-near" (Wikan 1991) approach that gives priority to the individual experiences of others and in which I try to use my own experience as a basis for better understanding theirs, I have found it extremely useful to have feedback from a part-time assistant and several anthropologist friends who have visited the SCH and met Michel.[15] I would add that the methodology of the study includes not only participation in Spiritualist activities but also many interviews. Moreover, observations based on various "unobtrusive measures" (Webb 1966) have their place in this type of research: for example, counting the number of individuals present at each gathering and the proportion by gender, observing decor, taking note of the turns of phrase used, and so on. In any case, I see the "experience-near" (Wikan 1991), "observation of participation" (B. Tedlock 1991) approach adopted for this research as one that corresponds to its object, the Spiritualist experience. Had my interest been, for example, the political life of this small congregation, more distant, objective methods might have had a greater place in the study. The question of whether my experience of Spiritualism is the same as that of other participants is worth discussing, and I return to this issue later.

The Closed Group

The closed group, or what the participants commonly call a "course in spiritual development," meets in the evening twice monthly, except for one group led by Michel that meets weekly. Most groups gather in the church, but several hold their meetings in private homes. All are directed by a minister–medium who decides who can participate. Groups are normally fewer than twenty in number, and some have only half a dozen participants. Members pay a modest fee (eight dollars, at this writing) for each class and commit to regular attendance for the duration of the course, from September through mid-June. The cost is kept low, according to Michel, so as to allow the unemployed to participate. The students in these groups are taught clairvoyance using various techniques; these include focusing on color, using objects (psychometry), using symbols (e.g., those associated with Christmas, Easter, spring, etc.).

Though pleased at Michel's invitation to join a closed group, I was somewhat anxious as to what I would find there. Scenes of possession from the films of Jean Rouch came to mind. I was initially reassured by what I saw. Members arrive on or before the group begins at 7:15 p.m., punctuality being de rigueur; the doors are locked unless someone is expected to arrive late. Joking banter and friendly greetings precede the opening prayers. Michel encourages these light moments as a way of shaking off the stress of daily life before entering into the evening's activities. Most group members try to arrive early, in time to say hello to friends and, sometimes, to have a private word with Michel. When someone mentions a personal problem, Michel often promises to see what comes to him in the way of clairvoyance over the course of the evening. Normally, I arrive early to have time for some personal exchange with others in the group, a number of whom are in my core study group, or, occasionally to do a short interview with Michel. The first time, though, I felt ill at ease; I knew no one there but Michel, felt unsure as how to enter into the conversations around me, was a bit self-conscious about my dual role (as yet unannounced to other participants), and above all, was anxious about what was to come.

The tone becomes quieter and more serious with opening prayers, the Lord's Prayer and a spontaneous prayer led by Michel asking for spiritual protection for the evening's activities. We hold hands, forming a circle. Michel assigns positions at the beginning of each year according to the aura of the individual, sometimes seeking to harmonize energies, sometimes to provoke a little creative dissonance.[16] For the first few months, I am seated about seven or eight places to the left of Michel. Some months later, several of us are asked to change places, and I find myself seated next to Michel, on his left. Being close to Michel while he is in trance, even a light trance, has a deeply calming effect on me. Moreover, it allows me to sense which spirits are coming to speak through him (perhaps cued by small changes of posture), as happens from time to time. There are regular visitors, like his native guide, Michel's main protector and "gatekeeper" spirit, the one who decides to let others come through or not—such as the nun who speaks in a high, sweet voice (a bit comical in the persona of Michel), the little boy who teases and laughs, the Chinese guide, and others.

After prayers we stand to do breathing exercises ("to open the chakras"), and then take our places, sitting with ankles crossed for meditation. According to Michel, the ankles are like another chakra, so this helps the quality of meditation. Michel provides guided imagery leading us to focus on themes that change each week, such as forgiveness, or changing the world. For about half an hour, we meditate, eyes closed. A single blue light tempers the darkness. Often I find myself quickly borne away into a state that leaves nothing but a few words or images in my memory, and I thus miss much of the guided meditation. Eventually, I hear Michel instruct us to come back to the group gently, to move our hands a bit. An exchange about the meditation follows: Michel calls upon a member, and in clockwise rotation, each tells what happened during the meditation.

Next comes a brief recess. If weather permits, some go onto the veranda behind the church to chat or have a quick cigarette. Otherwise, we stay inside. Most take advantage of the break to stretch, perhaps go to the lavatory. Members come from various parts of the metropolitan area, so the period before the class and this break give them a chance to catch up with each other's lives. Some never see the others outside the meetings of the group, but several who have been coming for a few years have formed friendships and see others socially. After the break we sit again for "active meditation", or clairvoyance. Now the blue light is replaced by a red one, a stimulus for our clairvoyant capacities. That first evening, when Michel instructs us to "see" something for two others in the group, I'm surprised. I feel paralyzed: even if I could see what is normally invisible in others, do I want to? Not that I expect to discover any clairvoyant gifts in myself. For the first few months, I feel, as most beginners do, that anything that popped into my mind was my imagination. I try to go along with the clairvoyance exercises, simply as a way of getting better acquainted with Spiritualists and better understanding their religious experience.

Typically, Michel gives guidelines such as, "Look for a color that the two people to your right need, and why they need it," or "See something physical [that is, part of ordinary life, not spirituality] for any three people in the group." In December he might suggest, "See a Christmas present for each of the two people on your right and explain what it means." Later in the year, students are asked to see via objects, a type of clairvoyance known as psychometry. Each leaves a personal object on a tray that is passed around, and each chooses an object without looking at the tray. Or the students may be told to write their name on a strip of paper. Then each draws a strip from a container and reads for that individual without knowing whose name is on the paper until after clairvoyance is given.

Normally, the students concentrate for ten or fifteen minutes on the exercise they have been asked to do. Usually, members have their eyes closed during this period, though occasionally they may be instructed to look at several individuals in the group for a minute or two and "enter into their aura." Sometimes Michel gets up to give healing to a few of the individuals present. After ten or fifteen minutes, he announces that time is up. He calls on a member of the group and this time moves around the group counter-clockwise. Each tells what they have seen and what it means. Afterward, he is likely to tell some of those present what he saw for them (time rarely permits giving a message to everyone). If he has conferred with someone before the class about a personal matter, he may discreetly give clairvoyant feedback (e.g., "Robert, what you asked me about *is* going to work out, I got that very clearly, but it will probably take a little while."). Finally, at about 9:30 p.m. Michel announces that it is time for the closing prayer; after Michel's improvised prayer of thanks, we hold hands and say the *Notre Père* together.

The Spiritualist closed group functions in ways that are reminiscent of psychoanalysis in that a series of firm rules circumscribes the context, creating a safe zone of freedom in which extraordinary experiences can happen. Members are expected to arrive on time and, usually, to pay for missed classes. People sit in the required posture for each activity, not leaving their places except for the short break in the middle of the meeting. When students give messages, aggressivity, even of a mild sort, is not tolerated. Members of the group speak in turn during the parts of the meeting devoted to verbal exchange, and otherwise only with Michel's permission. They sit in the required posture for each activity, not leaving their places except for the short break in the middle of the meeting. Generally, Michel enforces the rules with a light touch, first with humor, then with a quiet word in private, but repeated inappropriate behavior (speaking out of turn, sitting incorrectly, leaving one's seat, tardiness) is likely to lead to expulsion.

When participants recount what they have seen during the clairvoyance exercise, Michel usually remains noncommittal, reacting with a few words of acknowledgment: "Great, thank you!" Many new members see nothing for the first weeks or months, and this, too, is given support. Michel reminds the group that this is normal for many people. Little by little, what seem at first to be one's own imaginings take on another aspect. Unexpected words, images, and phrases come to mind. Some may experience actual visions or see spirit guides. Between Michel's nonjudgmental encouragement and the many rules that surround the context, a protective space of freedom is created where students are led to perceive impressions and sensations that might normally go unregistered.

It is, of course, difficult to assess the accuracy of one's own clairvoyance or whether it is improving with practice. Classes and church services give ample occasion to observe others over time; in general, their readings for me become more detailed and precise, and seem more accurate, as time goes on. My own readings for others in the classes have become far more detailed than they were in the beginning, and the impressions more elaborate (words, images, and very occasionally, visions that unfold like a mental video). I learned to recognize a strange feeling that comes when receiving an impression that is at odds with my everyday perception of the individual and leaves me feeling insecure. Quite often this leads to my giving a message that seems strange to me but is later confirmed by the individual concerned.

Consider this example from my own experience. Michel asks us to "see" something for the two people seated to our left and tell them what it means. I close my eyes and see Réjeanne, a fifty-ish home health care worker seated two places left of me. She is receiving a bird of paradise flower from a friend. I try to figure out the meaning. Could this be something unusual someone is inviting her to do? A week later, Réjeanne greets me before the class and says, "Guess what? Last week when I went home after the class, someone gave me a flower just like the one you described! The first time in my whole life that I got such a flower!" Conclusion: Sometimes a flower is just a flower.

Often, clairvoyance seems to involve emotional rather than factual truth. Messages may be about how a person is feeling now and in the near future. The following occurred while this article was being written and illustrates the anxiety one can feel when giving a message that might be taken as negative:

> We are supposed to go into the aura of the person on our left and see something they need. I concentrate on Arianne (slim blond artist, early thirties; we took the subway together once a few weeks ago, it was the first time we talked outside the class). Immediately the words come, emphatic: "Forget it." (I feel silly, this can't be a message, can it?) I try to sink into it, be open to the possibility that I am *able* to see. In this meditation I suddenly feel paralysis, it's as if I'm nailed to my chair. "Forget it," comes again. "It's too heavy, it was not your fault, you'll paralyze yourself with this, you have to forget it." Michel calls on me. I give the message, feeling foolish and embarrassed. I hope Arianne isn't offended. After the class,

she turns to me and says, I know you didn't know what your message was about but it was really important to me, I really needed to hear it. I realize that it (whatever "it" was) is still affecting me, even though it wasn't my fault. Thank you. Relief! (Fieldnotes, August 17, 2004)

Spiritualist writers often mention "thought forms," visible manifestations of others' thoughts that affect the person to whom the clairvoyance is given. My first contact with a "thought form" happened several months after I joined the group.

I am trying to see for Nancy (thirty-ish, divorced, two children; a massage therapist), but when I try to focus on her, there is a whitish cloud on one side of her, and it gives me a creepy feeling. I try again and again, but I just can't make myself look there; it repels me. When the time comes to tell what we saw, I hesitate. Does it mean something negative about her or that something bad is going to happen to her? Michel explains that what I saw was a "forme de pensée," a thought form, in this case the jealousy of others, and goes on in elaborate detail about a problem Nancy is having at work. Nancy nods vigorously in assent throughout his explanation. (Fieldnotes, March 26, 1999)

As several of the preceding examples suggest, seeing is one thing, interpreting another, and communicating what one sees, yet another. All three are part of clairvoyant inspiration in the Spiritualist context. After a while, Michel's new students are nudged toward interpreting what they see. "Ask your guides," Michel tells them.

When this happens to me, a few months after I enter the group, I am startled: "Push has come to shove," I think. "If you are there, please help me out!" While not disbelieving in spirit guides, an idea familiar enough from Catholic beliefs in saints and guardian angels, I was not at all convinced at this point that they were present in the room or interested in what I was doing.[17] In fact, as usually happens, the interpretation came immediately, and so this procedure became, in a sense, naturalized. A year or so later, I began to *feel* the presence of a certain guide from time to time (and not only in the Spiritualist group), most dramatically on one occasion:

Michel asks us to give healing to ourselves during the period when we usually do clairvoyant exercises. We are to put our hands over our hearts and close our eyes as usual. Good, I think, I need it. I am emotionally shaken by a disturbing event earlier in the day. Still feeling somewhat unsettled, I close my eyes, try to feel my heart beating. A heart starts beating thunderously under my hand, it seems to be popping out of my skin, like a cartoon image . . . and I can feel a large hand enclosing mine! Whose heart is this, I wonder, is it mine or his? It feels like the same heart, mine *and* his! I know whose hand it is, it's his . . . (Fieldnotes, March 21, 2003)

"His" refers to the guide who had become familiar to me, the one Michel calls "your native guide."[18] We return to this incident later.

"Picking up" (*capter*, in French) on things not usually visible is, from a Spiritualist point of view, a generally *human* capacity, one that is perhaps greater in some individuals than in others. Indeed, many people who do not consider themselves clairvoyant have dreamt of people or places before physically seeing them for the first time. To use an example from a novel in Anthony Powell's series, *A Dance to the Music of Time*, many have had the experience of suddenly thinking of a person from their past for the first time in years, only to cross paths with the individual shortly thereafter. I myself had had such experiences, and I was convinced, well before my acquaintance with Spiritualism, that some few individuals have clairvoyant capacities.

Opening myself to such experiences in a Spiritualist context was not only a means of gaining rapport. These experiences allowed me understandings that are fundamental for comprehending that clairvoyance is not reserved for a gifted few but is something open to ordinary individuals, including myself. However, it became clear early on in the research that I would have to accept my own perceptions if I were to participate at all. One who censors his or her own perceptions cannot begin the process of learning to see clairvoyantly. Decensoring one's own intuitions, sensations, and perceptions is an essential precondition for experiencing how clairvoyance is done. True, objective proofs are often lacking: I cannot prove to a skeptic that the hand I felt was real and that it belonged to my native guide. But as an observer of my own experience, I have to accept that his presence was very real to me, quite as real as happenings that are verifiable by conventional means.

Moreover, participating in the closed group led me to understand that mediumship need not involve strictly individual phenomena. The same things can sometimes be seen and felt by others at the same time. To my surprise, I found that what I initially thought was the exalted experience of the rare gifted individual often involves a common level of perception, a kind of intersubjectivity. Furthermore, I have discovered for myself the complex role of the body in healing and clairvoyance. The exercises in the closed group allow one to become attuned to what Csordas elegantly terms "somatic modes of attention" (1997, 67–70), because "seeing" clairvoyantly often involves the senses. Before going further into these matters, I turn to another kind of Spiritualist experience in which the body often serves as a vehicle: transmitting healing.

Spiritualist Healing

Influences such as Reiki, healing touch in nursing, and various New Age approaches have made Spiritualist healing appear less strange than it must have seemed when the Spiritual Church of Healing was first established in 1967 in Montreal. As mentioned earlier, healing in the SCH involves passing the hands over the body of the one seeking healing; this is done in silence while those waiting hear a guided meditation and soft New Age music. Initially, transmitting healing was not an activity I ever expected to perform. By the time I was invited to become an apprentice healer, about three years after I began to attend the closed group, I had received healing a number of times from Michel and others. Spiritualist healing seemed to help many of those who requested it, and I had certainly felt an enhanced well-being on the occasions when I received it.

Healing in the SCH is never presented as an alternative to medical treatment or psychotherapy. In fact, clairvoyant messages often encourage individuals to see a physician. Healing is seen as a support for dealing with physical malaise and trauma (illness, surgery, chemotherapy, etc.) and psychological issues such as stress, grief, depression, and so on. While in the past it was requested mainly for physical ailments, today one gets the impression that emotional distress often brings people to seek healing. One aspect of healing that appealed to me was that it is done by several people at the same time, such that there is less focus on the individual than when a medium gives clairvoyance before the congregation. Doing healing does mark one as something of an insider in that only those who have been part of a closed group for some time are likely to be invited to become healers. A few candidates are trained from time to time, not necessarily every year, in order to have enough healers for the clientele of the Sunday healing service.

The "training" to become a healer was much more limited than I expected; four of us, two men and two women, met with Michel for several hours of instruction. We learned, for example, that we were supposed to dress professionally (no shorts, no T-shirts, no short skirts, etc.), and that we should not give clairvoyance while transmitting healing, nor should we touch people. This last is partly because of a Quebec law that prohibits touching for spiritual healing, but also because, according to Michel, it is really not necessary, an issue I will return to shortly.[19] Except for a short demonstration by Michel on this occasion, our main instruction about what to do in healing would consist of watching others and doing it ourselves.

> It's my first experience of transmitting healing. I feel very awkward and anxious. How will I know what to do with my hands? The first person to be seated in front of me is a somewhat fragile-looking woman who seems to be in her seventies. I feel humble, touched by the trust and faith of those who come to sit in front of me and the other healers. (We are five.) At first I am so tense that my hands feel cramped. I try to move them over the zone around the woman as I've seen other healers do. Suddenly a tidal wave of heat that passes through me, from my feet through my head! Am I going to pass out? Then I feel a sense of awe, wonder, deep stillness . . . in short, ecstasy. I am still awkward but it is not the important thing . . . what is important is staying focused, staying in touch with It, this energy . . . (Fieldnotes, August 24, 2003)

Each time I have served as a healer, the experience has been different. But the sense of contact with another's energy remains and, in fact, becomes stronger and stronger with time. A few weeks after my first experience as a healer, I wrote the following:

> I'm sitting in church, waiting for the evening service to begin. I feel my hands buzzing. I have felt this often when I meditate in the last few weeks. Is it related to the healing? After opening prayers, Elisabeth is the first medium to speak. She goes straight to me. I must tell you, while you were sitting there before the service, your hands were surrounded by blue light. (Fieldnotes, October 9, 2003)

The buzz in my hands is a normal part of healing for me; others tell me they feel heat in their hands. However, healing is not the same experience from one occasion to the next, just as it is not the same experience from one person to the next. Over time, the sensation of healing energy feels less localized in the hands; sometimes it feels like a global sensation, sometimes very real, out there, like something I am touching. Yet the sense of contact with a different kind of energy is always there.

Giving healing often brings flashes of clairvoyance for me, which according to church rules should not be communicated during the healing service. (Apparently, it's OK to communicate these flashes to the individual if they remain after the service.) I have done healing outside the church context twice, both times at the request of the other person; these are the only occasions when I have received feedback from those receiving healing from me.

Bridget (an academic friend) is at a low ebb. Divorce, the ensuing legal wrangles, illness, work, stress, and money worries have left her exhausted. We agree that I will try healing on her. I give her a meditation tape to listen to and have her sit with her eyes closed. I work on her energy field as I would do in church. While I'm working near her throat, I get the sense that there is something funny here; she needs to say something. This surprises me; Bridget is so emotive and very communicative; what could she not be saying? Afterward I tell her about this. She says, "While you were doing healing I realized that I had to talk to X," a boyfriend she has broken up with. She needs to thank him for what he and their relationship have done for her in this difficult time. She says that she opened her eyes several times to see what I was doing and that she felt the air moving even when my hands were still.

Like the other individual for whom I had done healing outside the church, Bridget tells me that she felt cool air moving around her like a breeze. On the other hand, when Michel has given me healing, I felt heat. When I asked about this, he told me that some people have healing energy that feels cool, that one person who used to do healing in the church gave off energy that was icy cold. "Even sometimes from one month to the other there is different healing. . . . [E]verybody is unique . . . as long as they follow in front of people the laws of the church. . . . Not only every person is different, it can feel different from one time to another, also the state you are in on that day" (Michel, August 20, 2004).

Embodiment and Experience(s)

While, for the observer, Spiritualist healing looks to be the laying on of hands, appearances are somewhat deceptive. One can indeed feel healing energy in the hands, and in the church setting healers use their hands while giving healing. However, healing energy can be transmitted in other ways, depending on the healer and the situation: by thought and prayer, through the eyes, even through the breath. Jocelyne (fifty-two-year-old clerk in a large department store) has a Spiritualist friend who does healing silently while on the phone with her. Once I began doing healing, I found that I could feel healing energy while meditating, not only in the hands but more generally through my skin. Over time, it has become a kind of sensation that does not always have a restricted physical locus. From the Spiritualist point of view, healing energy has its origin not in the human body, but elsewhere. Like clairvoyance, it is a divine gift whose positive development is aided by spirit guides. In the end, it is a kind of energy, so diffuse that as Blaise, a Spiritualist in his early fifties who was born in West Africa, puts it, "It's in everything you do." For Blaise, healing has become an existential attitude. Yet, as my first experience of healing attests, somatic happenings may herald the extraordinary. Healing energy passes through the healer and also the supplicant. And after giving healing to a person, it is usual to wipe one's hands. (Paper towels are provided for healers in the SCH for this reason.) On the other hand, clairvoyance, which would appear to be a matter of the mind, is often a matter of the body as well. For Michel, clairvoyance is a kind of sensory bombardment: Sometimes he receives odors; for example, the smell of bread baking, tastes, or sounds, images, or visions. And sometimes he prefers to see in another way, through feeling.

> It all blends in, hearing, seeing, feeling . . . I see, hear, feel, all at the same time . . . from my guides, from the [spirits of] relatives all around . . . Sometimes I tell my guides that I'm just going to do clairsentience today, where I don't see, I don't hear, but I know. I can describe your spirit guides without seeing them. I can see them with my third eye, and I can tell you what you're feeling. Clairsentience, it's knowing . . . It's one of the strongest gifts, I find, and the least known, clairsentience, You just know, it's so strong, you know it's *there*. (Fieldnotes, Michel, September 9, 1999)

It was through bodily sensations that I first came to sense a different level of perception than usual . . . feeling heat on one side of the body and not the other, for example, or feeling sudden congestion in the throat. Bodily experience then becomes a medium for another kind of knowledge (McGuire 1996). Sometimes, it should be added, the image or idea of a bodily sensation is a vehicle. One may not see something as in a vision, but, rather, as Michel explains, as a mental image. The *idea* of an aroma or taste may act as a stimulus for clairvoyance without one's actually feeling and tasting it.

As McGuire points out, in daily life we deal with bodily intelligence in the form of "gut feelings" (1996, 112). In retrospect, I realize that my spontaneous impression of the SCH as authentically spiritual was based on a physical sensation, a rush of energy to the sinuses that I had experienced a number of times during long meditations with hundreds of others in an ashram. In closed groups such as the one Michel directs, one becomes able to catch and hold fleeting physical sensations or other impressions that one might normally miss, and use them to orient clairvoyant perception. The body becomes a point of departure for understandings that are not literal readings of corporeal happenings but rather leaps of clairvoyant insight for which the body serves as a springboard. An example of how this may work can be found in D. Tedlock's (1997) wonderfully vivid, moment-by-moment narrative of divination, where spurts of lightning-like energy in different parts of the ethnographer–diviner's body lead to clairvoyant revelations.

A Different Intersubjectivity

In social science, intersubjectivity is typically associated with the notion of scientific reliability: would another similarly situated observer observe the same thing? Spiritualism offers contexts for a different kind of intersubjectivity, one in which fields of knowledge and perception that are not available to everyone are nonetheless shared among several, sometimes many, participants. From the Spiritualist point of view, social sharing happens not only between mediums but between spirit guides and mediums. Of course, clairvoyance involves "picking up" things about and for other people, so in that sense it necessarily involves at least two people. Beyond this, several individuals may have the same or similar clairvoyant visions at the same time. Edith Turner offers several examples of shared clairvoyance among individuals participating in the same rituals and healing events in her Alaska research (1996) and, with her coauthors, from work with the Ndembu (E. Turner et al. 1992).

I have found such sharing is the case not only among gifted, experienced Spiritualist mediums but also among apprentices. Open groups held during the summer offer ample opportunity to observe newcomers attempting clairvoyance, since anyone who wants to come is admitted. These groups follow roughly the same format as the closed group, but clairvoyance exercises are a bit simpler. Time and again, I have witnessed groups of neophytes give very similar readings for the same person. It is extremely rare that messages for the same individual on the same occasion contradict each other. Occasionally, in the summer groups, those present are asked to see something for themselves and something for a person seated beside them. Quite often what a participant sees for him- or herself is very nearly identical to what their neighbor sees.

In the closed group, even more dramatic examples of convergence may occur. One evening, Jocelyne saw black tulips for Nancy. At the end of the evening, when the lights came back on, Carole (a business-woman in her late forties) pulled a gift-wrapped bouquet of black tulips out from under her chair, a birthday gift for Nancy. It happens quite often that person A feels a headache when reading for person B, who in turn is picking up on the real headache being experienced by person C. Mediums often work together in the church, and it is common to see one add details to what the other has seen. In the closed group, Sylvie (a medium in her sixties who gives clairvoyance at church services) and Michel often see the same spirits, as in the example given at the beginning of this article.

When I ask Sylvie about such incidents, she laughs: "Yes, it happens a lot, there's something between us, maybe you could say we're on the same wavelength; I don't have his level of knowledge, we're very different, but we connect on the level of clairvoyance."

Zaretsky has described the way Spiritualists talk among themselves as a "distinct system of communication," one that is often deemed "incomprehensible" by outsiders (1974, 167). It is not surprising that Spiritualist discourse would seem hermetic to a non-participating observer (the role Zaretsky adopted in his study). For example, color symbolism frequently comes up in Spiritualist readings. Michel might ask his students to see a color that another participant needs and explain why. Quite often, students perceive in terms of color even when this is not the objective of the exercise. The same color can mean different things for different people on different occasions. Green, for example, can mean love or healing, among other things. With experience, one learns to see clairvoyantly in terms of color, to interpret one's own color symbolism and to follow that used by others.

Spiritualism offers an ongoing dialectic of the idiosyncratic and the shared. Each clairvoyant medium sees a bit differently from all others, each healer works in his or her own way, though all frame their activities in generally the same terms, as spiritual gifts from God used to serve others and developed with the help of spirit guides. The SCH

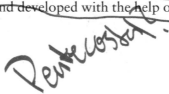

offers remarkably little in the way of community, as the term is generally understood (e.g., Hervieu-Léger 2001, ch. 5). There are almost no church-sponsored social activities or events other than church services, group meetings, and other occasional events of a religious nature. Yet a community of a sort is formed, especially in the closed groups that involve repeated encounters with the same individuals. Members of closed groups often don't know each other's last names, yet they share many moments of *communitas* (V. Turner 1975), deeply meaningful experiences that are shared with, or at least communicated among, participants.

Participating in a closed group over a number of years has allowed me to understand that such sharing, though limited to a few hours every month, can be felt as more profound, more vital, than the economic or social interactions usually implied by the term *community*. In the closed group, one experiences and shares deeply meaningful perceptions that would normally be censored, even within oneself, ones that often manifest in personal, corporeal ways (see Cataldi 1993). Further contributing to the special quality of this kind of community, such things happen in a sacred context where spirits, not normally considered to exist, are acknowledged as social actors. To what extent can a researcher share in the intersubjectivity that links other participants in such a context? This is the question to which we now turn.

Us and Them

The question of alterity has generated a voluminous literature in anthropology over recent decades, most of it focused on representation with little or no reference to how one does fieldwork, with a few notable exceptions such as B. Tedlock (1991) and Goulet (1998). As Tedlock notes, representation is not only a matter of how one represents the Other but how one presents oneself. Experiential ethnographers accept that it is necessary to "pay attention to their own lives, including their inner lives" when trying to understand the experience and belief systems of others (Goulet 1998, 254). For those of us willing to "coexperience" religious phenomena with those they study (E. Turner 1996, xxiii), certain questions remain: how do we know how others feel and perceive things (Leavitt 1996)? Can we assume that our experiences of the extraordinary are the same as those of others?

Some anthropologists believe their experiences of trance states are definitely different from those of their informants; others are convinced they are the same. Peters (1981), who worked in Nepal, finds his experience of trance "unproblematic" as a means of understanding the worldview of those he studied.[20] Desjarlais (1992, 14–15) notes that his cultural experience had not conditioned him for trance. In contrast, my background (experiences of meditation using a mantra, hypnotherapy) had prepared me to some degree. Still, the question remains: can we be sure that our experience of phenomena such as trance, clairvoyance, and healing is the same as theirs?

I would suggest that we cannot be sure; indeed, can we ever be sure that a common experience is shared identically by all participants? How can we be sure that our experience is radically *different* from that of others? The Spiritualists collaborating in my research have very different types of experiences from each other; one cannot speak of a homogenous "them" in this regard. My experiences are different from those of others, but from my dialogues with the Spiritualists I have interviewed, I cannot say that they are more different than anyone else's. True, having a research agenda affects how one experiences a situation, group, or context. Yet the nature of extraordinary experience is that it requires that that research agenda be bracketed, set aside, if only temporarily.

As we have seen, healing and clairvoyance happen differently for the same individual doing them from one occasion to another. While such variation is easy to see in a complex society, I believe that when Victor Turner speaks of getting to know participants in ritual processes as "unique individuals, each with a style and soul of his or her own," he was suggesting that heterogeneity and idiosyncrasy are part of religious activities (V. Turner 1975, 28–29, in E. Turner 1996, xxiii). Such is certainly the case with the Cape Verdean ritual specialists I have known. As for the Spiritualist research, I would say that my experiences of healing and clairvoyance are *comparable* to those of others, in the sense that we understand each other when talking about them. As mentioned earlier, some feel heat in their hands when giving healing, whereas for me, it is more like an electrical current. When I talk with Marcel (a French-born Spiritualist in his fifties) about feeling the presence of guides in daily life as being "like in clairvoyance," he nods knowingly. The way he feels clairvoyance is probably different from how I do, but it is an individual permutation on a common experience. This commonality in diversity is something similar to what Schutz describes when he writes of "the pluridimensionality of time" that is experienced simultaneously yet differently by each participant involved in "Making Music Together" (1964, 175); the musicians are attuned to each other without having identical experiences, nor necessarily identical interpretations of what the composer wrote.[21]

A number of factors blur the boundary between home and field, researcher and subjects, their experience and mine. First of all, there is considerable cultural proximity, in that the SCH is situated in the city where I have lived for much of my adult life. The working-class flavor of the Spiritual Church is a bit different from my usual frame of reference, and French is not my first language, as it is for most of the Spiritualists in my study, but we share many cultural referents. Moreover, my Catholic upbringing in the United States bears many similarities to the religious background of Québécois Spiritualists.

The fluid quality of in-group definitions in the Spiritual Church of Healing also makes the boundaries between self and others hazy. Who is "in" the church and who is not is not clear, even to church members. As mentioned earlier, membership in the SCH is not a matter of conversion but of helping to pay expenses (see note 7). Conversion in fact, is never mentioned. Adults are very rarely baptized. I know of no such case in this congregation. In Michel's words: most are already baptized as Catholics.

When asked if they would say "I am a Spiritualist," some active members who have participated in closed groups for years, including some who do healing and clairvoyance in church, replied, like Sylvie (a medium who has known Michel for decades): "I never thought of it that way." Members participate in church activities in very different ways. Some attend closed groups as a means of personal development but never attend church services, finding them too religious; some among the older cohorts attend church services but are uninterested in closed group activities or are uneasy about them; a few

Inclusivity

see them as vaguely "satanic." Moreover, as discussed elsewhere (Meintel 2003), some who are very involved in the SCH combine Spiritualism with another spiritual frame of reference (e.g., Catholicism, neo-Shamanism); even those who consider Spiritualism their religious affiliation say that they have not renounced Catholicism but simply added to it or gone beyond it. Neitz (2002) discusses a somewhat similar situation in her study of Wicca. The witches' notions of belonging were so nebulous and inclusive that they could easily include the sociologist, without her having to change anything in her way of life or beliefs. I suspect that had I studied Pentecostals or Charismatic Catholics, I might have taken a more distant role, as a defense against pressure to declare religious allegiance. In my work on Spiritualism, I have never felt obliged to go beyond the truth of my own experience or convictions; in fact, no one has ever asked what I believe. And so I have felt free to let experience take me where it will.

Accusations of "going native" have a quaint ring in present-day anthropology, especially now that so many "natives" are doing anthropology. But when the Other is just down the street, somehow the threat to one's credibility as a researcher looms all the greater, especially when the subject is religion. This was one of the factors that led Neitz (2002) to study Wiccans far from the university where she teaches sociology. There are now quite a number of anthropologists who have written about transformative spirit contacts or other types of extraordinary religious experiences occurring in the course of their research (see examples in E. Turner 1996 and B. Tedlock 1991). However, these anthropologists generally write about experiences lived in societies quite different and distant from their own. As the research on Spiritualism took form, I became anxious to find out whether other anthropologists' extraordinary experiences ever occurred on home turf, as was happening with me. Were such experiences compartmentalized, removed from the researchers' ordinary lives? I was encouraged to read Goulet's accounts of dreams and visions experienced in Ottawa, far from the Dene Tha reserve.

Stoller's *Stranger in the Village of the Sick* (2004) gives a brilliant account of how the author's long-ago apprenticeship to a sorcerer in Niger was revitalized to support him as a cancer patient in a modern biomedical setting. Moreover, Stoller makes it clear that he has used the divination skills learned in Niger to help friends in the United States from time to time. Edith Turner et al. (1992, 1996) allows her readers to see that healing and spirituality were not only field experiences for her and her late husband, Victor Turner, who apparently had considerable healing gifts. Moreover, the couple's conversion to Catholicism gave them a means to understand religious symbolism among the Ndembu, and for Victor Turner to develop the concept of *communitas*. All the aforementioned works show in various ways that the separation between the research context and the home context is not complete for the experiential ethnographer, even when the two are geographically distant from one another.

In another research project now under way, interviews with young parents in ethnically mixed marital unions has revealed that many of the subjects function with a view of world culture as one vast repository of human symbolic resources to which their children, by virtue of their multiple possible belongings, have wider access than if they were not of mixed origins. While their logic is not without contradictions (Meintel 2002), I see a similarity with the reasoning of anthropologists who find resources of value for themselves in their "real" lives in their contacts with "others." Such resources are likely to be all the more relevant to one's daily life when they are drawn from a symbolic system that is of modern origin and adapted to one's own society, as is the case with Spiritualism and the SCH.

Conclusion

I have tried to show here that the glimpses of the extraordinary Spiritualism has offered me have led to new understandings about healing and clairvoyance. Becoming an apprentice medium has allowed me to see that clairvoyance is a capacity that everyone has experienced at least to a small degree, one that can be developed, provided one is ready to suspend disbelief in one's own perceptions. Moreover, clairvoyance is a *social* experience. Apart from the fact that several people may perceive the same invisible phenomenon at the same time, there is the unspoken communion that is necessary in order to give clairvoyance to another. Participating as an actor in giving clairvoyance and healing has allowed me to perceive the importance of the body in these activities. At the same time, by doing healing myself, I have been able to grasp what is *not* visible to an observer: that the "laying on of hands," or any other visible gesture, is epiphenomenal to what is really happening: mobilizing and channeling a certain kind of energy. While such a statement might seem unverifiable to the skeptical observer, it makes sense to those who do healing, including my informants.

Furthermore, participation in the closed group has given me a very different sense of what community can mean; religious community is not necessarily a matter of structures that ensure sustained interaction outside of ritual activities. *Communitas* indeed seems a better word to convey the special quality of the sharing that happens in the closed group. For those I interviewed, these privileged moments shared in the group occur outside everyday social relations but give support and deeper meaning to them. Participating in Spiritualist activities has been advantageous for the research, but beyond this it has given deeper meaning to my work as an anthropologist, on the level where anthropologist and person are indistinguishable.[22] Giving and receiving clairvoyance, receiving and transmitting healing, feeling spirit presence and experiencing occasional ecstatic moments have enriched my life immeasurably and have greatly enlarged my sense of human possibilities.

Notes

1. Fieldnotes have been slightly amended for the sake of clarity. Pseudonyms are used for the individuals mentioned and for the church where the fieldwork is based so as to protect informants' privacy. Short quotes are transcribed from field observations; longer ones (indented in the text) are taken verbatim from tape-recorded interviews.

2. I spent a year in Cape Verde in 1972 and have visited several times since then, briefly in 1986 and for some six weeks of fieldwork in 1998. I continue to do occasional research among Cape Verdeans in Massachusetts and Rhode Island.

3. Financial support by the Social Science Research Council (through the Small Grants Programme, administered by the Université de Montréal) is gratefully acknowledged.

4. The name of the church has been changed; however, the real name is often shortened to "the Spiritual Church" by its members and so is used herein, along with the initials SCH.

5. SCH ministers have announced at church services that gay marriages will be permitted there.

6. Hell is not mentioned; instead, emphasis is placed on the continued evolution of the soul after death. This appears to be a widespread belief in Spiritualism (See Barbanell 1940).

7. As explained in Meintel (2003), becoming a member is not considered conversion; it is rather a financial contribution ($20 annually) to the church and entitles the individual to participate in certain activities, borrow books from the church library, and so on.

8. All the ministers are mediums and healers, but there are many mediums and healers in the SCH and other local Spiritualist groups who are not ministers.

9. Like McGuire (1988), who studied middle-class spiritual healers in New Jersey, I was surprised at the residential stability of those I have interviewed at the SCH, many of whom still live in the neighborhood where they grew up.

10. The Protestant version of this prayer concludes with a sentence absent from the Catholic version: "For Thine is the kingdom, the power and the glory, forever and ever."

11. Terms and phrases that are part of Spiritualist jargon are put in quotes only the first time they appear in the text.

12. *Accepter d'être inclus dans les situations où elle se manifeste et dans le discours qu'elle exprime* (Favret-Saada 1977, 43).

13. See Clifford's (1997) description of Karen McCarthy Brown's mobile study of a voodoo priestess and her entourage in New York City.

14. *L'ethnologue qui se distancie voit son objet lui glisser des mains; celui qui accepte une participation de près doit toutefois faire face aux risques de la subjectivation* (Favret-Saada 1977, 48).

15. My thanks to Judith Asher, Claudia Fonseca, Sylvie Fortin, Louis-Robert Frigault, Isabel Heck, Ilda Januario, and John Leavitt for their insightful comments at different points in the research; thanks also to J. Asher, I. Heck, Géraldine Mossière, and the editors of this book for their editorial suggestions.

16. When I asked Michel if he could see auras while walking down the street, he answered, "Yes, I could see them, but I choose not to, because I want to have a life."

17. Margaret Mead, an Anglican, believed that she had two spirit guides (Howard 1984).

18. The frequency with which native guides manifest in Spiritualism is a subject worth longer discussion than is possible here. Not only are they extremely common among the spirits perceived and channeled by members of the closed group in which I participate, but mention of them can be found in English Spiritualist writings of the late nineteenth and early twentieth century.

19. I have heard reports, which, so far, I have been unable to confirm, to the effect that Quebec law has been modified recently and now allows limited touching (i.e., of the head, hands and shoulders of the person receiving healing) by spiritual healers.

20. In fact, Peters presents himself as a "Tibetan Shaman" on his Web site: http://www.tibetanshamam.com.

21. Thanks to Jean-Guy Goulet for this reference.

22. I am reminded of an essay by Jorgé Louis Borges that speaks of "Borges" as being no longer separate from Borges-the-writer.

7. Prophecy, Sorcery, and Reincarnation

Inuit Spirituality in the Age of Skepticism

EDMUND SEARLES

Weber's famous 1918 lecture, "Science as a Vocation," describes modernity's rationalized approach to reality, in which "there are no mysterious or incalculable forces that come into play. . . . [O]ne can, in principle, master all things by calculation. This means the world is disenchanted" (Weber 1946, 139). Walter Benjamin, too, writes of the ontological effects of the emerging technologies of image and other forms of mechanical reproduction. These technologies altered "the limits of space and time to such a degree that they erase[d] the uniqueness and distance that alone might preserve the 'aura' or sacrality of things" (Carlson 2003, 208). What Weber and Benjamin are describing is a world in which "the modern human subject . . . through its rational and technological self-assertion, emptie[d] the world of mystical presence—precisely by taking over the very production or framing of that world" (Carlson 2003, 208).

But this disenchantment is perhaps the symptom of a larger process, namely the rise of a particular secular form of subjectivity and individualism, the capacity to know and define oneself independently of any explanation whatsoever provided by religion (Oberoi 1995). In this condition of modernity, the figure of the Other (a divine Other that cannot be confined to the finite or to specific categories of meaning) "is gradually replaced by the figure of the self who defines, controls, possesses and masters—that is, the modern subject" (Schwartz 2003, 138). In this context, our bodies, our selves, our actions, the images we have of ourselves, the image we imagine we are to others, are nothing more, nothing less, than objects in a universe of objects of measurable form and substance.

The secularization of the self is a source of both liberation and alienation. Released from the fetters of faith and fear of God, enlightened subjects have discovered a world free of the direct influence of God. New disciplines and doctrines have emerged from this impulse, culminating in novel understandings of mind, body, and history. The enlightened subject is now positioned to apply rigorous methods to the study of epidemiology and the transmission of diseases, leading to the possibility of longer and healthier lives. The enlightened subject is also free to imagine and enact new forms of commodification and exchange, and, with the right luck and ingenuity, generate unimaginable levels of wealth and power.

But all is not rosy with the modern subject. Loosened from a love and fear of God and the security of a faith-inspired, sacramental life, the self has become an object of self-loathing and self-deception. Obsessed with a heightened self-consciousness, the self becomes trapped in its own images of itself and in the projection of its desires and insecurities onto the world. The self now struggles to make itself an object of desire to others, a process that continues today in almost surreal proportions. Television is replete with shows offering a complete makeover of one's body and personality via plastic surgery, interior design, and a new wardrobe and hairstyle. In these conditions, the self seems lost in a world devoid of sacramentality, of mystic presence.

In this essay, I examine my own spiritual odyssey through various worlds of enchantment and disenchantment. Using my fieldwork experiences in the Canadian Arctic, the Alaskan Subarctic, and Guinea-Bissau, West Africa, as a guide, I explore how I have come to believe what I believe. I also analyze how my position as a person and ethnographer keeps changing in response to my questioning the taken-for-granted assumption that anthropology is a vocation in the Weberian sense of the term and that I am a secular subject.

Levi's Phobia

Several months into my dissertation fieldwork project, my fiancée (now wife—Michelle C. Johnson) and I encountered a fascinating reincarnation story, revealing to us a belief that still prevails strongly among many Inuit and non-Inuit living in the Canadian Arctic. We decided to take our host family's children to Iqaluit's community pool for an hour of recreational swimming. Aged nine, seven, and four at the time, Tukya, Noodloo, and Levi are the children of Mary Ellen Thomas and Udlu Pisuktie. Mary Ellen, a longtime northern resident, devout Anglican, community activist, and friend to many scientific researchers working in the Northwest Territories, had witnessed our trials and tribulations as struggling and now-desperate researchers at the local Science Research Center, built to provide logistical support and lodging for non-local researchers. Eager to make my low-budget fellowship stretch for a year, we became distressed when our rent suddenly increased from free to $30 a night per person, an amount we could not afford given all our other expenses. Not wanting to impose directly on Mary Ellen and her family, but knowing she was well connected in the community, we asked if she knew anyone who was willing to rent a room or part of a house to a young couple. Much to our delight, she invited us to stay in her newly built home, and she even gave us a room to ourselves. The house was already full; but that did not bother this family. For years they had been welcoming a constant flow of visitors, family, friends, and even the occasional visiting scientist, into their homes.

Ever mindful of the sacrifices Mary Ellen and her family made, we were eager to reciprocate their kindness and generosity as best we could by contributing to the household budget and by taking care of the children if either (or both) of the parents wanted or needed a respite. When Michelle and I offered to take the children to the local public pool, Mary Ellen enthusiastically supported the idea, and she immediately began to coax Tukya, Noodloo, and Levi into packing their bathing suits and towels. Although I was glad we could be helpful, and I knew swimming would be fun, I was also feeling anxious about the progress of my research and the quality of my research methods. Taking a bunch of children on an excursion of fun and swimming did not seem to be authentic ethnography, what real arctic anthropologists do while conducting research. My field notes at this time of my research reveal a deep ambivalence about staying with the Pisuktie family, and I devoted many pages to narrating these and other anxieties about not getting the right kinds of data and not pursuing the right types of informants and experiences. Shouldn't I be surveying hunters or documenting genealogies? Shouldn't I be making the most of this research time by determining average household expenditures on hunting, identifying Inuktitut terms for various plants and animals, practicing grammar? Although I constantly wrestled with these and other questions, I did receive steady support from my fiancée who was also my research partner. Despite my misgivings, she convinced me that every experience, large or small, is significant and within the scope of ethnographic inquiry. This is perhaps one of the more exhilarating and intriguing mysteries of ethnographic research; we often encounter the most significant insights and discoveries during the most unlikely, mundane moments.

Considering we were living in a small, isolated town in the middle of southern Baffin Island, just a couple hundred miles south of the Arctic Circle, I was surprised to find the pool alive and crowded with enthusiastic and accomplished swimmers. Tukya and Noodloo, we soon discovered, had already learned a couple of strokes, and they were soon off on their own, playing with each other and friends. Levi, on the other hand, was much more tentative, and although he was quick to enter the pool, he was unwilling to leave the shallow end, where he could stand on the pool's bottom with his head entirely above water.

When I offered him a chance to cling to my back while we swam to join his sisters, he reluctantly accepted my offer. I thought that piggybacking him as I swam around the pool would inspire him to become more comfortable away from the shallow end. But there were other factors at work between Levi and me, for we had been struggling with a rather tumultuous relationship. The first two months in Mary Ellen's home were difficult for me. Unfamiliar with the psychological complexities of Levi's moods and habits, and unprepared for his particular wrath, I was hopelessly unable to cope with Levi's mischief and moodiness. A familiar theme of my field notes at the time was how much he prodded and poked various parts of my body, and how helpless I felt in trying to make him stop. I was still harboring guilt about losing my composure on several occasions. When Levi refused to stop poking and punching me in my lower abdomen and genital region, I slapped him on the side of the head, a gesture that shocked more than hurt. Up to that point, I had restrained myself. I tried to apologize to a now-startled and sobbing young boy, but my shame was only intensified by a rather intimidating glare from his father, Udlu, who asked for a summary of our interaction.

As our relationship grew less tumultuous, a truce settled in, and we even started to enjoy one another's company. This swimming date would provide me an even greater opportunity to have fun with Levi. With Levi clinging to my back, I dropped below the surface of the water to take a stroke. Much to my surprise, however, he reacted violently to my movements and his grip on my neck intensified. I was also surprised by how strong he was; his nails dug sharply into my skin. As I rose to the surface, I realized Levi was genuinely terrified of getting his head wet. He was coughing and sobbing intensely. I immediately took him back to the shallow end of the pool and tried to comfort him. The sensation of standing on solid ground in the shallow end calmed him to the point that his tears of panic and fear transformed into smiles of joy and laughter.

Looking back on these experiences, I realize that they allowed me to really learn much more about Levi. Outside the realm of poking and prodding, they allowed me to experience a different side of Levi, one that was happy and vulnerable, more playful and less competitive. Swimming enabled us to find a social space of grace where we were neither annoying nor a nuisance to one another. But there was still much more to Levi that I did not know, and his unusual fear of the water was a personality trait I did not understand. On the subsequent trips that we (or I) took the children swimming, Levi never allowed his head to dip below the water. Although I never analyzed Levi's peculiar phobia too systematically, I was curious. But, then again, most children were mysterious to me, since I had grown up the youngest sibling, cousin, and neighbor. Levi possessed many peculiarities, it seemed, and this was just one of the many facets of children and childhood that I was just beginning to discover. If anything, I thought his phobia was attributable to his inability to prevent water from coming through his nose under water.

It wasn't until several months after the incident in the pool that I learned the local explanation for Levi's fear of water. Mary Ellen over-heard me discussing his phobia with his sisters, and she said, "Levi is named after Inookie's [another elderly Inuk whose family is related to Levi's] son Jamasee who drowned a year before Levi was born. Levi's namesake died in the water and transmitted this fear of water to Levi." I was partly amused but mostly skeptical. This was more the remnant of a bizarre folk theory than an explanation for a particularly psy-chological symptom. In fact, this comment made me more interested in analytical psychology and the role of memories and emotion in ex-plaining why Levi acted the way he did, a tendency I have retained. Perhaps it was a traumatic episode with water in his recent past that caused him to act the way he did. Surely, the explanation must be based on experiences in his own lifetime, not those of another.

I was unable, at the time, to really understand or appreciate the cos-mic significance of this explanation for his fear of water. I could not accept the veracity of folk theories that attribute causality and agency to name souls that move from one generation to the next. And be-cause of my skepticism at the time, I did not pursue the topic any fur-ther with either Mary Ellen or any of her Inuit in-laws, which I regret to this day. They would have been more than happy, I suspect, to ex-plain this and other features of a complex system of pre- and post-Christian beliefs about the nature of time, souls, and persons. It is only recently, however, that I have begun to appreciate the significance of this and other aspects of Inuit cosmology and spirituality, a universe replete with various types of supernatural actors and supra-sensible experiences, a point I will return to shortly.

Although the arrival of Christian and secular metaphysical claims somewhat weakened the power of these myths and the influence they have on everyday life, stories of shape shifting and soul cycling are still quite common, even among devout Anglicans and Roman Cath-olics. As a person increasingly drawn to the origins of certain beliefs and doctrines and willing to accept the ontology of mystic presence, divinity, sacrality, and profanity in everyday lives and in different parts of the world, I feel much more prepared to investigate saturated phe-nomena and meaning in the Arctic by examining several examples of extraordinary experience in the Arctic. Rather than regarding these pre-Christian beliefs and Christian doctrine as competing worldviews, or mutually incompatible, I am now drawn to them as resources for exploring how the Inuit make sense of their world, whether relying on Inuit eschatology or on the message of the Gospel.

My conversion process has inspired me to explore more thoroughly what I had previously discounted, the fact that Levi is the reincarnation of Jamasee Nowdluk, his namesake, or that his older sister, Noodloo, is the reincarnation of Mary and Joe Tigguk's son, who died a year prior to Noodloo's birth. Perhaps it was my destiny, like that of so many who had trouble finding their faith in a world of reason and skepticism, to suffer periods of doubt before I could reach a different plane of subjectivity, a greater willingness to be open to the enchantment of the world. Perhaps I was not ready in my mid- to late twenties to consider the possibility that I am not a self-made individual, always responsible for making sense of my life without religion or metaphysics but with resources of my choosing, desires, and fears emanating from within me. Rather, I am part, if I choose to accept it, of some larger plan, of some larger teleology, that makes us more curious about and enable to accept what is sacred, divine, and mystical. In the remaining section of this essay, I will explore several features of the supernatural (soul migration, prophecy, and sorcery) that I encountered while doing fieldwork in Iqaluit and at several outpost camps, beginning in the summer of 1990 and continuing intermittently.

Repositioning Subjectivity

Renato Rosaldo's essay, "Grief and the Headhunter's Rage" (1989), explores his own turmoil and transformation as a person grieving the loss of his wife while conducting research among the Ilongot. This life-changing event repositioned him with respect to the Ilongot, enabling him to understand more deeply their need to find a place to carry the anger that comes with losing a cherished relative or friend. Repositioning can also occur in the context of one's religious identity and spirituality. Frank Cushing, a scholar of Zuni culture and society, was initiated into the sacred order of the Zuni Bow Priesthood in

1881 (Green 1979). This event not only improved his ethnography but also inspired him to become an ardent defender of Zuni lands and religion. S. B., a Winnebago whose autobiography was translated by Paul Radin (1963), remembers his conversion as being rather immediate and intense. After ingesting peyote, he was deeply moved by the overwhelming presence of Earthmaker (God).

Victor and Edith Turner were repositioned by their research among the Ndembu in southern Africa in the 1950s. Returning to England, they joined the Roman Catholic Church, a decision that led to tensions with their friends and colleagues (Engelke 2000). Roman Catholicism, however, satisfied their hunger for ritual and shaped much of Victor Turner's future work on symbolism and ritual in various cultural contexts. More recently, Paul Stoller (2004) describes how the experience of cancer clarified his understanding of Songhay sorcery and allowed him to draw connections between his Jewish identity as a child and his quest to be a sorcerer's apprentice. Stoller states that his encounter with cancer deepened his faith, but he doesn't specify how. Perhaps this is a symptom of a bias in the academy. The Canadian anthropologist Roderick Wilson describes how his faith in Christianity "reinforced [his] own awareness of the sacred" and broadened his appreciation of modern shamanic practices (Wilson 1994, 207). At the same time, however, his faith made him feel deviant from the dominant society of the academy, a place where faith and religion are discussed only in appropriate academic contexts and seldom as an aspect of one's own identity.

The idea that having faith or being a Christian is a form of deviance resonates with my struggle to understand secularism and its grip on a disenchanted world. Perhaps this is why I feel tentative writing this essay. Nevertheless, I would be lying if I claimed that ethnographic research in Africa, my marriage to an anthropologist of religion, and my return to the Episcopal Church has not repositioned my relationship to Inuit spirituality. As my understanding of the world has changed, so has my belief that the world cannot be explained by cognitive and material forces alone.

Debates about faith and religious belief continue to pit philosophers against theologians, scientists against priests, spiritual healers against medical doctors. I hesitate jumping into these debates, if only because I am neither a philosopher nor a theologian. Rather, I want to explore Inuit spirituality in light of a renewed faith in God and in the reality of other mysterious, sacred phenomena. This essay is an attempt to recover lost opportunities, to revisit a world that I had largely over-looked and to perhaps provide morale for younger ethnographers: try to be open and as inquisitive as possible to the mysteries of faith and belief that we encounter in the field.

The Transformation of My Vocation

When I first went into the field to do my doctoral dissertation research in 1994, I was uncomfortable with my religious identity. Baptized into the Episcopal faith as an infant, and confirmed in the same church as a young adult, the mysteries of the sacraments and sounds of the lit-urgy never moved me. I enjoyed serving on Sunday as an acolyte, and I was proud to carry a torch during the procession and even hold the Gospel to my chest while the priest read from it in the middle of the congregation. But I did not believe all the central tenets of Episcopal belief and was often more mesmerized by the description of other re-ligious figures and texts, including those of Hindus and Buddhists, not to mention the many other religions loosely bunched under the label "traditional" or "polytheistic."

This ambivalence toward religion began to change when I met my fiancée in graduate school. She was raised in a large, devout Roman Catholic family and educated in Roman Catholic schools until her se-nior year of high school. She has always been fascinated by ritual and religion, and she chose to major in anthropology several weeks after enrolling in an Anthropology of Religion course at the University of Washington. Attracted to the works of Victor Turner and the study of initiation rites in West Africa, her interest in anthropology was merely an extension of her interest in the Roman Catholic rites in which she had participated in school, at Sunday Mass, and elsewhere, including during a year-long exchange trip to Spain.

In January of 1994, she joined me for the beginning of my disser-tation research, and since I had a generous fellowship, I decided to

ask her to join me, at least for half the year. We lived together in Iqaluit for seven months. We attended the local Roman Catholic church,
then under the direction of Father Dufours, who celebrated Mass in
three languages, French, English, and Inuktitut. A native of France,
Father Dufours had been a priest in the Arctic for more than thirty
years, and his knowledge of Inuit language and culture was encyclo-
pedic. My wife was reluctant to attend St. Jude's Cathedral, Iqaluit's
scenic Anglican Church, in part because of the rumors she had heard
about Protestant denominations. It made her uncomfortable to think
that Protestants had rejected much of what Roman Catholics hold
dear, the veneration of saints and an elaborate and extensive devotion to sacraments. I did not argue with her, nor did I try to convince
her to attend St. Jude's. I found myself more interested in attending
the Roman Catholic church anyway, if only because it seemed so different to me, even exotic.

  She started graduate school later that year, and in 1996, she was
awarded a twelve-month pre-dissertation fellowship to study initiation rites among the Mandinga of Guinea-Bissau, West Africa, a former colony of Portugal. Having had many unusual experiences in the
Arctic, we entered the field with a healthier appreciation for the unknown and the uncontrollable. Although Michelle had specific research topics in mind, that is, Mandinga initiation rites, we realized
we would not make any progress if we did not speak Kriolu, the national language, and Mandinga, the language of the Mandinga. The
Mandinga are the third-largest ethnic group in Guinea-Bissau, and
their language is one of the several dozen Mande languages spoken
throughout West Africa. Little has been written about the Mandinga
of Guinea-Bissau, however, and nothing had been published on their
initiation rites since the 1940s.

  After several months of intensive language study in a Mandinga-
dominated neighborhood in Bissau, the nation's capital, we indicated
to our Mandinga friends that we wanted to move to a village in the
Oio region, one of twelve administrative units in Guinea-Bissau. Oio
is considered by many to be the crucible of Mandinga history and culture in Guinea-Bissau, which is no larger than Connecticut and which
boasts a population that recently surpassed 1.2 million. Our language

instructor's cousin, Idrissa Camara, arranged for us to visit Bafata-Oio, a farming village several miles southwest of Farim—the capital of the Oio region. Having arrived in Bafata-Oio in the middle of the night with only a flashlight to guide our path, we had no idea what the village actually looked like until we awoke the next morning to the sound of children—students—reciting passages from the Qur'an. There was a mist hovering around the large compound, which consisted of a big rectangular courtyard circumscribed by a series of simple mud brick homes, some covered with corrugated tin, some with thatch. Shortly after we emerged from our room, donated to us by one of the teachers, we were led to greet Alhadj Fodimaye Touré, his three wives, and his numerous children and grandchildren. Alhadj asked us about the nature of our visit and decided to allow us to live in his village. He even granted us exclusive use of one of the village's unoccupied homestead, Camarakunda, which had been previously occupied by a teacher–student who had moved on to start his own school.

We hired local villagers to do some minor repairs and renovations, including building a new outdoor latrine, and we gradually settled into a routine of daily visiting and language study. The stories we began to accumulate about the village in general, and about Alhadj Touré, in particular, were both inspiring and impressive, and it was no surprise that several thousand pilgrims came to the village in late May for a three-day prayer vigil and sacrifice to celebrate the birthday of the Prophet Mohammed. The people of Bafata-Oio spend most of the year preparing for the annual ceremony, in which visitors from as far away as Mali, Morocco, and even France, arrive to receive the blessings of Alhadj on this special day. As a consequence, Alhadj's reputation has grown in the past several decades, and he is one of the most revered traditional healers in the entire Senegambian region, which encompasses Senegal, the Gambia, Guinea-Bissau, and Guinea.

Alhadj Touré is a devout Muslim who preaches peace and presides over a traditional Qur'anic school based in Bafata-Oio. The school is a place where children learn to recite the Qur'an by memory and to provide for themselves and for others by learning basic trades, like farming and animal husbandry—a combination of school and experiential learning not unlike Outward Bound and alternative education programs found in North America. One of Alhadj's more memorable proverbs sums up the mission of his school: *hakiloo warta* (open mind), *jusoo sumiata* (cool heart), and *sondomé ten kunta* (calm spirit). He had dedicated himself to a life of prayer, obedience to Allah, and a passionate concern for his fellow villagers and regular stream of visitors and pilgrims. I would even venture to argue that Alhadj's life is a manifestation of the true mystical life (Underhill 1995).

Interwoven into this particular form of Muslim piety, shared by his fellow villagers, is a strong faith in traditional Mandinga beliefs and customs, including beliefs in the mystical power of amulets and talismans, in the presence of evil and malevolent spirits, and in complex initiation rites for both boys and girls. Female circumcision, a rite that is not described anywhere in the Qur'an and not condoned in any way in any of the supplementary texts attributed to the teachings of the Prophet Mohammed, is still practiced in most Mandinga villages throughout Guinea-Bissau and in the capital of Bissau itself. The rite has become a sore spot for many Mandingas both within Bissau and beyond, as they have become targets of intense anti-circumcision campaigns promoted by the World Health Organization and other NGOs (Johnson 2000, 2002). Unfortunately, these attacks, which some argue is colonialism in a new guise, draws attention away from the achievements of the Mandinga and other Muslims living in Bissau, who continue to support peaceful interethnic relations, a unified resistance against Islamist extremists, and a commitment to civil democracy and a judiciary based on constitutional, and not religious, laws.

Fieldwork, in this context, led to many intense emotional experiences and seemingly fantastic stories, grounded in a world that included Islamic faith and a world of shape shifters and soul-eating witches who caused disease and even death. In addition to hearing claims about the healing powers of praying and adhering to the five pillars of Islam (faith, prayer, fasting, almsgiving, and making the pilgrimage to Mecca), we also listened to stories of a snake child who slithered away into the forest; amulets that could protect one against the ill will of jealous mothers-in-law or evil spirits; and how the people of Bafata-Oio survived eleven years of terror at the hands of Portuguese and pro-Portuguese militia forces fighting against a grassroots independence movement that liberated Guinea-Bissau in 1974. We learned how Islam and traditional Mandinga beliefs continue to be cornerstones of an enchanted world, suffused with the will of Allah and mystical forces and presences. Here was a world in which marabouts made secret potions that opened our minds and greatly enhanced our language-learning abilities. We surprised many with the speed in which we became proficient in Kriolu (Guinea-Bissau's unofficial national language) and Mandinga, although my wife's progress, our friends would say, always surpassed my own.

We also attended the dramatic, spontaneous performances of Kankaran on the streets of Bissau. Kankaran is a masquerade figure who mysteriously appears and disappears as he scares away malevolent spirits looking to eat the souls of boys undergoing initiation rites. Our neighbors warned us never to look at Kankaran with our own eyes, lest he decide to try to kill us. Some had died from his attacks. Moving furiously about the city, covered in a full-length bark-colored "costume," Kankaran always carried two machetes, one in each hand, and he would slap them together every few minutes, while issuing a piercing scream. The sound resonated for blocks, causing a collective sense of fear and excitement that lingered for hours, if not days.

On other occasions, we met people who were bewitched by *irans* (spirits that were invisible to everyone except *porteiros* or visionaries, those who had an innate capacity to identify them in a crowd). We listened as our neighbors in Bafata-Oio recited the legends of Amadou Bamba, a Muslim saint and mystic who lived in Senegal in the nineteenth century. He is still remembered for his heroic resistance to French colonial forces, who tortured him in order to show him the futility of his faith. During a month-long voyage from Senegal to an island prison colony somewhere off the coast of Africa, the French authorities refused to allow him to pray on board the ship. In response, we were told, he simply prayed outside the boat while he and his prayer carpet gently glided over the ocean, keeping pace with the ship. To this day, the place where he is buried, Touba, Senegal, receives millions of pilgrims a year on the anniversary of his death.

In Guinea-Bissau, I began to feel that there was more to the world than natural forces and human agency. The weight and loneliness of a secular self began to loosen its grip on me. I began to feel re-enchanted and reanimated by a world of mystic presence and spiritual agency. I began to experience the world as saturated with unseen forces, a world suffused with God and other invisible beings. I felt as if I were undergoing a slow and gradual conversion process, one actively transforming and shaping my understanding of the world and how people make meaning in it. My experiences in Africa drew me to a deeper interest in the power of prayer and pilgrimage in the Christian world (particularly Roman Catholic), and I became more attentive to stories of miraculous healing and other miracles associated with Catholic shrines in Europe and North America. I was also inspired to revisit stories told to me in the Arctic about the mystical presences of name-souls, spirit helpers, and shamans. My experiences in Guinea-Bissau enabled me to step outside my taken-for-granted view of the world and to learn why I refused to explore episodes of sorcery, prophecy, and reincarnation in the Arctic, and why I avoided discussing these topics with my host family or others.

Many a priest or spiritual counselor would argue that the commencement of a journey into the inner life is not the result of one's own will but rather an example of a mystical presence moving from the outside in (for a fascinating set of case studies, see James 1997). I feel that when I conducted research in the Arctic in the early 1990s, I was neither willing nor ready emotionally, psychologically, or spiritually to confront a world of infused with sacred signs and saturated with mystic presence. I was too committed to an independent, autonomous figure of my self and too preoccupied with the success of my research project. I do not regret what I accomplished in those sixteen months of fieldwork spanning four years, and I am proud of the results of this research, encapsulated in my dissertation and subsequent publications (Searles 1998, 2001a, 2001b, 2002).

It is difficult to admit that I avoided many opportunities in which I could have confronted my own preconceptions and stereotypes about the world. I jotted down notes about shaman-like activities, and also evidence of reincarnation and soul migration, but they informed neither my analysis of Inuit social experience nor my understanding of the Inuit world. I kept these episodes and narratives safely removed from any analytical or theoretical gaze. I was not going to sacrifice my credibility as a student of anthropology, and I felt I lacked both the necessary language and empathy to write about these events with any conviction. In short, I struggled with my particular vocation of anthropology as a science. Partly out of convenience, partly out of fear, I wrote about a world in the Arctic that was disenchanted and wholly devoid of mystical presence. I would explain accounts of extraordinary or mystical experiences with the tools of social theory, psychology, and history. I interpreted Mary Ellen's claim that Levi was a reincarnated being as the result of Mary Ellen's exaggerated faith in pre-Christian cosmology. His phobia could be explained as some acquired voluntary or involuntary response resulting from a prior traumatic experience in the water.

Looking back on this experience, I realize that I had some unresolved and unfocused anger toward a particular form of Christianity, which had colored my views of institutional religion. I was still disoriented by a disturbing and confusing experience I had had with an evangelical faith community in Port Alsworth, Alaska, in the spring of 1993, about six months before I began my dissertation research. Sent to do a field study of the subsistence practices of the residents in and around Lake Clark National Park and Preserve by the National Park Service and the College of Forest Resources at the University of Washington, I wanted to know how these residents were using forest resources for food, shelter, fuel, and medicine.

Port Alsworth was home to a small community of Park employees and small business owners. The town's loyalties were sharply divided between those who belonged to the local evangelical church and those who did not. Glen Alsworth, one of the original residents of the town, had built a mini-empire of bush planes, cabins, and airplane hangars with revenues generated by guiding an international clientele of outdoor enthusiasts on sport-hunting and fishing trips of all types, from brown bear to salmon. He lived in a spacious, multilevel log cabin with his wife and children. They were hospitable and gracious to me, offering me food and company on a number of occasions. Glen was the leader of the local church, an independent evangelical church, and he invited me to attend one of the Sunday services.

Attending that service was an uncomfortable experience, I later wrote in my field notes. I felt out of place and surprisingly alienated by this community of worshippers, considering I had attended church regularly most of my life.

The creed of this church was built on a particular incantation that all members were required to utter publicly if they were going to become members of the church: "I accept Jesus Christ as my savior." I quickly learned that they had no interest in my faith, my prior religious experience, my views on religion. On the contrary, they treated me as if I weren't Christian at all, but just another soul to be saved before the final showdown between good and evil as prophesied in the last chapter of the New Testament, the Revelation to John. Soon after the service, one congregation member invited me to a private showing of a documentary identifying itself as an authoritative interpretation of the Revelation. The documentary was dramatic and compelling, using graphic images and utterances to portray a world divided in a final battle between good and evil, Christ and the Antichrist. Followers of Christ would be saved, swept to heaven by an almighty lord; followers of the anti-Christ would be left behind, awaiting a fate of death and destruction.

I would not be allowed into heaven, my host assured me, unless "I accepted Jesus Christ as my savior." I decided to be true to my own beliefs and instincts and refuse to undergo their initiation rite. In fact, I never attended their church again. I never was able to transcend a sense of awkwardness around them, as if we were locked in a grip of mutual mistrust, even disgust. I decided to spend more time with another non-member of the church, John Branson, a natural historian of the park who lived alone with Sparky, his aging black Labrador retriever. He lived in a one-room cabin he had built and heated with wood acquired locally. He thoroughly enjoyed his solitude, and although his salary was small, he had no bills and no debts. What confused me was the presence of Christianity in this community. John's generosity toward strangers (me) and his lack of pretension and ostentation more closely approximated the life of Jesus and his apostles than did the lives of any of those who attended church. They valued commercial and economic success, and they were not shy about displaying the fortunes they had made. I felt that their brand of Christianity was inspired by selfish motives that made their church an exclusive social club. If I wanted to learn more about them, I had to aspire to be like them. John Branson, who belonged to no faith community in particular, seemed to embody the Gospel message of simplicity, poverty, and inclusivity. If I wanted to learn more about John Branson, I simply had to be with him.

My experiences in Port Alsworth spilled over into my understanding of missionary activities in North America and inspired me, I think, to avoid working with members the Anglican Church in Iqaluit. I regarded the work of missionaries in the Americas with a newly acquired suspicion of modernization and assimilation, particularly in the way those acting in the name of Christianity trivialized and even mocked indigenous belief systems and practices. I assumed that religious transformation in the Arctic was linked to rather sinister motives on the part of missionaries to disempower and even disenchant a world of spirits and supernatural forces.

After my trip to West Africa, however, I grew more interested in studying a growing body of scholarship that problematizes this simple view of contact history in North America, offering a much more complex narrative than the more simple stereotypes of bad missionaries and victimized Natives. Detailed descriptions and discussions of religious pluralism and syncretism in the Arctic can be found in the works of Fienup-Riordan et al. 2000, Goulet 1982; Laugrand 2002; Laugrand, Oosten, and Trudel; 2002, Tungilik and Uyarasuk 1999; and E. Turner 1994b, to name just a few. I learned that many indigenous peoples accepted Christianity as another doctrine that neither diminished nor conflicted with their own beliefs; rather, they allowed the systems of thought to coexist or even complement one another. Goulet's (1982) description of Dene Tha Catholics in northern Alberta provides a compelling example: in addition to attending Roman Catholic mass, praying the rosary, and so on, they believe in the reincarnation of humans, in the incarnation of spirit helpers in the form of animals, and in the power of prophet dances and visions.

Becoming more familiar with this scholarship propelled me into
an even greater appreciation for religion's role in shaping experience,
pushing me away from a wholly disenchanted view of the world, one
in which the secular self is the dominant source of meaning and agency.
Although I am not completely convinced about the reality of mystical presences, I do pray every day in some form or another, and I feel
I have much to learn in terms of my understanding of the world's religions and the role of sacraments, mystery, and the ineffable in everyday life. My deepening curiosity about the nature of the divine as
embodied in the sacraments, about the complexity of religious faith,
and about the enormous variety of religious experience has resulted
in a new set of questions and new interests about the nature of mystic presence and extraordinary experience in the Arctic.

Name-Souls and Mystic Presence

Much has been written about Inuit naming practices (e.g., Frederiksen 1968, Kublu and Oosten 1999, M. Nuttall 1994, and Williamson 1988). Anthropologists who study the circulation of names and
its overarching cosmology are drawn to the sociological, psychological, and mystical aspects of the practice (Guemple 1994, M. Nuttall
1994; for a counterexample, see most of the essays in Mills and Slobodin 1994). Lee Guemple treats naming as a window into Inuit cosmology and patterns of social relations, including how persons are
constituted through their material (*saunik* or bone) ties to other individuals in the community, living and deceased. The name confers
much more than a label, however. It provides the building blocks of
one's personality, of one's psychological and cognitive matrix (Guemple 1994, 111). The name or "*atik* embodies who the individual 'really is'; and it is from this acquisition that one's social relationships,
peculiarities—even skills which a child can manifest throughout its
corporeal existence—are acquired" (Guemple 1994, 112).

Mark Nuttall identifies naming as a practice that provides a sense
of continuity, sociability, and community, and notes that a person's
name "is a vital link in an overall chain of social, psychological, and

emotional support" (M. Nuttall 1994, 133). Nuttall explores the deep emotional and social bonds that are attached to namesakes:

> Once named, children begin to learn the identities of the people they are named after and acquire a knowledge of the various relationships that link them to an intricate pattern of genealogical and fictive kin. As the child is named after people who had previously occupied positions in the kinship network, to some extent roles and interaction between *atsiaq* [i.e., the person who receives the name of a dead person] and the family of the *aqqa* [the person who gives the name] are prescribed. However, this does not tell us of the person's own sense of identity and feelings of being named. Other people do the naming, ensuring that they continue to experience the memory of a deceased relative and loved and valued member of the community in the form of an *atsiaq*. (M. Nuttall 1994, 130–131)

Although I never heard my host family use specific terminology in conjunction with naming practices, the names used correspond to Nuttall's description of Greenlandic naming practices. What are the cosmological origins of such systems? This question has not been studied so extensively, although a recent article by Alexina Kublu and Jarich Oosten, building on the work of Knud Rasmussen, portrays the Inuit soul-complex as a complex yet comprehensible system of agents and actions (Kublu and Oosten 1999). Every being, persons and animals included, possess a *tarniq*, or that part of the soul that gives life and health. A tarniq might be coaxed into leaving the body through sorcery or when a person transgresses a taboo. The loss of one's tarniq generally eventuates in death, although shamans have the ability to call back one's tarniq, or replace it with another. The other part of the soul (in animals, it exists independently of the tarniq), the *inuusia*, is associated with warmth and breath (Kublu and Oosten 1999). Both the tarniq and the inuusia eventually leave the body when an individual dies. The tarniq might linger for a few days with the dead body and then either become reincarnated and/or go to the land of the dead. The latter is what happened to Levi's tarniq, which had dwelled in the body of Jamasee, then died, then entered the body of Levi, transferring to him memories and idiosyncrasies from his life.

In addition to tarniq and inuusia, there is another mystical presence, namely the *inua*, or owner of an object. Every object, animate and inanimate, has an inua, a spirit-being that controls the destiny of that object. A knife has an inua, a person has an inua, and so on. A hunter is successful, it is thought, only when the animal's inua is complicit. In this way, hunting itself becomes a spiritual act, an act of gift or grace on the part of the inua. Inua are sentient beings, and they study the actions of hunters and their families; they can withhold their gifts from those who are selfish or disrespectful. According to our host family, Kelli, Mary Ellen's oldest brother-in-law, was experiencing a streak of bad luck in hunting because he had grown self-absorbed and lazy, unwilling to help his father or his younger brother. The language and beliefs of the inua in the cycle of life and death, luck and bad luck, are sensed within the language of the sacramental rites of Holy Communion as practiced by Anglicans and Roman Catholics. In the sacrament of the Eucharist, Jesus Christ's inua, God, sacrifices his son to redeem a world of sinners, to make salvation a reality for all. In much the same way that the inua of animals offer a sacrifice to worthy and willing humans, so does Christ offer a sacrifice on behalf of willing and worthy followers, those who have been baptized into the Christian faith.

This collection of spiritual entities, tarniq, inuusia, and inua, provide the Inuit with mystical ties to the past, present, and future, creating a living, breathing, embodied link to their ancestors. The Inuit subject, reincarnated with name-souls and living in the shadow of inua, provides a striking contrast to the figure of the modern self who finds meaning not in reference to religion but to a world of individual desires mediated by social conditions and cultural constructions. For Levi Pisuktie, baptized into the Anglican Church several months after his birth, and the recipient of several name-souls, including Jamasee, the self lives in a much different register of meaning and agency. He is intimately connected to other souls through his own soul, and he is also a child of the living God, through faith and sacraments.

Ironically, because Levi is the reincarnation of deceased relatives, he is treated as an elder in some contexts, as an individual whose tastes and preferences are acknowledged, and when appropriate, indulged.

Levi's older sister Noodloo was given a pair of wristbands and a head-band by the parents of one of her namesakes. Their son, who shared Noodloo's name, enjoyed playing basketball and loved to wear wrist-bands and sweatbands. Students of Inuit childrearing practices often emphasize how permissive and patient parents strive to be around their children (Briggs 1998). There is very little admonishment or punishment, and very few demands are placed on children, although there are exceptions. I found this attitude toward parenting, this per-missiveness, frustrating at times, for I was raised to believe that hu-mans develop emotionally and psychologically if they are guided by rules that teach them self-discipline and restraint. Because children are reincarnated, there is a tacit assumption that they are born with accumulated wisdom that is hidden but that gradually emerges as the child awakens to his reincarnated identities. It would have been very wrong for me to train Levi to be comfortable putting his head under water. His family believed that this was not a problem to be resolved but a habit to be tolerated, even valued. His family did not judge him based on how well he developed according to a set of psychological and educational criteria.

Perhaps the most detailed and breathtaking description of nam-ing comes from Alexina Kublu, a longtime instructor of Inuktitut for non-Inuktitut speakers in Iqaluit. Kublu describes how the choice of a name is often precipitated by visions and dreams, unusually in the form of visitations from deceased relatives. Far from being a static system, however, the practice of naming is integrated into a world where name-souls have a direct impact on the everyday reality. Kublu describes how changing an individual's name can protect that indi-vidual from sickness or death, a custom that Alexina Kublu reports is still being practiced by members of her family (Kublu and Oosten 1999, 75). It also creates much space for children to experiment and learn from different names. When Kublu's daughter was five years old, she demanded to go live with her mother's midwife and her hus-band. The daughter had been given the name of their son, and she was convinced that she was their son, and when she moved in, they called her *irniq* (son). Later, she grew tired of this arrangement and returned to live with her mother. Naming is also a source of fun and amusement, as adults tease and teach children about the various personalities behind the names. Levi's father's cousin, Elijah, would try to trick Levi into thinking that he had had the tip of his index finger removed. Levi's namesake was nicknamed Tiggittuk (he "killed" his index finger), because he had lost the top half of his index finger in a hunting accident long before Levi was born. Naming combines the playful and the serious; it is a vital, vibrant source of enchantment and spirituality in the everyday life of Inuit and non-Inuit alike in the Canadian Arctic.

Levi's and his family's active participation in the Anglican Church has neither trivialized nor eliminated their belief in reincarnation but rather has supplemented them, providing a means to infuse their lives with multiple perspectives on the nature of souls, salvation, and sin. Furthermore, both Anglican and pre-Christian systems of belief accept that Levi's destiny is not entirely a matter of his own will, his own choosing. Both admit that his life path is influenced (but not determined) by an interconnectedness to the sacred that long preceded his birth and that will outlive his death. This is not to deny that Levi has a will of his own, or that he might reject these doctrines altogether. He would not be alone in making such a choice. Given the abuse that occurred at residential schools throughout Canada, it is not surprising that many indigenous Canadians are rejecting the Roman Catholic and Anglican Churches as sources of authority and support. He may not develop an interest in mystic presence or a desire to deepen his faith in Christ; I have not had the opportunity to converse with Levi regarding these matters. But I look forward to such an opportunity. The fact that this tradition remains strong and active, that Inuit are even incorporating biblical names (like Levi, which is an Old Testament name) into the available pool of soul-names, attests to the strength and vitality of this system of beliefs—a topic ripe for more exploration.

Prophecy

When I first met Meeka Mike, I was impressed by her knowledge of hunting and outpost camps. She immediately became interested in my project, a study of an outpost-camp family living some 250 miles from

Iqaluit. She was convinced that the only way to really learn is experientially, when body, mind, and soul are pushed into new realms of self-awareness and emotional intensity. She wanted to hear stories of our adventures at the outpost camp, and she was somewhat unusual in that respect. Most other residents thought it bizarre that my wife and I would want to spend most of our time at a tiny hunting camp, far from the familiar faces and conveniences of town life, confined to cramp quarters, and constantly constrained by weather, wind, and shifting sea-ice patterns.

Meeka's autobiography is overflowing with mystic presence; extraordinary experiences provided coherence and consistency to her life story. Although she did not belong to a particular church, she was raised Anglican by her parents in the town of Pangnirtung. Meeka had recently separated from her partner, and she obtained custody over her daughter, then nine years old. She was finishing a public administration class at Nunavut Arctic College, and she would soon be offered a job as executive assistant at the Baffin Regional Inuit Association. But she was also a mystic (my label, not hers), full of intriguing narratives and an unshakable faith in the presence of supernatural forces in the world.

Although I did not think she was a quack or a con, I did not know how to respond to her descriptions of near-death experiences or encounters with deceased persons. She had had enough tragedy and emotionally intense experiences in her life to make me think that she was sincere in her beliefs and fully capable of distinguishing the real from projections of her own ego. She had lost all vital signs for several minutes during the birth of her daughter, and she describes having an out-of-body experience in which she was able to pass through walls. In fact, she felt that she had been without a body, merging seamlessly into the tunnel of light in front of her. When she saw her body lying on the gurney the hospital room, it was dirty and constraining. She sometimes wonders why she came back. I am glad she did, because she is a help to many in the community, including residents of outpost camps. She is now a guide for ecotourism excursions to outpost camps, and any net income she makes goes straight to the outpost camps.

She had recently participated in a search for a five-year-old boy who had become separated from his father during a snowstorm. She "freaked out" the father of the boy because she was able to describe in detail the position of the body and the clothing the boy was wearing when they found him. The image appeared to her as if on a television screen in a shop window—she thought her friends were playing a joke on her because it seemed so real.

What is interesting about Meeka's spirituality is that it involves a combination of passivity and activity. When I first met her, her involvement in so many different activities and programs in Iqaluit impressed me. She had recently started her own business. She was a counselor in the local outward-bound program that takes high school students on multiday excursions of hunting and camping. She had been nominated to sit on Nunavut's Wildlife Management Board, which oversees the regulation of both subsistence and commercial hunting and fishing activities in Nunavut. At the same time, she believed that her destiny was not entirely in her hands. She illustrated for me the concept of *ajurnarmat* or *ajurnaqtuq*, meaning "it cannot be helped." Inuit use it to refer to difficult situations in which few options exist. When someone is trapped in a snowstorm, the only possible solution is to sit tight, because it cannot be helped. Some confuse this attitude with a sense of futility. Meeka regarded it as both empowering and disempowering. She remembered one story of a hunter who was alone and trapped in the ice. He knew that if he were not rescued within several hours, he would not survive. He was able to survive, and he described being pushed and helped to safety by a mysterious force. He had let go of a world in which he was in control, because he knew it could not be helped. *Ajurnarmat* can lead to feelings of anxiety and fear but also to feelings of tranquility and comfort.

I am now much more curious to learn about these visions and other extraordinary experiences in the Arctic, both in terms of how they frame her life and how they reveal a particular variety of religious experience, which is both similar and dissimilar to my new-found appreciation for the Episcopal Church and its creeds of inclusivity, generosity, and love. I feel prepared to approach all these topics with a new frame of mind, one less inhibited by the conceits and preoccupations of a secular self and more open to embracing a world of religious pluralism and enchantment.

Conclusion

Following the insights of Johannes Fabian (2001), the best ethnography is often done when the ethnographer is least self-conscious and most free from internal controls. In this essay, I have tried to expose the internal controls, conscious and unconscious, that made me unwilling to take seriously spirituality and faith as expressed by my informants. I analyzed and wrote about Inuit social experience as if beliefs in reincarnation, extraordinary visions, and God were only of secondary importance for understanding the people I was studying. I assumed the world to be a disenchanted one, devoid of mystical presence, and filled only with repressed desires, concealed motives, and historical conditions. I accepted the model of the secular self, in which one's identity and destiny is a matter of individual will and sociocultural circumstances, not a product of divine or other supernatural agents. My consciousness began to shift as I took on new opportunities and new challenges, including marrying an anthropologist of religion, doing ethnography in Guinea-Bissau, West Africa, and developing a greater appreciation for the power of sacraments and faith in my life.

The various components of Inuit spirituality discussed in this essay, including prophecy and reincarnation, are just a small portion of an enormous corpus of knowledge and thought about cosmology and eschatology. I have given the reader a small glimpse of religious pluralism in the Arctic. Being open to varieties of faith and religious experience can both improve our ethnography and illuminate the choices we have made in our lives and research, choices that open doors to some avenues of thought and close the door on others. I am not sure exactly where my faith life or interest in ethnographic research will lead me, but I am confident that it will be neither boring nor disappointing.

Part Three

Epistemological and Ethical Thresholds

In three distinctive essays, we focus on what anthropologists "stand to gain by taking up challenges posed by ways of knowing alien from ours" (Wikan 1991, 296) and explore the merits of various epistemological and ethical frameworks within which to act and think, once in the midst of our hosts in their homes and homeland. Together these essays make the critical point that the experience of the field carries on well beyond the geographical and temporal boundaries of one's fieldwork. Over the years, the full impact of one's engagement with others in their world unfolds. As it does, one gains significant insights into one's own personal and professional life, the meaning of events lived while in the field, and of the relationships between one's self in and out of the field. Far from being a single experience of transformation in the field, fieldwork is here seen as an integral part of continuous personal and professional development.

In "The Politics of Ecstatic Research," Bruce Granville Miller illustrates how "experience-near," or ecstatic, anthropology builds on an idea of collaborative ethnographic research that takes local ideas of knowledge, power, experience, and the transmission of knowledge seriously. His own field experiences with Coast Salish people and communities reveals the practical and political advantages of this approach. Among these are the consequent unexpected insights into worldview and community processes, the creation of new questions, new sources of data, and an enhanced sense of beauty. Most significantly, he inverts the commonsense understanding to argue that it is the failure to participate in the belief systems that may be politically naive rather than the converse. There are other, darker consequences, however, to this participation, including the entry into worlds of violence and danger, the creation of obligations that are difficult or impossible to meet, and the risks of depoliticizing and exoticizing indigenous experiences. Miller nonetheless argues that these risks themselves lead to new opportunities for engagement.

In the following chapter, "Moving Beyond Culturally Bound Ethical Guidelines," Jean-Guy Goulet addresses the question raised by the Canadian Tri-Council Policy Statement: Ethical Conduct for Research Involving Humans, particularly as it pertains to research with aboriginal peoples. The question asked by the Canadian Research Tri-Councils is the following: What does it mean to involve "other humans" in a research project when investigators and aboriginal peoples belong to two different cultures? Goulet argues that this question is best answered once we have considered the significance for one's research project of one's radical participation as a human being with other human beings in their world. He shows how novel ethical issues arise when the investigator is incorporated in an aboriginal world that includes interaction with spiritual beings. Based on Spiro's concept of culture as a set of propositions (or beliefs) held to be true by members of a society, Goulet proposes an analysis of this account that sheds light on the conditions for mutual understanding within and in between different lifeworlds.

In "Experiences of Power among the Sekani of Northern British Columbia: Sharing Meaning through Time and Space," Guy Lanoue starts with his shared experience with the Sekani of northern British Columbia (Canada) of what he was conditioned to consider as "unscientific" and thus "unknowable" and what they consider "unsayable" (but not unknowable). He describes Sekani experiences of power (which is a special state of being that is not considered the result of empirically verifiable conditions) and examines how these notions are communicated without recourse to semantics, leaving open the possibility that meaning, arising out of each person's individual interpretative frame, can be shared through "mythical" means. Lanoue shows how transformations in one's personal life may lead to powerful insights in the cultures of others. It is only when he abandoned his own spatial meanderings, moving from city to city, across continents, for personal and professional reasons, that he understood what space meant to the Sekani in terms of acquiring power. He therefore reminds us that fieldwork is not bounded in place and in time, and that the prolonged contact of field research continues to operate well beyond the boundaries that define the formal aspects of contact.

8. The Politics of Ecstatic Research

BRUCE GRANVILLE MILLER

My purpose in this paper is to make some observations about research that takes seriously the views of reality and the knowledge possessed by indigenous peoples, not simply as objects of analysis but also as part of a mode of anthropological understanding and a way to address larger questions.[1] In so doing, I problematize the interesting discussions to date concerning the topic of ecstatic anthropology by adding an explicitly political note to the orchestra. Previous work on this issue has focused on epistemologies, meta-models of reality, problems of interpretation, research methods, empirical tests of strange experiences, the transformations of the researchers themselves, and the nature of culture. Examples appear in the work of Young and Goulet (1998) and of Mills and Slobodin (1994). Yet others have considered the history of anthropological theorizing as it relates to indigenous epistemology. Faris (1994, 11–16), for example, described the emergence of research that takes the Navajo "how and why" seriously, following, sequentially, periods emphasizing comparative religious studies, Jungian archetypes and their application to indigenous thought, the "sophisticated functionalism" of Kluckhohn (which moved between economic and psychological determinism), symbolic analysis, and essentializing linguistic analysis that sought core principles. Valentine and Darnell (1999), however, argue quite differently that Americanist anthropology has been characterized by the internalization of indigenous concepts.

My questions are different than those of these predecessors and are, in brief: What are the responses of indigenous peoples and communities to the topic we refer to as the anthropology of extraordinary experiences? What is the play of power within communities and between communities and the outside world that must be accounted for in such an anthropology? I examine these issues and provide illustrations from my own experiences with members of the Coast Salish communities of Washington State and the province of British Columbia over the last thirty years.

There are some fifty Coast Salish communities concentrated in Puget Sound, Washington, and along the lower stretches of the Fraser River and on Vancouver Island and the adjoining mainland in British Columbia (Miller 2002). My work in these communities has focused on justice and legal practices, tribal political life, and relations with the mainstream societies of Canada and the United States. As the co-director of a graduate ethnographic field school sponsored by my own university, the University of British Columbia, in conjunction with the *Stó:lō* Nation, a Coast Salish tribe, I've had the opportunity to spend eight summers in a longhouse, the site of winter spirit dancing, with community members and hosted by a band chief and ritualist. In part, the field school participants and I were invited in to help keep spirits out of the longhouse during summer months, but spirits clearly pervade the location, and anthropology graduate students, particularly those who are themselves indigenous, have had complex, sometimes disturbing, relations with the spirits in this location.

As I will indicate in the last part of this paper, my family and I have had our own relationships with the spirit beings there and in other longhouses. I wish to consider my own examples of extraordinary experience to make my related argument that an experience-near anthropology may no longer be seen as a fringe activity, but, rather, as increasingly in touch with changes in social science methods that are more responsible to indigenous peoples' concerns and perspectives. I also must add that I do not find it unusual for anthropologists to have experienced the "extraordinary" events I recount here. Indeed, it is probably more often the case than the other way around. Nor am I suggesting that only indigenous peoples engage in such events and processes. Clearly, other peoples have well-known cultural practices such as second sight. However, social scientists ordinarily do not yet directly account for these in their written record of fieldwork. These are edited from most reports or, perhaps, taken as hallmarks of the peculiarity of anthropological work.

 My argument is that participation in or the failure to participate in the belief systems of the members of this community is not politically neutral. There are significant and unexpected reasons that one might adopt the approach of "experience-near" anthropology that are neither naive nor evidence of scholarly failure through "going native." One might draw an analogy between giving anthropological testimony in court as an expert witness and making the argument I am making here. In that setting, if one does not understand the legal language imposed by other participants (lawyers, judges, and others), they can unwittingly and easily testify to something they did not intend. The legal practitioners may *use* the same language as anthropologists, but often with different meaning; for example, "tribe," "fish," or "time immemorial" may have specific content deriving from case law and have limited connection to current anthropological use.[2] In both the courtroom and the longhouse, one's presence has unintended political consequences if one does not participate in the local legal culture in the Geertzian sense of a local, dense system of meaning (Geertz 1983). This perspective stands in contrast to the more usual and converse view that engaging the beliefs of non-Western communities as something other than the object of analysis is politically suspect. From my perspective, it is naive empiricism and unfettered positivism that is intellectually and politically untenable in the emphasis on examining local beliefs within a foreign framework. And such a position is frequently simply not useful. Mills and Slobodin (1994), for example, tell of a Paiute man who observed that anthropologists sometimes fall short because they don't know what questions to ask. Similarly, I've worked with health researchers who refuse to consider what they regard as uninformed or misplaced local views concerning health, well-being, and disease. As a consequence, they produce expensive research reports carefully calibrated for reliability and validity, but which fail to speak to the health problems as understood locally and which have no impact on the lives of community members. In addition, such research alienates community members who regard the work as evidence of mainstream societies' failure to take indigenous lives seriously and to ask the right questions.

In contrast, Fabian (2001) describes good ethnography as the outcome of both time spent with collaborators that engages our conscious senses, and time in which our inner control is relaxed. He argues for an ethnography that moves beyond passive and contemplative knowledge to active sharing resulting from experience "out of mind." This approach might enable anthropologists and other researchers to escape a great variety of problems, some with unexpected political dimensions, as revealed in several examples.

Spirituality and/or Atheism

Many scholars have observed that members of indigenous communities may not draw distinctions between the validity of knowledge derived from visions, the intervention of immortal beings, and forces, intuition, dreams, and sensations of various sorts on the one hand, and knowledge gained in "everyday life" on the other. Both are regarded as experiential and meaningful. If this is so, one might question what our indigenous collaborators make of researchers who do not share this epistemology. A few years ago, a Canadian First Nations intellectual and Coast Salish tribal cultural adviser with whom I work gave me an account of a time when he was distraught because an anthropologist who formerly worked in his community had unexpectedly announced that he was an atheist and did not believe in spirits or spirit helpers. By implication, this anthropologist did not accept any of the accompanying explanations, and it appeared that there could be no meaningful discussion or communication about the cultural realm. The culture adviser felt betrayed because the anthropologist had not revealed his views earlier and because he felt that, despite the keen interest the anthropologist showed in the First Nations cultural practices, they were rendered as "specimens" of something improbable and fantastical. The gift of knowledge given by the culture adviser appeared to be wasted, unappreciated, and even intentionally slighted. Even more to the point, the adviser observed that researchers should have some sense of spirituality. In his words:

I can't see how an atheist who doesn't believe in any form of spirituality is able to respect [our beliefs]. I'm trying to think of a way to respect that belief [atheism]. Without an individual's own spirit there is no way to connect to the metaphors, the teachings of others which allows us to relate to others' beliefs. Atheists have nothing to look at for similarity or for understanding metaphor. A Christian has a soul. Someone who is not a Christian [an atheist] doesn't believe in a soul. A Christian can relate to our *shxweli* [spirit or life force] and the connections to rocks, trees, and fish. A person without that belief can't relate to it and that must affect their understandings and interpretations.[3]

I have not known indigenous people to subject researchers to purity tests of spiritual orthodoxy (in part because there is often no orthodoxy in indigenous practice), or to ask them directly to accept the epistemological basis of life as understood by indigenous peoples. The cultural adviser holds the position that "it's not a question of having some [particular] belief," adding, "One of our teachings is to respect the beliefs of others. I don't want to say that our culture is the best or that we are the most spiritual. But our beliefs have developed with the land and resources here, and aboriginal rights and title comes from this respect" (interview, March 11, 2004). In this case, the spiritual adviser brings up an eminently practical consideration regarding how researchers understand spirituality, arguing that tribal claims to aboriginal rights and title rest on their own notions of the landscape and epistemology, and human relationships to other entities. In indigenous theory, then, although not from a Euro-Canadian viewpoint, denial of this epistemology, through failure to understand, jeopardizes land claims.

Part of this issue concerns the nature of the political process. Recently, a newspaper reported the case of an indigenous band that had won a land claim case in court. The band leader proclaimed the judgment a defeat because the band had been forced to contest the case in a court that was outside its own indigenous system of law, and the court had not recognized the basis on which the band made the claim to the land. In this case, the band members regarded their control of the land as an outcome of their spiritual connection to the landscape and other spiritual entities. The band won, but on the wrong grounds and in the wrong venue. Indigenous epistemology, in this case, asserts that the human system of reciprocity includes non-human beings, which have to be considered. Failure to do so is dangerous.

Recently, I participated in a friendly and revealing conversation between a prominent psychologist who has carried out valuable studies of suicide in Coast Salish communities and an indigenous psychologist who is herself a member of one of the communities. The mainstream psychologist explained that although he studies suicide, suicide itself is unimportant because it is symptomatic of the greater problem of the large number of people who have become despondent. Suicide, he concluded, was the moment in which a small number of these people made the conscious choice to end their lives. To the indigenous psychologist, this viewpoint missed the mark. She responded that, in her community, suicide represented the communities' failure to support the spiritual nature of the deceased rather than an individual decision by the suicide victim. She placed the psychology of suicide within the domain of Coast Salish notions of spirit beings that establish relations with human beings and become part of one's being. Separation from these spirit beings, the failure to create a proper relationship, spiritual harm, and disruption in one's spiritual life could cause the death of a human. The complex of winter ceremonials and spirit beings is social, rather than merely private and personal, and family members and other winter ceremonial dancers who have helped someone create and develop the relationship with the spirit beings have a continuing mutual obligation. The pathology that results in death, then, cannot merely be a private matter. And, for those community members who have not obtained a spirit helper, they still live within what the Coast Salish theorize as the embrace of the extended family within the animated universe.

This exchange reflected significant epistemological differences, even though both psychologists argue that culturally intact communities would have lower rates of suicide than ones with little active indigenous cultural practice. The differences in position, though, suggest differences in what might be done to diminish the likelihood of suicide or the impact on the community when it did occur. It also reveals the outcome when researchers don't account for local beliefs and ways of organizing community experience. In this case, the indigenous psychologist thoughtfully offered an encapsulated version of a perspective different from that held within mainstream psychology. The unspoken implications of her comments were that safety for the community lay in understanding the roots of depression and suicide and that danger lay in approaching these from the wrong angle.

Learning to anticipate and avoid danger

Goulet (1998) has observed that indigenous people impart to researchers only what they believe them to be able to understand (although the first case I mentioned suggests the cultural adviser missed or was misled into missing the mark). It's interesting to consider carefully what this idea might mean, "what one can understand": it suggests that as researchers grow in their understanding of the others' cosmology, their ability to comprehend the immediate world, the world of daily experience, grows accordingly. As comprehension grows, one can engage the spiritual world without creating manifest danger to oneself and anyone else. The issue of danger is a significant one; and I recall the case of an archaeologist who refused to dab on ochre while excavating a sensitive burial site, despite the request of the community officials and elders. The ochre is part of a local system of spiritual practice and imparts protection to those wearing it. These tribal people were not particularly worried about the archaeologist, but they were openly worried about the possibility of people being bothered by spirits that might be agitated by the excavation. In particular, inadequately prepared or weakened humans, the elders, the feeble, the sick, and children, were vulnerable to spirits that might take their souls.

This example reveals that it is barely enough for researchers to simply set aside their own systems of belief; rather, one must anticipate danger and difficulty to live gracefully with indigenous people in their environment, just as the indigenous peoples themselves must. In fact, it has been observed that a defining characteristic of adulthood is the ability to anticipate danger and avoid it. This idea shows up in Basso's

[handwritten margin note: Ability to Understand]

(1996) work with the Apache, for one notable example, and Ortiz's (1969) studies of his own home, the Tewa Pueblo community.

In the Coast Salish world, it is a mark of one's status as an adult of significance to skillfully encounter the spiritual world immediately surrounding the human world or to know when to back away. Miller (1991) has glossed "Real People" from Tshimshian, but the idea has applicability in the Coast Salish case as well. Real People are those with spiritual training and knowledge sufficient for them to intercede with the outside world on behalf of kin. In this case, the outside world includes members of other families; other human communities; the leaders of the animal world, especially the salmon; and many other entities, including spirits. While some people are known for this knowledge and ability and are called upon to help on ritual occasions or during times of difficulty, to some extent everyone, including visitors such as anthropologists, have these skills. This is similar to what Ridington (1990) referenced in the Dunne-Za phrase glossed as "little bit know something," which speaks to the knowledge derived from direct experience, dreaming, and the vision quest.

At sundown in Coast Salish territory, shades are pulled in family homes to avoid harm from ghosts or other beings; it is only reasonable, but consider: if one does not share these beliefs, one might not pull the shades or take other prudent actions to safeguard others. Similarly, at spiritual burnings following funerals or other important events, where ancestral spirits are called forward to feed on meals provided them (but consumed in fire so that the spirits can participate), ritualists commonly call on those in attendance, including anthropologists, to move out of the path of the spirits. Failure to do so could result in soul loss and illness on the one hand, and concern and alienation on the other. Not all ritualists can carry out this work, and it requires judgment to determine if one is ready and able to do so.

I don't wish to render indigenous people exotic, spooky, and mindlessly spiritual by these descriptions. I recognize the mundane features of their lives. However, there are complex understandings that cannot be discounted and that are overlooked at one's peril. Another brief story illustrates this point: a man in his seventies frequented his Coast Salish tribal community's biweekly elders' lunches held in the tribal center. He was given to teasing widowed elders, to their great dismay, about his prospects of marrying them under a provision of the local kinship system, the sororate. He is a gruff former logger and semi-professional boxer, and a bon vivant. He is irreverent by nature and gave no sign of spiritual or religious inclination in my presence until one afternoon when a non-indigenous tribal employee pushed her rationalist perception of the world too hard, arguing for the merits of the economic development of the region. She suggested that a noted feature of the local landscape, a rocky outcrop, might be removed. At this, the elder exploded, in his only show of rage I've observed in the years I have known him, shouting: "The rock is alive!"

I conclude from this that it is continually unclear what mutual expectations might entail. Goulet gives us that the Dene Tha insist on the primacy of experience in learning and that they expect anthropologists to learn in the manner they learn. This is likely a widely shared idea in indigenous communities; after all, as I have suggested, protection and safety arise only from power and knowledge. But indigenous people recognize other forms of knowledge and ways of learning as well, even if they contest them in their own communities. For example, community members with a post-secondary education are sometimes scorned and thought to have lost their ability to understand indigenous knowledge, but they are also valued in other contexts.

The problematic assumption of the posture of learner

Academics are similarly problematic. Anthropologists commonly position themselves as beginners or learners in another's culture (Guédon 1994). We assume this posture because we genuinely do not know and because we hope it will cause others to explain things to us. It seems intellectually honest, and it suggests that we will learn and that, at some future date, we will have progressed. Learners, after all, learn. We seem to learn oddly, however, and to learn odd things that do not fit with local epistemology. An example might be knowledge of the demographic structure of a community. We do not necessarily learn things that suggest our maturation, how to think and behave, from the community viewpoint. The anthropologist–indigenous relationship sometimes might be more properly said to resemble a wardship.

But we are not actually children, after all, and don't really look like children. Fogelson tells us that "wardship suggests immaturity and vulnerability. On the other hand, the relationship suggests definite obligations on the part of the more powerful protector to assist and defend the interests of the ward" (1999, 78). This construction might enshrine us in what might appear to be our preposterously slow learning. Wards might grow in knowledge, but at some unanticipated and far-off time. There is danger in remaining a ward, however.

My own illustration of this concerns an occasion when I was called as a "witness" at important "work," or ritual, in a Coast Salish community. This event was held in an earth-floored longhouse and attended by several hundred people from all over the Salish world. While often many more witnesses are called, on this occasion only four were asked to speak and carry from the occasion a memory of what was said and done so that this could be substantiated later, if necessary. In effect, witnesses act as legal repositories of the spoken documents of the occasion. One witness was called from an outside community, another from a nearby group, and a third from the local group; I served as the "elder" of the academic and non-indigenous world. This posed a considerable challenge to my limited abilities as a speaker within the Coast Salish idiom, and it was not appropriate (although there would be no sanctions other than, perhaps, disappointment) to speak in an academic voice. I attempted to emulate local practice in establishing connection, in tone, in composition, and in drawing attention to relevant people and issues. Local forms of discourse, in brief, entail an awareness of local epistemology. Afterward, an elder who had first taken me some years earlier to a winter ceremonial said, "I was so worried about you. You never knew how to speak in public. I'm surprised by you! You sounded like a real speaker!" This elder clearly expected I might never end my period as a ward, but nevertheless thought I should eventually learn something and sound like a speaker or endanger myself by my own presence in her world.

The proposal for "radical participation" or experience-near anthropology is attractive for many reasons, including because we wish to understand how indigenous epistemology works. We find experiences beyond our own understanding to be compelling, and we want to talk with our collaborators. This sort of anthropology might let us fit community expectations of learners and join those who have a sense of what is going on, who are not a liability, who pose little risk to the health and safety. These are obvious advantages, but I wish to explore other advantages and also risks, traps one might fall into.

Within an experience-near framework we become more easily interpretable, more predictable, to our collaborators; they more readily understand what we are trying to do and why (Goulet 1994a). There arises a common language of motivation that might allow relationships to deepen, to be more genuine. A trivial example from my own experience: one hot summer day some years ago I sat working in my office at the University of British Columbia. No one else was around except a single secretary. I heard someone walk up my corridor and was startled when a man walked into my office. He told me he had found a wallet in a phone booth and wanted to return it to its owner, and for some reason he couldn't explain, he thought he should come to the anthropology building at UBC. The wallet belonged to Professor Cyril Belshaw, a previous occupant of my very office. I took the wallet and put it in my desk for safekeeping. While my back was turned, the man disappeared, or perhaps, vanished. I mentioned this strange story to a few First Nations people, who offered their own understandings of the event, and what I might do in response. One noted First Nations scholar told me that possessions find their way back to their owners. My office, in effect, continued to attract Belshaw things. In addition, the man who brought the wallet might not really be human, but instead a spiritual entity. Someone else, a Coast Salish person, suggested that I spiritually cleanse the room so that this sort of thing wouldn't happen again, and hang cedar over the door. This would involve bringing in someone qualified to conduct such work. This suggestion hinged on the fact that Professor Belshaw had once been tried in a foreign country for the murder of his wife, a charge he was cleared of, but which nevertheless was associated with his name. Belshaw items might themselves be spiritually dangerous.

There are several things of interest about this. One is the assumption that indigenous interpretations were the ones that mattered, even though this was an event apparently involving three white men: Belshaw, the man who found the wallet, and me. My observation is that, in recent years, there is an increased expectation by indigenous people that their understandings be foregrounded. Perhaps all the examples I have given indicate this. The whole debate about experience-near approaches to anthropology could be seen in this light. It is no longer necessarily a choice made by anthropologists sifting through structural, functional, symbolic, or semiotic models and methods. This development is analogous to political change elsewhere, to indigenous movements to control the landscape, education, justice, and so on. We ought not be surprised that there would be a push to extend indigenous thought into this domain as well. Indeed, when I began the planning for a ceremony to honor a *Stó:lō* chief, Frank Malloway (whose "Indian" name is Siyemchis), the host of the UBC ethnographic field school for several years, members of his community assumed that although the event was to be in a university museum at UBC, it would be in Coast Salish idiom. No one seemed to question whether I might be able to pull off hosting a complex Coast Salish ceremonial occasion, although when I requested help, it was provided.

Subsequently, I engaged the services of two "speaking chiefs," who advised on protocol and spoke at the ceremony. I purchased blankets to drape over the speakers and the guest of honor, arranged for the calling of witnesses, and hosted a feast with appropriate foods and a surplus sufficient to allow guests to take food home with them. The day before the event, an important chief requested that the protocol for the event, and even the concept (originally analogous to a naming ceremony but now being treated as an honor ceremony), be revised (Miller 1998). Among the things I learned was a level of detail about ceremonials that exceeded what I had recorded in my notes from many other occasions, the considerable extent to which ritualists differ in their interpretation of how "work" should proceed, and the sheer difficulty and expense of putting on such an event. Of greatest importance was the connection between the epistemology and the politics of the community. All this was part of my education about the Coast Salish world.

This example reveals that the text of interpenetration between indigenous and mainstream worlds is not solely ours in anthropology and the social sciences to read. This development is related to a widely held view in indigenous communities that "Western" society is woefully, dangerously short of values, is spiritually deficient in its emphasis on rationalism and universalism, and that we are "people without culture" (with apologies to Eric Wolf). In this purported absence of spiritual strength, perhaps it seems an obvious path to insist on those indigenous views that have depth and that are thought to produce a life worth living. Goulet (1994a, 88), for example, writes of a Dene man who regarded whites as having lost their souls, a point that he may have meant both metaphorically and literally.

In the same vein, Cove recently noted, "By the mid-1980s, Maori claimed to have their own science. . . . It was asserted to be theoretical and more comprehensive than its Western counterpart insofar as the former included a spiritual dimension, denied the validity of human/non-human and nature/culture distinctions, and fully integrated basic and applied research (Cove 1999, 115). The members of Coast Salish communities have not stated their position in these terms but have advanced a theory of learning and education (Hilbert 1985), of ethnohistory and archaeology (Carlson 1997), and have positioned their own approach in contrast to Western approaches.

The second issue arising from the "Belshaw wallet caper" is the presumption that I could understand what I was told and might be motivated enough to take action, in effect, believe their accounts, rather than simply hear them or find them interesting. This relates to the new sort of insistence on the recognition of indigenous presence and values I just mentioned, even or especially those that appear in contrast to Western values and epistemologies.

The third issue is that different indigenous people provided differing interpretations of the wallet story. Part of this could be ascribed to their differences in origin; in this story, one was a prairies person and the other from the West Coast. The variation in response is itself, in positivistic terms, interesting data; or, more humanely, it provided insight into different perspectives, into cultural themes, including, potentially, pan-Indian perspectives. But Bierwurt (1999) and others have written about the need to fracture the authority of anthropological accounts and, more generally, the authority of single narratives, and to seek the individuality of interpretation, in Barth's (1995) terms, the individuation of culture, or "culture in many modalities." This experience provides a way to do so. This fracturing places the story of the wallet more clearly in line with Coast Salish understandings, which themselves recognize diversity as suggested by the cultural adviser regarding Christian and atheist anthropologists.

Local concepts of power and sources of conflict

There is a related problem, however. Curiously, the literature of the anthropology of extraordinary experience runs the risk of promoting a kind of timelessness, of dehistoricizing experience, by an implicit notion of "authenticity" of experience. And what is the situation if the indigenous people with whom we are working speak within a pan-Indian idiom? Are we as prepared to take the spiritual view as seriously as we might regard a practice known to have existed in situ for longer periods? One might wonder what the political costs are of evaluating one experience positively and overlooking an emergent spiritual–political movement. An example is the recent diffusion of the Medicine Wheel into Coast Salish territory from prairie communities. Some community members disparage this spiritual development, holding it to be outside or even in contradiction to the traditions of their own community, and therefore potentially dangerous (McIlwraith 1996), while others embrace it as an "authentic tradition." These differences in perspective are the sources of conflict, particularly as they are manifested in problems of representing Salish culture to the outside world.

Let me provide less trivial stories than that of the story of the wallet. The understanding of local concepts of power, and how it is employed and received, is a central concern to contemporary anthropology. One story reveals the connections between the lived experience of power and experience-near anthropology. A tribal politician described to me his fears about a spirit power he had inherited and that had manifested itself to him. He did not want to establish a relationship with this spirit helper because this would require him to take the winter off from his busy work schedule in order to enter into spiritual training as a "baby," or initiate, in the winter dance society longhouse. Further, he would have to place himself in the hands of ritualists, some of whom he did not trust politically, in order to receive instruction. He would be required to travel throughout the Salish world to dance his spirit power in the presence of hundreds of others. He preferred to carry out his work less publicly and in the economic and political, rather than the spiritual, domain.

As is consistent with the cosmology of his community, bad thoughts are regarded as capable of causing harm, and, in his case, motivated this unbidden entity to take malevolent action against a political enemy. This elder political enemy and spiritual leader was "struck," hit with spirit power, while out fishing. He toppled out of his boat, the victim of an apparent heart attack. The two separately told me their own accounts of what had happened, and they were the same on the central point that the leaders' uncontrolled power had caused the damage. The elder withdrew his political challenge. The politician had the spirit helper "lifted" off, temporarily removed spiritually by a ritualist. The process and the two accounts provided a glimpse into community life. They show the fear of dangerous people and beings, and the dangerous outcomes. They also reveal the alienation experienced by those who believe themselves to be outside the political channels of the community; the sense of isolation experienced by members of small families such as the man who was "struck," and the difficulty of belonging to a divided community, both for the dominant and the subordinate. Here, community politics and indigenous epistemology are not detachable. Whereas, as an anthropologist from outside the community, I am not an obvious target of dangerous spiritual work, my ability to understand this is connected to my ability to comprehend the nature of political life and to avoid carrying information between community members in a manner that could endanger someone else.

There are some instances of ecstatic experience with more direct political implications for me. In the late 1980s and early 1990s I worked for several years on major treaty-linked litigation with a Washington State tribe. Part of my task was to compile genealogical information in order to connect the ancestors of present-day tribal members with those who used particular resource-procurement sites. One night, during the most intense part of this research, I was visited in a dream by three visitors, ancestors, who came to the foot of my bed and told me their names and names that I needed to find. This was not scary, nor did it seem wholly otherworldly, although the experience was outside the ordinary for me. Information from ancestors and dreams is an appropriate source of knowledge in the community, for some at least. While I did not widely broadcast the news of this experience, it was readily understandable locally. It struck me that this experience suggested that it was good that I was doing the work; I felt that way about it. No one disputed this or proffered this opinion (I did not share this thought). But people more matter-of-factly suggested that these experiences do happen (are part of daily experience and, hence, experience-near) and that it showed that the ancestors maintain active interest in the community of today. The experience, in this interpretation, was about the community and the ancestors, not me. The benefits to me, however, were that I was encouraged in my work, and I could relate an experience that conformed to local understandings and that suggested respect. Further, what I was told was a source of raw data, albeit data that needed confirmation from another source to be used in a legal setting. The reactions of community members were a source of unexpected insight into culture. I could see more clearly what knowledge meant and how it might be obtained. I might add that this experience conveyed something of the beauty of this society and its systems of knowledge and meaning. This was an "ecstatic" experience, and the local connotation was that good comes along with it. I experienced it that way. I am not sure it means that I have learned enough, that I am progressing in knowledge, and that I truly share this epistemology or ought to. I may be somewhere in transit.

Positioning oneself between modes of knowing

Let me consider the risks and costs to being positioned somewhere between modes of knowing. This approach to knowledge, as I have suggested, runs the risk of exoticizing, even while finding out something of the ordinary, day-to-day worldview of others. Concerning the story of "power" and the injured fisherman, I recall that community politics operate in domains other than that of spirit-powers. Tribal politicians rely on the support of their large families, develop strategies for re-election, and curry the favor of followers, as in elections elsewhere. One cannot overlook demographic factors and political processes, the political economy and resource competition, while embracing the "ecstatic." One might hope to find a balance between the sense of mystery and the statistical in the understanding of the perception and play of community power. On the other hand, if the ecstatic leads away from an easy interpretation, then this is an achievement, as long as the various sorts of knowledge and data remain in view.

Another issue is where one might take a relationship based on "ecstatic" experience. Within this mode of thinking, one assumes reciprocal obligations that are difficult for anthropologists from a "university world" to fulfill. In fact, these obligations to humans and non-humans alike are difficult for indigenous people to fulfill since they, too, live in a capitalist, Western world. A notable example of the difficulties anthropologists face in engaging in moral and reciprocal relationships is that of Wade Davis, an ethnobotanist who worked with Haitian voodoo practitioners (1985). According to his own account, although he had an initial interest in simply discovering the active ingredients used to create the state of human zombification, he eventually discovered that furthering this research required his direct participation in a religious practice with important connections to political life of the community. Voodoo is both a religion and the political act of creating conformity to community norms and creating a means of applying pressure on political opponents. Davis eventually withdrew from the activities that might have prepared him for the priesthood, understanding that he could not fulfill the subsequent lifetime of mutual obligation with other practitioners. I suggest that his disengagement at this point was the right choice since it did take seriously the epistemology and its relationship to political affairs. Strangely, entry into the priesthood, in this case, would not have taken indigenous epistemology seriously. Similarly, Toelken (1996) has reported his own disengagement from research into Navajo oral traditions regarding witchcraft because of fear of danger to himself, his family, and his friends.

At one point in his inquiry into the subject he was asked, "Are you ready to lose someone in your family?" and was informed that this is the price one must pay for pursuing this topic (Toelken 1996, 11).

Participation in ecstatic experience has costs for indigenous community members as well. Some Coast Salish communities, for example, have difficulty maintaining a Shaker church; the obligations of the minister and the congregation in general are immense; one must participate continually in healings, funerals, and other events. Another example is the tribal politician I mentioned; he does not wish to engage the spirit power because of the immense obligations of time and effort that entails, and the consequent difficulty in doing his political and economic work. The practical difficulties are considerable. One can envision this as a sort of liminal phase that cannot be maintained.

There are implications for embracing ecstatic experience for academics out of the field as well as in it. Our university lives require us to assume a fixed status, not a disrupted one, and to have a "university voice," rather than to be voiceless or wrong-voiced winter-dance initiates. I recall the experiences of a valued colleague who is an able learner, who has matured in the sense I mentioned earlier, and whose embracing of an indigenous epistemology has caused her to both have a deep cultural understanding and to be misread by university colleagues who devalue the effort. The disinclination of the academy to seriously consider indigenous epistemology has implications for the university as well as for individual scholars. There is now a broad understanding that universities and colleges are commonly hostile environments for indigenous people, including students and professors. Many of these people have expressed the view that the university suffers the same malaise that mainstream society in general experiences, namely, an absence of spiritual understanding of human existence and a devotion to destructive values and practices. Fabian (2001, 32) has suggested that there is utility in employing "passion" (the ecstatic side of a critical approach to knowledge) in dealing with peoples who have been subject to brutal domination and oppression. Similarly, indigenous scholars have suggested to me that institutions of higher education would likely create an environment more attractive to non-mainstream people and academics if anthropologists and others on campus attached credibility to indigenous knowledge through their own approaches to research.

This is not a question of embracing cultural relativism, which has no real requirement of obligation or reciprocity, and which is, instead, based on an ethnocentric assumption that does not require we take the other's worldview seriously and demands that we respect beliefs because they are totally other (Wilson 1994). Neither is it a case of "going native," which has no requirement of maintaining a university persona, and which, as Goulet (1998) points out, makes us unable to fulfill the hermeneutic task of interpreting one culture to another. This is a more difficult proposition entirely. It is a proposition that risks taking oneself much too seriously, of appearing too self-concerned or asserting a false insider status, the position Toelken found himself in. However, this position can provide a sense of appropriate activity, of knowing when one is violating rules. Otherwise, we are akin to that tiny minority of people who do not experience pain and have no sense of dangerous injury.

Issues of experience-near anthropology do not apply only to those whose research interests focus on visions, dreams, reincarnation, ritual, and religion. Those who wish to think about politics and justice, for example, might consider the same issues. This is in part because, in indigenous discourse, these categories of experience cannot be easily separated, in part because our time in a community takes us to a variety of settings, and, finally, because members of communities have multiple roles; ritual leaders might be political chiefs. But because one's focus might not be on ritual or religion per se, the idea of ecstatic research might play out somewhat differently.

Nor do issues of ecstatic research relate only to the embodied perceptions of the researcher. Research is commonly carried out in a context larger than that of researcher-community. While I have given the example of a vision in my own experience, I have been more attuned to my children's experiences of the extraordinary. One child, then aged three, walked for the first time into one particular dimly lit winter dance house (there are no windows, and only the light from the doorway illuminated the interior of the 120-foot-long, 50-foot-wide earth floor structure). He immediately headed across the floor, pointed to a cedar pole positioned on the wall, and asked "What's wrong with that pole?" The longhouse owner, an "Indian doctor," described this pole as a place where malevolent power was concentrated, and a location that winter dancer initiates had to avoid, or else they would suffer from disturbing dreams. My son had correctly noted that there was indeed something wrong with the pole. (Despite this experience, this son is now fifteen and an avowed empiricist.)

Another of my children, then aged ten, experienced a vision while I was attending a naming ceremony at a winter dance house a two- or three-hour drive from home. Two years before this occasion, I had found a number of "Indian" names long forgotten in an archive. These had been recorded on a genealogical chart sixty years earlier by an anthropologist and provided English names back four or five generations and names of a few generations of people who had lived before there had been white contact with their location. These names dated back perhaps to the late eighteenth century.

In the Coast Salish world and on the northwest coast generally, these names have great significance because they are tied to control of particular resource locations and to ancestors. Names are given to those who are thought to embody some of the traits of the previous holders, and some names are those of highly revered ancestors. Kan (1989) described a similar naming practice among the Tlingit to the north of the Coast Salish as central to the creation of a system of "symbolic immortality." Among the Coast Salish, as with the Tlingit, names are associated with ideas of reincarnation. For these reasons, names are freighted, deeply connected to the epistemology of the community, and, ostensibly, beyond the reach of outsiders. One of these names was being "brought out," that is, given to a young person. I was invited to the ceremony as an honored guest and wrapped in a blanket with money pinned on to it as is the local practice. I was asked to eat with elders, which I felt too young to do. Although I was happy for the families involved and pleased that the naming was taking place, I wasn't especially happy to have my contribution noted, and I felt distinctly uncomfortable. During the naming I was asked to comment on where the names came from and on how old they were, and I gave what immediately seemed to me to be inept answers. The dissonance I felt emerged out of the inconsistency between the ideas of immortal names and beings and historical, datable, lost, and retrieved names. I felt as if I was peering, or being asked to peer, too closely behind the curtain, although community members did not appear to share this concern.

As I prepared to leave the ceremony, I went to the kitchen attached to the longhouse in order to have some food for the drive back home. There I choked on fry-bread, rendering myself completely unable to breathe. I dimly heard people around me saying, "He's choking; should we try the Heimlich maneuver?" With great difficulty, I recovered and stumbled out of the longhouse into the night, covered with sweat.

Late that night, while I was attending the ceremony and long before I returned home, my son arose from his bed because, as he told my wife that night, he heard and saw me. He called out to me, desperately concerned for my well-being and convinced that something was wrong. When I arrived back home at three in the morning, my wife anxiously inquired how I was, and informed me of my son's actions and worries during the night. I thought I knew what the local interpretation would be; nothing happens for no reason. I had felt out of synch and, in this case, danger had ensued.

Conclusion

My argument has been that there are practical and political dimensions that support the adoption of an experience-near approach to research. This approach is not akin to going native, and neither is it a cultural relativist stance. This position allows scholars to avoid engaging in dangerous activities that threaten community members' health, political and legal initiatives, and engagement with the mainstream world. Such a stance enables anthropologists to move past the child or ward role and to directly engage in what are seen locally as appropriate forms of learning and adult modes of behavior. Embracing experience-near research helps reveal the beautiful, powerful, and engaging features of local cultures. The presence of researchers who adopt this approach can begin to transform academic life on campus and make universities less hostile to indigenous students and faculty and more open to their contributions. In addition, our current period is one in which indigenous community members view mainstream society as defective in significant ways and demand or simply assume that we take their views seriously and begin to engage the world in what they take to be better ways.

There are also risks to this approach to research. Researchers may overlook other, more mundane dimensions of life, and they may depict communities as ahistorical, timeless, and "authentic." Researchers may enter into long-term reciprocal relationships whose entailments they cannot fulfill. In this case, it is disengagement rather than engagement that may be the most respectful route and the one that most fully acknowledges local epistemologies. These risks can be managed, however. And, as the story of my son's vision reveals, I might not believe in spirits, but they believe in me, or perhaps more accurately, my family. It's hard to overlook and harder still to imagine why we would want to.

Notes

1. This is a revised and expanded version of a paper to appear in the Acts of the XXVI International Congress of Americanists, following the May 2004 meetings in Perugia, Italy.

2. In legal arguments, "time immemorial" is a phrase that may specifically reference, depending on the jurisdiction, the date when the British Crown assumed control or the year when a treaty was signed between the U.S. government and tribes. It does not refer to the deep past, in the way that indigenous people and some anthropologists occasionally use the phrase. Similarly, legal proceedings have turned on nineteenth-century terminology that included whales in the category of "fish." Anthropological use of "tribe," within a neo-evolutionary scheme of social organization (bands, tribes, chiefdoms, states), is very different from legal terminology, which references specific holders of recognition by the state.

3. Personal communications, Sonny McHalsie, cultural adviser to the *Stó:lō* Nation, February 4, 2003, and March 11, 2004.

9. Moving Beyond Culturally Bound Ethical Guidelines

We do not spontaneously and effortlessly comprehend human phenomena in a changing sociocultural environment other than our own by birth and upbringing.[1] In a foreign milieu, whatever our research objectives, we are bewildered by the multiplicity of actors and the inevitable interplay in significant events of social, cultural, economic, political, and religious factors. In such circumstances, we are likely to unknowingly substitute our own assumptions and categories to those shared, reaffirmed, or contested by local people. Substitution of this sort voids any possibility of understanding others, first and foremost, as they understand themselves. Ethical interaction with others presupposes that we first come to terms with their reality, in their lifeworld.

I use the expression "lifeworld" as defined by Schutz and Luckmann (1973, 3) as "that province of reality [as opposed, for instance, to the province of reality of art, science, or religion] which the wide-awake and normal adult simply takes for granted in the attitude of common sense [as opposed, for instance, to the attitude of the artist, of the scientist, or of the mystic]." In any lifeworld, as adults we conduct ourselves on the basis of "the general thesis of reciprocal perspective," assuming all along that for all practical purposes "the world taken for granted by me is also taken for granted by you, my individual fellow-man, [and] even more, that it is taken for granted by . . . everyone who is one of us" (Schutz 1967, 12, emphasis in original). As noted by Rogers (1983, 36) in each finite province of meaning, we deal with "meaning-compatible experiences," that is, "experiences unified by a 'cognitive style' that stamps them as belonging together."

To engage in research of any kind is to suspend our ordinary sense of reality and to join a community of scholars committed to the advancement of a specific kind of knowledge. Epistemological concerns are therefore at the heart of any discipline. In Schutzian terms, as scientists or investigators, we work within a historically constituted and evolving province of reality distinct from that of our everyday life. To operate in the scientific or professional domain, we shift attitude but also presume that within this domain, "every one who is one of us" is committed to certain values and goals. For instance, we take for granted that everyone agrees on research methods and that everyone's work is submitted to peer review and evaluation. These standardized processes allow for the critical assessment of knowledge claims, without which a discipline simply does not exist. Within this province of reality, in the investigation of any phenomenon, we are all expected to distinguish between personal bias and professional, substantiated claim. As noted by White (2003, xxvi), there is general agreement among social scientists that while "a person's religion, gender, political orientation, or race may affect what problems they wish to do research on . . . they do not necessarily influence, nor should they influence, the research design and scientific assessment of the findings." In brief, to engage in research is to leave one's daily concerns behind and join the ranks of the initiated.

Among anthropologists, the journal article and the monograph concerning a particular people are the vehicles through which knowledge claims are made publicly available. These are the product of the fieldworker, someone who has taken on a profession created to generate accurate and reliable observations about others in the world. The goal of participant observation as a research method was to improve on the unsystematic information gained otherwise through travel literature and the writing of missionaries and administrators. In other words, it was thought and taught that "anthropology became a science when it left the travelogue behind" (Fabian 2000, 241). Fieldworkers were expected also to bring back to the metropolis objects of various sorts to display in museums as illustrations at the synchronic level of the diachronic evolution of human cultures and civilization. The juxtaposition in a museum of Huron or Hottentot artifacts with those of Europeans illustrated in the minds of the viewers a "sequence of historical cultures," from the most primitive, to the most advanced (Zammito 2002, 236). At the end of the nineteenth century, for ethnographers and museum visitors, to travel in space was to travel in time. Encountering the primitive other was literally to come to face with an earlier version of oneself.

Anthropologists no longer live their quest for direct observation of others as a gate to the past. Fieldwork is nonetheless still privileged as the most reliable means to encounter others in their environment. Our participation in the lifeworld of others ought to be deep enough to enable us "to describe reality as it is confronted by our hosts, to describe all that they cannot wish away and that, therefore, must enter any reasonable and moral account of one's actions and those of others" (Goulet 1998, 258). Like many other anthropologists, I maintain that the more radical our participation in the lifeworld of our hosts, the better positioned we are to describe it as it is.

Immersing ourselves in the world of our hosts, as they confront it, we inevitably undergo various degrees of personal transformation associated with a heightened awareness of the human potential. These changes result from our interaction with others who act on the basis of ontological, epistemological, and ethical assumptions that differ from those in the light of which, more or less consciously, we originally thought out our research agenda. In the light of such transformations in the field, we move beyond the canons of modern ethnography that rest on the assumption that We (Westerners) are not They (the ones we anthropologists variously referred to as the Primitive or the Traditional) (Watson and Goulet 1992).

In this respect, Favret-Saada (1980, 191) notes that the "Great Divide between 'them' and 'us'" was a device used by modern ethnographers and their audiences to protect themselves "from any contamination" by the object of anthropological study. This point is reiterated by Shweder (1991, 191), who reminds us that "one of the central myths of the modern period in the West is the idea that the opposition between religion-superstition-revelation and logic-science-rationality divides the world into then and now, them and us." This central myth—or belief, in Spiro's meaning of the term as explained further in this paper—is so deeply embraced by Europeans and Euro–North Americans that they cannot spontaneously embrace, as Native North Americans do, the experiences of elders visiting in one's dream.

This paper is concerned, therefore, with the following two questions: How does the ecstatic side of one's journey in the field illuminate the scene and the people one seeks to understand and interact with ethically? What are the limitations in the field of foreign-bound ethical guidelines? To ask questions such as these is to push the boundaries of conventions within the anthropological profession. Answers to these questions allow us to respond appropriately to Native North American ancestors who intervene to inform and direct one's actions in this world, the world in which we are born and eventually die, the world of everyday life in which land claims are settled in court and term papers are submitted in a university setting.

Embracing Aboriginal Cognitive and Spiritual Maps

For all the reasons mentioned above, and more, epistemological and ethical questions related to fieldwork are generally complex, especially among indigenous or aboriginal peoples. They are the descendants of those inhabitants who were living principally from hunting, gathering, and foraging all over the world, before they experienced contact with European explorers and colonizers. Since then, everyone who shares in this context of life participates in a complex interaction of social forces and cultures. These have developed in a process of "co-formation" through which identities remained differentiated while being altered (Kahane 2004, 37). In the literature, the term *aboriginal* is therefore used with a clear understanding that "there is no one 'Aboriginal' identity, just as there is no one 'non-Aboriginal' identity" (McNaughton and Rock 2004, 57, note 2).[2]

Notwithstanding their distinctive philosophies and histories, on all continents, aboriginal peoples are increasingly aware and critical of what others have written and write about them. More and more they expect anthropologists to write in a fashion that respects their epistemological assumptions and ethical values. Hence, the call for a decolonization of research methods and a critical evaluation of Eurocentric assumptions and categories governing the allocation of research grants and the design of research projects (Brettell 1993, Duran and Duran 2000, T. L. Smith 1999, Battiste 2000, Cole 2004, Lovelace 2004, Long and LaFrance 2004). In other words, in the field of research, as reiterated in *Walking a Tightrope: Aboriginal People and Their Representations* (2005), aboriginal peoples and aboriginal scholars challenge forms of ethnocentrism shared by Europeans and their descendants.

Decolonization of one's ethnographic endeavor leads to its redefinition as the advocacy of the truth value of stories other than the ones with which Europeans are familiar. In his presentation of the Tutchone account of the creation of the world, for instance, Legros responds to this expectation by acknowledging the validity of aboriginal criticism: "When they read Us," he writes, "they also read in our choice of the word 'myth' [to refer to their stories] the arrogance of the so-called enlightened scholar—of the unbeliever towards the believer" (Legros 1999, 21). Striving to make the Tutchone "oral text coeval with Christian sacred books" (Legros 1999, 1), and wanting at all costs to avoid the term *myth*, with its negative connotations, Legros opts for "more neutral terms such as sacred narrative" (Legros 1999, 21) or "religious oral text" (Legros 1999, 16). "Such change," Legros (1999, 18) writes, cannot originate from an initial personal theoretical reflection but from imposed "changes in the praxis and politics of anthropological research and writing" (Fabian 1983, xi). Rooted in a new sociopolitical reality, Legros's atheoretical publication reflects the Northern Tutchone band council request that, as a condition of his research among them, he "now research and write for Them, not on Them for Them in the outside world, 'down South'" (Legros 1999, 19).

To raise epistemological and ethical issues within the framework of a paradigm of decolonization of research is to propose new criteria and obligations, including that of conceptualizing one's research on the basis of "Aboriginal cognitive and spiritual maps" and of adhering "to Aboriginal protocols at all stages of its enactment" (McNaughton and Rock 2004, 52).

The mention of such criteria concerning newly defined appropriate ways to design and implement research projects involving aboriginal peoples is significant in and of itself. As underlined by Weber-Pillwax (2004, 80),

> When a researcher assumes that the ethics guidelines of a hypothetical "research community" can take precedence over those of a real community of people (real faces and real bodies) situated in space and time, this surely constitutes a breach of ethics and ought to raise serious questions about the research itself. Where a researcher cannot discern and does not recognize what lies in the space between the ethical world of the hypothetical "research community" and the ethical world of the real community, s/he will be unable to take such critical information into account in the research project being conducted. Logically, the existence of such a knowledge gap would call into question the findings, results, products, and outcomes from such research.

The process alluded to here is one of discernment leading to a shift in research paradigm. In the following pages, I illustrate what it means to act upon critical information received in situ, from the real people among whom one acts as human being and research. The case material is offered as one contribution to ongoing efforts to formulate national ethical guidelines for research involving aboriginal peoples that takes into account their concerns, priorities, and many realities.

With the publication in 1998 of the *Tri-Council Policy Statement: Ethical Conduct for Research Involving Humans* (TCPS), the three Canadian Research Councils announced that from then on they would "consider funding [or continue funding] only to individuals and institutions which certify compliance with this policy regarding research involving human subjects" (TCPS 2003, I).[3] When it came to research involving aboriginal people, however, the councils determined that it was not yet "appropriate to establish policies in this area" since they had "not held sufficient discussions with representatives of the affected peoples or groups, or with the various organizations or researchers involved" (TCPS 2003, 6.1). In 1998, the *Tri-Council Policy Statement* therefore called for an extensive dialogue between interested parties to define ethical guidelines that would protect the rights and interests of all involved.

Launched in 2002 by the Social Sciences and Humanities Research Council (SSHRC), this dialogue involved key aboriginal organizations and individuals. Following the submission of more than fifty briefs, participation in an extensive dialogue on a Yahoo! site with more than three hundred individuals—the majority aboriginals, and the preparation of two major synthesis papers, McNaughton and Rock (2004, 59, note 23)remark that "within the Dialogue there has been some ambivalence around the need for national ethics guidelines." Participants in the dialogue have argued that research guidelines and protocols were best defined at the local level. Defining them otherwise would demonstrate a lack of respect for the legitimate differences rooted in distinctive local cultures and practices. "For example, the Blackfoot emphasize approval by responsible individuals, not community political representatives," whereas, "in other Aboriginal communities approvals are given by families who are responsible for various kinds of knowledge" (McNaughton and Rock 2004, 59, note 23).[4]

Determining how to ethically conduct research involving aboriginal peoples is complex. In 1998, the three councils had already recognized that "in Canada and elsewhere, aboriginal peoples have distinctive perspectives and understandings embodied in their cultures and histories." "Debates may arise," noted the three councils, "because of different definitions of public and private life," different "notions of property," or, "competing interests among different sections of the community" (TCPS 2003, 6.2). Reading through the *Tri-Councils Policy Statement* and SSHRC recent synthesis papers, it becomes clear that progress toward establishing culturally sensitive ethical guidelines goes hand in hand with a critical examination of the ontological and epistemological assumptions that aboriginal and non-aboriginal parties bring to the table.

These assumptions, I argue, have profound implications: First, at the level of describing the world within which one is to conduct research; second, at the level of ethical decision making with aboriginal peoples in a social environment that encompasses the presence of both the living and the dead. For as Chief Seattle of the Dwanish tribe of the Pacific Northwest reminded us long ago: "Dead, I say? There is no death. Only a change of worlds" (McLuhan 1971, 30). This is a truth that contemporary aboriginal peoples subscribe to. In this paper, I write an ethnographical report with this truth in mind. In other words, I follow as closely as possible the Dene Tha "cognitive and spiritual map" in deciding how to interact with others and reach appropriate ethical decisions in their midst. The outcome, I hope, is a modest contribution, in conjunction with the contributions of other papers in this book, to the development of an ethnographic genre that moves beyond the constraints of classic, modern ethnography.

Not Stealing Someone's Opportunity to Learn

Anthropologists want and need to write.[5] The question is how, for whom, and in terms of what epistemological and ontological assumptions? Anthropologists meet others where they are "at home." In a process of immersion in a new social environment, mishaps, misunderstandings, even confrontations with one's hosts in their home, are unavoidable. Why? Because the foreign anthropologist has so much to learn: the expectations one is to meet on a daily basis given one's age, gender, and economic status, for instance; the positions one occupies relative to one's hosts and relative to other local and regional actors—including local spirits and ancestors; the language, verbal and non-verbal, through which communication flows effortlessly between members of the group.

In the anthropological profession, rejection from the people whom one wants to understand and/or study is perhaps the most dreaded fate. A degree of hospitality in the midst of others is the necessary condition for the anthropological endeavor. Social acceptance, however, is not a temporal event as is, for instance, one's arrival in such and such a place at such and such a time. Social acceptance is a continuously unfolding process within social relationships. In most cases, initial acceptance leads to a long process of learning by trial and error. In such circumstances, investigation is never initiated by "turning our gaze on objects," or human subjects, available to unintrusive observation. Inevitably, investigation involves "*confrontation that becomes productive through communication*" (Fabian 2001, 25, emphasis in original).

Everywhere, home is a social environment in which people govern themselves according to a wide body of assumptions and injunctions, however implicit. Among Northern Athapaskans, for instance, when it comes to learning, the general expectation is that one learns "first from personal experience, second by observation of people who know how to do things, and third informally by hearing mythical, historical, or personal narratives"(Rushforth 1992, 488). To appreciate the significance of such an injunction, we must see the intimate connections established here between epistemology and ethics. As I was to learn among the Dene Tha, their "way of knowing and living is an expression of great confidence in the human ability to learn to live responsibly and competently without diminishing other people's opportunity to live in the same way" (Goulet 1998, 58). The Dene Tha view is similar to the one reported for the Yurok of northern California, where "people in training tend to view explanation as a mode of interference with another's purpose in life, comparable to theft, '*stealing a person's opportunity to learn*'" (Buckley 2002, 104-105, my emphasis).

According to this ethically grounded view of learning, to hear a narrative and to follow with probing questions to ascertain the meaning of what one has heard is offensive. Initially, when with the Dene Tha I sometimes failed to meet the expectation that I was to learn as the Dene themselves learn.[6] On one such occasion, when I did question what I was being told, I was immediately reminded of my position: "If you do not say the right words, and we don't like it, you are in trouble. Like you write what we tell you, we could walk away, we go away, what do you do? Nothing, you can't write anymore" (Goulet 1998, xxiii–xxxiv).

The speaker refers to my practice of writing down verbatim the content of parts of conversations with Dene Tha in their homes. Dene Tha who accepted the practice would often slow their narrative down so that I could record it accurately. The same individuals would, however, tell me at times to put my pen down and to listen carefully to what was for my ears only. I would listen and they would often remind me that what I had just be been told, I was not to tell others, *"edu keda-dondi ile."* We would then resume the conversation and the recording on paper of what I could write about. Had I failed to respect this injunction about proper ways to conduct research, I would have had nothing significant to write about. To be at home in the field meant learning new ways of being, of knowing, and of writing.

In the following pages, I examine basic ethical issues that arise from unanticipated and unintended dream experiences on the part of anthropologists living in different Native North American communities. The productive outcome of such experiences shows the limitations in the field of ethical guidelines defined in a foreign culture. The awareness of these limitations lay the ground for an anthropological discourse that incorporates the fieldworker's firsthand, experience-based knowledge gained in interaction with others in their lifeworld.

"Ask the Elder!"

Injunctions, however short and concise, implicit or explicit, rest upon the bedrock of assumptions about reality and true or valid knowledge without which social life could not proceed. The degree to which these assumptions vary between Native North Americans and Euro–North Americans becomes obvious in the following account of interaction between myself and a student in an introductory course in anthropology I was teaching in Ottawa.

The event took place in the early 1980s, in the month of September. For the fourth consecutive year, I had returned to teach in my hometown after six months of immersion and work among the Dene Tha of Chateh, in northwestern Alberta. A student who had spent a year in an aboriginal community, in northern Ontario submitted a paper in which he described how local elders had dealt with a relative who had committed a serious violation of the community's values. The elders and community members could have reported the culprit to the Canadian courts and/or the local priest. They chose not to do so. In a process similar to the one described by Ryan (1995) for the Dogrib, the guilty party had been confronted by a group of elders who, following their traditional judicial practices, passed and implemented a sentence.

The nature of the breach, the decision by the Cree elders in council, the fate of the culprit, and the circumstances under which he eventually resumed his social life in the community, were all richly described in the paper the student handed in. I was so enthusiastic about the material that I suggested it be published in a journal where it could shine as a prime example of aboriginal justice enduring despite decades of government and Church assimilation policies. Hearing my suggestion, the student hesitated. He reminded me that he had been told this story by a Cree elder who had been his teacher and mentor in the Cree world. The story, therefore, could not be published without the elder's authorization.

"Well, then ask him!" I said. "But he is dead," the student retorted. "It does not matter; ask him anyway," I insisted. As soon as I had spoken these words, we both fell in deep silence. Clearly our conversation, in an Ottawa university classroom, was not proceeding according to standard Euro–North American canons of academic exchange. Far away from the homeland of the Cree and of the Dene Tha, what was going on? I realized that I was speaking out of Dene Tha convictions that I had inadvertently come to share with them over the years after countless conversations and experiences with them in their world. The student also realized that I was addressing him from a vantage point with which he had also become familiar among the Cree.

Startled at the turn of our conversation, we nevertheless carried on. The student asked, "Well, how do you ask someone who is dead?" I answered, "I don't know how the Cree would do it, but I do know how the Dene Tha would. They would take some tobacco, pray with it before going to bed, and ask the question that they would want an answer to and then go to sleep with the tobacco under their pillow. Then they would see what happens." The student said he would do the same. A week later, he eagerly came back to me with the answer: the Cree elder did not want us to publish his account of the events in his community.

How did the student know? He had done as I had described for the Dene Tha, and he had slept with tobacco under his pillow for three consecutive nights. Each morning, as he woke up, he remembered a dream image. The Cree elder would look at him while holding a pipe in his hands.[7] The elder, who wore a kerchief around his neck, would look directly at the student, smile at him, and shake his head from left to right three times. The image would then vanish. The student told me: "I was so stupid; it took me three nights to understand. He was looking at me and saying no." On that basis, we decided to respect the elder's answer and not publish an extraordinary account of indigenous justice and Native North American self-government.

A growing number of anthropologists incorporate in their ethnographies experiences such as the one described above. In this account of interaction with a student, I wish to highlight the challenging task of reconciling contrasting experiences of oneself in two original life-worlds. In many respects, the dominant culture in the world one has grown up in as a child and the dominant culture in the world of others one enters in adulthood as an anthropologist (the world in which they are at home) differ dramatically. These worlds are nevertheless two human worlds, two among so many other versions of dynamic meaningful coexistence created by humans, over time, all over the world—all of them open to understanding, each one of them a partial expression of the human potential.

From that vantage point, it is eminently reasonable to welcome the teaching of Dene Tha elders and community members. Acting on the basis of knowledge acquired among the Dene Tha is exactly what I did when I responded to the student's objection that he could not consult a Cree elder who had passed away with the injunction: "Ask him anyway!" I knew this was possible on the basis not of book knowledge but of experiences lived with the Dene Tha. To speak otherwise would have undermined the integrity of our similar experiences among the Dene Tha and the Cree. The epistemological position we took is fully consistent with the aboriginal view expressed by Buckley (2002, 90): "A person does not come to 'believe in' his discovery; he makes them or not, knows them by experience or remains ignorant of them, acts them out in what he does or knows nothing."

From an anthropological viewpoint, the interaction with the student also demonstrates that "communication across cultural boundaries creates a problem of identity" (Fabian 2000, 278). This problem is experienced not only when in the field, in the midst of "strangers," in their home environment, but also when we ourselves are back "home," behaving "strangely." The apparent contradiction is between the need to maintain an identity, without which interaction and communication is impossible, and the need to abandon an identity that would preclude new forms of communication and, therefore, new insights and information. In other words, "Because action needs an agent, we must maintain our identity. And we must abandon it, because no action—certainly not the action of exploration and ethnography—is possible if we keep a rigid hold on our identity" Fabian (2000, 278). Letting go, we enter into the ecstatic, that side of the ethnographic endeavor that is beyond the known and the taken-for-granted. Doing so, as illustrated above in every other chapter of this book, we also learn to "think of identity as a process rather than a property or state" (Fabian 2000, 278). As a result, accounts of dreams and of other "subconscious processes are well on their way to securing a place in this recasting of the ethnographic field" (Salamon 2003, 250).[8]

"The stories are wet with our breath."

For the anthropologist, the issues involved in living and working with Native North Americans in their world are complex. Bruce Miller (2000, 6) observes that "in recent years, there is an increased expectation by indigenous people that their understanding be foregrounded. . . . It is no longer a choice made by anthropologists sifting through structural, functional, and symbolic models and methods" to determine the best framework in which to present their findings to fellow professionals. If so, what happens to classical anthropology when indigenous understanding is foregrounded? Does the anthropology recede in the background or, does it even disappear altogether? Trigger (1995, quoted in Legros 1999, 21) suggests this much when he asks: "Can non-Native scholars write a history of Native people of North America? Will the Cambridge history of the Native people of North America be the last scholarly account of Native peoples by non-aboriginal scholars?"

To ask the question in these terms is to suggest that the assertion of the aboriginal voice goes hand in hand with the negation of the voice and perspective of non-aboriginal scholars. The outcome of such a stance for the anthropologist is clear. One moves out of the field or, moves "from studies on the Other to research for the Other" (Legros 1999, 19). In this manner, in his long-term research relationship with the Tutochone, Legros relinquished the "academic study [that] would destroy the whole allure of their narratives, the authority of their storytellers, betray their band council's aims, and even more so Mr. Mc-Ginty's." To avoid destruction and betrayal, Legros became "a scribe to Mr. Tommy McGinty, one of the most learned elders in Tutchone culture and a long-term friend" (Legros 1999, 19). In this kind of transformation, from analyst to scribe, the professional voice of the anthropologist necessarily gives way to that of the other.

Francesco Spagna and Guy Lanoue take a different view and argue for a transformation of the anthropological voice. The time has come, they write, to "reaffirm indigenous discourse" and incorporate it within the anthropological endeavor. This anthropological repositioning that seeks to tell the story of Native North Americans from their point of view has been encouraged by the Italian Association of Canadian Studies (AICS) and the Centre of Americanist Studies (CSACA). (Spagna and Lanoue 2001, 14). In this changing context, anthropological accounts consistent with aboriginal thought and experiences are seen more and more as evidence that aboriginal perspectives are valid.

It is premature to assess to what degree, in the eyes of indigenous peoples, anthropologists may succeed in this endeavor. Some indigenous people and indigenous scholars may not view this project as a legitimate one to embark upon. Others might prefer to tell their own story, make their discourse public and let it stand by itself on its own merit. This paper nonetheless proposes an anthropological understanding of human experiences that is informed by indigenous perspectives. Others still may welcome accounts by contemporary anthropologists who acknowledge the value of aboriginal practices and thought. As Navajo elders remarked to Toelken after his analysis of Navajo stories was well received presentation by a Navajo audience: "Now the whites are admitting that our stories are important and that we ought to listen to them. This is a significant change. If the whites are going to know about our stories, then it's even more important for our young people here to listen to them, too" (Toelken 1996, 6).

Anthropological accounts consistent with aboriginal thought and experiences, as the one presented by Toelken to a largely Navajo audience, are seen as evidence that the aboriginal perspective is valid. In no uncertain terms, in different places around the world, anthropologists are told again and again: "Don't try to save us physically unless you are willing to see that we keep our culture" (Navajo woman, quoted in Toelken 1996, 6). Aboriginal peoples around the world would agree with this Navajo woman when she adds: "We Navajos will live as long as the stories are wet with our breath!" (in Toelken 1996, 6).

To tell a story based on personal experience is to speak a truth. Our hosts in aboriginal communities listen to accounts of our experiences among them and examine how these accounts are consistent with their own stories. For instance, Miller had a vivid dream when in the midst of an intensive research project to compile vital genealogical information that would give tribal members grounds to claim their ancestral rights to access resources in specific sites within Washington State. In the dream, the visitors identified themselves as tribal ancestors and told Miller their names, names that he had to find to complete his research. The next day, when Miller shared the experience with local tribal members, they were not surprised. In their view, the dream "showed that the ancestors maintain active interest in the community of today and in the role of the anthropologist therein" (B. Miller 2000, 9). In cases such as this one, we clearly see that "dream reports and dream interpretation are inseparable from the social and political situations in which they occur" (B. Tedlock 1992, 28).

Notwithstanding the truth about the dream, Miller and tribal members recognized that this information "needed confirmation from another source to be used in a legal setting" (B. Miller 2000, 9). Soon thereafter, at the University of Washington archives, Miller found not three but thirty-two Indian names that had been lost to the band. Miller "hand-recorded this material and brought it to the elders. This information was . . . useful in litigation and the names were later 'brought out' in naming potlatchs" (personal communication, April 25, 2002).

In this instance, the strengthening of the legal basis of the aboriginal claim went hand in hand with a deepening of the anthropologist's on-going relationship with tribal members in their world.

Miller's account of his experiences in a Native North American world raises a larger issue. How are anthropologists to conduct themselves with Native North Americans in their world? Will they stand as outsiders who prefer unintrusive observation to radical participation? As illustrated in the events described above, to speak of the ethnographer's radical participation in the lifeworld of his or her host is to acknowledge "the fact that the interaction promoted through long-term participation produces not only 'observations' but also conceptualizations and insights that are clearly a joint creation of the anthropologist and his/her local partners in interaction" (Barth 1992, 65). Stories offered by anthropologists or their hosts authorize, found, and set in place "ways of experiencing the world" (Cruikshank 1998, 1). This is more crucial than the mere documentation of the range of ideas found in any culture, for it is in the context of interaction with our hosts that "new materials for internal reflection" become available (Barth 2002, 35). These materials are relevant also for conversation with our hosts in their home environment, and with our fellow anthropologists, who may or may not have lived similar experiences.

In this light consider the following conversation I had with Alexis Seniantha in the early 1990s. Alexis Seniantha, the head prophet of the Dene Tha, was living in Peace River approximately six hundred kilometers south of his home community in Chateh, northern Alberta.[9] With a few other Dene Tha elders, he spent the last years of his life in a retirement home and palliative care center in Peace River. There he was looked after by local staff and visited by Dene Tha relatives and friends. When I entered his room, we greeted each other as we customarily did and I handed him a pouch of pipe tobacco. As I sat next to him on his bed, he held the tobacco in his right hand with much delight and in a strong voice said: "This is very important!" He then spoke at length, in a reflective mood, about his life and the many experiences he had lived as a hunter, trapper, healer, and dreamer.

He began with a question: "Why is it that once in a while we have visions?"—literally, "things appear before our eyes." Alexis Seniantha thus led me once again directly into the consideration of the nature of beings, human and non-human, of the role of spiritual entities who manifest themselves in the land and lives of the Dene Tha, and of the reality of the inner life of human beings whose very soul or spirit dwells in the body when it is not on journeys of its own to explore the other world.

In the course of this conversation, I had the impression that Alexis Seniantha was still astonished as he recollected how his own life had been shaped by a series of extraordinary experiences. He obviously knew the traditional answer to the question he was asking. Yet I thought that he was not asking that question solely for rhetorical purposes. As he spoke, Alexis Seniantha knew what every Dene Tha knows: that in one's sleep one's soul wanders away from the body, acquires information about this world and the other world, and returns to the body with new experiences and knowledge; that death does not establish a barrier to interpersonal communication between the person who passes away to the other world and the ones left behind in this world to grieve; that interpersonal communication between here and the beyond takes on various forms including that of dreams and/or visions; that animals are sentient, intelligent, and powerful beings in their own right who give themselves as prey to human beings who show them respect, and who manifest themselves to chosen ones to become their animal helper, giving humans access to a font of knowledge and power to use to better their own lives and that of others in need of assistance when mentally and/or physically sick.

Knowing all this, Alexis Seniantha was nonetheless still asking: "Why is all of this unfolding as it is?" Despite all the traditional knowledge at hand to account for these experiences, Alexis Seniantha was still in awe of it all. His was an attitude of respect of the experiential dimension of his life. He does not attempt to explain and reminds me that explanation must remain secondary to the immediacy of lived experience. This is a challenge for anthropologists immersed in many aboriginal cultures. How is one to learn to know with a minimum of explanation? Buckley quotes Kroeber who saw this aboriginal refusal to explain things "as evidence of Yurok deficiencies in intellectualization" (Buckley 2002, 106). Conversely, Yurok saw Kroeber's questions "as both impolite and unproductive of real understanding" (Buckley 2002, 105). "White people explain too much," said Robert Spott, a respected Yurok. Spott maintained that he "had tried to teach Kroeber, . . . [who in the end] just couldn't learn" (Buckley 2002, 106).

Conversations with colleagues about ecstatic experiences and their content, as suggested above, depend on how anthropologists decide to conduct themselves when they return home and sit down to write the results of their anthropological work for fellow professionals to read. One option, perhaps the one preferred by the majority of anthropologists, is to do as Robert Lowie and many others since have done, to produce classical scholarly work that leaves aside all experiences of dreams and visions that flow from radical participation in the Native American world. Much of the anthropologist's findings and experiences in the Native North American lifeworld are then written out of one's ethnography. These decisions reflect epistemological and ethical concerns. How much do we bring forth in the public record as anthropologists? On what basis do we decide to exclude or include certain kinds of data or accounts of experiences? Every anthropological paper, journal article, or book published expresses a decision on these matters and determines whether within anthropology, foregrounded or not, the aboriginal perspective will be visible and visibly respected.

Living According to "True" Knowledge

In the course of this paper, I have referred to propositions that are widely held to be true by Native North Americans. First, when learning, do so from personal experience, personal witnessing of people and events, and careful listening of other people's accounts of their experiences and observations. Second, when in doubt about publishing an account obtained from an elder, ask for his authorization to publish, even if he has passed from this world to the next. Third, ancestors maintain an active interest in the well-being of their descendants. And so on. At face value, depending on the identity of the reader, these statements will stand either as assertions of facts or as assertions made in good faith that demonstrate the tenacity of traditional beliefs, however erroneous, in the life of certain individuals.

To account for the fact that these statements may be true for some and false for others, I have found useful Spiro's definition of belief. Spiro (1987a, 163–165) defines a belief as a proposition or a statement that is held to be true by the members of a society. The proposition may be about oneself or about other entities, whatever they may happen to be, fellow human beings, God, spirit, atoms, or germs. In other words, to hold a proposition as true is to believe. Beliefs held to be true may belong to any realm of experience: science, politics, economy, religion, or another body of theoretical and/or practical knowledge. To live with others and to conduct one's professional activity one has to hold certain propositions as true. No one is not a believer and "the role of the 'will to believe' in the acceptance of scientific ideas is as prominent as the role that William James attributed to it in the acceptance of religious doctrines" (Spiro 1987b, 103). To hold beliefs with others in a society or in a professional body is to share with others a worldview and an ethos.

Spiro further distinguishes various degrees of belief. To learn about an assertion that someone or something exists is a first level of belief. To understand the meaning of that assertion is a second level of belief. To believe that the proposition is "true, correct or right" is a third level of belief (Spiro 1987a, 164). To act upon this assertion is a fourth level of belief. The statements held as true are then "genuine beliefs, rather than cultural cliché" (Spiro 1987a, 164). The fifth, deeper level of belief, involves a deep emotional attachment to these truths. One's life is then lived as the emotionally satisfying enactment, as a member of a group, of a set of propositions that one knows, understands, and holds as conforming to the way things are and/or ought to be. The interaction described above between myself and a student illustrates that we were behaving on the basis of assumptions or propositions learned from aboriginal peoples, in a manner that was satisfying to us.

The analytical value of Spiro's conceptual framework allows us to distinguish between contemporary Native North Americans and Euro–North Americans according to their degree of familiarity with aboriginal propositions or beliefs. Irrespective of their ancestry, individuals may believe in Native North American propositions at the first three levels of belief, but not at the deeper levels where they would inform their day-to-day lives. Dene Tha recognize this much when they insist that it is only through personal experience that one truly knows. Dene Tha acknowledge also that the juxtaposition of traditional and scientific propositions poses a special challenge. A Dene Tha young man in his early thirties, for instance, told me about the day he came back home from school to tell his father that the Earth was revolving around the sun, and not the sun around the Earth. The father replied: "How come then the bear snared the sun one day? Unless the sun went somewhere, it would not have its path." The man then asked his son: "If that story [about the bear snaring the sun] was not true, how could you be here now?" The young man understood his father to say: "Why create a new school of thought, why reinvent the wheel, when there is already a school of thought that works?" (Goulet 1998, 86). In a sense, the father is reminding the son that the province of science is not the only province of meaning accessible to human beings. He is inviting his son to move out of the realm of scientific knowledge to reconnect with the realm of traditional Dene knowledge on the basis of which his parents and ancestors had lived since time immemorial. It is in interaction with aboriginal peoples, in their world, that the kinds of ethical issues discussed in this paper arise.

Spiro's conceptualization of belief applies also to the anthropologist. For instance, the proposition that one ought to conduct fieldwork as the basis of one's anthropological research is a belief. According to Spiro, one may know about fieldwork, intellectually grasp its meaning, and believe the statement to be true without ever engaging in fieldwork or ever really wanting to do so. The proposition about fieldwork is then held to be true at the first three levels of belief without being a genuine belief. For more than a century, however, anthropologists have engaged in fieldwork and truly valued the qualities of human coexistence and cooperation it generates. The proposition that fieldwork constitutes an integral part of research may be held by some anthropologists as true, or believed, at all five levels. Similarly, the proposition that one may consult deceased elders or that one may be visited by them is also a belief that can be accepted at various levels. This may be a proposition that one knows about and understands as being part of the lives of others—Native North Americans, for instance. Knowing and understanding this, one may believe the proposition to be false. For many Native North Americans, however, and for many Euro–North Americans and Europeans also, the proposition is true at a deeper level. As illustrated in the ethnographic material presented above, this proposition may also shape one's behavior and inform one's feelings and unexpectedly open the door to genuine interaction between Euro–North Americans and Native Americans in their world. Such occurrences reflect the fact that the field experience becomes, to a significant extent, "the center of our intellectual and emotional lives," the process through which we are, "if not 'going native,' at least becoming bicultural" (B. Tedlock 1991, 82).

Barbara Tedlock's suggestion that many anthropologists become bicultural through the process of fieldwork enables us to account for the manner in which a student and I pursued a conversation on the basis of aboriginal epistemological and ontological assumptions, ones that we had not been truly familiar with before we became familiar with our Dene and Cree hosts. Burridge had clearly thought through this issue when he wrote the following:

> Every anthropologist has experienced "culture shock": a temporary inability, when moving from one culture to another, to grasp and act and think in terms of the assumptions upon which the newly entered culture is based. Not only is this shock experienced in fieldwork, while one learns the ways of a new culture, but it is experienced even more disconcertingly when one returns to one's own culture. Mind and emotions are confused: two different worlds have met in the same person. One alternative is insanity. Another is to comprehend one world in the terms of the other. (Burridge 1969, 163–164, in Fabian 1979, 9–10)

Beyond the stark alternative of going insane or comprehending their world in term of ours, there is still another possibility. We may, as contributors to this book do, compare and contrast competing epistemological and ontological assumptions as experienced in and beyond the field. The task at hand consists in describing and analyzing the experiences of communication when one "learns the ways of a new culture" and "when one returns to one's own culture." Contrasting epistemological and ontological assumptions as they compete with each other within the same person serves to highlight the fact that they are, in a sense, irreducible to one another. Contrary to Burridge's suggestion, it follows that we cannot simply comprehend one set of ontological assumptions (a worldview) in terms of the other.

Native North American understanding of many practices and experiences challenges the canons of Western reality and of modern ethnography. If we do not totally devalue the experiences lived in dreams and/or visions, what may we do with them, ours or that of others, within the profession? Shall we argue then with Gregory and Mary Catherine Bateson (1987) that one can act "as if" the elder had actually talked to us, leaving to others the worry about the ontological status of the Elder's appearance in a dream. Shall we take a more radical stance and maintain with Goodman (1990, 55) that "ritual is the rainbow bridge over which we can call on the Spirits and the Spirits cross over from their world into ours." Elders and spirits, however, are not always benign. This led Stoller and Olkes (1987, 22) to state that "ethnographers can go too far. They can pursue the other's reality too hotly, crossing a line that brings them face to face with a violent reality that is no mere epistemological exercise." We risk ignoring that we are living in sorcery's shadow at our own risk. Similarly, it took Toelken more than thirty years to learn that his research among the Navajo between 1954 and 1984 had actually been "more endangering than entertaining" (Toelken 1996, 14).

Multivocality, the hallmark of postmodern accounts of human activity and history, characterizes the anthropological domain also. Authors speak and write and agree to disagree. In this context, we ought at least to take note of the beliefs espoused by our colleagues, beliefs understood here in Spiro's sense of propositions held to be true. In the end, whatever position one espouses on the issues raised in this paper, that advocated by Trigger, by Spagna and Lanoue, by Bateson and Bateson, by Goodman, by Stoller and Olkes, or by Toelken, the "will to believe," the decision to posit this as opposed to that as a meaningful gestalt in terms of which to make sense of one's experience has to intervene.

From that perspective, I can listen attentively to colleagues who claim the following: You did not know what the elder wanted. Contrary to what Cree and Dene Tha may think, the dream of the Cree elder was not to be taken as an apparition of someone addressing you from beyond the grave. To think so when you are awake is to delude yourselves. Once awake, you ought to set aside immediately absurd notions of nightly communication with those who have passed away. Moreover, in your day-to-day life, you ought to at least keep in mind that the injunction to "say the right words" that governs Dene social interaction also ought to shape your interaction with fellow professionals.

These colleagues may enjoin me also to follow in the footsteps of great anthropologists, such as Robert Lowie, who carefully kept from his peers and from the public at large the many experiences of dreams and visions that so helped him in his work with Native Americans. The accounts of these experiences became known after only his death when his wife published them posthumously in *Current Anthropology* (1966).

To these admonitions I reply that the practice followed by Lowie and many others undermines the integrity of the ethnographic record and postpones indefinitely the public, scholarly exploration of such experiences. On the basis of personal experiences and firsthand accounts of numerous credible colleagues, I maintain that I am most comfortable with the proposition that our capacity to communicate with each other is also expressed in dreams and visions. In some instances, dreams or visions enable us to respond to events occurring in an intersubjective world in a most appropriate manner. I have described elsewhere how, in the middle of a Cree ceremony, I had a vision of myself fanning a fire with my hat, which was exactly how the action was to be performed (Goulet 1998, 231–242). Cree and Dene elders with whom I shared my experience were not surprised, for they know that this is how one is instructed in the midst of their ceremonies. They simply say, *sindít'ah edahdí,* "with my mind I know." The experience reported by Gardner in this book is of the same order. Time after time he correctly guessed in which hand participants in a hand game had hidden a piece of wood. Following several rounds of this, someone in a back corner of the tent suddenly called out, "You are cheating. You closed your eyes, so you can see."

In the end, one realizes that if it is true that "so-called natives do not 'inhabit' a world fully separate from the one ethnographers 'live in,'" (Rosaldo 1989, 45), it is equally true that the ethnographer and his or her hosts are both human beings. The experiences described earlier in this paper, my own and those of Miller, occur in a world that comprises our contemporaries and our predecessors, those who have passed away but who live in our memory. In such a world, praying with tobacco and then dreaming with the tobacco under one's pillow enabled a student to experience the visit of a Cree elder who had died. Clearly, anthropologists enculturated in Euro–North American scientific and rational traditions who nevertheless immerse themselves deeply in a Native North American world cannot spontaneously report, as Native North Americans might do, their own experiences of meeting Native North Americans ancestors in their dreams. This reticence to do so is understandable. The following comment by Jung, in this respect, is revealing: "I am convinced that if a European had to go through the same exercises and ceremonies which the medicine-man performs in order to make the spirits visible, he would have the same experiences. He would interpret them differently, of course, and devalue them, but this would not alter the facts" (Jung 1920 [1960], 303, in Young 1994, 169).

It is perhaps appropriate then to share the following dream. It is one with which Alexis Seniantha would have had no difficulty. A number of years ago, a close friend of ours was dying from cancer. My wife, Christine, was away for a few days in Vancouver when our friend died. A few hours before receiving the long-distance phone call announcing her death, I had a dream in which I saw our friend dressed in a hospital gown step out of her bed and begin walking in my direction. She kept her balance with the help of a cane held in her right hand. As she passed to my right she waived and smiled at me, saying: "I'm on my way to see Christine." I had a clear sense that our friend had passed away and that somehow Christine would soon know. Half awake, half asleep, I remained in bed with our two-year-old son.

Early in the morning, the phone rang and a friend asked to speak to Christine. When I said that she was away, I was told about the death of our friend. I responded, unintentionally and matter-of-factly: "I know." Surprised, the speaker asked how this was possible. I shared my dream, after which the speaker asked for the telephone number at which Christine could be reached. I hesitated for a moment and said I preferred not to give it. Shocked, the speaker insisted that Christine would want to know what had occurred. I agreed but maintained that following the dream I had in the morning, I felt that our friend would soon let Christine know. This made no sense to the speaker. Out of respect for her, I asked for time to think about the matter. I assured her that I would call within twenty-four hours. I did so and maintained my earlier position. I did not give out the phone number. To do so, in my view, was to destroy an unfolding form of communication that was proceeding in ways beyond our ability to fully comprehend.

The next day I received a phone call from Christine who reported sitting by the ocean beach and seeing our friend rest peacefully, horizontally atop the waves. This simple image had comforted her immensely because she "knew" that her friend had died. I then told her about my own dream, the ensuing phone call, and my decision not to give out the Vancouver phone number where she could be reached. In our experience, everything had fallen into place at the right time.

In the light of such interpersonal experiences, I feel much at ease sitting with Alexis Seniantha on his hospital bed. With him, I can consider the very fundamental question: "Why is it that, once in a while, things appear before our eyes," in dreams or in broad daylight, as described elsewhere (Goulet 1998, 8–9, 178–180). Like Alexis Seniantha, I do not have a truly intellectually satisfying answer to such a question. The experiences of such visions and annunciatory dreams are nonetheless real. They arise out of deep emotional involvement with significant others, as illustrated in this paper and that of many others included in this book. Why and how such knowledge arises eludes us. In the end, we may be wise—with the Yurok, the Dene, and many other aboriginal peoples—to learn to simply live responsibly and ethically in the light of such experiences with a minimum of explanation.

Conclusion

An anthropologist and a student decide on the basis of the student's dream not to publish an account of a Cree judicial process. Is it sufficient then to say that they then acted ethically, for, in doing so, they did not undermine the Native North American understanding of the event? An anthropologist listens to three local ancestors who visit him in the night to assist him and the local community in their land claims. Following the visitation of these three elders, is it sufficient to share the news with tribal members and later on to write that "this [Elders speaking in a dream] is an appropriate source of knowledge in the community, for some at least" (B. Miller, personal communication, April 26, 2002)? How can we European and Euro–North American anthropologists truly deal with these questions as they arise from our living and working cooperatively with Native North Americans in their world?

To answer such questions, ethnographers often shy away from radical participation in the world of their hosts, claiming that such intimate association with others is not a prerequisite to penetrate the reasons for which they account for their behavior within their sociocultural universe. In this vein, Augé writes the following: "I see no inconvenience whatsoever in considering that the observer is recording fictions, narrations that are quite foreign to him, but the reasons of which he can penetrate. The expression participatory ethnology has no other meaning and presupposes no kind of mystical fusion with others" (2004, 44). Broadly speaking, fiction is to be understood here "not as fiction opposite to the truth of the narrative the historians claim to be true, but as narration, a scenario that obeys a certain number of rules" (Augé 2004, 34). In this sense, living fictions is the characteristic of human lives everywhere. No one is ever not living a fiction, including the ethnographer interacting first with his or her hosts, and later on with his or her readers. Nonetheless, in Augé's insistence that "no other meaning" be attached to the notion of "participatory ethnology", we see operating the fear of going native, of crossing over the boundaries of rationality into the world of mysticism. This fear unduly constrains the range of ethnographic experiences that may be included in one's accounts from the field, and in so doing diminishes the range of meanings that may be attached legitimately to radical participation as a method of investigation.

Extraordinary anthropology originates with the recognition that "Western styles of knowledge, which typically give priority to detachment over engagement, textuality over vocality, mind over body, are to be exposed to radically different ways of understanding and inhabiting reality" (Orsi 2005, 195). Such a change of priority may involve giving oneself genuinely to aboriginal ways of learning and knowing, including full participation in rituals understood "as a means of gaining knowledge of the world" (Garroutte 2003, 108). Through radical participation in ritual we experience changes in the life we then live and of which we are witnesses. "Unlike Galileo's contemporaries, who refused to look through his telescope, experiential ethnographers are brave enough to stand inside what may be to them a foreign means of encountering the world" (Garroutte 2003, 108). What is involved in this process is not "mystical fusion with others" (Augé 2004, 44) but rather a modification of "our previous cognitive structures to include those new features of the environment learned through new or unexpected perceptions" (Fuller 2006, 83). Accounts of extraordinary experiences in the field become part of the larger stock of knowledge revealed through a "tracery of stories, intrigues, and events that involve the private and the public sphere, which we tell each other with greater or lesser talent and conviction (Listen, you're not going to believe this, but something wild happened to me . . .)" (Augé 2004, 32–33). The content of this chapter and of every other chapter in this book provides such moments when the reader is invited to expand his or her intellectual and moral horizon.

Notwithstanding our desire to enter the world of others, our minds and hearts (like those of Native North Americans and of countless people around the world) are firmly anchored in our familiar world: the homeland, the friends, the loved ones, and the profession to which we return. Initially, when entering the world of Native North Americans, we discovered the possibility of opening ourselves to human potentialities as they are actualized in that world, their world. This potential to experience life differently creates a context in which communication with deceased elders through dreams become a fact of life. Ecstatic moments experienced in the field become moments of personal and professional transformation.

When leaving the world of Native North Americans to join fellow professionals, the issue is twofold: First, to find the means of conveying a sense of what it meant to really be there among Native North Americans. Second, to begin to explore the larger anthropological theoretical issues involved in accounting for reports of experiences of communication with others in dreams. When we leave these conversations with fellow anthropologists to turn toward our hosts and friends in aboriginal communities, we accept to journey more deeply with them in their world. In the end, it is with them that ethical guidelines in the light of which to conduct one's research must be generated and acted upon.

Notes

1. I gratefully acknowledge financial support for my research among the Dene Tha between 1979 and 1985 from the Social Sciences and Humanities Research Council of Canada and Saint Paul University's Canadian Research Centre for Anthropology, in Ottawa. See Goulet 2004b and Goulet and Harvey-Trigoso 2005 for description of recent developments among the Dene Tha of Chateh.

2. In Canada, the term *aboriginal* includes Indians or First Nations, Metis or Mixed Blood, and Inuit (formerly known as Eskimos). In the 2001 national census, 976,305 respondents identified themselves as North American Indian, 292,310 as Metis, and 45,007 as Inuit (Canada 2001).

3. The *Tri-Council Policy Statement* is available at www.ncehr-cnerh.org/English/code_2. The three councils are the Medical Research Council (MRC), the Natural Sciences and Engineering Research Council (NSERC), and the Social Sciences and Humanities Research Council (SSHRC). See MRC, NSERC, and SSHRC 1998. The main criticism directed at the policy statement is that it has universities establish ethics review committees through which "the university or granting agency passes on liability to the researchers and the researchers pass it on to their subjects" (Lambeck 2005, 232). In Lambek's view "this is not merely non-ethical, but unethical." On this and other related issues, see also van den Hoonaard (2002) and Gotlib (2005).

4. McNaughton and Rock submitted a first version of their paper, "Opportunities in Aboriginal Research. Results of SSHRC's Dialogue on Research and Aboriginal Peoples," in October 2003 to the SSHRC's board members and senior management. Their paper was preceded by two other reports, one published online in 2002, "SSHRC Synthesis of Briefs Received from the Fall, 2002 Consultation on Policy Directions Related to Aboriginal Peoples" (L. Davis et al.) and the other, "SSHRC's Dialogue on Research and Aboriginal Peoples: What Have We Heard on What Should Be Done?" published online in 2003. These

papers, along with discussions of participants in the national dialogue, are found at http://ca.groups.yahoo.com/group/Aboriginal_Research.

5. The following three sections are revised and expanded versions of published material for which I have retained copyrights (Goulet 2004a).

6. Fieldwork and teaching in Ottawa followed each other for five consecutive years, with approximately six months spent in each place each year from January 1980 to July 1984.

7. The ceremonial pipe so prominent among the Cree and other aboriginal populations is absent among the Dene Tha and other northern Athapaskans. See Paper (1989) and Waldram (1997).

8. For examples of recent work that incorporate in this manner the subconscious processes (perceptions and dreams) of the investigator in the ethnography see Sylvie Poirier 2001, 2003, 2004, and 2005, and David H. Turner 1987, 1989, 1999, and 2002. Both authors have conducted extensive and intensive fieldwork among the Australian Aborigines.

9. See Goulet 1996 and 1998, 194–212, for a presentation of Alexis Seniantha's dreams and visions that led him to the status of head dreamer or first prophet among the Dene Tha.

10. Experiences of Power among the Sekani of Northern British Columbia

Sharing Meaning through Time and Space

GUY LANOUE

Our feelings and definitions of alterity as anthropologists are produced to a significant degree by direct and prolonged contact with
our hosts. Our indigenous cultural beacons, however, sometimes not
only fail to illuminate but produce an ultimately enriching confusion
that challenges the very postulates by which we have carefully constructed our anthropological and personal selves. In this paper I take
a position that differs with the theme announced by the editors. This
theme emerged from the notion, first advanced by Fabian (1991), that
our best ethnographic fieldwork is often carried on while we are "out
of our minds," temporarily deranged by the strangeness of it all. According to the premise advanced by the editors of this volume, the
clash of viewpoints obliges us to confront deep epistemological, political, moral, and other issues, because the boundaries of the ways we
constitute knowledge of the world and of ourselves are brought into
sharp relief by prolonged contact (Goulet 1994b). I argue that fieldwork is not bounded in place and in time and that the prolonged contact of field research continues to operate well beyond the boundaries that define the formal aspects of contact.

While it is not for me to second-guess other people's thinking, it
seems to me that this position, which privileges the spatial dimension
of the encounter at the expense of the temporal, is a refinement of the
earlier postulate of cultural relativism that dominated postwar anthropology. It opens the door to the same problems that anthropologists have been trying to avoid for the last two decades. Briefly, in the
1960s, anthropologists couched the issue of relativism in exclusively

moral or ethical terms that, in effect, depoliticized the encounter with the other. The reminder that "they" were every bit as sophisticated as us, despite appearances, created a vicious circle: the more disgusting bits of our encounters with the other (see, for example, Turnbull's famous description of the Ik, 1972) were automatically attributed to cultural contamination or interference by other cultures. Cultural relativism was therefore a tacit admonition to seek out "uncontaminated" societies (witness the debates in the 1970s and 1980s over the Kalahari San, "Bushmen"), which, in the end, reinforced the idea that each society had more or less impermeable boundaries.

Then came Foucault. Suddenly, everything was politicized, everything was evidence of identity wars between a colonializing Us and a resentful Them. There was more, of course. Foucauldian politicization of the anthropological encounter gave a voice to the other, and therefore fundamentally changed the relationship between anthropologists and their hosts. If, before, we had been (or tried to be) sensitive to them, it was nonetheless still in the anthropologists' power to decide the how to be sensitive, which parts of their culture were to be trotted out in evidence of "their" relative accomplishments. Perhaps the most famous example, still perpetuated in a host of contemporary textbooks, is the Nuer kinship system that allegedly functioned "like" a political system, which meant, of course, like a Western political system was supposed to function (see Geertz 1983). Afterward, anthropologists were no longer so sure that it was in their power to decide. Not only was fieldwork to be carried out under more or less contractually explicit terms, but knowledge was no longer ours to produce. It was to be a collaborative effort, a dialogic relationship.

Naturally, this was not the end of fieldwork or of anthropology. It was merely another step in the complex evolution of a discipline that almost from its inception has struggled with its colonial demons. Fieldwork, always the cornerstone of the discipline, has, however, been strongly affected by these debates of the last three decades. One effect is seen here, in the theme of this collection. As fieldwork becomes more collaborative, it becomes more pressing to identify the moments of epiphany that are properly the anthropologist's, and this I understand to be the aim of this volume.

There are, however, problems with this formulation. Situating the moment of epiphany in the field ignores the dimension of time. Aside from suggesting that understanding is generated in an atemporal dimension, that the flash of insight is not the result of a cumulative process, situating sudden insight in the field experience reproduces some of the essentialisms that anthropologists have tried very hard to identify and confront over the last several decades, especially the notion that "the field" is a *special* instance of space and time. It *is* different, true, but to what extent do the differences noted by anthropologists transform the field experience into a special, *bounded* instance of space and time? Is it possible that anthropologists project their later, post-fieldwork interpretations onto the past, thereby canceling not only the present but also the evolutionary process by which they arrive at understanding? I think the answer is yes, and the result is the further exoticization of "fieldwork time" and therefore of "the field" as a special space, a separate instance in time, when in fact the experience is better described as a moment in the developmental continuum of our lives. I think that the intellectual value of the special moments in which we are "out of our minds" in the field is something we can discover only much later, since epiphanies act on our emotions much more than on our alleged understanding of events by means of intellectual struggles within a well-established body of doctrine (no matter how critical and self-reflexive it may be). By situating "understanding" in intellect and in time, we recreate the very boundaries between Us and Them that we otherwise work so hard to overcome.

There is another essentialist dimension attached to the fiction of fieldwork as a special time. Anthropologists often think we need to ask the "proper" questions to get answers, and that the special times when we are "out of our minds" will yield better, more insightful questions, to which we will receive richer answers. Undoubtedly, this is true in some cases. This, however, precludes instances in which dialogue is not a normal or even respected form of interaction (for example, see Basso's well-known article on silence among the Apache, 1990), no matter how precise the initial hypotheses may be. Asking questions, no matter how insightful or provocative the answers they evoke, is sometimes so inappropriate that it will tacitly frame the apparent exchange of questions and answers between anthropologist and host as a hierarchical relationship. By asking questions that emerge from a series of insights temporally bounded by the field experience, anthropologists may be contributing to reproducing an institutionalized form of anthropology that needs its hypotheses to obtain funding. It may be possible, in other words, that the best insights come from forgetting we are anthropologists while in the field and from confronting our emotional reactions to the field after the fact. It may be that the condition of being "out of our minds" is an artificially produced condition unique to the anthropological endeavor. Perhaps we should pay attention to what transpires while we are out of our minds at other times, in other places.

I am not denying that being "out of our minds" in the field occurs and leads to rich and immediate insights that would otherwise be inaccessible. Here, however, I would like to explore how one can be "out of one's mind" long after the fieldwork experience, and suggest that the triggers may have little to do with the strangeness of the field experience bounded by time and place and more to do with the anthropologist's emotional condition. Specifically, I would like to describe an encounter with one trait of Sekani culture, "power," that took me twenty years to understand, although "understanding" became possible only when I changed my definition of understanding and therefore inadvertently came closer to Sekani thoughts on power. This, however, was not so much the result of being "out of my mind" in the field as it was the confluence of many coincidences and the inadvertent result of many choices made over a twenty-year period. To help readers better understand the process, I will briefly describe some aspects of power as it is experienced by the Sekani and by other northern Athapaskan and Algonquian-speaking peoples, reminding the reader that this description is the result of twenty years of struggle.

Sekani Thoughts on Power

Power is not the correct word for the quality I wish to describe because it implies relations of force, and a Western notion of agency. Force and agency are different for the Sekani, as I argued recently (Ferrara and

Lanoue 2004; Desgent and Lanoue 2005). Nonetheless, "power" is a commonly accepted though ambiguous word that Athapaskan scholars use to describe a special relationship to a transcendental or immanent quality said to be unique to animals.[1]

The Sekani are now classified as speaking a dialect of an Athapaskan language, Sekani–Beaver, though Sekani was considered a separate language when I was doing my fieldwork (see Denniston 1981). They live in several communities in north-central British Columbia, Canada, mostly concentrated in three reserves in the heart of the Rocky Mountains. Their homelands have been almost destroyed by the provincial government's decision to build a dam on the Peace River, completed in 1968, which created a huge artificial lake in the valley where two tributaries of the Peace ran through Sekani territory. The consequences of this unilateral decision have been described elsewhere (Lanoue 1992). In fact, some of these consequences were of capital importance in the process that led to my understanding power. One community, Fort Grahame, was completely destroyed by the flooding. The southernmost, McLeod Lake, was physically untouched, although a large part of its homeland was flooded. The northernmost community, Fort Ware, was relatively untouched by the flooding though people had to adjust to the influx of refugees from Fort Grahame. Overall, a government policy favoring the exploitation of the forest lands made accessible by the new lake led to the creation of several new towns (for Sekani, the two most important were Mackenzie and Hudson Hope) meant to house and service the thousands of workers needed to process the wood products that would be made accessible by water transport. These people, for the most part unskilled workers used to migrating as the economic frontier moved back and forth with the prevailing economic winds, were often a significant source of problems for the Sekani.

First, alcohol became freely available (before, local traders had generally limited the supply so as not to jeopardize trapping and hunting). Second, some whites entered into status competition with the Indians, in my opinion hanging around the reserve because other whites often shunned them. Compared to the Sekani, however, they were fabulously rich. These whites often sought to entice the younger Sekani into drinking so they could feel superior, as providers of booze and rides into town. Third, many whites (usually not those who hung around the reserve) in the new towns used the forest as a sporting arena for their snowmobiles and for hunting, though not hunting in the unobtrusive way the Sekani had practiced. The presence of these sport hunters made the bush unattractive for Sekani, who had no desire to run into representatives of the people who, in their opinion, had ruined their way of life. Fourth, intensive logging of the Sekani homeland destroyed habitats for beaver and moose, disturbing Sekani habits of displacement over the homeland. Fifth, the region was transformed from forgotten backwater into an administrative zone that had to be "normalized" (apologies to Foucault) by imposing a "regular" form of government administration. This meant, at the very least, hunting and fishing regulations that further weakened Sekani desires to hunt and trap. At the worst, it meant welfare for the "unproductive" Sekani, most of whom chose not to work in the new economic sector of logging. The Sekani also became the target of various government social service agencies that needed a clientele to justify their existence. Almost overnight, programs sprang up for everything, from teaching bush craft to training the Sekani in the new skills they needed, it was believed, to survive in the new politicized environment. It seemed that McLeod Lake was quickly becoming a welfare community where few people worked in the new economy and most ceased regularly hunting and trapping.

The result was massive discouragement. Some would call it alienation, but whatever the term, the results were shocking. Alcoholism became a major problem. Violence and tension were endemic. These are all classic signs of a people in distress and are important to the subject at hand since they led to a cleavage between the generations and, in particular, to a crisis in social reproduction as older people stopped trying to impart their knowledge to the disinterested young. Between 1962, the year work began on the dam, and 1978 (ten years after its completion), the year I arrived in McLeod Lake, one-seventh (thirty-five people) of the population died from violence or accidents related to drinking. Dozens moved away seeking new lives in other Native communities or in white towns. The community, once composed of nearly two hundred people, was reduced to about seventy-five people. Had this occurred in a non-Indian population, I am sure it would have been classified as genocide by the media. No doubt, Sekani feelings of despair were exacerbated because they were ignored, left to fend for themselves except for government retraining programs mostly aimed at the young who spoke English fluently. The relationship between traditional knowledge and social continuity was irrevocably broken. Old and young no longer lived in the same world.

Contrary to some contemporary ideas of how culture is transmitted in Indian societies, the Sekani placed no great stock in orality or on the role of "elders" as repositories of knowledge, nor did they have any concept of "tradition" as such. It was not normal for "elders" to give explicit instructions in the lore and practices younger people would need as adults. In fact, it is arguable that the category "elders" is a response to the politicization of Indian bands by federal-government policies that have created a new Indian elite (Bousquet 2002) whose political constituency and power base is more attuned to interacting with various Euro-Canadian government power structures than it is to solving problems of spatial organization, the normal domain of power in these hunting peoples. These "new" politicians often seek legitimacy by extolling their links to "tradition" and so claim a continuity of political practices by appealing to the older generations, who are generally excluded from the new power structure by choice and culture. Sekani learned by doing, especially since it was believed that knowledge was keyed to individuals and could not really be shared except at the most banal levels such as teaching someone about topography. Parents saw their roles as placing children in situations that would lead to learning by experience. For example, young men had to learn to acquire power by entering a particular sort of situation.

Acquiring power was based on Sekani beliefs concerning the special and indescribable qualities that are part of the transcendental dimension of animals, which is thought to be a holdover from the beginning of time. Sekani are ambiguous about the creation of the world but clear about the Transformation, an epoch in which a Trickster-like creature (a beaver for the Sekani, although it takes many forms among

Experiences of Power among the Sekani

Athapaskans) appears and gives the world the form it has now by the inadvertent consequences of his actions, usually motivated by greed, gluttony, and disproportionate sexual desire. In the past, animals were larger ("monstrous" or "giant," according to most accounts), spoke, and sometimes married and hunted humans. For their part, humans are often represented as weak and unable to defend themselves from the depredations of various monsters, including the monstrous animals. In other words, animals were superior to humans, a belief that many Sekani still profess, since animals live in the same environment as the Sekani yet survive without weapons, society, and language.

The Transformer imposed on each species a smaller, limited, and weaker biological form that reduced the giant animal's ability to express its powers—it could no longer talk, marry, or hunt humans. However, the Transformer did not alter in any way the innate capacities or natures of animals, just as he did not significantly alter human physical abilities by making them stronger or better-armed, as in many classic culture-hero tales from other parts of the world. In brief, the Transformer conjoins humans, who become less animal-like (because they acquire culture through rule-driven behavior), and animals, who become less humanlike (because the Transformer gave them the physical bodies by which we know them in the present, thus making them unable to express their natural superiority over humans). Not surprisingly, it is believed that hunting is possible only if animals give themselves to people since they are still naturally superior.

The Acquisition of Power by Men

To come into contact with this now-hidden dimension of animals, hunters transform themselves into symbolic prey, calling into being the pre-Transformer dimension of animals. Hunters can dream this contact, but the more usual way is what has sometimes been called a vision quest, which among the Sekani and many other northern nomadic hunters is not so ritualized as versions found among the semitribalized peoples of the plateau or the plains. Immobile, without food or weapons, and alone, the hunter creates a ritual space by these inversions of normal experiential reality (hunters normally walk to hunt;

244

they carry some food and, of course, weapons; they hunt in pairs). A man on a quest thus metaphorically evokes the pre-Transformer epoch, when animals hunted humans. Because an animal's biological nature would normally urge it to flee humans, any animal that approaches the hunter in this temporary ritual space is assumed to be under the sway of its primordial, non-biological nature. In these special circumstances, in which the human has become prey and the animal has in a sense become a hunter, a metaphoric link develops between the hunter and the animal. Some of the animal's power can be passed to the human.

In fact, the favorite metaphor used to describe this is a "conversation" or "talking with the animal doctors" (the widespread Native English name for the act of engaging the invisible dimension of animals). It is in fact a form of contamination, in which some of the animal's innate essence is transferred to the weaker human. The transfer is seen as normal, because everything in Sekani culture (including the Transformer tales) urges people to believe that equilibrium is a natural condition. If someone has food and another does not, the food is given to the hungry person not in the spirit of generosity but because it is the "natural" thing to do, like water seeking its level. By the same token, animal power "naturally" gravitates to those who do not have any, although there are many dangers associated with this transfer. Just as the Sekani say that a person who is too hungry or too thirsty should not eat or drink too much, a person who is without power should be very careful not to become too contaminated with a force over which he can exercise no control.

All men are expected to be able to achieve contact with power, though not all do so. Women cannot because they already possess an essential quality of the transcendental, the blood of reproduction and of species survival, the same blood that superior animals willingly sacrifice to ensure the survival of individual humans. In one sense, women are symbolic animals and are more perfect than men, just as animals are more perfect than humans. Men are thus the semiotically marked category that is subjected to the ritual transformation of the self by means of the vision quest and its rules; women are unmarked because they are "naturally" superior.

Just as the Transformer did not alter the essences of humans or giant animals, people who come in contact with the transcendental are not necessarily transformed in any fundamental way. They have access to the transcendental and its pre-Transformation powers, and these acquired powers usually cause men to become more successful in the hunt. While it may be tempting to think of enhanced abilities as resulting from contact with some spiritual force, in reality people become more "efficient" because they feel more graceful and confident. They simply feel better because they are attuned to themselves and to the people and natural environment around them. Again, while it is true that these beliefs enable the Sekani to shift agency from individual abilities to a wider and invisible dimension, it is also important that people who are said to have received power have achieved a balance between themselves and others, and between themselves and the natural environment. In other words, "power," hunting "luck," and the Transformer's actions are perfect metonyms of balance and harmony: in each case, potential polarities (contemporary humans versus the transcendental; contemporary humans versus contemporary animals; early humans versus early monstrous animals) are attenuated by bringing the two poles closer to one another (contemporary humans obtain transcendental power; contemporary humans eat animal flesh if the animal sacrifices itself; early humans move closer to animal perfection, and early animals move closer to human imperfection). The ideal is always integration that does not sacrifice or eradicate the elements that define the opposition. In other words, Sekani notions of integration favor placing elements in a relation of complementarity rather than on a hierarchical ladder; or, put another way, they create an arbitrary hierarchy to reach a state of equilibrium.

In brief, acquiring power is the result of an experience. It is not something that can be taught. Nor is power a gift in the usual sense of the word, even though it is acquired from animals, who, after all, are enticed into the contact that results in power. Power can be thought of as a disease, a contamination by a force stronger than the individual. The trick is to limit contact, which Athapaskan hunters do by a series of prohibitions and taboos, such that people do not become dominated by the force they are actively seeking. One such prohibition is

talking about the experience and about acquired powers. With the
threats to cultural continuity from the consequences of the flooding
of the southern Sekani homeland in 1968, the possibilities of learning this traditional knowledge became more than limited. People no
longer came into contact with "animal doctors," who, as the Sekani
say, now refuse to speak to the Sekani because of the inequilibrium
that became typical of post-flood life. In simple terms, how could animals be enticed into "infecting" willing hunters after people stopped
hunting? If they no longer acted as hunters, how could men transform
themselves into symbolic prey?

The situation in the north, however, was very different. After spending nearly eleven months in the south, I went to Fort Ware in 1979,
nearly 250 kilometers north of the southern community of McLeod
Lake. People in Fort Ware still hunted and lived a more "traditional"
lifestyle. Some people were still in contact with animal doctors. Unfortunately, the old rules were still in effect, and people would not
talk about power (though everyone knows the powers attached to individuals by their "luck" in particular hunting situations). Ironically,
some older people in McLeod Lake had willingly talked about this
subject precisely because they believed that it no longer mattered as
much, with the animal doctors refusing to communicate with people;
they were too "far in the bush" to hear humans breaking the rules
of silence. I was therefore in a situation of having glimpsed a "traditional" and somewhat exotic way of thinking in one locale and then
living its effects silently (and ignorantly) in another. For an anthropologist, it seemed ironic.

The Dog Looked at me Patiently

I was not much interested in questions of power at the time, however. It seemed much more urgent to understand people's political responses to the horrific situation into which they had been plunged
by the building of the dam. I struggled to understand the violence
that seemed to rip apart McLeod Lake by contextualizing it against
the "traditional" harmony of Fort Ware. The result was that, for the
next two decades, I struggled to understand the Sekani way of living

power without ever contextualizing it in an academic venue by publications or conferences. I rarely spoke about it, since I, too, was considered contaminated.

I had many strange dealings with animals, but one stands out enough that I've carried the image with me for twenty years. One day, a woman came to my cabin with a large dog on a leash. That was unusual, since women usually have nothing to do with dogs, which the Sekani consider to be work animals used only while hunting. These dogs are never allowed to stray since they are aggressive. I was sitting on the steps in front of my one-room cabin. It was near sunset and my workday was over. I was thinking that it was time to get my notes in order, make some bannock bread, split some wood for cooking and heating. I concentrated on the stick I was whittling instead. Time to do all that later. I was tired.

I was quickly brought back to reality as Marie approached. The dog, which had no name, weighed more than she did and was fairly aggressive, I knew. Now, it was following her quietly. This dog, like the others in the community, recognized only one master. To put them in harnesses, one needed to out-alpha the alpha male and have no fear. This dog was a fine specimen, half wolf, it seemed. He never barked, like the other large work dogs in the community. They would impassively regard passersby, apparently with a neutral look, but I knew better than to get too close and try to pet them. I had once tried to tame one by feeding it every day for nearly two weeks. Every day, I got closer and closer, and the dog began recognizing me when I came out of my cabin with a piece of bannock. He would sit down on his haunches. Just when I thought I had tamed him (he waited without growling till I tossed him the food), he nearly took my hand off. It was not his fault. The Sekani had told me not to play with dogs. The only other breed in the community was a small Chihuahua-like monster (undoubtedly a Tahltan bear dog) with an even worse temperament.

As Marie came closer, the dog sat down quietly and cocked its head in my direction. Marie told me that the dog had bitten a fishhook that had been stuck in a piece of dried fish she was feeding it, and asked me to get it out. The hook had gone clean through the upper gums on the right, just behind the canine (what else?). It was a nasty thing, nearly two and half inches long. I told Marie I could do nothing, since the only way I knew to get it out would be to cut the thing with a pair of pliers. My Swiss army knife was not so equipped. She simply repeated, calmly, that I do something. The dog looked at me patiently. The eye of the hook was too large to push it through the bone. I decided to start cutting the gums below the hook. The dog's black lips and gums seemed to magnify the size of its white teeth. The dog was immobile as I sawed away. At any moment, I expected a nasty bite and mentally calculated how many stitches I would need (which I would have to do myself since there were no medical people around; strangely, as I had already found out, normal thread works fine in an emergency). I got more nervous as I hit bone. The dog's right eye looked at me, but it stayed quiet. Finally, I got the thing out. The dog shut its bloody mouth, got up, took a few steps toward Marie and sat down next to her. Marie picked up the leash and walked away with the dog in tow.

I never forgot the patience of the beast when I was mutilating it, nor its large eye looking directly at me (obviously, I was only inches away since I was working with both hands in its mouth). Afterward, I wondered why Marie had come to me. I had no particular talents with animals. I was a mediocre hunter, as far as the Sekani knew. In fact, I never killed because I thought what was a necessity for the Sekani would be for me merely a vainglorious confirmation of being in an exotic field locale. My old Lee Enfield was a backup gun, in case the first hunter missed. No one ever did, so no one knew that in fact I was a very good shot. For the Sekani, I was "their" anthropologist, a white man whose questions and presence they tolerated with grace and humor. I could occasionally solve a few bureaucratic problems for them, but no one would have ever asked me to solve one of "their" problems. It remained a mystery, even after I had asked Marie why she had come to me. She had merely shrugged.

I often wondered about my alleged power (I had other strange experiences with dogs), especially since dogs normally do not confer power (only animals that hunt are thought to have power). But, as some people told me, who knows, for white men? One day, in 1997, it came to me. There is no climax to my story, no sudden flash precipitated by a particular event. I was not out of mind because of a transcendental epiphany in the field. I had begun working on a book about Sekani mythology (Desgent and Lanoue 2005). I also had long been exploring various aspects of my model of political culture in various domains and culture areas, so I obviously had the benefit of thinking about the problem of what constituted power from different points of view.

I think the major factor in understanding what had been before my eyes all this time was the fact that I had been a nomad for twenty years, even after I had begun working full time in Montreal in 1994. For reasons too complex to explore here, I had been moving around all my life, from city to city, language to language, country to country, continent to continent. Initially, most of these moves were for the usual reasons, for middle-class white men of my generation: jobs and career. Later, in my thirties, it became a habit and an emotional necessity. I remember when I got tenure at my university, normally a huge step in one's career. My boss told me the news and then, she added: "I know you are disappointed because it means you cannot move around anymore."

In fact, I got tired of it all. Moving no longer made sense on an emotional level. For years, moves had not been related to career, which, in terms of North American middle-class upbringing, had, at least in the past, furnished a ready-made and somewhat satisfying justification. I no longer felt the emotional and psychological engagement arising from displacement. In simple terms, I felt European while living in Canada and Canadian while living in Europe. The usual metaphors of place no longer made sense.

Space is a major metaphor for identity everywhere in the West. It is, however, so polysemic that it is not a simple sign of social or personal identity (see Geertz 1996). Space as a metaphor also refers to psychic conditions, depending on how it is politicized according to larger ideological frames of space and time. The apparent importance of space *or* time varies only according to whether people engage an explicit discourse or tacit but nonetheless shared meanings. People in Native North American band societies, for example, profess values that are discursively situated in terms of territory but not in terms of time. Nomadic hunters constitute themselves and their social organization as users and owners of territories, not as inheritors of a tradition. These people, however, situate themselves in local hierarchies and networks on the basis of who was living (and therefore working) with their parents in the previous generation.

Briefly, the Sekani have primary and secondary brotherhoods very similar to those described by Turner and Wertman (1977) for the Cree, in which children of people who worked closely together are considered close kin who should collaborate closely, especially in the early stages of a person's life. "In-laws" (the secondary brotherhood) are the network from which partnerships (usually, wife's brother or wife's sister's husband) are formed during adulthood. In both cases, partnerships are always hierarchical (a junior and a senior partner define a hunting group). In the final stages of a person's working life, junior partners are selected from the senior's hunting group of origin (usually, sister's husband or sister's son), even though this has long ceased to function as a unit. In fact, the offspring of parent's secondary brotherhood are a child's primary brotherhood, which roughly defines a circle of collaboration and incest that provides an initial point of reference for defining other potential bonds, marriage, and partnerships acquired through marriage.

Time, in the sense of history, is meaningless since it is not politicized as a meaningful category that structures the present. The past, in other words, is very much in the present since parents are still active when younger children begin hunting and trapping, transforming the potential partnerships of the primary brotherhood into social capital to develop a secondary brotherhood. Although there is no history in our Western sense in these societies, time is everywhere embedded in space, even though individual memories cannot be easily grafted onto a larger semiotic dynamic defining time as an ontologically independent category (Lanoue 1992).

Place, however, is highly politicized. First, the physical limits of the homeland are defined by the sum of the extent of the displacement of individual hunting groups. Second, even hierarchy is linked to space, since it is the role of the headman to suggest displacements to individual hunters that will bring them into areas of the homeland that have been temporarily abandoned; such areas are dangerous invitations to occupation by neighboring groups, potentially leading to conflict. Finally, displacement defines the normal habitus of the hunter's daily life. Hunting and trapping are activities that require continual displacement. Space is therefore the main trope for expressing the survival of the band.

When people argue that place is constructed (as in the two collections edited by Low and Lawrence-Zuniga 2003 and Feld and Basso 1996), they mean that space is inscribed with complex meanings that become powerful metonyms and metaphors for social life. Space is a metaphor than can be "embodied" (Low and Lawrence-Zuniga 2003, 5), in the sense that it is felt as a subjective condition. Space is thus not only a metaphor inscribed with social life, it is also an active agent that "spatializes" social life and individuals. It is linked to "time" only indirectly through the intersubjectivity of daily life.

Here is what I am trying to say: I was struggling for years to understand a notion, power, that seemed to be linked to *time* because I had conceptualized it as a holdover from before time began as such. I thought of power as a survival of an atavistic force. My obsession with time prevented my seeing what was under my nose all along, since it was clearly a mistake to try to understand power in terms of time in the context of a culture that neither places importance on time to conceptualize and organize daily life nor uses it as a metaphor for social reproduction. My temporal obsession was clearly a product of ideological interference, since I had long worked out the importance of space for the organization of hunting and for social reproduction (Lanoue 1992).

The real clue to understanding power lies in the artificial contrast between a hunter's normal mobility and his ritual immobility that transforms him into symbolic prey, which only *then* metaphorically evokes the animal's powers that survived from the pre-Transformer epoch. In this sense, these powers are, literally, time-less since they are unchanged by the passage of time and never explicitly created; they just *are*. That is the point of the Transformer stories, dealing with the transformation of Giant Animals' physical bodies and not their spirit, that I had been missing: if things are "timeless" (to use an expression from our society), then they are not "time-ful" as they are in the West. They are simply unmarked for time.

It was only when I abandoned my own spatial meanderings that I understood what space meant to the Sekani in terms of acquiring power. Only by understanding in very personal terms that space and place no longer meant anything to me as means of understanding myself was I able to see that space and place were fundamental in defining power for the Sekani. Power is linked to time, but time is, and can only be, metaphorized in spatial terms. Access to power can be evoked only by immobility, which is a meaningful trope only in the context of people who have somatized the need to move continually over the homeland to survive and to politicize territory. My coming to understand the phenomenon was far from the interplay of elements that define the "ecstatic side" (as the editors put it, in their call for contributions) of fieldwork. I did eventually understand something about power by "relaxing [my] controls," but it was a form of control and agency that was so somatized and part of my being that I was completely unaware of it when I did my initial fieldwork. I suggest that anthropologists listen not so much to the voices of fieldwork but to the echoes that may still be reverberating many years later.

Notes

1. Among Athapaskan speakers, this power is called by several names: *nadetche* by the Sekani (according to Jenness 1937, 68, although the Sekani in 1978–1979 never used the word); *zhaak* (which Legros 1999 translates as "grace"); *ink'on* among the Dogrib and Dene-Tha (Helm 1994); and *nitsit* among the Kaska (R. McDonnell, personal communication). Discussions of the same concept are found also in Sharp (1987, 1988) for the Chipewyan, in Ridington (1988b) for the Beaver, and in Goulet (1998) for the Dene Tha.

Part Four

Keeping Violence and Conflict in View

At the time of launching this book project, Edward Abse reminded us that we ought also to pay attention to the darker side of the exploration of other forms of knowing and of fieldwork entanglements. This darker side is expressed not so much in "ecstasy" as in its opposite, "paranoia," from the Greek *para*, "beside" or "beyond," and *noos*, "mind." Engaged in the world of sorcerers and healers, authors note that "the insider/outside dialectic of ethnographic fieldwork (Thom 2004, 117) produces a wide range of emotional and intellectual responses to tensions felt in the context of competing loyalties: to competing hosts and to one's profession; to one's previous identities and to one's emerging, more complex self transformed through narratives and experiences of the dark side of life.

In "Don Patricio's Dream: Shamanism and the Torments of Secrecy in Fieldwork among the Mazatecs," Edward Abse reflects on the study of shamanism and encounters with sorcery among the Mazatec Indians of southern Mexico to explore epistemological and ethical quandaries involved in the pursuit of ethnographic knowledge. The narration of a fieldwork experience describes a gradual shift of emphasis in research activity away from relatively detached observation and structured techniques of inquiry, toward an unwitting (and unwilling) intensive participation in the tortuous social dramas of his hosts, in which he finally appears as the alleged victim of aggressive magical attacks. He explores the ways in which co-participation in a culturally specific form of paranoia ultimately became the intersubjective method of his field research, as well as the trembling grounds for relative objectivity. With regard to the more ethical aspects of this endeavor, he also touches upon the various complexities of "informed consent" and its ever-renegotiated production through a dialectic of mutual and self-deception and revelation on the part of, and between, fieldworker and hosts.

In "Clothing the Body in Otherness," Janferie Stone shows how the choice of a field site may evolve from a series of chance encounters that in hindsight seem to form a pattern. She suggests that while we think that we actively catch the moments when the familiar opens into the exotic and explore it until the exotic becomes familiar, we are more often than not caught or perhaps even chosen by our subject worlds. To demonstrate this is the case Stone describes her interaction for more than a decade with a Kaqíchikel Maya weaver from highland Guatemala. Given that this weaver wears *traje* (traditional dress) even when she comes to California to teach her art, Stone explores the Kaqíchikel Maya presentation of oneself as an *indígena* and the use of the tales of the "ancients" to explain one's personal power and ability to traverse distance and hardship. Stone focuses on the relationship of one of the most quotidian of practices in Maya society, the act of dressing, with Maya representations of women who have undressed beyond their human flesh, becoming *nawales*, their "animal others." She ties such tales of transformations to the spiritual development of individuals within their life cycles and to the sociopolitical histories of the Maya peoples during *la violencia* of the Guatemalan Civil War and genocide.

Duncan Earle writes from the perspective of a consultant to an international NGO working with Quiche' Mayas in Guatemala. He describes how they took him deep into their world, more than he ever dreamed possible. His is an account of the transformation of an applied anthropologist who goes to the field thinking he knows how to fix at least some of the problems of the world. When deeply settled in the field, however, he came to the realization that he himself was in need of fixing first, to better take on the task he originally envisioned, and second, to come of age as an anthropologist. Quiche' Maya diviners, recognizing the esoteric signs of destiny, insist on teaching him the ancient shamanic teachings of the "count of the days" (the

Maya calendar) and its use in divination and healing. They show him how this is the first move in a nuanced understanding of their whole life way, the basis of any notion of planned change. The way his account is told itself suggests the process of personal and professional transformation.

11. Don Patricio's Dream: Shamanism and the Torments of Secrecy in Fieldwork among the Mazatecs

EDWARD ABSE

The American Anthropological Association's "Code of Ethics" is prefaced by the statement "In a field of such complex involvements and obligations, it is inevitable that misunderstandings, conflicts, and the need to make choices among apparently incompatible values will arise." And when such conflicts of interest do arise, we are told that "the interests of the people with whom we work take precedence over other considerations." Why? Because "the anthropologist's first responsibility is to those whose lives and cultures they study" (AAA 1998). This statement leaves an important question unanswered: which of those people's interests determines our responsibility when the conflict of values confronting us is between them? This is precisely the sort of ambiguous situation I faced among the Mazatecs, when I found myself involved in a disagreement between shamans, provoked by my presence and activities in the field. Here I shall only obliquely address this question, for which I can provide no good answer, certainly not one that is adequate to forestall the necessity for my individual atonement or that other ethnographers might find at all useful in resolving similar ethical dilemmas of their own.[1]

Instead, this problem serves as the indeterminate and overdetermined context for the recognition of ethical-cum-epistemological difficulties inherent in the fact that anthropology is (and anthropologists are) necessarily two-faced, that is, at least in the sense that knowledge of our host cultures, gained or invented through the intimacy that characterizes personal relationships in the field, is then represented, circulated, and consumed in the impersonal realm of a public academic discourse back home. The "two-faced" metaphor is the Mazatecs' own, what they call *b'éenkoa* and sums up in one word essentially the same meaning as that of our own idiomatic expression. What I allude to has everything to do with the sorts of misgivings voiced by my hosts, which they had to overcome (again and again) if they decided to be among those who cooperated with me in what was for them a very strange project. This was an effort made especially difficult for them since knowledge as a value in and of itself does not in any way correspond to their own indigenous forms of understanding, wherein, as Kenneth Morrison has said of Native Americans generally, "knowledge as power derives [in part and in an important sense] from a cautious scrutiny of the other that seeks evidence of good intention in actual behavior" (1994, 12). Indeed, certain areas of inquiry are refractory both to cooperation itself and, even where limited collaboration is offered, to preconceived eliciting methods intended to bring such relationships to fruition.

On the one hand, then, this chapter explores some of the unanticipated complexities involved in the implementation of a recently elevated ethical tenet of social science research, that is, of "informed consent." I argue that, rather than abiding the polite fiction of a once-and-for-all, decided contractual agreement, such consent and the working alliance that it enables might more realistically be perceived as the ever-renegotiated effect of a dialectic of mutual- and self-deception and revelation between and on the part of fieldworker and informants. On the other hand, I seek to call into question the efficacy of any idealized solutions to what are in fact the intractable problems involved in overcoming the distance between self and other in the collaborative production of ethnographic knowledge.

In the mid-nineties, when I was preparing to embark on fieldwork, an emphasis on "dialogue" and its transparent representation in ethnography was still being promoted by many anthropologists as a corrective for the distortions of power inequalities methodologically constraining and morally compromising our professional endeavors. And yet, the ideal and the practice of dialogue itself present obvious problems from the very outset of one's research, from developing competency in the native language to establishing rapport with host subjects. One issue is especially acute in particular situations such as

I experienced in the field: the problem of secrecy. The Foucauldian or so-called postmodernist insight into the Gordian entanglement of power and knowledge is a basic cultural principle and an implicit working assumption of social life in many Native American societies. This idea is probably not so exotic as it might at first sound; after all, it is one that guides plenty of our own decisions and behavior in everyday life about what to say to whom. Even so, the Mazatecs and other Amerindians do appear to be especially adept at either concealing or carefully imparting potentially efficacious knowledge by evasion, dissimulation, formal pretense, ellipsis, euphemism, and other forms of indirect speech, including the telling of half-truths, and the lie. Also worthy of mention is every Mesoamericanist's favorite, the wall of "*Quién sabe?*" ("Who knows?"), a common-enough response to the ethnographer's questions when it appears that almost everyone except you does indeed know.

Secrecy is not a thing in itself but an aspect of human sociality and as such always culturally specific in its attributes; furthermore, it is subject to different rules and takes on variant qualities at the boundaries between distinct spheres of communication within any given culture. I am not concerned with the full range of Mazatec secrecy in this chapter. Rather, I foreground the issue of esoteric knowledge that pertains to shamanism, both because this is the domain within which the more general principle of secrecy operative in Mazatec culture becomes most explicit, in the form of voiced imperatives, for example, and because it was the focus of my own field research and presented me with the most difficult ethical problem.

However, let the reader beware (as I should have) that what I pose here as the special problem of secrecy in our terms, that is, as if it were simply that which impedes the transfer of certain information, finds no equivalent in Mazatec language or ideas. For them, what is at issue is not so much knowledge of what is secret but of who is party to the sharing of knowledge, where what is most importantly hidden and revealed is not so much the object or content of secrecy but rather the intentions of one's interlocutor. For this reason, the question of access to the esoteric in the Mazatec case is densely interwoven with the more widespread and most pressing existential problem of *confianza*, that is, of establishing and maintaining mutual "trust."

In this chapter, then, while offering few clues to a solution of the ethical problem I encountered, I attempt to provide a concise ethnographic description of the emergence of an entailed intersubjectivity of shared ambivalence between fieldworker and host subject. I begin by introducing the cosmological and social context out of which the moral quandary developed, endeavoring to convey a sense of the predicaments of contemporary Mazatec social life in which I participated—while also foreshadowing the inevitable consequences. Then I present what is admittedly an elliptical narrative illustrating how I inadvertently became the catalyst of a local conflict that led to deeper insights into the ethnographer's dilemma and into the social and psychological dynamics of Mazatec sorcery.

Appearance and Reality in the World of the Mazatecs of Southern Mexico

The Mazatecs are an indigenous Mesoamerican people who live in the extreme north of the state of Oaxaca, Mexico, within a territory of about 2,500 square kilometers, with some further settlements in adjacent areas of the neighboring states of Puebla and Veracruz. There are between 170,000 and 200,000 Mazatecs inhabiting more than 400 communities, the majority of which are either draped along the steep hillsides, perched atop the narrow ridges, set beside the rivers, or nestled down in the lush valleys of the Sierra Madre Oriental, while others are located further to the east, on the coastal plains that stretch toward the Gulf of Mexico. These places range in size from the smaller *rancherías* of perhaps two dozen people, made up of a cluster of households related to one another as a single patrilineal, patrilocal extended family, to the exceptionally large *Ciudad indígena* and municipal center of Huautla de Jiménez, inhabited by more than a score of thousands.

Further details of demographics or of geographic setting would hardly begin to express the Mazatecs' conception of the world and their own place within it. Objective descriptions of this sort do not correspond very well to the Native's point of view—what is in this case a kind of pained "double vision" in the proud certainty of revealed cosmological continuity, on the one hand, and a poignant awareness of irreversible social change, on the other. That sensibility is better expressed through a version of things presented to me by a Mazatec elder, Don Agustín, while we stood together atop *Nindo Chikon Tokoxo*, also known as *el Cerro de la Adoración*, the "Mount of Adoration," abode of the supreme Earth Lord spirit and topographic center of the Mazatec cosmos. At the summit from where we watched the rising sun and enjoyed a view extending in every direction of much of the landscape of the Sierra, Don Agustín said to me:

> You know how the shaman sings in his prayers, *'Ngo kjoabinachjaón tjiná 'ngami*, they say, that "there is a life that is in the sky." *'Ngo kjoabinachjaón tjiná so'nde*, that "there is a life that is on the Earth." *'Ngo kjoabinachjaón tjiná ndachikon*, they say, "there is a life that is in the ocean."

> Look around you: The earth is the flesh, the body of the world. The trees, the great forests, the great jungles are the blankets of the world. The cornfields are the clothes, the *huipíl* dress, of the world. Its muscles are the mountaintops, the hillocks, and the small plains and dells. Its bones: the rocks, the crags and stones . . . Its veins are the rivers, streams, springs, the waterfalls and wells. Its heart is the rain it receives, cast down from the sky above . . . And its blood is all the water that flows over the ground, the oceans, the seas. Its lungs are the caves and caverns, because by means of these it breathes. The volcanoes are from where it smokes its cigars, the World. And that which might be its bellybutton, although protruding, is the Mount of Adoration, and here [where we are standing] is the most sacred place . . .

> But our elders say *"Je kjimajchaya so'nde,"* "Already the world is becoming old"; *"likui tik'oakjini jokji ngas'a, nga ch'indeyasakji,"* "Already it is not like before, like when it emerged, when it was tender."

> Before, there was an abundance of wisdom. Enormous! And the people knew how to live well together. But with the emergence of the dominion of man, well . . . There has come to be more and more of us. Things go turning upside down. Already now there is always strife, they are discontent, and already now they attack one another . . .

Now, when I heard this in January of 1997, relatively early on in my fieldwork, it was far from clear to me exactly what kind of troubles Don Agustin was talking about.

Indeed, when I first arrived among the people of the Sierra, I had been very happily surprised by their conviviality. I left home for the field anticipating a difficult encounter with the embodiment of a stereotypical image of Mesoamerican Indians derived from my reading in the ethnographic literature of the region, conjured up from descriptions perhaps half-misremembered that seemed to portray them as gruffly taciturn, closed, and xenophobic. Portending even worse, soon after my arrival in Mexico I had been told by various persons—most of them bureaucratic functionaries with whom I had dealings in the state capital of Oaxaca—that of all the indigenous peoples in the region, the Mazatecs were known to be the most *canijos*, that is, calculatingly inscrutable, stubborn, and evasive, in short, very difficult to get along with. But when I finally came into their company, I found them to be hospitable, generous, and visibly well disposed toward me. Among themselves, they were obviously gregarious and displayed a great love for music, dances, games, and fiestas. What I witnessed from day to day at first was a lot of playfulness, frequent laughing, and the telling of jokes—even at one another's expense, and without anyone seeming to take serious offense. I confess, then, to having seen them in the beginning only hazily through the smokes of an orientalist's pipe dream, while looking forward to a relatively easy time of it in the field.

Later, however, time and again, in conversation with people of the Sierra, I heard expressed the idea that they find themselves currently in a situation of acute social crisis, caught in a predicament apparently without solution for the simple reason that, as they so often say, "Already now the people don't know how to live together." And, indeed, the way they speak of this problem more generally is as if they were faced with the irremediable loss of some sort of knowledge, what we might refer to as the ethical capacity for peaceful coexistence. In its stead, Mazatecs posit the theory of an inherently violent asociality, and its elaboration has become an obsession that takes center stage in the contemporary moral imagination. This is an idea that is regularly expressed in the insinuating hushed tones of gossip and always with an emphasis on the word *kjoaxíntokon*, referring to a kind of hideous malevolence often concealed behind the mask of friendship. *Kjoaxíntokon* can be literally translated and resolved into its component meanings as "[nominalizer] emoting apart [from others]," a term bilingual Mazatecs spontaneously translate as *envidia*, or "envy," in the natural discourse of unmarked code-switching from their native tongue to Spanish.

Envidia, however, is for them a concept with a range of connotations that includes but surpasses the meaning of what our English word suggests, and so *kjoaxíntokon* is something not easily interpreted in terms of rationalist social science models of cognitive orientation along the lines of, for example, the "Image of Limited Good."[2] Rather, this species of envy is emically understood to be directed against another person's possession and enjoyment of whatever quality or object, or—and this is the peculiarly paranoid genius of Mazatec social thought—to emerge suddenly and unprovoked as a spontaneous response to no particular quality or object at all. *Kjoaxíntokon* is, ultimately and in essence, a conscious indigenous theory of the irrational, albeit never applied to oneself, who is always the actual or the potential innocent victim of the acts of sorcery this foul emotion might inspire others to commit. Indeed, this negative force of asociality is feared especially as the pervasively immanent, dreadfully imminent motivation that will lead others to hire a mercenary shaman to perform destructive rituals against one's person, family, and/or property.

Although sorcery attack can be the straightforward consequence of a mutually acknowledged quarrel between the parties involved, in many of the cases that I was able to observe or to reconstruct in any detail, the effects of sorcery were traced back through shamanic divinations to their alleged instigation by someone who circumstantial evidence would strongly suggest was the elusive object of the victim's unrequited (and unacknowledged) desire for a more active, positive relationship. But, however interpreted, the predatory reach of envy was most often revealed as straining against the grain of relations of spiritual kinship, the elective affinity of *compadrazgo* ritually contracted to establish an enduring bond of obligatory reciprocity in the provision of social and psychological security and support, aid and comfort. Sorcery, then, represents the ultimate betrayal and violent inversion of that *confianza*, or "trust," which the *compadrazgo* relationship is intended to epitomize.

The current discourse of *kjoaxíntokon* or *envidia* bears witness to a sharp increase in the suspicion of its occurrence, suggesting epidemic proportions on a scale not unlike that of the ravages of previously unknown diseases that have afflicted populations in the highlands in recent years. People claim that, like the local outbreaks of cholera in the 1980s and 1990s, the predominance of *envidia* in their lives is something new in their experience. Taking seriously their comparison of past and present, which structures this widespread discourse of plaintive nostalgia, I have been able to discover plenty of historical evidence indicating that the uneasiness manifest in this kind of talk finds its source in something beyond any sort of collective forgetting or the moral deficiencies of this generation as compared with previous ones. Instead, these anxieties and their consequent cultural expressions testify to a contemporary social experience of unprecedented, unbearable ambiguities that have resulted from radical transformations and ruptures in traditional, institutionalized forms of authority, association, and exchange among the Mazatecs. While these changes have occurred over the past century, they appear only recently to have arrived at a point of crisis.

All they say is simply that there is too much evil in the world nowadays. This malignancy is discussed with vague reference to any number of now-prevalent sins, but primarily in terms of what they perceive as an intolerable increase in sorcery activity among themselves. This is what I eventually learned Don Agustín and others really mean by the common expression that "people no longer know how to live together." Furthermore, many who are farmers often speak of how, in the not-so-distant past, harvests were much more abundant than they are now. Decreasing returns on agricultural labor are taken as a sign confirming their increasing awareness that the Earth itself— its fertility and thus its capacity to support the regeneration of life— is rapidly becoming exhausted. "Our Mother Earth," understood to be an organic entity, indeed, a sentient being, "is getting tired" and "drying out," they say.

On the one hand, they speak as if this were the result of ineluctable natural processes of entropy, a measure of the diminishing good available in the universe with the passage of time. On the other hand, such speculations are almost always peppered with insinuations of the role taken by irresponsible and unthinking human agency in hastening rather than forestalling such an inevitable fate of the world, mixing their nostalgia with remorse. Natural and social explanations are intertwined in their blaming the meagerness of harvests also on the fact that the people no longer carry out the proper sacrificial fertility rituals for cornfields. And this, in turn, they say has happened—not only because many shamans have lost the knowledge necessary to perform these rituals—but, more importantly, because people are afraid that if they were to perform these rites, they would incur their neighbors' envy, with dire consequences for their crops and family.

It would be difficult to overemphasize the importance in the past of the agrarian dimension of shamanic practice now virtually lost. Indeed, the abundance of vegetal metaphors in contemporary shamanic curing ritual discourse—a range of human–plant analogies used to describe actual or desired states and attributes of persons undergoing treatments—suggests that this aspect of shamanic practice, ritual specialists' contribution to agricultural reproduction, was in some way fundamental to the Mazatec shamanic complex. Until recent decades, an annual round of ritual interventions, prayers, offerings, animal sacrifice, and so on, that focused on the cornfield and directed toward nature gods and spirits, such as the Lord of Thunder and the Owners of the Earth, was observed in adherence to the traditional Mazatec calendar, or *Chan-chaon-yoma*—a system of time reckoning consisting of eighteen counts, or *veintenas*, of twenty days each (plus an extra count of five inauspicious days at the end of the year)—which scheduled both farmers' labors and associated collective rituals presided over by shamans (Weitlaner and Weitlaner 1946; Cowan 1946, 37–38; Carrera and Van Doesburg 1992).

At the same time that shamanic activity has withdrawn from cornfields, shamans' divined attribution of affliction has changed. In the past, more severe cases of illnesses and suffering were most often attributed to spirits associated with the sacred topography, nature spirits, and Owners of the Earth. The paradigmatic instance of what is called in Mazatec *chi'in*, the encompassing category for "sickness," was apperceived as a rupture in the established order of things as the result of some imbalance or transgression in human–spirit relations. Through the process of divination and other forms of performative and visionary diagnosis, the shaman usually led the afflicted to understand that he or she was suffering as the unfortunate consequence of his or her own actions. For example, by associating their memories of everyday-life events with what was revealed to the shaman in reading the positions of corn kernels tossed onto a cloth or the smokes of burning *copal* tree-resin incense, a patient was likely to remember that on some occasion they had crossed a stream at midday, the very hour when the spirits—the *chikones* or "owners" of the place—come out to eat, and, as a result, he had "stained" their table. Or perhaps, equally typical, it turned out that the patient had cut down a tree in the territory of a *chikon nindo*, a spirit who lives in a nearby cave, without asking permission, that is, without first presenting the appropriate offering. In either case, he had provoked the ire of the spirits who, at that moment, had seized his *sén-nizjin*, literally, his "day image" or "reflection," the soul that remained trapped there in that very place as punishment. For this divined reason, then, the patient had been experiencing all the debilitating symptoms of soul loss. The shaman who discovered the explanation then worked to calm the spirits' anger by praying in negotiation on behalf of his patient and then paying a ransom in the form of ritual offerings.

The fear and dangers of soul loss at the hands of the spirit-owners of nature are these days for the most part only an aspect of older persons' memories. In contrast to this emphasis on supernatural forces beyond human control, the meanings associated with contemporary experience of illness tend to evince that it is the behavior of fellow humans that has come to be more difficult to predict, more worrisome, and potentially even more dangerous. In an overwhelming majority of cases I documented over the course of three years of fieldwork, the preponderant cause of illness and other misfortunes is thought to be the malicious action of others in the immediate social environment. Obviously, then, the relationship between oneself and others in the community is displacing that between humanity and the spirits as a source of preoccupation and is therefore more often now subject to the visionary scrutiny of shamans.

There is a further, deeper sense in which the subjective experience of illness is something quite other than it used to be. Suffering is no longer understood to result from one's own actions as punishment for violation of the sacred and forbidden, however unwitting. Now one has done nothing wrong to incur the illness: one is instead the innocent victim of a neighbor's usually unprovoked, spontaneous envy. Consequently, in contrast to the past, there is now no transgression and, therefore, no redemption, no way to put things right again with the offended party and source of one's misfortune. To suffer in this way, then, marks the awareness of radical evil. Even the imagery associated with soul loss has changed. In the past, divinations matched to a patient's memories of his or her actions prior to an illness event led to the location of the missing soul, represented as trapped in one of the many named sites of the sacred topography inhabited by spirit beings. Lost souls used to be found on mountaintops and in caves and streams. Today, the predicament of the soul caught in the snares of sorcery often places it altogether "off the map" of those more prominent, well-known features of the landscape. Instead, the soul is now more likely discovered to be entrapped inside a tree trunk, in a ditch, under a small rubbish heap, or simply wandering lost somewhere out there in the *jñá*, or "wilderness," in one of many hidden spots scattered across an oneiric and discontinuous geography of nowheres. Alternatively, in cases of mortal illness, dreams or divinations reveal that the soul has been directly "delivered over to death," with no hope of rescue: the sorcerer has either buried the person's soul in the graveyard or has affixed it to some macabre location at the shadowy borders of the cosmos, for example, crucified upon the "Black Cross in the West."

These ideas and experiences appear to represent a historically new vector, at least in terms of the proportional and absolute number of such cases and their directionality, of limiting or extreme representations that are extending the range of the Mazatec imagination about the displacement of the soul. The presenting symptoms of soul loss have remained constant, whatever the cause: it leaves one deprived of the intentional faculties of the will, and of the source of one's renewable energy or "strength," both of which are necessary to the capacity for effectual activity in the world and, ultimately, to physical survival itself. The most immediate and unmistakable signs of soul loss refer to a disturbed state of mind and waning sense of self. The more commonly reported complaints are a strange tiredness that overtakes one early in the day, general listlessness and a sense of heaviness in the body, a lack of appetite, nightmares, and any one of a number of debilitating phobias. Furthermore, chronic bodily symptoms may also be attributed to this condition, whether indirectly, because of the resultant decline in physical resistance to disease, or directly, as a manifestation of the actual location of the displaced soul. For example, erysipelas, a deep red inflammation of the skin accompanied by high fever, is associated with graveyards, and may be understood to arise from a sorcerer's having deposited one's soul there among the dead.

The details that bring out in sharp relief the more subtle and elusive dimensions of change manifest in the sufferers' anguish are most vividly described in dreams that present the experience of soul loss from the externalized soul's point of view. Visions in the sleep of the afflicted reveal a complex symptomatology transcending that of the body, while at the same time providing the significance of waking-life complaints. I was often told by shamans and others that "while the body rests, the soul wanders," and that dreams are effectively the extra-corporeal adventures of the soul. Sometimes, however, to dream is to wake up to the fact that the soul is already elsewhere and in peril, lost and/or immobilized in some way that prevents it from returning to the body. In such unfortunate circumstances, the perceiving soul of dreams, captured in the designs of sorcery, almost invariably experiences itself as trapped, somehow forcibly contained in a certain evil, enchanted, and enclosed space, far from the familiar surroundings of home and the company of fellow human beings. The sensations or emotions that stand out in the telling of such dreams are a near-suffocating claustrophobia and the terror of being alone, in trouble, and cut off from communication with others.

There is a very real sense, then, in which the fate of the soul in sorcery-provoked soul loss precisely mirrors the bizarre and threatening qualities of asociality intrinsic to the culprit's *kjoaxíntokon* or "envy" and from which the anomic state of the victim is believed ultimately to derive. The disjuncture between the soul and body of the afflicted is analogous to that between the hidden intentions of the envious neighbor and his outward gestures extended toward others; both are implicated as divided selves in a situation of estrangement from positive participation in the lives and society of others. Thus the current re-elaborations of Mazatecs upon the age-old theme of soul loss or capture can be understood as the magnifying refractions of those ever-more-profound fears and apprehensions now permeating their social experience.

Caught Between Two Shamans: Ambivalence, Dilemma, and Dream

The possession of special knowledge is the defining characteristic of Mazatec shamans. The Mazatec word or phrase for shaman is *chjota chjine*, literally, "person who knows." What they know, for example, are varieties of divination techniques and healing rituals, and details of cosmological reference and principles necessary to their efficacy. They may also control dangerous knowledge about deadly ritual methods of sorcery, something allegedly acquired not through practice but through visionary investigation of attacks on victims whom they attend as patients.

All shamans claim that their special knowledge comes to them directly from the deities and spirits in the course of their own individual visionary experience. Ordinarily, this knowledge is jealously guarded from rival practitioners. I was often told by shamans that each first acquired his or her healing knowledge during initiatory ritual ordeals that culminated in being presented by either God or the spirits with his or her own *Libro de Conocimiento*, or "Book of Knowledge."[3] The phrase neither refers to a literal object of printed leaves sewn and bound together, nor is merely a figurative expression; instead, it attests to the revelation of a kind of supernatural entity—typically addressed in Mazatec by many names, as in the lilting repetitive sequence in this excerpt from a recording I made of a shaman's celebratory *alabanzas*, or "praise" chants and songs:

Xon tsje	Pure [clean] Book
Xon naská	Beautiful Book
Xon nizjin	Book of the Day
Xon xoño	Book of the Morning Dew
Xon fate	Shining Book
Xon én	Book of Language

This "book" (*xon*) somehow encases or embodies knowledge of special ritual languages and healing techniques. These teachings are made manifest to and are assimilated by the shaman only "little by little" (the oft repeated expression in Mazatec is "*tjobi, tjobi*" or, in Spanish, "*poco a poco*"), as they gradually are made available in the form of divinely revealed solutions realized in the attempt to cure specific cases of illness. Knowledge is something one actively accumulates with experience over time, even though in some sense all of it is always already there in the Book of Knowledge pertaining to each shaman.

Many ritual practitioners are wont to insist that each shaman's book is entirely different from those of others. Yet the claim that such knowledge belongs in any exclusive sense to the individual shaman is belied or at least attenuated by the fact that there are many similarities and even equivalences between the various shamans' specific practices. In each case, these are for the most part apparently a selection from a common extensive repertoire of ritual forms that even have the same names. Indeed, experienced patients who consult with different shamans are prone to misrecognize as evidence of sorcery whatever minor idiosyncratic elaborations they might discern in a given shaman's practice. All this suggests that the transmission of shamanic knowledge moves along channels other than or in addition to the visionary. For example, most shamans I interviewed referred to members of their extended family who were also *chjota chjine*—a grandparent, an aunt, or maybe an uncle. There were almost always small children present bumbling about during otherwise solemn ritual occasions. And, of course, adults and children witness and participate in healing ceremonies as patients, including those who will later become shamans in their own right. From this perspective, then, it is ironic that shamans are very jealous of their knowledge and busily guarding from one another secrets that, to a significant extent, they all in effect share. Indeed, the shared nature of their beliefs and practices is what allows us to speak of "Mazatec shamanism" as such, and could be taken as evidence for arguing that the use of this shamanic knowledge appertains collectively and exclusively to all Mazatecs, as something that ought to be guarded against appropriation by outsiders.

Normally, Mazatecs are not troubled by the implications of this inherent contradiction between their individualist model of the production or acquisition of shamanic knowledge and their insistence upon uniform standards in the evaluation of its performance. Perhaps the occasion for thinking about this issue did not arrive until I did. The conflict of values latent in this context came to a head as I found myself caught between two shamans with opposing views on the disposition of sacred knowledge. One is Don Nicolás, an elder shaman, renowned for his great powers and a long career of community service, whom I had approached with a proposal of collaboration that he firmly refused. The other is Don Patricio, a younger shaman who had already cautiously begun to discuss his knowledge and experience with me.

One day when I was away, Don Nicolás sought out and publicly berated Don Patricio for working with me. This constituted an unusual event, given that Mazatecs, unless they are extremely drunk, normally avoid public displays of anger. According to those who later told me of the incident, the older man had vehemently accused Don Patricio of "shameless" involvement in something that was, he charged, "entirely a business." Don Nicolas furthermore declared his not wanting to have anything to do with it himself. He voiced as well his opposition to any other shaman's speaking with me about such "delicate" matters—employing the usual euphemism for what we would call "sacred" concerns. From what I could gather, he was asserting that such ritual and cosmological knowledge rightfully belongs to Mazatecs alone, principally their shamans.

The gist of Don Nicolás's harangue was that Don Patricio had allied himself with me "just for the money." This is an accusation of sinister resonance for a shaman, given the central place in the Mazatec imagination of the lure of lucre in the formation of the *chjota chjine tjaon*, or nefarious sorcerer, the sort of ritual practitioner who uses his or her powers to injure rather than to heal others, a good shaman gone irredeemably bad.

Shamans who remain true to the spirit of the gift of healing will not explicitly request payment for their services. Indeed, it is generally recognized as the most important characteristic of an authentic and just shaman that he or she will expect nothing more from those whom they benefit than, as they say, "that which springs forth from the heart." In contrast, it is believed that acts of sorcery have a specific price and that the shaman who will carry out such rites demands at least ten times what one would usually expect for legitimate practices. Thus, to be accused of receiving disproportionate fees in connection with one's status as shaman is to fall under the shadow of larger suspicions.

It is true that the financial arrangement between Don Patricio and myself was without precedent and thus open to question. As far as I am aware, this particular community had never been visited by an anthropologist before, and my appearance there was peculiar enough; my relationships with specific individuals among them were even more of a mystery, and subject to much speculation and inquiry. During my extended periods of residence elsewhere in the Sierra, some families had sought to remake my unusual presence in their lives in the image of a more recognizable role by extending invitations to become a minor *padrino*, or "godfather," to their children, and so to sponsor some element of a celebration in honor of a son's or a daughter's passage through one or another stage of life. In this manner, they were able to formalize our relationship and to ensure in a way not blatantly coercive more substantial (and more publicly visible) gestures of reciprocity on my part, and I was very pleased to be given the opportunity. For instance, as *padrino de los mariachis* at the coming-of-age fiesta of one of my *ahijadas*, or "goddaughters," I was entrusted with arranging for and paying the group of musicians who played at the event, and also with keeping them going all night long with liberal servings of *aguardiente* sugar-cane liquor while everyone was dancing.

In my new location I was the guest of the village doctor, a young man from a neighboring community who had received four years of medical training in a faraway city before returning to the Sierra to practice among his own people, and who wanted to take part in my research there in order to learn more himself about the shamans whom his patients also consulted for their health complaints. People often asked what he was getting in return for allowing me to live with him in his home. With a shrug and a smile, he would always humbly answer *nada*, "nothing." This was true. He would not accept any rent or other payment from me, although I was able to provide food for our table from the local shopkeepers. But when the time came for him to marry, I seized upon the chance to be the couple's *padrino del toro*, "godfather of the bull," the one who would procure the large animal to be sacrificed in preparation for the ceremony and then butchered to make ready *caldo de res* soup to feed all the company. In this way, I was able to return a gift to my friend while not inciting the envy of others, since they all shared in it: more than half the community was present, and there was enough meat and broth to feed more than two hundred people for two days.

Reciprocity with Don Patricio was of a different order, made neither in public nor in kind, but in regular installments of Mexican *pesos*, in exchange for his time and help. Prior to this point in my fieldwork, my experience and working alliances with other shamans had been much less formal, but out of my growing concern to be even more straightforward and easier to understand in my dealings with ritual specialists, I decided to try proposing a more "professional" arrangement from the outset; in short, it was my idea, and Don Patricio was well pleased with it. And yet he was unsure of just what his contribution was to be or why I wanted it, despite my repeated attempts at explanation, and surely it was even harder to comprehend for others who were not directly involved in our negotiations and who could only imagine what it was all about. Certainly, for a shaman to be compensated for anything other than divinations and healing was as anomalous as it was novel. But our odd relationship was soon brought within the orbit of more familiar, traditional forms of Mazatec association. We became friends, exchanging gifts and unpaid visits to one another, and not long afterward, he became my protector in the aftermath of

Don Nicolás's confrontation with him, during which the elder shaman engaged in more subtle gestures of hostility and social avoidance
toward both of us. This ultimately resulted in a situation of two-fold
irony, given Don Nicolás's claims and intentions. Subsequent unusual
events, Don Patricio's dreams, the untimely death of his mother, and
the development of certain physical symptoms of my own were interpreted as indicating that it was Don Nicolás who was himself practicing sorcery—and against us! Furthermore, as a result, Don Patricio
was led to reveal to me two especially secret healing rituals as part of
his effort to cure and shield us from the effects of these attacks.

To compound the irony even more, before Don Nicolás challenged
Don Patricio and so sparked suspicions of the threat of sorcery, my
working relationship with him was not going so smoothly as the older
shaman might have imagined. Up until that point, Don Patricio has
been somewhat reluctant to answer the questions I put to him and
was instead more interested in interviewing me, not only about the
nature of my work, but especially with regard to what the other shamans I had worked with in other communities had shown and told
me. Perhaps he was in part testing me, to see whether I might be capable of such betrayal.

Later, after we had established an easier rapport, he told me a dream.
This event marked a new level of trust in our relationship, one that
sustained us throughout the drama of sorcery and counter-sorcery
that ensued. This was the dream:

> He is cutting firewood, down in the forest on the hillside below
> his home. Suddenly he is working on something else: he is harvest-
> ing coffee beans. "Then the owner/master of the land arrived and
> said to me, 'Don't cut this coffee, because this coffee is mine.' And
> I answered him, 'How can it be yours? The land is yours, yes, but
> I planted these coffee trees.' And the owner/master said, 'No. But
> don't you cut them.' Then he, the owner/master, disappeared again."
> Then Don Patricio finds himself walking on a road, and he notices
> that the road is filled with mud. He arrives near the top of the road,
> where the muddy stretch comes to an end. "And after that I saw
> Eduardo up ahead. I don't know what he was doing, but the point

is that he was talking; he was speaking in English. And I wanted to talk with him, and he did not speak to me. He turned and went away from me, over the top of the hill and out of sight." (Field-notes, April, 20, 1998)

I heard this dream as the expression of Don Patricio's ambivalence, his desires and fears, about working with me. In trying to understand the dream sequence as a whole, I find that certain elements appear transparent if we view the imagery presented in each of the three episodes as referring to that contained in the others in the development of similar or contrasting themes. From the outset, we can gain interpretive purchase on this dream if we first also take into consideration the more obvious features of Mazatec symbolism in its manifest content.

The dream begins with Don Patricio cutting firewood, a condensed symbol of his labor to provide for his home, a morally appropriate activity free from ambiguity or conflict. The second part of the dream appears to express both his moral qualms and his subsequent rejection of them. "Suddenly" he finds himself picking coffee. Coffee, the chief export commodity grown in the Sierra, is, for the Mazatecs, the most powerful image representing exchange value (as opposed to the use value of firewood in this case) and access to the accumulation of hard cash, much like the money Don Patricio continues to receive by working with me. This association is made especially compelling by what immediately follows in the dream, which appears in contrast to the fact that in waking reality Don Patricio owns the land where his coffee trees grow. Therefore, the relationship in this episode of the dream must refer to something other than that between Don Patricio and a landlord in the strictly literal or mundane sense. I contend that the "master/owner of the land," who shows up to warn him against harvesting the coffee, represents what we might understand to be a kind of cultural conscience, opposing Don Patricio's desire to take something of value from the land to exchange with outsiders for money.

Don Patricio refers to this figure using the same phrase conventionally used by Mazatecs to refer to Earth Lord spirits of the mountains, the ultimate "master/owners of the land" in the Sierra, and divine stewards of the people's prosperity. Is Don Patricio not asserting his right to cut the coffee, that is, to work with me, in effect exchanging a cultural property, his shamanic knowledge, for cash? Is he not disputing the figure of cultural conscience's command by insisting that, yes, the land belongs to the "master/owner" but that it is he who planted and worked the coffee and so he may cut it if he pleases? Don Patricio recognizes a cultural patrimony, symbolized by the land, which among Mazatecs is transferred through patrilineal inheritance—and, in this case, Don Patricio came to his shamanic vocation just as he came into possession of his land, that is, as passed down from his father, and before that to his father from his grandfather—as belonging to something bigger than and beyond himself, perhaps to the Mazatecs as a people, or to the Mazatec "Geist." However, he is the one who cultivated his own branch of knowledge, and so it is his to harvest and to sell. The dream episode is thus an assertion of Don Patricio's sense of individual entitlement as against the restrictive claims of a partially internalized cultural conscience. We recognize in this an echo of his earlier confrontation with Don Nicolas in which Don Patricio gave a defiant reply similar to the one in the dream.

The same theme of ambivalence and internal conflict is represented in the final scene of the dream. Don Patricio is walking up a muddy road. This is an unmistakable conventional image from Mazatec shamanic initiatory visions, an ordeal of temptation presenting the choice between two roads that lead either to benevolent virtue in healing practice or to illegitimate accumulation of wealth and ultimate damnation in the practice of sorcery. As one shaman described the correct choice: "On the straight road we find just a quiet path, upon which only the sound of birds, the continuous babbling of a stream, the murmur of a river, like a new dawn, is heard, that and the songs and conversations of angels." The evil way, in contrast, is visualized as a miry and wide road of soft and deep mud.

Again, then, Don Patricio's "selling" of his knowledge to me provokes him to question whether he has thus entered into an immoral undertaking. The concluding incident of the dream is when he finds me, Eduardo, standing at the top of the road and beyond the mud, where I am not listening to him while speaking in a language that he cannot understand. This imagery suggests his misgivings about the cultural distance between us and indicates his feeling something between hope and despair about finding somewhere or some way for us to speak together beyond the morally ambiguous terrain muddied by the question of pecuniary self-interest. That is, he might very well wonder whether he can avoid or overcome in his association with me what could amount to a betrayal of the sacred commitment to pursue the path of altruistic good in his shamanic vocation.

Overall, the sequential unfolding of Don Patricio's dream manifests a kind of teleological movement through a hierarchy of motives, from the at least partial resolution of ambivalence and guilt about working with me toward the expression of his anxious desire for communication, recognition, and continued friendship. He does not want me to turn my back on him and walk away. I must admit that at first I took solace and encouragement from his placing my image in the dream at the top of the road, at a spot free from mud. Nonetheless, is there not also in this image the hint that Don Patricio suspects I was in some sense actively deceiving him and perhaps all other shamans and Mazatecs who so generously provided me with their knowledge? Certainly, at least, it contains the premonition that his involvement with me was something that would lead finally to disappointment and that I would abandon our hard-won relationship in order to pursue further my own purposes, which were unintelligible to him. This foreboding is clearly there, again, in Don Patricio's memory of how the dream ended: "I don't know what he was doing, but the point is that he was talking, he was speaking in English. And I wanted to talk with him, and he did not speak to me. He turned and went away from me, over the top of the hill and out of sight."

There is more in this final episode of the dream than Don Patricio's accurate intuition that the very motivations that lead us (at least at first) to develop close relationships during fieldwork are the same ones that will take us away from them—that is, eventually we leave, perhaps never to return. It also points to a more general ethical problem of anthropological interpretations and representations entailed in the fact that we speak about our host subjects in languages they themselves might not understand (for example, in the terms of a style of dream analysis very different from their own). Furthermore, even while talking together with them, we do not necessarily share our hosts' beliefs about the world, yet we must show ourselves to be conversant in the issues that most interest us in order to provoke deeper conversation about these topics. This priming the pump often involves feigned adherence to attitudes and ideas foreign and even contradictory to our own. Certainly, in research on esoteric traditions, rarely will anyone tell you but just a little bit more than they at least think you already know and have properly understood, or, in our terms, "believe."[4]

From the Mazatec point of view, insofar as I understand it, my preoccupations about the problem of honesty in this regard would be seen as futile. For them, I would imagine, the question ought to be framed not in terms of belief or faith versus the doubt or skepticism we must admit informs our complex anthropological (re)interpretations, but rather in terms of knowledge about the world around us versus ignorance. Accepting their own categories of understanding, then, perhaps removes this particular issue, at least, from ethical consideration. For the Mazatecs, pretending to be knowledgeable when one is in fact ignorant is not so much a problem of deceit as it is one of foolishness.

That said, we must still consider the ethical quandary of choosing between honoring Don Nicolás's claims that Mazatec shamanic knowledge is a collective cultural property not to be shared with outsiders and accepting Don Patricio's gift of that knowledge, which he feels is his to grant, or perhaps even to sell. My acceding to the elder shaman's moral demand, while never addressed directly to me but made to the younger shaman, would have implied either going native or burning my fieldnotes and going home. It may be impossible to decide who is right and who is wrong: Don Nicolás or Don Patricio? In the end, I chose not to relinquish the responsibilities I had assumed in my role as ethnographer, a decision that may appear only to beg the question but which was made in the sincere belief that it is not my place to judge an issue between Mazatecs. What I did, then, was to continue to pursue my research with Don Patricio and the other shamans who were still willing to work with me, while risking the hazards involved.

That is not to say that I am free from ethical responsibilities concerning secrecy and the issues of consent, confidentiality, and exposure. I want to be clear that I will never disclose anything any Mazatec shared with me and asked me not to repeat or publish. My hosts requested that I keep silent in many ways. For example, some of them asked me to preserve only their anonymity, while others insisted that I never publish transcriptions or translations of their sacred chants. Inevitably, then, my ethnographic record of Mazatec shamanism must remain somewhat incomplete. Will this lead to distortion, some sort of misrepresentation by omission, in the published results of my research? My answer is a qualified no. That is, I do not believe the issue of secrecy poses a special case in the problems of ethnographic representation. After all, even if we felt free to tell all that we know about our host culture, all that we can say must fall short of the subject, or even of the way we ourselves conceive of it, both of which always remain to some degree refractory to representation. Indeed, it may well be that this quality of elusiveness and inexhaustibility is what the outsider's ethnographic insights and insider's secrets have in common, and what in some significant degree determines their compelling efficacy as forms of symbolic knowledge.

Conclusion: The Play of Shadows of a Doubt

I have so far presented a reading of Don Patricio's dream from an analytic perspective involving the discovery of meanings latent in the symbolism of the text as recorded in my fieldnotes. What I have yet to mention is that the shaman provided his own equally cogent interpretation of the dream at the time of its telling. For Mazatecs, the conventional understanding of a dream wherein a person turns his back on you is that the person has doubts about you. It indicates that there is a hidden lack of trust toward the dreamer on the part of the dreamed. After recounting his dream, Don Patricio was careful to insist that the usual explanation was inappropriate in this case, that there was no real problem of trust between us, that we have no doubts about one another. Rather, he said, the dream indicated that "there must be *'ntjao*, an evil wind. That is, from the people who see you coming here [to my home]. It is because the people remain with the doubt." In other words, Don Patricio meant that the suspicion and busybody speculations of others had taken the form of an invisible sinister influence that works to break our relationship of mutual trust, or *confianza*, by entering into our dreams.

What I find most interesting about this episode—insofar as it might shed light on other cases of the fear of magical aggression—is that it signals the emergence of a kind of paranoia that would later develop into the apperception of sorcery attacks against us by Don Nicolás. In general, Mazatecs seem unwilling or unable to think that internal conflict is inherent to the self, or that ambivalence is intrinsic to social relationships. When either makes an appearance, as in this dream, it is instead construed as a contingent evil coming from without, threatening to affect the integrity of the self or of social relationships. In retrospect, I now believe that the sense of sorcery's presence, as it developed later on in this case, was really born out of Don Patricio's sense of guilt—disavowed and so turned inside out, as it were—derived from his working with me. Even so, it must be said that it would be a mistake to reduce his desire to collaborate with me to motives of mere profit. For one thing, the bottom line for him is drawn at a different level than that. Given the risks of sorcery attacks and even death, the stakes were way too high to have been worth it for him had it been only a question of positive economy.

The doubts expressed in Don Patricio's dreams are obviously his own, and are at least in part manifest as a kind of self-accusation and guilt, but in his brief interpretation of them, they are projected onto a diffuse Other, as the malignant force of slanderous rumor. It is just this externalized doubt and self-reproach that will later take on the more tightly focused shape of a condensed hostility coming from the outside, in the image of Don Nicolás and his imputed sorcery attacks against us. Indeed, the way toward that transformation appears to have been opened by Don Patricio's decision to name the meddlesome agency as *'ntjao*, Mazatec for "evil wind." But, then again, perhaps, as suggested by Don Patricio, evil winds were simply the form taken by multiple *chismes*, the result of many different people's mischievous talk and uncertainties, literally, a kind of malevolent "gossip" on the breeze.

Notes

1. The first section of this chapter is derived from a revised version of a paper presented at the American Anthropological Association meetings at Chicago in November of 2003, as part of a panel on "Indigenous American Conceptualizations and Transformations of Alterity," while the substance of the second section was in large part presented at the 2000 AAA meetings in San Francisco for a panel on "Forms of Power/Knowledge." The field research was carried out with funds provided by the Wenner-Gren Foundation for Anthropological Research. Many thanks especially to Jean-Guy Goulet, and to Julie Thacker Abse, Susan McKinnon, Elizabeth Abse, and Michael Kaufman for their contributions to earlier drafts. Also, I am very grateful to Don Patricio Hernandez for his bravery and protection and for his efforts to further my understanding of Mazatec shamanism. I owe the greatest debt to Antonio Briseño of San Martín de Porres (Chilcholta), Oaxaca, who was my steadfast friend and co-researcher throughout many a harrowing adventure in the Sierra and without whom none of the fieldwork experience directly related to this chapter would have been possible.

2. For earlier theoretical debate among Latin Americanist scholars regarding envy and the "image of limited good," see, for example, Foster 1965, 1966, 1972; Kaplan and Seler 1966; Gregory 1975; Rubel 1977; and Dow 1981. For more recent ethnographic descriptions that convey subtleties of indigenous Latin American concepts and experiences of "envy" analogous to those characteristic of the Mazatec case briefly described here, see especially Monaghan 1995, 131–136, and Taussig 1987, 393–412.

3. Benjamin Feinberg has provided a historically sensitive and politically astute interpretation as to why the vehicle of Mazatec shamanic knowledge and claims to legitimate authority should be objectified in the form of a "book" (Feinberg 1997).

4. For a comparative example, Goulet has stated essentially the same thing as true to his experience with Native Americans in the context of fieldwork with the Dene Tha of northwestern Alberta, Canada: "Dene tend to exclude those who are not perceived as knowing from those among whom they discuss experiences of dreams, visions, and power. Such discussion occurs only between those who are "in the know." To one who "knows" and understands, Dene offer a degree of explanation according to their estimation of his or her understanding. This estimation of the ethnographer's knowledge, more than the investigator's own research agenda, determines the flow of information between the two, information that most often takes the form of stories, the significance of which at first simply escapes the ethnographer" (Goulet 1994b, 114).

12. *Clothing the Body in Otherness*

JANFERIE STONE

Late one January evening in 1992, I went to meet with a Kaqʔchikel Maya woman from the area of Lake Atitlan, in Guatemala.[1] Vera had been visiting the northern coast of California and teaching backstrap weaving at an art center. I wound my way along the roads of the California coastal range to the house of her friend Alyssa, where, over cups of tea and with much laughter, Vera plied words as deftly as her fingers moved when they worked the warp threads of her loom; she formed a portal through which we left the familiar world to enter another reality.

Vera's native tongue is *Kaqʔchikel*, lending cadence to the Spanish used as the lingua franca in market towns around Lake Atitlun, where three different Mayan languages are spoken. I asked questions in English, and Alyssa translated into Spanish. I sought to draw out the story of her life that Vera had recounted a few days earlier at a small grade school. There she had created a marketplace for the children, evoking her pueblo where narrow streets lead down to Lake Atitlun, suspended between volcanic cones. I had been so intrigued by Vera's aura of quiet confidence and the identity she established through her *traje* (traditional dress) that I had sought this further meeting. As the night went on, our conversation moved across a divide of difference, working on the assumption that we held a common reality based on experiences such as childbearing, familial interactions, and the dynamics of power between women and men. If I did not completely understand her answers, Alyssa translated, but Vera understood English as well as I understood her Spanish, and she interjected explanations that spun off into one tale and then another. These were bursts of stories, like rain showers, that I could feel but barely comprehend. Stories of houses and saints, of cargoes, cloth, foreseeing, and dreams. A story of caves, a black man, an abducted woman, the *coates* (feathered serpents), and sacred lances. The sentences were double-woven coupleted phrases within the flow of a Mayan tongue, laying out the twinned drives of tradition and change. While their simplicity carried emotional force across three languages, these stories were simultaneously as layered as the brocades that Vera wove.

Asked how it was that she was the first person to leave her town to come to the United States, Vera launched into a tale that cited what I have come to call a lineage of spiritual power going back to her grandparents. Just as one might present one's line of descent to establish rights to land and material property, so one may cite the occult powers of one's ancestors, thus claiming the ability to dream truly, to have prescience, to move in otherworldly ways that affect the reality of the day to day. According to Vera, to be born with such abilities in her society, manifesting from a young age, bestows more authority than any knowledge that one might gain by being apprenticed to a teacher. But training is necessary to be able to control one's natural powers. The following synopsis of Vera's tale, "Shapeshifting Wives" demonstrates this.

Part I: The Transforming Wife

It was in the time of my grandfather. Yes, my grandfather. He was married first to a bad wife. This wife had no children; she was barren. She was a woman who went out into the night and ran wild like a lion. The husband grew to be afraid and suspicious even though she gave him something to make him sleep as if he were dead. One night he awoke anyway; his wife was not beside him. She had left a grinding stone in her place. He went out of the house, taking his machete. He waits and he waits, and then it is big, crying *Aieee, aieee* in the night and it is coming close, it is coming closer, it is as big as a horse and he slashes with his machete; he slashes his machete and she falls, she dies. He knew and yet did not know that it was his wife. The head of the animal, which was now human, uttered words. The pieces of her body kept moving, moving, trying to come back together. In the morning, her father and brother came, and her husband, furious, protested, "How was I to know? You did not tell me she was like this! You should have told me she had this problem!" They gathered up her body and returned to the house of her father, where she finally died.

Part II: Dreaming with the Wife in the Green House

Her grandfather had need of a wife; after all, who would make his tortillas? As no family in his town would allow him to court their daughters, he thought and thought. What was he to do? One night he dreamed that he needed to travel to the next town where he would find the good woman in a green house. When he did so, he was annoyed to find that this woman was already married and had children. He thought to himself, "Well, this is bad, but after all, I too have been married." That night he dreamed and traveled into the dreams of the sleeping woman to talk with her. He said that when she awoke she should tell her husband that a man had come to her in her dreams. Her husband would become enraged, suspecting her of infidelity. He would threaten her and when he did, the house would shake; she should leave with her children and return to her father's house where he, the dreamer, would come to claim her. And it all fell out according to what he said. The grandfather came down the road in the morning to present his case to her father. He had found the woman with whom he could make his house, to continue his bloodline, to pass on his power and knowledge. The family that came from this union included the granddaughter who was telling the tale.

The Work of the Tale

Thus we returned to the present, where the tale reverberated as we continued to talk. When I pressed Vera to relate how the civil conflict in Guatemala had affected her life, her answers grew elusive and disjointed. The hour late, the flow was spent.

I left our meeting stunned, thinking that I had experienced beginner's luck. I had caught complex, magical tales on my tape; I had them to study. But I was deluded, for if anything, the tales actually had me. Over the next few years, the tales surfaced at various moments, always associated with Vera's image and the cadence of her voice, rising and falling. I began to interpret the tales, as I shall presently convey, but these ideas were but strands I followed across a field that came into being over years of study and Vera's friendship.

At first my research followed standard folklore lines, focusing on the historical–geographical distribution of the tales and finding versions recorded since the Spanish Conquest in Mesoamerica. The Franciscans, on a conquest of the souls of this heathen world, detailed accounts of idolatry and beliefs that humans could shapeshift into animal others, a belief that has been called *nawalism* (Coe and Whittaker 1982, 63–68, Sahagún 1979, vol. 4). Such accounts were traces of alternate realities and power sources, hidden behind the masked faces and laboring bodies that the indigenous peoples presented to colonial authorities. The Inquisition in the New Indies sought to identify recalcitrant beliefs that prevented the complete Christian conversion of subject peoples (Few 1997, Obregon 1912). After the Independence movements of the early 1800s, state authorities sought to track subversive forces that might fuel rebellion (Brinton 1894, Bricker 1981).

From the nineteenth century on, anthropologists and linguists working in Mesoamerica have recorded variants of such narratives about *nawalism* (for an overview of scholarship see López Austin 1988, I: 362–275, II: 283–284). Since the mid-twentieth century, epigraphers have made progress decoding ancient Mayan hieroglyphs, a labor that suggests deep roots for such representations of relationships among humans, animals, and power (Houston and Stuart 1989, Klein et al. 2002). Tracing tales and beliefs, I sensed that the archival record did not present an unbroken continuity of custom and belief from the Pre-Columbian to the present but rather showed how tales, as a genre, were employed to recount experience, tapping core beliefs pertinent to moments in sociopolitical movements, representing actors and their choices, and potentially changing the course of events.

Academic literature provided models for interpretation of the tales, but these were framed within the disciplinary flows of Western culture. I had thought to collect and study tales, to describe them in academic terms and to use theoretical tools forged in Western understandings of individual development, feminism. and functionalism. While I intended to keep a proper academic distance from both the tales and the culture, I grew increasingly uncertain of how truly my theoretical approaches mapped the worldview of the people who told the tales. Methodologically, I experienced constraints to engaging in a comprehensive field research project. Unable to schedule extended fieldwork (because of family obligations), I had only short sessions in the field in Guatemala; my ability to immerse myself in the language(s) and culture was limited. Over two summer visits, I spent time conversing with women from Santiago Atitlan and San Pedro la Laguna (towns on the shores of Lake Atitlun), thereby gaining an understanding of the lake as a region where community is constituted through languages and tales, and learning that symbols woven or embroidered on cloth represent condensed ritual and secular practices. In each tongue, there are specific terms to describe people of force, both good and evil. There are also terms to denote saints, ancestors, and the native deities that hold otherworldly power at specific named sites.[2]

More importantly, I gained a sense of the vital relationship between the appearance, dignity, and traditional dress of Maya women, and the way they tell the world to themselves and others, even if conjunctions of tellers and audiences are rare. The time that can be spent in idle conversation is all too short in lives bent upon modernization and development after many years of civil conflict. As the years passed, Vera had commitments to another marriage, three more children, and her matrilineal family to honor; she was too busy as a householder to pause for long. Short bursts of gossip and asides of information interspersed her daily round when I was there. But a major factor in her ability to sell her weaving was the circuit she had established with weavers in North America. Visitors to Guatemala came to her house to buy textiles. Feeling it necessary to maintain and develop these contacts, she made journeys northward, but now brought one or two of the children with her as necessary. I came to appreciate a field of engagement that was formed bilaterally, for with each of us traveling long distances, we established a trade in cloth, representations of other culture and multiple fashionings of knowledge. While I have experienced dislocation and a heightening of the senses while visiting her culture, I became the coordinator for her work in California. In the process, as I shall describe, what I take as my known world has sometimes been shot through with uncanny experiences that defy explanation. Such a long-term engagement in fieldwork, while piecemeal, has opened the process of interpretation to consultation over an extended period in our developing life courses. The exchange has become increasingly dialogic as Vera and I discuss ideas about the phenomenological versus the real, and ways that the Mayan peoples around Lake Atitlun speak about and practice time and space.

While worldviews and templates for behavior within Maya societies are instilled in multiple ways, I would hold that one of the more powerful modes has been the telling of traditional tales. Certainly, for tellers such as Vera, it is the chosen genre to convey complex metaphors and beliefs and to frame the relationships among humans, society, and nature. At one level, the two episodes of her *Nawal* tale describe a set of positive and negative values for women, thereby delineating the balance of power between woman and man deemed necessary for the reproduction of family and culture. It contrasts the first wife as an asocial being, incapable of human reproduction and wild with power, with the second wife, who was a worthy partner to engender a lineage, "the house" of the grandfather. Viewed in this manner, neither woman had much agency or control over her desires. Such a tale seems to function to control the social power of women, confining their labor to the domestic sphere and requiring their bodies in the reproductive strategies of a male hierarchy. In this narrative, this fate is denoted by the woman's return to the house of the father in each episode.

The anomaly about the tale's performance is that Vera, telling the tale, was a twenty-four-year-old woman who was moving far outside the spheres of the good wife as described in the story. On the contrary, Vera was seeking employment to help support her infant son after she left her alcoholic husband. She went to work caring for the child of a *gringa*, an American woman who eventually invited her to come to California. She left her infant son in the care of her maternal family.

The actual course that her life had taken could be juxtaposed to her own presentation of what and where it was proper for a woman to be. While this discrepancy posed a question of cognitive dissonance for me, it did not seem to phase her, for (to work a weaving metaphor) the tension on the strands of her life was a tension that opened the sheds of possibility. She carried through the border crossings the interior calm and dignity of a woman of her family and society, signified by her outer dress. The choices she made as a young woman within this space led her to a new design for the life of a *Kaq?chikel* woman, encompassing roles as a mother, weaver, artist, and trader. While others in her community have begun the long migratory labor circuit to North America, none have been able to achieve her balance of cultural conservation, artistry, and service within the family. Although physically distant from her loved ones, she insisted that she was able to maintain spiritual contact. One night she dreamt that her infant son was ill and close to death. She telephoned the next day to ascertain the truth of her dream and immediately booked a flight to return. She told me, "He grew well because he knew I was coming." As the granddaughter of dreamers, she lays claim to the power of prescience but also to the power to weave new patterns in life based on traditional values.

I propose that the *Nawal* tale may be seen as a template for roles and behavior within the span of a human life, a template that moves through the generations, affecting behavior and perception in the day to day, but also empowering its carriers to grasp opportunities as they arise, thereby changing the courses of both family and community histories. A deep understanding of the tale involves a discussion of traditional Maya spirituality, of the frame provided by the particular historical moment of the telling and of the Maya approach to oral history, in short, an undertaking of book-length proportions. But one common thread in these explorations is the attention to the immediate appearance of things against the background of alternate and greater realities. I use the phrase "clothing the body in otherness" to characterize the relationship of one of the most quotidian of practices in Maya society, the act of dressing, with Maya representations of women who have undressed beyond their human flesh and transformed into *nawals*, spiritual animal others. Realizing that in both the tale and the field of interaction, more than one reality was interweaving, and that the appearance of things was crucial to understanding the multidimensionality of knowing, I concentrate here on the relationship of dressing, specifically between the traje that Vera always wears and the manifestation of the power of another dimension of her world, demonstrated by belief in and representations of *nawalism*, "animal transformation."

Belief in the ability of humans to change themselves into animals or their association with an animal spirit is recorded in Maya hieroglyphic writing, in sculptural media, and the iconography of the *tzolkin* (the Sacred Calendar round of the Maya). The deep background of Vera's tale refers to the relationships between humans, *itz* (magical power), and the *chíulel*, or *tonal*, an elemental or animal co-essence connected to each human by the moment of birth (Chouinard 1995, 73–79). A human's ability to actually transform into an animal (not necessarily their *tonal*) is a manifestation of force that may be for good (that is beneficial to the community) or for malice and selfish gain. One term often used in Maya communities and in the literature for this ability is *nawalism*, and in many Maya communities it has carried a strong negative connotation, giving rise to charges of *brujeria* (witchcraft), shaped by five hundred years of Catholic and colonial agendas. Humans, by changing appearance, have the ability to deceive others, and their motives are to be suspected. In one story that Vera told, she posed the dilemma of interpersonal relations: "Who can know why? Perhaps it is jealousy, perhaps they are angry, perhaps they want something? Your land, your house?" A transformed being can enter the private areas of the house and cause bodily harm to its inhabitants. The contrasting roles of the two wives could also be described as statements about clothing and posture, about upstanding social behavior versus the incomprehensible behavior of an animal or an animal in the wrong place.

The contrast of animal to human behavior, the way of telling experience and the warping of the perceptual field in the aftermath of violence come into sharp focus around an incident that occurred in

May of 2000, when Vera visited California with her infant son and her five-year-old daughter, (little) Alyssa, namesake of her American friend. Unfortunately, the end of Vera's visit overlapped with a previous commitment I had made to travel overseas with my mother. Because I would not be able to take Vera and her children to the airport, I contacted Alyssa who was living to the northeastern interior of Mendocino County. While she was extremely busy working on environmental campaigns and felt disconnected from her Guatemalan past, she agreed to help.

After Vera taught her class on the Mendocino coast, we drove seventy miles up into the interior. The heat was intense and the air crackling and dry, so that we arrived headachy, our energy sapped. As I prepared to leave, Alyssa suggested I wait a half hour more, passing the time in her garden. We trailed out across the hills, the five of us and her dog. I was moving ahead on the path when I heard screaming and turned to see that the dog had little Alyssa down on the ground and was slashing at her face. I did not think but ran past Vera, who was holding the baby up out of the way. I pushed the dog off and lifted little Alyssa high above my shoulders. The dog leapt up on me trying to get to her. I began moving swiftly back toward the house, thinking that Alyssa (elder) would get the dog under control, and Vera would bring the baby. I wanted to distance the little girl from the dog and clean her to see how badly she was hurt. Fortunately, the dog was a hunting breed, soft-mouthed for retrieving birds, and there was only a small puncture wound near Alyssa's mouth that nevertheless produced a great deal of blood as she sobbed quietly. Back at the house, we were completely disoriented by the sudden eruption of violence, and Alyssa's children were further disturbed by what might happen to their beloved family dog because of the attack.

What force had animated the dog? The attack could be attributed to a number of factors. The dog had been on put on medication a few weeks before. Talking with friends afterward, I heard two accounts of otherwise sedate family pets suddenly attacking five-year-old children; the size and movement of the young human triggered some ancient wiring, breaking through the dog's breeding and training. Perhaps the busyness of our lives had stressed all the beings involved.

But in the midst of the incident I had a flash of vision—the image of the dog on little Alyssa overlaid by images of the Conquest and the use of the Spanish dogs as instruments of terror. The dense brocade of little Alyssa's *huipil* had functioned as an impenetrable shield for her torso when the dog knocked her down, but her face had been defenseless. I could not rid myself of the sensation that another layer of reality had mapped onto the one we had walked.

I did not share this with the others; it seemed an excess of imagination, with our senses wide open and the emotional atmosphere so tightly strung. Little Alyssa's wound was treated. Time stretched out, one hour, two, as we calmed and tried to settle what should happen. Alyssa and I went outside the house while Vera rested with the children. Alyssa tried to explain why she was so reluctant to engage deeply in Vera's life anymore; she told me the story I have called "A Dark Illness."

The second time that Vera was living in Guatemala, when her children were young, she came to Alyssa one day, complaining and complaining of deep pain. Alyssa offered to take Vera to the doctor, but Vera said, no, no it was not that kind of illness. She could tell by the duration and quality of the pain that active human ill will was behind it. She explained that a jealous woman, suspecting that Vera was involved with her husband (although it was not true) had consulted a shaman (Alyssa's term) to send this illness. Vera would need to go to a diviner herself to try to counteract the pain that would otherwise kill her. Alyssa agreed to pay for it. They went to a powerful healer in the town of Santa Catarina, who did rituals and gave Vera medicine to take.

That night Vera slept, and dreamed. She dreamt she was a bird, a hawk soaring. She saw another hawk below and swooped down to engage it in battle. They fought, rising and falling in circles, until the other bird tumbled from the sky. Vera awoke in the night, and the pain was gone. In the morning, agitated, she telephoned someone in the part of town where the other woman lived. She was told that the woman had tumbled down some stairs in the early morning, breaking her arm.

Alyssa now found this incident from their past to be evidence of superstition and the dark jealousy and underlying violence of Maya nature. I did not know how to reply. I had read narratives (Laughlin 1976, 5–6) that followed the pattern described but found it interesting that in this account it was the women themselves who had engaged in spirit battle, when usually it was the shamans who fought for the *souls* of their patients. I thought this might have to do with Vera's own powers, dormant while she was in the childbearing phase of her life. Alyssa's revulsion for the superstition and the dark magic that had resulted in actual injury seemed compounded by her complicity in paying for it. Moreover, I sensed that she had distanced herself over the years because she had a genuine fear of being caught up in the malice, something to be considered when the bond between the self and native contacts is weak or broken.

Favret-Saada (1980) describes such a fieldwork dilemma, in which life-threatening danger arose as she explored witchcraft in the Bocage region of France. The inability to cope with the inexplicable may lead the person external to the culture to put distance between the self and the field. But on this hot June evening, I found it fascinating that Alyssa had switched to a narrative mode, echoing the cadences of Vera's voice, to try to resolve some of the issues that had arisen in that moment. I also felt that telling the story had lanced some of the venom from the situation. Whatever the current state of their relationship, Alyssa and Vera had long been friends, and we would all have to trust that it would work out for a few days. Reluctantly, I did leave Vera's family there, the issue of the dog unresolved, so we might all get to our separate flights.

Incidents such as this one resist easy interpretation. In the life courses of the people involved, they remain sore until, as in this case, time can heal the anger and fear. Four years later, in May of 2004, when Vera and little Alyssa visited again, Alyssa was once again living on the coast while her daughter attended high school. She, her daughter, Vera, and little Alyssa spent time together reestablishing the sense of extended family. Little Alyssa does, however, remain afraid of dogs.

I could not readily absorb this incident into my work. Such experiences resist academic description, obtruding like rough stones in a deductive flow. The perceptual warp we experienced in the aftermath of the incident made me ask what it was that each of us had seen, and I understood better how people come to believe in supernatural forces. That Alyssa resorted to a narrative citing Maya metaphors and beliefs to ease the situation emphasized the instrumentality of tales in human interaction. But perhaps most importantly, the dreamlike pace of this small act of violence had induced the imagination that opens understanding. The overlaid image of the terror of conquest evoked the entrenched structural violence in Guatemala, forcing me to seek deeper historical patterns. To ignore the currents of violence in Guatemala is to completely misrepresent the conditions of production of the Maya self and culture. But equally, to do justice to Maya worldviews and their tenacity in the face of oppression, emphasis must be laid on the positive aspects of Maya self-representations. Ultimately, I needed to find ways to reconcile the contrast created between the enchantments of clothing and the magic of the tales and the undercurrents of violence that the same tales brought out.

Dressing in Alternate Skins

On the most recent visit, in May 2004, I awaited Vera and little Alyssa at the San Francisco airport until they appeared, exhausted by post 9–11 security woes, delayed five hours in immigration, but still upright and beautiful in their *traje*. Again I was struck by the centrality of the cloth to their very being and over the next weeks watched them at two conferences for textile artists in the San Francisco Bay area as they wove the magic of presence, productive on their looms and through the weaving, in the world.

Guatemalan Maya women are expected to have command of the idiom of clothing (Goffman 1959, 74), and dressing is an "everyday secular performance" to be judged for its "aptness, fitness, propriety, and decorum" (Goffman 1959, 55). As Vera's *nawal* tale conveys, there is a significant contrast between the valued performance of a woman dressed in the hand-woven products of her labor, keeping still in her house, and the ambiguous role that she occupies as the other, a transforming wife. Such *nawal* figures have lost moral and social agency, having chosen to move outside the sphere of the house, when the term "house" encompasses both domestic space and lineage.

Many tales involve a man, a trader, on the road overnight, who is forced to take shelter in a strange house, or near ruins or a cemetery. Overhearing people talking, he recognizes the voice of his wife, making pacts with other "masters of the night" to bring destruction to the townspeople. While it may be necessary for a man to be out in the night, it is never acceptable for a woman (see, for example, *Ya kta?l q?iisoom*, "*Catarina la characotel*" from Santiago Atitlan, Petrich 1999, 86–90). Women, transformed into their *nawals*, are seen as agents of destruction for both family and community, and ultimately, they must be expelled from society.

The two images of women, the one in *traje*, highly valued and indeed valorized, the other as *nawal*, an anathema, are actually both instances of dressing, when the appearance of women is represented as crucial in the construction of everyday sociality. These accounts must be contextualized within the historical development of Maya spiritual and political power. Furthermore, drawing on the work of Kay Warren and a historical model proposed by Gary Gossen and Richard Leventhal, I suggest that within the context of *la violencia* (the Guatemalan civil conflict) these images of women as *nawals* represent extraordinary spiritual performances that marked movement toward widespread social change at a particular moment. These performances may not have been recognized as such within the society.

Clothing the Woman, from Labor to Reproduction

For women, cloth has been the product of female labor, key in their contributions to the household, town, and the national economies of Mesoamerica. This has been so for millennia. Many studies of Maya textiles have focused on their technical excellence, skill, and mastery of design, yet imputed Spanish influences and institutions of control, to the development of significant markers of clan, village, and linguistic regions (Shevill 1985, 20–22). But Irma Otzoy insists that the Maya had more control over the socio-cultural trajectories of their production. She explores the complexities of signifiers on cloth, beginning with ancient portrayals on ceramics, codices, and the stone monuments of Classic Maya cities (Otzoy 1996a, 142–143). As more

Maya writers take the myths and legends of their peoples into publication, often in poetic forms, a worldview emerges in which it is necessary to mark identity and underline the centrality of cloth to power. As both practice and ideology, weaving is one of the defining arts taught by Jich Mam and Jich Mi (the grandmother–fathers of the Jakaltek Maya) that Victor Montejo (2001, 7) highlighted as a trope of identity tied to place, ancestry, and spirituality:

> And our women, with skillful hands,
> wove blankets, skirts, belts and blouses,
> and made with pride all our clothing
> which they dyed with bright colors
> using indigo and the blood of the annatto

The art of weaving has been and is an art of possibilities, a dynamic and conscious series of choices tied to sacred beginnings (Otzoy 1996b, 26). She cites the words that the *Kaq ʔchikel* ancestral grandmother–father, *Q ʔaq ʔawitz*, spoke to the hero *Q ʔaxq ʔanul*: "the heart of a hero must not be afraid, and then your victory shall be the victory of the whole pueblo" (Otzoy 1996b, 27). Otzoy draws a parallel between this injunction and the daily valor of women who continued to wear *traje* despite the racist legacy of colonialism and the danger during *la violencia*. Since the Conquest, women have felt a responsibility to transmit Maya knowledge to future generations through their weaving, confronting the discrimination of the dominant society. Similarly, Rigoberta Menchú claimed that "it is the same to speak of the *tejidos* (weaving) as it is to speak of the earth" (quoted in Otzoy 1996b, 32) tying *traje* to the fight for resources and social justice.

But for Maya women, the identity constituted through *traje* is also a bodily practice, linking persona to sensory being and perception. Vera explained: "I tried wearing other clothes, jeans and T-shirts, but I didn't feel right. I couldn't move or carry my bundles of cloth." Habits and postures are assigned worth according to the body's ability to produce, to labor, and to carry Maya culture. As a weaver and conserver of Maya culture, Vera articulates what it means to dress and be a *Kaq ʔchikel* woman. When traveling in California, she continues to wear her *huipil, corte* (skirt), and *tzute* (head wrap), cutting a line of glorious color through a street or shopping mall. This teaching is compounded when she travels with her daughter, as she conveys to the next generation the need to proudly wear iconography and colors that refer to her people and place, despite the blandishments of other kinds of distinction deployed by global Western culture. While American response to her being varies, factoring in the viewer's class and ethnicity, individuals do pay attention (if only through a momentary glance) and many engage in exclamations of beauty, compliments, and questions about Vera's place of origin.

Ways of dressing are formative in bodily habits that are instilled through repeated injunctions to children about their clothes and behavior. Young girls, as they are wrapped in their *corte*, are taught how to fold the layers of cloth over the gathered *huipil*, and then to align their *fajas* (belts), drawing the spine into an erect posture. The female's shoulders should be squared so that the entire design on the *huipil* may be read. Correct performance is assessed in the eyes of others, for there are few mirrors or large plates of glass in rural Guatemala to encourage the habitual self-evaluation in which members of Western societies indulge. Marks of distinction scripted in bodily coverings renew motifs and stake claims of belonging to families, organizations of people, and their places. While public schools may require uniforms for boys, many accept *traje* for girls. For women, wearing *traje* while selling goods in the market is an essential part of the display, read as carefully as a label upon their goods. Contemporary local contests to choose the queens for processions extol traditional dress and values for girls and are part of a secular process of defining and displaying indigenous presence against Ladino institutions (Hendrickson 1995, 92–94, 116).

In sacred venues, dressing the saints or the Virgin is an act of devotion for the wives of the Cofradias. The process creates a path of knowledge, power, and encoding that travels through the generations. First, a weaver may invest the piece through iconographic signifiers, as when Irma Otzoy traces, in the work of Asturias de Barrios in Comolapa, the way in which weavers "transform objects of a ritual character into woven motifs and are thus designing for survival" (Otzoy 1996a, 153). But the woven piece then carries instrumental energy, for the impulse for such new designs or for the revival of old ones may come in a dream, signaling the spiritual onus such a task may carry. The work is highly honored, and according to Vera, the clothing of the saints has been preserved over the years in the houses of the Cofradias. While the clothing of the saint or of the Virgin represents the most sacred deployment of *traje*, the annual cycle of saints' days and fiestas gives those who throng the streets an occasion to display best clothing as marks of distinction and status. Dressing to be seen at the procession is an act infused with excitement and social meaning. Posed against the Westernized clothing of the numerically inferior but politically dominant Ladino population, "*traje* is animated not only by the person wearing it[,] but women wearing *traje* give the gift of presence—signaling to the world that they intend to preserve *costumbre* and participate in a dynamic Maya community" (Hendrickson 1995, 167).

While the image of the *indigena* dressed in *traje* has been carried to the world by such ambassadors as Rigoberta Menchú and through countless reproductions of beauty and cloth in travel brochures and postcards, the covering of women takes place (as with the tales) within historical trajectories and specific political contexts (Nelson 1999, 128–205). At present, as urban Maya nationalists within the Pan-Maya movement assert, it is more important for women to continue to wear traditional dress than for men to do so (Warren 1998, 108). This continues the trend that began with the Conquest when men abandoned loincloths and capes for the pants of the Spanish, while the form of women's costume remained virtually unchanged. Over the last century, men, as itinerant workers on the coastal plantations, were subjected to increased pressure to abandon their *traje* when it was stigmatized as backward and feminized. During the decades of conflict, it was not only socially problematic but also dangerous to be marked as a traveler on the road, outside the supporting community. And certainly in our contemporary world labor market, with anonymity required of border crossers, the pressure for young men to dress in a mode of dominant culture–homogeneity is constant.

Against this background, the production of cloth and woven identity becomes even more highly valued for its inscription of tradition as the communities of production necessarily devote energy to other practices and educational strategies. As clothing carries such significance within the momentum of contemporary Pan-Maya activism, it becomes obvious that the appearance of the body simultaneously constrains and empowers the individual as the body moves through the spaces of the house, town, and world. The early 1990s were years of transition. How might one draw out the relationship of a young woman, wearing *traje* and traveling in California, to the stories she told of transforming beings and the dream narratives that described correct behavior and ideal female roles and yet empowered her to seek new paths of interaction with the world? And how did these tales relate to the time in which they were told, when the civil conflict in Guatemala was moving toward the peace accords, a period of détente characterized by deep emotional exhaustion?

Cultural Reproduction in a Time of Death

Vera told this tale when Guatemala was emerging from a forty-year-long civil conflict, peaking in the late seventies and the eighties, when more than 200,000 Maya were killed and 440 villages destroyed in a massive repression by the Guatemalan Army, authorized by the government (Montejo 1999, 4). The Commission for Historical Clarification (CEH), the UN-appointed truth commission, reported on the extent of the terror and its racist–ethnic basis in 1999.[3] Knowledge of the genocide is still obscured for many of the Maya people who did not directly experience the violence, although it happened across the lake, up in the mountains, or just down the road. In 1992, when asked directly, Vera claimed to have no knowledge of violence in her town. However, when she began to relate one incident, she cut it off, saying that "after all, not much had happened." In recent conversations, Vera admitted that there are things she is willing to talk about now, across elapsed time and at a distance, when she is in the United States but not when she is at home, where her words might be overheard. As a woman, enclosed by household activities, she is aware of the small ears, older ears, and male ears that may listen and judge. Conversation is always in flux, taking all possible audiences into consideration. When Vera and I talked, we were in a small cabin in the hills east of Mendocino, California. Her daughter, Alyssa, was present. As she told some of the tales, she said that usually she would not talk of things of such force before children, but she felt that at some point it was vital to be sure that stories were passed on. Traveling with her child, now a highly responsible nine-year-old, created a special bond and opportunity. Even so, as she began to describe the violence, her voice dropped. She admitted, "At night you would hear the sound of pickups along the road. But you did not look out of the house. There were vehicles moving on the highway. Or if it was a group of men, who knows? It was too dangerous. Once when my brother was traveling between towns he came upon bodies. He could see where they had been mutilated." Her hands brushed the spots on her body as she named the wounds, seen through slashed and bloodstained clothes. The people spoke in hushed tones within the walls of the family compounds of mutilations to the breasts and sexual organs.

The peace process that has been ongoing since the 1990s raises questions about what the individual, the community, and ultimately the state can or will acknowledge and then what narrative forms they may use to do so. While folklore is often dismissed as trivial, Henry Glassie, working in Ireland in the midst of the troubles, framed the act of telling oral history by saying, "When the neighbors gather tonight, they will speak of the past to discuss a present too horrifying to face directly. They will tell themselves the story of their place, saying what they know to discover what they think" (Glassie 1982, 5). One approach to the question of truth in speaking about violence is to explore the capacity of narratives about transformations to open a space for both listeners and tellers to review the conduct of individuals and groups in such times of crisis. Within the circle, all could adopt a posture of unknowing that simultaneously acknowledged individual consciousness and social contracts. In a time when it was dangerous to do so, the names of those suspected of betraying others could be obliquely referred to as husband or wife, allowing the community to address and to some extent redress malicious actions.

According to narratives collected in the nineties, the people of Santa Catarina say that it was the protection of their Lady, Santa Catalina, that kept the violence away from the center of their town. The town became a bounded zone of safety that was sustained through prayer and public silence (Petrich 1997, 27–28, 30). But the violence was present around Lake Atitlun, flaring into open battle in Santiago Atitlan and in frequent gunfire exchanges in the hills and on the roads. The connection of such tales of *nawals* to *la violencia* is made explicit by the work of Kay Warren in the Kaq?chikel town of San Andrés. She has written a detailed analysis of similar tales of *nawalism* that she has come to call "Peel Off Flesh; Come Back On," that she recorded on her return to San Andrés in the late eighties, when the violence had diminished (Warren 1998, 101–108). She was amazed to find that the most progressive people, catechists who had dedicated themselves to Catholic Action and political consciousness–raising, were discussing rumors and stories of shape-shifters, usually women and wives. One woman insisted, "This is really true; this really happened, Kay. My niece saw a woman as she was transforming herself" (Warren 1998, 101).

The stories featured a woman, who had previously lived harmoniously with her husband, exhibiting signs of illness. Despite his loving care, she does not improve, and he begins to watch her more carefully. It turns out that she is drugging him into a deep sleep each night so that she may change into an animal and roam the town. Her aches and pains are the result of beatings she receives in her animal form. Once he has witnessed the process, the appalled husband consults a diviner and resolves to be "an assassin of the flesh" by salting the human skin she leaves behind. Thus, one night, returning to the house, the wife is unable to re-clothe herself in her human flesh and disappears in her animal form into the night. In these tales, the ideal behavior of a wife is posed within a state of harmony in the marriage; this performance, by preceding the transformation, casts the wife's moral choices in a negative light and her actions as betrayal. In the outcome of this version, the ambiguous other, unable to return to the human fold, is expelled into nature. There is no episode leading to an account of lineage, the positive and ongoing outcome presented in Vera's tale. The unknown fate of the *nawal* parallels the inherent uncertainty that rules during a state of violence.

When Kay Warren recounted the Trixano *nawal* tales to North

American audiences, they responded with comments that focused on gender relations: "a woman's desire for autonomy but apparent lack of control over the consequences of her actions and a man's anger and violence towards a woman" (Warren 1998, 105). But when Warren conveyed this response to her talebearers, they were surprised, and denied such implications, stating rather that these narratives were one way to speak about the pervasive fear and trauma generated during *la violencia*. With the people gathered, often at wakes for those who had been caught in the crossfire between the army and the guerillas, the teller, without naming any one person (for that might bring further repercussions) nevertheless evoked the dilemma with which they all lived. Framing the larger social betrayal of people trapped by civil conflict as actions within the idealized bond of marriage emphasized the depths of the uncertainty and distrust that state violence had created. The tale performance itself served as a ritual to unify a community, reinforcing the norms of what it is to be human and social, to have standards of behavior and movement to regularize relations between people. These were essential in a time when movement in the night, outside the fragile houses that sheltered families, might be the army or the passage of guerilla forces.

The tale performance created a parallel between marriage as the basic unit of social order and the town and its relations with surrounding pueblos, symbolizing rings of commitment, all vulnerable to possible betrayal. At this level, one town might direct the army to the pueblo down the road, stating that the guerillas operated from there, thus hoping to deflect military attention from their own community. And at another level, the tales raised questions of existential doubt, as individuals, faced with brutal violence, pondered their ability to make ethical choices or the limits of their resistance to torture and pain. Asked for names, under torture, what might one utter? If, to live, one betrayed others, she or he would ultimately betray a self that is constructed within a communal whole (Warren 1998, 101–104). While these are vital metaphoric trajectories for the tales, the image of the fleshly body, dressing and undressing, also has a physical materiality that is significant against the backdrop of violence.

Warren states that Trixanos particularly focused on the moment

when the woman was in the midst of transformation, with her flesh
coming off and the bones appearing:

> She opened the door and was transforming herself when her hus-
> band saw her. She was transforming herself but she was there with
> four legs, she was talking, talking, talking. But what was she say-
> ing? Now she was there half changed and the part below was what
> was left. Now she had the upper body of a ram. But yes, she spoke.
> Then she was saying, "Peel off flesh, peel off flesh." When the man
> looked again, she was an animal, a ram, a male goat.

> [Later] a longhaired ram entered. Then it leapt twice and said,
> "Come up flesh, come on up." First it was peel off, peel off. As it
> leapt it took the form of a skeleton. It wanted to become a person
> again. "Come up flesh, come on up," it said. Little by little the
> flesh rose up, and it became a woman. (Warren 1998, 103–104)

Warren focuses on this moment of transition, being half woman,
half (male) animal, as that which is most abhorrent to the Trixanos.
The story frames the nexus of betrayal by linking such transformations to certain persons, known as *rajaw aʔqʔa*, "masters of the night,"
humans with the ability to become spiritual animals, with malicious
intent. The bones dress in flesh in order to deceive. But focus on this
moment, when the human strips to her bones and descends to animal
posture or its reversal upon return also evokes the ambiguous states
before birth and after death. Bones, detached from their coverings of
flesh and cloth, reveal gender only with study.

The skeletal figure has deep roots in Maya culture; it is found on
ceramics and in glyphs from the earliest periods of Maya civilization.
The power of the skeletal being is animated in contemporary times
through stories of *calaveras*. Such beings may appear as fleshly women
to unwary drinkers out on the road at night, luring them into the forest for sexual escapades, only to reveal their skeletal selves in order to
devour the hapless men. The tie between sex and death is emphasized
by one tale that Vera told recently: a *calavera* (male) knocked on the
door of a newlywed couple's house to engage the husband in a deadly
battle; the *calavera* (leaping and turning in the air each time) transformed from one animal into another and then another and another,

each time the human bones appearing and disappearing beneath the fleshly forms. The young wife was rendered cold and immobile as the battle waged; she barely recovered later, after days of illness.

Examined against the *calavera* figure, the *nawal* wife, at the skeletal moment, is an image of death, decay, and metamorphosis, an image that takes on a deeper significance in a time of massive unrest and both individual and communal denial of violence. Such an image, triggering fear and spurring rejection, creates a holding on to and evocation of the idealized domestic union, the space of fertility and reproduction. It is no surprise that images of death, unrecognized as such, should be symbolically expressed against the fertile and childbearing feminine other amidst the disappearance of so many earthly bodies, the lack of knowledge about where they were buried and angst about the destiny of their souls, undirected between the layers of existence without rites of burial, unable to join the ancestors. But reference to the space of the ancestral generations behind any society at a historical moment suggests that the role of the woman as *nawal* may actually be a manifestation of power at a deeper generative level. Power tapped from the layers of existence beyond the mortal is dangerous to those who come into contact with it, but it may also be essential in a world moving through destructive chaos. The appearance of women as *nawals* may indicate ritual symbolic roles arising in a time of widespread violence and need. To argue thus it is necessary to briefly trace the public performance of male and female roles in both familial and historical cycles.

Women control the domestic sphere, and their power, while effaced in verbal interactions with men, emerges in the ceremonial roles that they take within house compounds to mark life-cycle transitions such as birth, marriage, and death. They tend babies, weave the cloth, and prepare the food for daily presentation and for ceremonies; they wash and clothe the dead for the last bodily journey. Furthermore, the influence of women expands beyond the domestic sphere as they coordinate the number and status of attendees for community celebrations marking seasonal transitions. Vera stated that it is as a married couple that the senior members of the Cofradias sponsor celebrations within the seasonal and sacred cycles, for both husband and wife have crucial roles to play. Indeed, a man could not accrue enough service, status, or wealth to rise in the hierarchies, whether of the local civil government or the Cofradias, without a wife.

Gossen and Leventhal (1993, 185–217) suggest that the insistence on male dominance in public secular venues responds to a reality in which childhood and adult life for men are initiated in the female locus of the household. However, the power that accrues to the feminine from their submergence in the domestic sphere emerges publicly in sacred performances through symbolic images, the cloth and ritual objects they have fashioned, and their honored roles as mother–fathers in festival. Occasionally, over the centuries of Maya resistance to colonial and then nation–state domination, women have risen to prominence in public affairs as leaders and symbols in movements based on native "priesthoods" and values (Bricker 1981). In the context of *la violencia*, the appearance of Rigoberta Menchú as an international spokesperson might be viewed as one instance of this phenomenon. Historically, such female moments in power have been brief, with their reigns preceded and rapidly succeeded by those of men. Gossen and Leventhal, studying how Maya communities construct narratives to describe these historical movements, propose a model that is carried out on every level, from the local to the state to the cosmos.

The action begins with an initial state of nothingness, and then describes the coexistence of mutual adversaries and growing pessimism and despair. An awareness of plight or war arises, and expectations rise to meet it. A female divinity or principle appears, rallying the forces, but quickly her voice is supplanted by that of a male broker, who wrests mystical power from the female, leading to male ascendancy, the slaying of enemies, and a period of societal intolerance of otherness. Two outcomes are possible: one is the triumph of the forces who rose up against the status quo and the creation of a new steady state, now purged, in which patrifocal elements reassert their control over society. The second possibility is that the rebellious protagonists are defeated, but in the narratives and histories, instead of being killed, they transform into their *nawals* and disappear into the mountains. In such an ambiguous ending, they maintain the possibility of mounting a new threat to the steady state of the victors, and they may function in the future to initiate a new cycle of uprising, another impulse toward change. Thus, narratives that describe such movements come to inhabit layers of enactment. As Bakhtin suggested, "Each word tastes of the context and contexts in which it has lived its socially charged life" (Bakhtin 1981, 293). Whether performed through tales or festival activities, the particular telling consciously invokes text within text, all of which have become available to the audience through constant retelling and embodiment. If narratives recount uprisings of Maya power that ended in failure, then the unrest and resistance will accumulate below the bar of oppression until the power wells up once again. The underlying premise is that if Maya peoples can endure, change will finally be affected against the oppressive state that exists as a legacy of conquest and colonialism.

Placing tales of shapeshifting wives against the background of *la violencia*, one may see that female symbolic dominance is manifesting in the public sphere when change is imminent. The appearance of a female spokesperson, Rigoberta Menchú, on the international scene, and the telling of the *nawal* tale within communities signal a surge of force that aligns with the long historical cycle of resistance to colonial and postcolonial administrations, of male political and military engagement, and finally, against the convulsive civil war and repression, of change. Within the chaos of genocide the storytelling itself was a ritual movement to work balance, to set ethical standards for the community, and finally, to harness the power of the uncontrollable sacrifice that was taking place. The extent and rupture of this sacrifice ultimately affected the structural changes that had to come in the sociopolitical reality that is Guatemala, through the kind of inversion posed by Carol Smith when she stated, "One would hardly have expected Maya self-determination to be the rallying cry to rise out of the ashes of Guatemala's holocaust" (Smith 1991, 29). Victor Montejo has suggested that when the violence was at its height, an ancient Maya stirring was set into motion that had its own momentum and destined outcomes (Montejo 1999, 13).

The centrality of sacrifice in Maya views of land and history was poetically invoked by Miguel Angel Asturias when he wrote that "those who sow the earth with maize for profit leave the earth empty of bones, because it is the bones of the forefathers that give the maize, and then the earth demands bones, and the softest ones, those of children, pile up on top of her and beneath her black crust, to feed her" (quoted in Menchú 1984, 38). But it is necessarily women who carried the burden of bringing those children into a corporeality. That was, and is, anything but poetic in practice. The lives of Maya women are shaped by a deep want that makes the beauty and drive of Maya expressive culture more penetrating.

During *la violencia* the presence of women in *traje* assumed a greater significance, contrasting characterizations of women as *delicadas* (weak, frail) with women as *valientes* (Hendrickson 1995, 133) for carrying the markers of Maya culture when men had ceased to do so for fear of being picked up by the army on conscription or guerilla sweeps. The everyday secular performance of women came to carry a higher political stake in the context of state violence. But the role of women as *nawals* took place against a deeper Maya ideology. Supporting the proposition that the *nawal* describes an alternate role to that of the idealized woman in *traje* are the words Asturias used to describe *nawalism*: "becoming animal without ceasing to be a person" where "animal and person co-exist in them, through the will of their progenitors at birth" (quoted in Menchú 1984, 38). In the Maya worldview, the progenitors of society, both mythically and in their current embodiments as leaders in the towns, are named as the mother–fathers. At the end of the tale told in San Andrés, the wife as *nawal* has been driven into the spiritual realm inhabited by the ambiguous and ancestral forms from which the communities must make themselves anew after the terror. Rigoberta Menchú defined the *nawal* of a child as "a shadow, his (or her) protective spirit who will go through life with him [or her] . . . the representative of the earth, the animal world, the sun and water, and in this way the child communicates with nature" (Menchú 1984,18).

The deeper metaphorical burden of the *nawal* tale, beyond its messages of violence and distrust in the affairs of humans, is to carry the regenerative power of women back into nature, into the earth, so that humans may renew society in the aftermath of *violencia*. The woman as *nawal* fulfills an extraordinary spiritual performance. Only thus shall there be granddaughters, dressed in the *traje*, to represent lineages of spiritual power while telling the tales.

Working and Being Worked in the Field

There are many ways to come into knowledge. Studies within libraries and archives have their own well-deserved claims to academic authority. Other ways of knowing, opened to the extraordinary, to the sensations of otherworldliness that may be experienced in the field, more personal and indeterminate, also deserve their place in the discipline of anthropology. Such experiences often remain unacknowledged because they elude description, logic, and boundedness. Yet they obtrude within memory, belying the appearance of obvious solutions; they call for more encompassing understandings of the forces in play. In this work with Vera and her tales, I have been challenged to reconcile the difference between the ideal appearance of women and the negative connotations and the violent emotions aroused when a woman changes radically in form and behavior. But more than that, I have had to work toward deep changes in the way that I approach my studies and to grow more comfortable with the space between catching and being caught, recognizing this as the space of creative imagination and understanding.

A tale carries a fascination wherein the energy invested and values proposed move and change the people who carry and otherwise work with it. In a sense, a tale cares for itself, opening the consciousness of its carriers and driving them to create spaces where the tales may be unbundled to do further work in human affairs. While much of my work has been to write about what I make of these tales, I have also had to consider what they have made of me. Challenged by the inherent logic of the tale world to perceive a different way of being, I have become part of the weaving of the tale, seeking to do justice to its telling, its bearers, and the loom of their culture.

Notes

1. Lake Atitlun, at an elevation of 5,125 feet, is situated between the coastal plains and the highlands in the mountainous Department of Sololu, in the southwestern part of Guatemala. The lake region forms a corridor between the Pacific Coast, the Highlands, and the

interior. See Kay Warren (1998, 12–18) for a presentation of contemporary Maya communities (KʔicheʔΤ, Tzeltal, QʔanjobʔΑ, and others), and of the indigenous movement promoting a global identity to unify efforts in a general struggle against racism, marginalization, and poverty.

2. John Watanabe called such a matrix of practices an instance of a "recombinant syncretism" that conventionalizes the historically emergent social identities of communities (Watanabe 1990, 145–146).

3. The UN-appointed Commission for Historical Clarification (CEH) estimates that the number of persons who have been killed or who have disappeared as a result of the fratricidal confrontation exceeds 200,000. CEH documented unspeakable atrocities: murder, mutilation, rape, torture and held the Guatemalan state responsible for acts of genocide against Mayan communities. See http://shr.aaas.org/guatemala/ceh/report/english/toc.html.

13. Dog Days

Participation as Transformation

DUNCAN EARLE

Statuesquely iconic of the method and air of anthropology's historic posture of inquiry is the observing, well-mannered, and fundamentally removed character of the ethnographer. Peering out from the tower of our temporary presence in places nobody else goes, we seek some balance of engagement and autonomy that is fitting of this raucous science, and this posture always has an aroma of what they call, in the land of *Star Trek*, "the Prime Directive": an ethic, nay esthetic, of non-engagement, of the space traveler under strict orders to not undo the locals with something beyond their evolutionary stage of development, a kind of intergalactic Herbert Spencer meets Boasian cultural relativism. Yes Data, when among the natives, don't do anything to stand out. We would hate to disarticulate the cosmic sociocultural equilibrium and piss off Starfleet Command.

Ancient Changes

Yet, many times this half-life of removal is undone. The unexpected, the out-of-control, the crisis, throws the proprieties and distances aside, and we must plunge down the rabbit hole. We do not necessarily, however, reveal in print such radical "border crossings" as they like to call them in the recent craze, and they can take on the status of the taboo, the secret sin not to be reported to the Federation of Planets. Yet these transgressions challenge the posture we are normally asked to assume, and, in that tear, both notions of our profession and of self boggle and stumble, that usually reliable self that is the negotiator of differences, working out the details of the directive. They examine our adequacy in navigating the culture we authoritatively represent by putting us to the test, so to speak. We are asked to shift the focal axis of our presence in the field. Rather than participate to better observe, taking the posture of the good-guy spy, we are expected to observe to better participate, leaving the notebook behind for a time to cohere with locals in a radically new way. This stepping out into deeper engagements, for me at least, speaks to a movement breaking with the inherent asymmetries of origin, in a landscape deeply scarred with what colonialism grinds into memory, so as to break into a multidimensional reciprocity that goes further than the normal posture in illuminating the nature of the studied, the studier, and the studying.

Thoughts Move

My own career is punctuated by these liminalities, some brief, some enduring, some operative even now. But only now am I authorizing myself to reveal my apocryphilia. Maybe because the tenure packet is in. Or because bolder people have cut the trail, like Tim Knab and the Tedlocks, fellow travelers in the really magical lands of Mesoamerica. Or because, as my compadre Lucas would say, I am getting to the point in life to where the whole village receives the mother–father, where the cargo carries the totality, for Earth's sake, the place where everyone is kin. *¿Quién sabe?*

Incoming Cut

The first disturbance was a stumper. I was in Guatemala imagining I was there to help, living with some local Kʔicheʔ by chance, or so I thought. A gardener for one of the other expats, he takes me home and asks the folks if he can keep me. I am fed up with the gringo compound and the Save the Children mentality lurking about it, and someone shows up to take me away. My strategy is careful ethnographic observation as a check on how well our development project is going, all the better it turns out because the guy is traditional, someone who will give a more conservative perspective on the efforts at rational change. It gets quaintly domestic, off on the agency motorcycle at eight, after the morning breakfast of tortillas and chile around the comal, back by five or six for more of the same. The language starts coming, I am removed from the dining room and relocated to the kitchen, somewhere between the teens and the newly married in the food serving order. After six months I find I am almost the wall fly, helped, I have come to believe, by my enthusiastic participation in anything and everything when home, including a lot of religious activities. I am careful to get my own offerings and keep up with the Joneses as regards offerings made to the Sacred Earth, among other hungry entities, and I follow along with the treks to this shrine and that, some local and some farther away. Sometimes a project vehicle gets procured for a difficult peregrination, and sometimes it is just the old shaman and me, on a dirt bike, leaping through the landscape to some millennial shrine.

Inner Earthquake

Then, one Sunday afternoon, amid the lights and shadows of adobe, beams, and tiles, the melodious voices of children and the slap of the loom beater, old Don Lucas takes the divining table out, and in a strangely excited state, casts, again and again, those shiny red and black beans across the cloth. *Shajenam*, always the same. Validation through repeat identical outcomes of a demonstrably random procedure. Likelihood, initially one out of four times, continues to diminish with each throw. I once saw him do twenty-three throws with the same outcome, but that is another story. "You see," he says to me, "no change, the same message, the same news. You have to receive the bundle, you have to gather the path." "Do it again," my feeble *reposte*, in my panic and surprise. *Lo mismo. Shajenam.*

Shaman's Ambush

How about a second opinion? My head rebounds with this possible way out. I have already asked my compadres, Don Lucas says, with a tickled sort of resignation. Here is where I learned that compadres are made in shamanic initiations, not just weddings and births, but that, too, is another story. No, not ritual relations (God knows what obligations those entail!); how about someone more powerful, from another community, doesn't know you, doesn't know about me? Ah, but it is expensive, and a waste of time and money, Lucas replies. Not a problem, my treat. Surely this high-level shaman from a rival village will expose the self-interest in this offer. Many of the locals don't ever get initiated. Me, because I have access to a car, resources, power. This will be my tactful escape, debunked by the meta-*brujo*, the trance shaman, the *aj meís*, where cross meets the table. I decide to bring a second gringo, one entirely hostile to religion, as my anchor, in case things get too magical.

Left Crazy

A party assembles for the long sundown journey deep into Chiche'. Father, two sons, two daughters, me, and the gringa, weaving among the towering cornstalks, down and up shallow canyons of ancient ash, finally to the holy house. A huge room, many other clients sitting on benches along the walls, a whole affair at the far end, a curtain, a table, a pair of crosses, and an altar facing the crosses along with the rest of us. Pine needles for a floor, with an island of earthen floor sown in beeswax candles, before which kneel three women, all kin. More people, hours, offerings of flowers, finally, the man slips in, sits behind the curtain. It is close to midnight, and the usually hypertense gringa has become unresponsive, deeply asleep, rubber. Now they are chanting a prayer, now singing an eerie melody; now the candles are extinguished, now the strange breathing starts, like someone speaking through one of those masks they wear in the Conquest dance, but more rasping, like my dead grandmother's emphysema, and a high-pitched voice inside this wind, *ayeee miijo, ayyeee mihijo* (oh my son, oh my child), and banging on the table. Somewhere near, a dog whimpers.

Strong Wind

By this time I'm seriously spooked, there is no visual locus in the thick darkness, the copal fills my brain, the renewed chanting of the three women is like sirens of the psyche, the disembodied voice comes from every direction, close and far, above and below, and somewhere in there is the thin snore of the gringa. I cannot even draw assurances from my adopted family, even though they are somewhere close. Reyna, still a child, grabs my arm, and alarm runs up into my neck from the electrified grip. All the liquids in my body want to fulfill their gravitational imperatives. My lips can't find each other.

Night Place

Don Lucas, always one to dive into the breech, asks the female attendants if the Mundos (world) would fetch his mother, before he inquires about me. The request is made, the voice goes down a hallway, opens an auditory door, brings forth the sounds of an aged woman who complains about being bothered during her siesta, but who lets herself be brought back to the table. It is just past noon down there. Don Lucas asks how she has fared in Shbilbaj. I could picture clearly her wrinkled face, recalled her giving me her last good *corte* (skirt), one of the old green style of fine *icat* of half a century ago, saying they would just toss it in her box, what a waste, when she died, which she planned to do the following Friday, on 13 Dog, a lucky day to go out. I remember her titter. Now not a month later, and she sounded the same. Complained about the belt Hurricane Owl had insisted she wear, a *canti*, a nasty viper, always biting, biting, because she did not teach the kids to weave. That is why it is good about the classes, where they learn to weave. Reyna is translating for the parts I don't catch, gasping. You thank Don Tun Ka?an for me (that same titter) about the weaving (she and the kids always made a joke about my name, because in Kíicheí it sounded like "angry ass," a condition that often befalls the bowels of outsiders). The dead woman was referring to the weaving project I got started with money from the Marsden Foundation to teach women in the community who had stopped weaving when cheap commercial fabric came in, now that that same fabric had become dear. But how did the Mundo man know all this? Could I have fallen asleep somewhere along this path? No, I can *see* in my dreams!

Netted Burden

Before I could put my head in order, she is escorted away, and the *capitan* of the Earthlords is called forth, to consider my case. The chanting builds, peaks, then ceases. My sweat glands have lost control. The Mundo greets me. *Shuíaqíaí,* "good night," is all I muster, shakily. The room is without any sound, one of those instants that temporarily seems eternal. Then the raspy voice cackles out something sharply in *Kíichei,* too quick and complex for me to grasp, except the word for dog, *tzíií,* and in response there is a murmur of laughter, the first exhale of humor since sundown. The gringa groans, yawning, and we wash out of the room into the icy brilliance of a moonless night, a mile high without a light, and catch a pace along the roof beam of the Milky Way, surfing the joke of the Mundo. The gringa wants to know what she missed, I want to know what the shaman said, and everyone else can't speak, only more laughter with every try. I console myself with the idea that this is probably a tactful negative, or why yuk it up? I'm *asustado* (alarmed) but content at my escape.

Snake Bite

Finally, back across the line into Chinique township, the son Manuel manages to translate. "If you have a dog [laughter] in the house [more laughter] who does not know who your friends are, he could just bite anybody." Another round of laughter, giggles, shawls over faces. I am used to being laughed at; it is part of my rapport. Now I am in the dark as to what this cryptic message means, except to see that likening me to a dog constitutes a good example of local humor. Not until later do I find out that this meant that I must be taught: dogs are considered "natural" shamans, but, like a dog, I was sort of socialized but not entirely (recall what dogs do in the street) and a potential loose cannon on the spiritual plane, if left untutored. Don't let it swell your head, cranky ass. Carrying the whole thing further, they named a dog after me, one that had one blue and one brown eye. I was stuck now. And no, unlike so many of my own generation raised on Carlos Castaneda, unlike my elder colleagues over in Momostenango, I was not at the time in the least interested in becoming a calendar diviner.[1] I was an applied anthropologist with worlds to fix.[2] No one had ever explained to me that in addition to the divinations (check), the dreams (check), the special sickness with the appropriate visions (check), all these "impersonal recruitment" indicators, the one other sure sign of divinatory destiny besides my sacred calendar birth day is extreme reluctance to take up the beans, to count the days.

Death's Opening

The world changed. Now every day was like a flavor, not just another day, or the simplicity of weekday versus weekend, as I had previously lived time. Now all of time had another frame placed around it, in twenty-day rounds, and with the dance of the thirteen intensities. Deer days hard to get on top of, Dog days of desire and intuition, Bird days of fortune, so many influences to look for, so many signs to read, ponder, read again at the table, at the chair. Magic and meanings everywhere, everywhen. Now through the focusing lens of Maya time and holy space the opaque world of traditionalism emerged, and when I looked out on the projects we were attempting from the borrowed vantage point of my compadres of the table, it seemed suddenly all wrong, culturally misaligned, illogical mistake upon ignorant mistake, half a dissertation's worth of well-meaning disasters. But that is, or was, another long story.

Healer's Mount

Not long before leaving the Forest People, after I had quit Save the Children in disgust, but before the time of the evil men and their genocidal violence, I was walking alone in the area where Robert Carmack had discovered some of the early Kíicheí settlements, taking my vision to the ethno-archaeological map to see what arose. I was brought out of my intellectual reverie about the Place of Dawning in the Popol Vuh, the far mountain peak where I was initiated, and, locally speaking, time as we know it began, by a small agitated man with limited Spanish, requesting my help in the aid of a sick child.[3] Now, in Guatemala, I had often been approached by people seeking medical advice under the assumption, often correct, that we knew something about medicine. But this man was different. He knew who I was. He was in the vast compadre matrix, that spiderweb of initiates and their families who spoke with the World, who counted the days. He was asking for spiritual assistance for a medical case. Now what?

Yellowing Harvest

Off to the hut at a trot, forcing myself out of my thoughts into action, out of the shadows of participating to observe, to observation in participation. I was the ayudante, the apprentice of a known healer–diviner, and this was an urgent matter. As I approached the last rise to the house, I was already taking charge, sending children out for herbs, instructing neighbors to pool offerings, erecting an altar, and checking on the girl. Who has argued with this one? I asked plaintively, who has forgotten her permissions? What ancestor may be livid? What do you have to pay up? She had a fever, not too high but there. *Pericón*, *tagetes lucida*, relative of the marigold, an old Popol Vuh incense offering that cuts fever gently. I knew this because I had been thus cured when I had what this girl looked to have, an illness owned in the Xibalbaj underworld. I was also conversant with the illness in the medical literature and knew the best thing was good food, rest, lots of *pericón* tea, and attention by her family. There are no medications for food-borne hepatitis, once it shows in the eyes. I took note of the day, Home, heading for the Holy Earth day, interrogated family about any past failures to ask for thanks for issues of the household from the World. Another house was being built close by, and there had not been a proper ceremony of permission. This would have to be rectified, I knew the rite, I was completely engaged in it, I had taken on old Lucas? persona for a spell, to *do* the healing, render a cure.

Pay Day

The beans revisited the house, someone was angry, conflict with ancestors, a permission missed. A cross word to the sickly child had to be forgiven, with penitence before the altar, back and forth on the knees, in view of the patient, while I mumbled, swung the censer, did the ritual chewing out. Whose heart hardens to the child, hardens to all. And a chicken, a substitute had to be given up, it was too late to stave off the ancestors and the lawyers of the world with just copal and candles. That part was clear as rock crystals, clear as before we were blinded, when we all could see clearly.

By dusk, pure white feathers caught in the breeze danced toward Jakavitz, the early K'iche' citadel.[4] Why all the body signs, blood jumps, in the cheek, up to the eyelid. What did she see, ripe, harvest, yellow of course, yellow eyes. *Q'an bok'och*, the name of an underworld Lord, and the sickness he rules. A confirmation? Cost?

Dog Day

After some tea, she looked better. The family had her healing in focus, finally, and when I left she was eating a stringy leg with interest. The light of life, reemerging as dawn, after the sacrifice, after the confession. I had done what I could conjoining two traditions, while flying on automatic, while calling on Lucas for guidance at every step. But let's not make it a habit, I said to myself, in comforting darkness, on the trail back toward *Patojil*. This is way too out of bounds, way over the line. One blue eye and one brown.

Wrap Up

I found out later, through the web, that she had recovered; it was Lord Yellow Eyes, may I never have to make such a diagnosis again in the field. She was on to some more life in the shadow of Saqiribal, to the east "where it dawns," where all are initiated, even gringos. Me toward an awakening to even more fascination with how help works in other cultural latitudes, the calling of healing at the next level, how to have something at least approximating a profession as guide when messing with the poor. How to be a spiritually inspired ally of reason and hope, of learning and wisdom, asking always how to help without hurt. After all the hurt I witnessed inflicted by aid groups in Guatemala in their attempts to help, my soul wanted to take the lesson to the text, let the world learn something about what mistakes tell those who listen. A way to wrap all these lessons into a bundle, texts.

Journey's Path

I started out trying to help those who seemed obviously in need. But they were gentle on me, despite colonialism, and let me see gradually, despite my resistance, how differently I would have to be and understand what was before me, to know even the first thing to do, the first thought in the pathway of help, the first question to not even ask, the first move in any planning procedure. So I was the one come to study with and from them; they would send me back seeing where to walk, where to fly. I would meet those in flight, over the border in the heat of Chiapas, then, and write about it, another text of exodus. They came to meet those who had left the tiny plots of Altos traditional life to colonize the jungle frontier, there they mixed, there they worked, some went back, some stayed. I came back. I continued north, to the border with the United States.

Home Made

I have made full circle. From dogs and homes and time in Guatemala, to seeking shelter away in new lands, new homes, back toward home with those in migration, finally to the meeting place where bleak mountains ring the pass of interior history, of royal roads and westward rails, the end of the Rockies and the start of the Mother mountains, where the edges bleed not into the pitiful ditch of our separation, but across all walls of it into the veins of our breath, our thirsty cells and bushes, here in the desert where the path to cross now awaits the hungry for work, the thirsty for a living wage, dodging death, now the Mayas head for where the anthropologist hides out writing, and I watch them getting on the Southwest Eagle nonstop to Phoenix, tossing them a tamale *mas* for the road. I return south to those who have not left, return to the spiraling movement of the *caracol mandala*, to the heartlands of the Zapatistas, to help in consulting on helping, answering needs, asking questions, listening and talking, watching a new place being made, with *la palabra*. A word I can speak here when I return.

Sacred Ground

This is the beginning story, ending. In my learning always this lesson, word, taking the Dog day way of going over there. But as for the start of how I crossed the line, learned about the amazing Maya *mundo*, and came back somehow somebody else, that adventure began in the Dog days, when, for a short period in my life, I thought I knew where I was going, and what I was doing. *Ayeee Mundo!!!*

Notes

1. Dennis and Barbara Tedlock (known to my compadre as *tenisibarbara*). She is author of *Time and the Highland Maya* (Albuquerque: University of New Mexico Press, 1992); he is editor and translator of the *Popol Vuh* (NY: Simon and Schuster, 1985), and more recently, *Breath on the Mirror: Mythic Voices and Visions of the Living Maya* (San Francisco: Harper, 1993), in which I appear as a character named *Tunkan*. My compadre also appears in that story as the storyteller up on Patojil Mountain, not far from the Dawning Place.

2. As a "coauthorial" applied anthropologist, my recent titles include "Acompañar Obediciendo: Learning How to Help in Collaboration with Zapatista Communities" (with Jeanne Simonelli), *Michigan Journal for Service Learning* 10, no. 3 (summer 2004); "The Irrational Efficiencies of Planned Globalization: Alternative Development and Plan Puebla Panama in Chiapas" (with Jeanne Simonelli), *Journal of the Steward Anthropology Society* 28, nos. 1–2 (2004); "Disencumbering Development: Alleviating Poverty through Autonomy in Chiapas" (with Jeanne Simonelli), in *Here to Help: NGOs Combatting Poverty in Latin America*, ed. R. Eversole (NY: M. E. Sharpe, 2003); a book to come out in early 2005: *Uprising of Hope: Accompanying Zapatistas with Alternative Development in Chiapas* (Walnut Creek CA: Altamira Press) (also with Jeanne Simonelli); and fourteen other articles in the last dozen years on development subjects in the region.

3. The Dawning Place is where, in the sacred book of the ancient K'iche?, the *Popol Vuh*, the people gathered to see it dawn for the first time, dividing what we might call mythic time from historical time in the document. Once it does "dawn," most of the rest of the book is a history of the accomplishments of the K'iche Maya, whereas before it is largely about cultural heroes fighting deities of death and pride, and such things as the creation of the world and humans. Today this same location is used for the initiation of daykeeping shamans or *aj q?ij* for the nine municipalities that share a border at the peak or close by, and has shrines and caves associated with the rites of initiation, which the author experienced.

4. *Jakavitz* is about four miles from the Dawning Place, an early K'iche? city.

Part Five

Apprenticeship and Research Practices

In the closing chapters of this book, three contributors explore what they have discovered about the strengths and limitations of conventional research methods and agendas once they ventured on the ecstatic side of fieldwork. In these essays we see more explicitly how experiential ethnographers weave themselves, "or are woven by others," into the communities they study, "becoming cultural actors in the very dramas of the society [they] endeavor to understand" (Cooley 1997, 18, in Goulet 1998, 254). A common thread running through these essays is that of apprenticeship, of truly learning from people we engage with and who become our mentors.

In "A Pathway to Knowledge: Embodiment, Dreaming, and Experience as a Basis for Understanding the Other," Denise Nuttall describes her apprenticeship as a tabla player, in a musical tradition that is found in Indian Hindustani (classical Northern) tabla (percussion) communities as well as within the South Asian Diaspora in North America. In her discussion of this journey as an apprentice to a master, she shows how this indigenous way of knowing contrasts sharply with that of Western knowledge systems in the teaching and learning of not only artistic but other forms of knowledge. In Indian ways of knowing, oral tradition is privileged over the Western focus on textual knowledge. The ideal of the *guru/shishya* relationship promotes a total embodiment and mimesis of the master. This pathway to experiential knowledge includes much more than simply attending classes and practicing one's craft. The intensity of learning a tradition in this way often leads to the phenomenon of dreaming of the guru, his art and his life. Experiencing the dreams and spiritual side of a musical tradition deepened her connection to those she lived and studied with. This led her to an avenue of investigation in discipleship among tabla communities that she would not have looked at otherwise.

In their joint chapter, " Field of Dreams; Fields of Reality: Growing with and in the Field of Anthropology," Jeanne Simonelli, Erin Mc-Culley, and Rachel Simonelli demonstrate how learning and teaching anthropology in the field requires a special set of skills and insights, some of which can be gleaned from books, and others, as one of her mentors said, are figured out when you get there. This chapter provides a vivid account of apprenticeship of anthropological fieldwork. Throughout this examination, Simonelli, McCulley, and Simonelli ask important questions. First, how has our perception of this professional apprenticeship changed since the days when our "anthro-cestor," Malinowski (1967 in Kuper 1973, 28), in a fit of depression, saw the "lives of the natives as something as remote from [him] as the life of a dog"? Second, how have we modified and crafted the experience of fieldwork to meet changing perspectives on what anthropology is all about? Third, and most fundamentally, can we teach fieldwork, or does it teach us?

In the last chapter, "Dancing Lessons from God: To Be the Good Ethnographer or the Good Bad Ethnographer," Millie Creighton offers three significant segments of life stories heard from informants who represent different aspects of marginalization in Japan. The information offered by these Japanese women concern a *Hibakusha* (atomic blast survivor), a resident Korean, and a *Burakumin* (member of a discriminated-against hereditary group). None of these stories were told in response to specific questions, nor were they directly related to the specific primary research agenda of the author. To address the contradictions between the model of rigor, under which these stories might not have emerged, and the model of vigor, which recognizes the validity of seemingly peripheral discoveries, Millie Creighton argues that ethnographic fieldwork is not just about the collection of facts, but the meaningful interpretation of human experience that is sometimes revealed in unexpected ways. Being the good ethnographer in terms of rigorous adherence to specific project goals can lead to being the bad ethnographer in terms of long-term contributions of knowledge from the field.

14. A Pathway to Knowledge

Embodiment, Dreaming, and Experience
as a Basis for Understanding the Other

DENISE NUTTALL

This paper locates the study of indigenous or Indian knowledge systems in the *guru–shishya parampara* (master–disciple institution) within and beyond the borders of the South Asian diaspora in North American and Indian Hindustani (classical Northern) tabla (percussion) communities. I draw on fieldwork carried out within tabla communities (1994 to present) in Mumbai, New Delhi, Vancouver, Seattle, and San Francisco, to focus on an anthropological and musical journey into the world of tabla. Apprenticing as a student first under Ustad Allah Rakha Khan and later under his eldest son, Ustad Zakir Hussain, has led me to question anthropological beliefs, traditions, and models concerning how we do anthropology in "the field" and subsequently how we produce our ethnographic texts upon returning from "the field."[1]

Deriving from my dissertation, "Embodying Culture: Gurus, Disciples and Tabla Players" (Nuttall 1998), this paper both adopts and builds upon anthropological models of lived experience that see everyday experience and the acquisition of performative knowledge as central to how people reproduce or transform their cultural lives and traditions.[2] Because we live our lives in and through our bodies, any theory of lived experience must take into account the primacy of our relation to others as bodily. Similarly, ethnographic texts must somehow correspond with and communicate the embodiedness not only of self and other but of anthropological, personal, cultural, political, and possibly spiritual knowledge. The guru–disciple relationship is complex, ever changing, intimate, and intense. In the beginning I did not realize how different my life would become in taking up the practice and performance of this instrument. And as I continue on the journey of learning to be a tabla player both in India and in North America, I continue also to learn anthropologically.

Embodiment, Experience, and Apprenticeship

Apprenticeship, as one form of participant observation allows the researcher to experience and communicate the embodiedness of self and other. Adopting the apprenticeship approach to the study of others moves the discipline toward a reconceptualization of the fieldwork process itself. It questions the basic assumptions about how we do what we do, the doing of anthropology. How do we learn anthropologically? How can we simultaneously go beyond and work within the problematic of postcolonial fields? Apprenticeship demands that analysts begin with embodied experience. As a tabla apprentice I came to realize that the anthropological field is not "out there," connected to a piece of land or a bounded geographical site. In an anthropology of apprenticeship, the body becomes the field site.

Gurus and Disciples

Originating from the Indian Brahmanical tradition of religious study, the guru–shishya or *ustad–shagird* (Persian, used as a form of address for Muslim masters) tradition is a culturally specific form of learning. This apprenticeship offers no easy translation culturally, spiritually, or philosophically. There seems to be a certain tendency today in India to have a guru, or multiple gurus, who guide others in all aspects of life, be it in a trade, an art form, a spiritual pursuit, or otherwise. Ranade (1984, 31) suggests that the relationship of guru and shishya is qualitatively different from the usual student–teacher relationships. Traditionally, disciples were expected to participate in the *guru-kula* system of learning, where the student would travel to and live with his or her master to apprentice in a craft, trade, or discipline. In this everyday world of apprenticeship, disciples would then be close to the master, come to know him in an intimate way, and learn to embody his knowledge, style, and way of being.

The relationship between guru and disciple is highly personal, close, and tightly bound. Just as the master gives of his time, love, and dedication, so, too, the disciple must give of herself or himself in similar ways. Ideally, in a *guru-kula* context the *shishya*'s learning necessitates a deep devotion to the craft or art form as well as to the master. This devotion often translates into service such as making tea or *chai*, running errands, and the like. The tradition is based on two central concepts, implicit faith and unquestioned obedience, found in Hindu religious texts such as the Upanishads (Mlecko 1982). It is crucial that the guru is seen to hold and pass on absolute knowledge accumulated throughout his career. My teachers have told me that the *shishya* must believe without question in the tradition, style, and discipline of the master (Hussain 1995, 1996). This emphasis on blind faith and unquestioned obedience serves to create a distinct type of student–teacher relationship. Disciples often struggle physically and emotionally as they learn a tradition in this way.

The attitude to the guru in Indian cultures is one of extreme reverence. Respect for the guru has evolved into a kind of devotional form similar to that held toward God. Touching the feet of the master symbolizes the disciple's complete submission and service to the master. As gurus are the mediums through which God speaks, or communicates, there exists a belief that the guru provides a path to spiritual or divine knowledge and experience. The gods said, "We can give you the knowledge . . . but only the teacher can show the way" (Mlecko 1982, 37, from *Chandogya Upanishad*). As Mlecko states, "To be near the guru and reverently serve and obey him is to find, to know and to experience the way" (Mlecko 1982, 37). However, while the guru is supposed to provide this kind of knowledge to a *shishya*, the Upanishads also suggest that it is not so much that the teacher shows the path but that he embodies the path (Gupta 1994, 27). Experiencing this pathway to knowledge relies upon the *shishya*'s ongoing cooperation, respect, and unquestioned obedience.

Among disciples in tabla communities, the guru is often described as divine, as being similar to a holy man. His life is held as the ideal way of being in every aspect from how he creates his image as a performer to how he walks, talks, and generally lives his life. The following selection from an interview with a senior disciple of Ustad Allah Rakha provides a good example of the spiritual dimension attributed to gurus by disciples.

> Going through all that with great control, getting over every hurdle and being successful in every mission he [Abbaji] has had to sacrifice a lot.[3] Every artist has to do this. They reach a stage where they become very vibrant. It becomes like a discipline, just like the spiritual one. Your only aim is God and nothing else. Similarly, Abbaji's only aim is tabla. So even when you are sitting around him there is this magnetic field of tabla *bols* going around and you just get engulfed with it. That is my observation. Even though he is just sitting he is looking at everything in musical and rhythmic terms. From his balcony you can see the sea. When he sees the waves the rhythm of the waves is fascinating him also. He is getting inspiration from that or he is creating something from that inspiration. When he sees the sun or the movement of the sun in that also there is *lay* (rhythm). He sees *lay* in everything. (Yogesh Samsi 1996)

The Masters and the Music

The classical music system in India is divided into two distinct regionally based categories, the *Hindustani* or Northern classical style originating within the Mogul court system and the *Karnatic* or South Indian style. Tabla, known more for its accompaniment of various instruments such as the sitar and sarod the Northern style of classical dance, kathak, has progressed in recent times to the status of a solo art form (Kippen 1991). Ustad Allah Rakha Khan, Ustad Ahmedjan Thirakwa, Ustad Amir Hussain Khan, and others have been paramount in this reinvention of tabla as a solo instrument both in India and around the globe. The generation of tabla players who followed these artists, such as Ustad Zakir Hussain, Pandit Anindo Chatterjee, Trilok Gurtu, and Pandit Swapan Chaudhuri continue to recreate this complex art form as they and tabla travel around the world.[4]

In the 1960s and 1970s as an accompanist to the sitar maestro Ravi Shankar (sitar) Allah Rakha brought tabla and Hindustani classical music to millions of people around the globe. Events at Woodstock and Monterrey, California, in the United States were, in part, crucial for the development of the study of tabla outside India, in North America and Europe. When Allah Rakha passed away in February of 2000, his eldest son, Zakir Hussain became head of the Punjab *gharana* (school).

The popularity of Zakirji as a performer, celebrity, and composer continues to reach new heights year after year. Zakirji's concert schedule includes more than 150 events around the world per year. On top of this, he dedicates much time to numerous Indian classical music recordings, world music and fusion recordings, performing, advising, composing, and acting in feature films such as Bertolucci's *Little Buddha* and Anita Desai's *In Custody*, Merchant Ivory's *Heat and Dust*, and, more recently, Rahul Bose's *Everybody Says I'm Fine*. Because of his many talents and amazing skills as a musician and tabla player, Zakirji's popularity has soared in India. In India, Zakirji is a much sought-after celebrity for consumer endorsements such as Taj Mahal Tea. This includes media coverage in the form of commercials as well as billboards and posters. In addition to this grueling schedule, Zakirji also teaches for a number of months in the Bay Area, California, and periodically in Mumbai at the Allah Rakha Institute of Music.

As I, too, travel around the world, I inevitably take part in tabla discussions of Zakirji's latest accomplishments, and his strength and great skill as a master of tabla.[5] There are many stories circulating about his "otherworldly" abilities as an artist and composer. Many students, whether they are from the Punjab school or not, take up tabla after seeing him perform in concert. For many young boys in India and elsewhere, he has become a tabla idol, worshiped daily as the ideal tabla player. From among those who follow his career in North America and Europe, I have heard some refer to him as "my favorite rock star." I traced some of the fiction surrounding Zakirji to stories recounted in Mickey Hart's *Drumming at the Edge of Magic: A Journey into the Spirit of Percussion* (1990). Hart recounts in his text Zakirji's stories of his own apprenticeship that includes a *chilla*, a kind of ritual retreat instigated by the master where the *shishya* is secluded for forty days and nights. During the *chilla*, the disciple is expected to practice, increasing the hours of practice to most of the day and night as time goes on. During the *chilla*, Zakirji has visions; it is a time of great self-awareness and knowledge. Upon reading Hart's book, some tabla students in North America and Europe have attempted to perform their own kind of *chilla*, albeit a shortened version without the master's knowledge.

The learning of tabla then necessitates a complete and total commitment both to the instrument and to the master of the art form. The instrument itself consists of two drums, the *bayan*, the left-hand drum made of aluminum or copper, and the *dayan*–tabla, the right-hand drum made of a variety of types of woods such as *shisham* or rosewood. The tabla heads are generally made from goat or cow skin with a *gab* (iron filings and rice paste combination) placed strategically in the center (*dayan*) or to the side (*bayan*) for optimal sound. The tabla belongs to one of the most complex and intricate percussive rhythmic systems in the world today, requiring the coordination of both hands, with each finger playing a particular set of sounds or *bols*. *Bol*, stemming from the Hindi verb *bolna*, meaning to speak, refers to the strokes the fingers make on the tabla or the basic grammar of the tabla. For every *bol* or stroke played on the tabla, there is a corresponding sound made by the voice. The *bols* are onomatopoeic syllables used by tabla players as an aid for the memorization of compositions. Technically, they are sounds or basic units that, when strung together, create phrases, and these phrases can be used to develop a composition. For example, the *bols ghe, re, na, ge* (pronounced ghay, ray, nah, ge) are frequently heard together as a phrase in all types of compositions. In the Punjab school the *bols te, ke, te* are strung together to create the phrase *terekete* (tey rey key te) or *tetekete*.

Often, class may begin with the master voicing the *bols*, or the sounds of the compositions, before actually playing. Very early on, I was told that to really understand a composition one must be able to voice it, remember it in the hands and the mind simultaneously. The knowledge of recitation also depends upon the ability to count out the composition within a certain *tal* or rhythmic structure. Counting is shown by using the thumb of the left hand as a marker, moving upward to each groove in the finger beginning and ending with the smallest finger. Again, knowing here relies upon both seeing, feeling, and hearing where the *bol* falls in relation to the time structure, to the *tal*. Gottlieb (1990, 140) notes that the word *tal* comes from the practice of counting time by clapping hands. There are many different *tals*, each having a certain number of beats. For example, the most widely used *tal* in Hindustani music is *tin tal*, which has sixteen beats. Others include *jhap* (10), *rupak* (7), *ek* (12), *dadra* (6), and *kherava* (8).

Unlike in the Western music system, where musicians begin counting with the first beat of the bar and end on the final beat (for example in 4/4 time you begin with 1 and end with 4), in Hindustani music, counting begins and ends with 1, the *sam*. Tabla players, as the timekeepers of the *tal*, use various *theka*s or rhythmic structures to keep the beat in instrumental and vocal compositions. The *theka* outlines the structural form and also provides the division of the *tal*. Each *tal* has different *thekhas* and each *thekha* consists of a specified number and arrangement of *bols*; however the structure of the *thekha* can and is elaborated on in performance.

Along with learning a variety of rhythmic outlines, tabla players must also learn to play a number of different compositional types. Students usually start their *talim*, or learning, with a *kaida* composition, a type of pattern that always has a theme of fixed *bols* followed by a number of variations based on those fixed *bols* ending with a *tihai* or *bol* phrase that is repeated three times. The *tihai* pattern is also found in other types of compositions, such as *chakradhars* (from Hindi, meaning "wheel"), which can be a more complex rhythmic pattern with fixed *bols*, and *tukras* ("a segment" or "part of a piece"), a type of short composition in solo tabla playing and classical performance.

Apprenticeship and Anthropology: The Method

An anthropology of apprenticeship necessitates theorizing and reflecting on ideas of experience. Jackson (1989, 1996), Stoller (1995), and Bourdieu (1970, 1977) note the importance of adopting William James's essential idea of describing the other in a radically empirical way. Jackson stresses that the importance of radical empiricism is that it highlights "the ethnographer's interactions with those he/she lives with, and studies, while urging us to clarify the way in which our knowledge is grounded in practical perspectives and participatory experiences in the field as much as our detached observations" (Jackson 1989, 3). Jackson goes further and notes that the method of participant observation is built upon the idea that the experiences of the researcher are crucial in ethnographic knowledge production. Here the experiential field is defined as one of "interactions and intersubjectivity" (Jackson 1989, 3). Focusing on lived experience in this way allows for the inclusion of diverse forms of knowledge acquisition and recognizes indigenous ways of knowing and doing, such as the possibility of dreaming about tabla and the master, his compositions and/or highly complex rhythms.

Re-evaluating what we mean by participation, action, or involvement in the ethnographic way of life is an important but difficult task. Traditionally, the experiences of the participant–observer have been presented in ethnographies as a way of maintaining and gaining authority in the discipline. I know the other because "I was there." The crisis in the anthropological representation of others has moved its practitioners toward reflection on ethnographic authority. Clifford (1997), Van Maanen (1988), and Geertz (1988) are among those who have pointed to the use and abuse of the anthropologist self as a textual strategy in knowledge production. These writers have, however, offered little discussion on the importance of theorizing anthropological practice as an embodied, contextually dependent mode of doing. As Fabian (2001) rightly points out, the anthropological focus on representation, to the exclusion of other critical issues such as knowledge production, has created a discourse that does not attend to experiential knowledge in any significant way. "If it is true, as we have said, that the question of ethnographic objectivity has been displaced by a shift of emphasis in critical thought from production to representation, then our response should be to explore again body and embodiment as involved in objectification and the grounding of objectivity" (Fabian 2001, 30–31).

Re-evaluating the meaning of ethnographic experience and knowledge production must begin with our assumptions about the relationship of the fieldworker self and the subsequent textual other. Engaging in an apprenticeship, in an experience with other cultural selves, is an engagement of a student to a master. Seen in this way, the power relations between self and other becomes crystal clear, the master has the knowledge, power, and skill; the anthropologist becomes the apprentice.

The apprentice approach demands that the anthropologist explicitly challenge the rigid subject–object dichotomy of old. In her work on the rise of narrative ethnography, Barbara Tedlock addresses the issue of intersubjectivity by looking back at the old accusation of "going native": "What seems to lie behind the belief that going native poses a serious danger to the fieldworker is the logical construction of the relationship between objectivity and subjectivity, between scientist and native, between self and other, as unbridgeable opposition" (B. Tedlock 1991, 71). This idea that the fieldworker must somehow effectively participate in and observe a new and somewhat strange way of life, in the Malinowskian sense of observation as detachment and objectification of the other, serves only to create a personal and ethical crisis in the doing of ethnography.

Although the apprentice approach to participant observation in anthropology has been most frequently used by ethnomusicologists and dance ethnologists (Neuman 1974, 1980; Kippen 1988; Chernoff 1979, 1993; Sudnow 1978; Zarrilli 1984, 1987), there is a growing interest in the practice of apprenticeship within the wider discipline (Coy 1989, Stoller 1987, Cooper 1989, Goody 1989, Dow 1989, Taussig 1987). Past studies of apprenticeship have neglected to examine the significance of apprenticeships where the anthropologist creates and sustains concrete ties binding the student to a master or larger social organization and culture over time (Lave and Wenger 1991, Dow 1989, Cooper 1989). Researchers have reported a type of schizophrenia arising from the problematics of engaging in a double role of apprentice in a skill or trade and as an anthropologist–ethnographer. The apprenticeship is seen as "pretense" or "play" because what the anthropologist is really doing is gathering data "with an eye to use in publication, explanation and testing theory" (Dow 1989, 207). A successful anthropology of apprenticeship is not based on a form of "play." On the contrary, in the case of tabla communities, the researcher–apprentice must learn the knowledge and learn it well; otherwise, the field literally disappears.

Looking for the Field

In the fall of 1994, I left Vancouver for my first fieldwork trip to study at Gandharva Mahavidyalaya, an institute of music in New Delhi. Not knowing any tabla masters in India, I assumed that I would find contacts through starting my studies at a musical college. Like many first anthropological trips to the field, my entry into Indian culture and the life of tabla players was short-lived. After my first week in Delhi, besides the intense culture shock I faced, the plague (both bubonic and pneumonic, or so it was thought) broke out in Surat to the south of Delhi and started to spread rapidly throughout the country. A week later, when the airfields opened up, I left India without having met a tabla player, teacher, or other musicians. My feeling of defeat was short-lived. A few days after returning to Vancouver, I went to an Indian classical musical concert, where I met a tabla player by the name of Satwant Singh. Satwantji agreed to teach me until I could return to India a few months later. Rather than continue with my original plans, I went, at Satwantji's urging, to Mumbai to see his teacher, Allah Rakha Khan, whom he referred to as Abbaji. And so I traveled to Mumbai to meet Allah Rakha Khan not knowing much about his history or school or life. When I first met Abbaji at his home in Malabar Hills, he welcomed me with open arms as a student of Satwantji's. I was already in the school, and now I was being welcomed as part of the larger family of the Punjab *gharana*. I was already an apprentice.

After some time, I met Zakirji at his father's home on his birthday. By this point, I was used to welcoming all who were senior to me in the musical world by touching their feet. As I attempted to touch Zakirji's feet and wish him well on his day, he shook my hand and welcomed me to Mumbai. I asked him if I could learn tabla from him, and he remarked that he only teaches in Seattle and the Bay Area of California, as his father teaches in India. The following descriptions provide a taste of my musical and anthropological journey following Zakirji on the West Coast of North America. The ethnographic selections I present here are, in part, a response to Stoller's (1995) call for sensing ethnography, for attending to the cultural in every sense.

Sensing Tabla I: Vancouver and Seattle 1996

Stefan had been learning tabla from Abbaji, Zakirji, and Satwantji, a senior disciple of the Punjab *gharana*, for three years now. In the process of doing so, he had become a dedicated disciple. His love of and passion for tabla was taking him on a new path, providing him with a new direction in his life. When we first met in 1994 he had been out of high school only a few years and was working as a sales clerk at a record store in Vancouver. The job barely allowed him to pay the bills, but it meant survival by day so that he could practice tabla (*riaz*) by night. *Riaz* was fast becoming his only activity outside work. At times I wondered whether this was a passion, an obsession, or an intimate type of dedication. His every waking moment centered on learning and practicing tabla.

In the summer of 1996 we began to practice together in anticipation of Zakirji's upcoming classes in Seattle. We usually met at his home before leaving for class. One day as I entered his room I noticed its arrangement was similar to the rooms I had seen of other tabla players while in India. It was filled with tabla; a *lahra* machine, which players use as a metronome for keeping time to practice playing in Hindustani classical style; powder canisters; and an altar dedicated to Zakirji and Abbaji. The altar consisted of a large picture of Zakirji and a separate one of Abbaji, lovingly placed on the top of a table and surrounded by rose petals, a carefully selected assortment of stones that Stefan had picked up by the ocean, and burning incense. I remembered also that Satwantji had carefully selected photos of Abbaji and placed them on the walls of his tabla room. Whenever I went to visit Satwantji, Abbaji's presence in the room was a very comforting feeling. Here, too, in Stefan's house, our teacher's presence was always felt. As I practiced *dha ge tin na ke na na ge dhin na ge na* over and over again, I would glance over to their pictures on the table.

Traveling to Seattle from Vancouver by car took us through rocky mountain passes along the Pacific Ocean. We listened to tabla solos, recited our own compositions (or tried to remember them), and talked of Zakirji's latest recordings, concerts, and movies. Zakirji had always been a major topic of conversation with most tabla players I had met, but speaking with Stefan and Zakirji's other students about him took on a new significance. Always they spoke of him with much love, joy, and excitement in their voices. We all intensely desired to be around him, learn from him, walk with him, and talk with him about tabla and life.

After arriving in Seattle, we drove directly to the home of Emam, a senior student of Zakirji. Although Emam had been learning from Abbaji since 1979, he shortly thereafter took up studies with Zakirji as well. Emam and Zakirji have formed a deep and close friendship over the years. Emam followed Zakirji to classes in California; spent time with him on tour in India, protecting him from over zealous fans; and now, along with another senior student, Tor, was helping set up classes in Seattle. Emam greeted us, as he usually did, with a big hug and a smile. Eventually, we got out our tabla to practice. The afternoon went by quickly as we sat cross-legged on the floor in front of our tabla playing with rhythm.

Soon it was time to pack up the tabla and powder and head out to class. We made our way to the University of Washington campus where our tabla lessons were to take place. We found the music room on the second floor, left our shoes at the doorway, and claimed our spots on the wooden floor in front of a portable blackboard. The room was empty except for a riser at the front by the windows. Others wandered into the room, set up their carpets and tabla, and started to warm up. Emam brought in Zakirji's tabla, a carpet for Zakirji to sit on, pillows, and some food to eat. He took special care in setting up Zakirji's space on the riser at the front of the room. In fact, Emam always made sure that Zakirji was comfortable. Was he getting enough sleep? Was he eating well? He always looked out for his teacher and friend. He made it his job to see to as many details as possible so that Zakirji could rest and relax.

Tor walked in with his tabla. Constantly telling stories and cracking jokes, his robust laughter filled the room. He knew everyone in the room. It took him a while to get by everyone to the front of the riser. Most of the people in the room were his own students from Seattle. Others had traveled from Portland and points in between. They were Americans of all types, some were Japanese American, some Irish, and a few were of Indian origin. Tor had been in the tabla fusion scene for some time now. He had been a student of Zakirji's in the early years in California and was one of the original members of Zakirji's percussion ensemble, The Diga Rhythm Band. It seemed that in North America, as I experienced in India, tabla culture was as much a complex of stories as it was a complex of rhythms, *bols*, and social interactions. There was one story in particular I heard Tor recount in various places. It was a story of a dear and close friend of his, Pete, who had taken up tabla many years ago, around the time of Tor's initiation into the world of tabla. His skill was amazing, intense, beautiful, and encouraging to Tor and to others.

I had heard of similar accounts about Pete from Zakirji's youngest brother, Fazal. Pete would travel to Mumbai to learn from Abbaji and was in the house day after day practicing, reciting, and performing compositions. Seeing this American fellow who held such a deep love and passion for tabla caught Fazal's attention. This, indeed, must be something special if someone from North America traveled to live and study with his father. Pete and Fazal would compete whenever they got the chance to do so. Pete would begin practicing tabla before Fazal left for school and would still be practicing when he arrived home later in the day. Fazal stressed that his speed was always a little bit faster than Pete's, and this would make Pete practice even more. Unfortunately, Pete's tabla career was short-lived. He died in the mid-1980s. Both Fazal's and Tor's deep friendship with Pete lives on through telling Pete's story to the younger generation of tabla players.

When Zakirji entered the room, he took off his shoes by the door and stopped to chat with the students before he proceeded to take his place by the window. As usual, he wore a *kurta-pajama*. This one was made of cotton dyed dark blue. Always he joked with us to help us relax and get reacquainted. Because of his hectic performance and recording schedule, Zakirji has decided to teach for only two months a year. There is an expectation that serious students travel to India in the winter months to attend concerts and be in the scene to digest and observe as much as possible. In our conversations, Zakirji stressed the necessity of watching and observing what other tabla players do in performance. Learning to accompany others begins by sitting with

335

your teacher during concerts. The general tendency in teaching tabla, though, is to teach it as a solo artistic form. Learning to accompany is an ongoing process.

The first group of students to play had formed a semicircle around Zakirji's tabla. Everyone was playing something different as they warmed up, waiting for class to begin. It sounded chaotic and loud to my ears. Each tabla was tuned to a different pitch, resulting in a collage of tabla noise. Class was divided into three sections, beginner, intermediate, and advanced levels. The students who were ready to start made up the beginner level. Behind them in my row were the intermediate students, and behind us sat the more advanced students. In the first two groups, I noticed that five of us were women. This seemed more or less consistent with what I had observed the previous year. Many others sat chatting in smaller groups, renewing their friendships.

As Zakirji began to play, everyone turned his or her attention to him. All eyes were on his hands. *Taka terekete taka terekete.* Soon everyone picked up the exercise and attempted to play along with him. Under our breath, we recited the *bols* so that our hands would remember the sequence. Where was he stressing the pulse? What was the intonation of this *bol* or that one? Where were the accents? Just as soon as I felt comfortable and in the groove of the moment, he changed the phrase by moving accents around and changing tempo. There was no time to think. We had to attend to the moment with all our concentration and just do as he did. It was a game of follow-the-teacher-if-you-can. He abruptly stopped the class and said, "Watch and imitate. Get your wrists to fall down. It's just a matter of getting used to the drum." He started again slowly moving the accents around and around, changing our conversation with each other, changing the feel of the exercise. Our tempo was all over the place. We consistently sped up after each cycle of the exercise.

I remembered the thoughts Zakirji had expressed the year before when the same thing happened. One of the students asked why it was that we always speed up. Zakirji responded:

> It's a natural tendency to rush. We are always trying to catch up to something. We always want to get paid more than someone else and we always want a better car than somebody else. We always

want a nicer house. I don't know—who knows? We just want to go forward. I have always noticed that when I have my students play with a tape they are always rushing. They are ahead of the tape by a couple of steps. I don't know why. There is just a natural tendency to drive it as opposed to just letting it relax. We always drive it. Always there is this drive.

The student remarked, "And you are steady?" Zakirji immediately replied:

I don't think I'm steady! I am also driving it. It's just that I have a little bit more control over how much drive. It's just not as much as someone else, right? I have seen drummers who naturally tend to relax so much that they are actually dragging it. There are such drummers who drag it, but then there are others who drive it. Although it seems to be moving forward, sometimes it doesn't really move forward as much as it actually seems. It just means that it has an up feeling. I've rarely found drummers who are steady. In Indian music, it's a natural tendency to start very slow and end up very fast. (Hussain 1996)

As class continued, Zakirji led us through various types of exercises. He would stop once in a while and comment on someone's hands. Oftentimes, he didn't need to speak but signaled his displeasure with a student's laziness of the hands, body, and lack of concentration with various gestures. He looked at his hands and then looked at ours and shook his head. "Do your hands look like this?" Zakirji yelled out over the motion and sound of twenty-five tabla students. The next moment he would have us write down the *bols*, all the while telling jokes and making us laugh. Emam and Tor would chime in as well, creating a very relaxing and welcoming atmosphere once again.

Zakirji played on, introducing various *tihais* that we could use in our tabla repertoire. He would present one *tihai* and then using a similar pattern and the same *bols* to develop it into another one by changing the rests and accents. He questioned us on our knowledge of a *tihai*. What was it supposed to do? When do you use it? How could we define it? Not entirely happy with the answers given, Zakirji took great care in explaining the structure and beauty of a *tihai* in various compositions.

Eventually, the first class came to a close and our group moved up to the front. It was getting hot in the music room. Many were beginning to use more and more powder to counteract their sweating, sometimes nervous, hands. When my hand started to sweat I could feel the tabla bending under my touch. I would dip my hands in powder again and again but it didn't seem to do much good. My fingers kept sticking to the black *gab* in the middle. Large bits of black ink stained my fingers. Stefan nudged me to look at Zakirji's hands as he started the class using the same *tihais* played moments before. The tempo was picking up. Stefan again whispered to me to watch Zakirji's hands and the placement of his fingers on the top part of the *gab*. "Look at how they move; check out where the hand sits." Indeed every gesture, every movement, began to take on a new meaning, a new intensity.

Zakirji started to teach a new *kaida* composition phrase by phrase. Eventually, the whole of the composition was revealed to us, but our accents were not right; it did not feel right in the body or sound correct when we played it. "Now recite it," Zakirji yelled out to us. After much reciting, I could tell Zakirji was happier with our rhythm and interpretation of the composition. "Now play it just in the same way as you have said it," he remarked. We attempted to play as Zakirji had asked. Five or eight minutes into playing the *bols*, concentrating only on doing what our teacher was doing at the same time, I felt an overwhelming sense of connectedness to Zakirji and everyone playing in the room. It was a kind of energy I had heard about from other students but had not, until then, experienced. Was it an illusion that what was coming out of his hands was directly going in my eyes and out my hands? Nevertheless, there was some kind of energy transmitted around and among tabla players at that moment that somehow allowed for an extraordinary unified sensation. Mirroring our teacher visually through the hands, and listening to his sound and interpretation of the composition in a focused way, ignited a kind of total communication between us. I felt a similar kind of energy or altered perception such as this only once before during one afternoon of practice alone. I was working on a composition for well over one year and had finally reached a significant speed in the process of doubling it. When I began to play the headline at slow speed, I was playing faster than my normal speed so that when I doubled it I increased the speed to what I thought was far too fast a tempo to control. However, to my surprise, my hands took off at lightning speed. Were these my hands? I could feel the rest of my body being pulled to the left of the tabla while my hands proceeded to perform without the rest of me. I wasn't thinking or reciting but simply observing my hands playing faster and faster. Time went by very slowly. In fact, what seemed like hours was only minutes. Time had slowed down; my breathing slowed down but my hands were playing faster than they had ever played before. Usually, my heartbeat increases when I double a composition, but this time my body fell into a kind of stasis, a kind of pause. It was an interesting experience and is one I have never felt since.

After we finished playing the composition, Zakirji showed us how to take it apart, phrase by phrase, to make smaller types of exercises for our *riaz*. The beauty of the structure lay in its simplicity. We could easily section off *bol* sequences to practice *tin ne* or *dhin ne* using *dhin ne na ge*. I realized that although Zakirji covered a number of *bols* by teaching certain compositions in the advanced classes, in the first two groups he consistently stressed *ne* and *ti*. *Ti* is played on the top of the tabla *gab* using the first bony section of the middle finger. It should be played strong, and sound crisp or tight. Essentially, the finger should just drop and hug the top part of the *gab*. The key in *ti* is to keep the finger near the top and not to move it down into the center spot.

One of the main elements of tabla playing that Zakirji continuously stressed was the use of space. He emphasized that the hand on the tabla should move within a specific range. Indeed, there is no need to come down from this central position unless a *bol* requires this (for example, *dheri dheri* or *di*). Many tones and *bols* can be played from the top part of the tabla, such as *tete, terekete, ti, na, tun, tin*, etc. Always, he showed us the hows of "doing," so that we could effectively get the job done. Positioning the fingers correctly does allow for the development of clarity and then, of course, increased speed in tabla playing.

There were many times Zakirji simply talked about the necessity of placing the hands correctly. His message to us was always to concentrate on the hand posture and positioning first, which comes in part from keeping the back straight and shoulders relaxed, and to worry about the sound later. The positioning of the hands leads the player to the right sound. If the hand positioning and subsequent wrist action is right, the sound will come. Here, the sense of touch, which leads to proper sound production, becomes a central focus of body memory and cognitive learning. Touching the tabla *bol* by *bol* creates certain bodily and hand sensations. After much repetition, the body begins to remember these sensations or feelings in the fingers and arms. Slowly, and with much practice, playing the *bol* correctly with the hands gives way to a stronger, clearer sound. Listening to the teacher play in class, in concerts and on tapes also figures in training the ear to hear what the sounds of *na* or *dha* should be. Eventually the ear "tunes in" and remembers the tones, the crispness, the softness or hardness of the *bol* sounds.

When it was time for the advanced class to play, we retreated to the back of the room with our tabla and carpets. Often, Zakirji took the time in between these sessions to play what he had just taught us, or a composition he wanted to work on at lightning speed. After passing on a few more compositions, Zakirji thanked us for our attention and ended class. Four and a half hours had passed. Many began to gather around Zakirji, wanting his attention or advice over this or that. He always took the time to talk to his students about their lives, loves, and desires. If they needed him, he was there for them. I realized that Zakirji played different roles for different students. For some he was their friend and teacher, for others he was like a brother, and for yet others he was a father figure, or a larger-than-life mythical master. Nevertheless, all highly respect him as a man and as a master of tabla tradition and culture.

Sensing Tabla II: Bay Area, California

In the fall of 1995, Leen, who had traveled from Belgium to study with Zakirji in California, came to visit me in Vancouver. We spent much time just getting to know each other and Vancouver by doing the things that tourists do. I found myself captivated by her tabla playing. I watched her technique and tried to absorb all that she was doing. She played with much emotion, intensity, and feeling. She played with her soul and was not obsessed with playing fast as many other tabla students I had met had been. She encouraged me to return to California with her and get to know some of the tabla players in the Bay Area communities.[6]

Leen took me to Oakland to stay with her friends Tim and Andrea. Andrea was a clothes and textile designer. Tim, then in his early forties, had been bitten by the tabla bug fifteen years earlier. Originally a Western percussionist, he had taken up tabla playing first under Ustad Allah Rakha Khan and Zakirji. Eventually, he connected with and became a disciple of Pandit Swapan Chaudhuri, a master of the Lucknow *gharana*, at the Ali Akbar College of Music in San Rafael. When we first arrived at Tim's house, there was much talk about Leen's trip to Canada and discussions about tabla. They acted like brother and sister, laughing at each other's jokes and teasing one another. Tim and Leen had met in Mumbai many years before, during the winter concerts.

Tim and Andrea lived in a Victorian-style house. It was spacious and had wonderful high ceilings. The neighborhood consisted mainly of lower-rent housing. The house was unusually large and grand in comparison. Across the street stood the local Baptist church, where on a Sunday morning we would awake to the choir's soulful calling of the Lord. Tim had constructed a magnificent tabla room in the central part of his old Victorian house on the first floor. It was here that he taught his private students and where many tabla players would gather and practice or perform for each other. There was always much tabla activity in the house from morning to night. Each morning Tim woke us up by softly playing a *kaida*. In the late morning and early afternoon, he taught classes, and later we practiced alone and then together. When we passed each other in the hall or gathered in the kitchen away from the tabla, we recited compositions for each other, counted them out, or talked of instrumentalists, concerts, and people in the music scene.

It was in this house where I first met Zakirji's students Peter and Dorothee. Dorothee had come from Germany for the summer months to study tabla. Peter, an "all 'round" musician, had been playing piano since he was a child. He had picked up cello and tabla by his early university years in Chicago and was now living and performing in San Francisco. Peter had, like Leen, traveled to India many times to study with Zakirji's father, learn Hindustani music, and follow Zakirji on tour. He often spoke of the classical music culture in Mumbai, telling us stories about learning to accompany with Hariprasad Chaurasia's *bansuri* (Hindustani flute made of bamboo) classes. Hariprasad Chaurasia, affectionately known as Hariji by many and as guruji by his own disciples, is one of the most popular *bansuri* players in India today. As a master of his instrument, Hariji attracts many disciples from around the world including Israel, Japan, America, France, and Canada.

There are many more opportunities to learn about the music in India. Being there counted in a multiplicity of ways. Although there were fewer chances to learn about the music in the larger scheme of things in California, in my newly found family there were daily opportunities to learn about tabla. Just being around older, more skilled students affected my skills and my aesthetic sensibility toward tabla.

We talked at great length about learning and performing tabla as non-Indian artists. The reality is that serious artists in India begin to study between the ages of five and seven, whereas many drummers in North America and Europe take up tabla in their early, mid-, or late twenties and thirties. Very few tabla players of non-Indian origin choose to compete in the professional classical market. The challenge for those who take up this instrument as a way of life outside of India is to somehow bring together classical tabla with their traditions, be it jazz or types of musical fusions.

Now and then, when the house was quiet, I had a chance to talk with Leen about her relationship with her teacher. Zakirji was a constant topic in many conversations anyway. It was not difficult to get his students to open up about their life with their teacher. Leen's very first encounter with Zakirji was in a dream. He woke her up in the middle of the night playing loudly, frantically, intensely. Leen did not know anything about this man or the instrument at the time of her first dream. This "calling" instigated a long search, which eventually took her to India. On her journey, she went from one tabla teacher to another but knew that she really should be learning from this master that she saw and heard in her dream. In her travels, she came to realize that it was Zakirji who had been present in the dream. Many friends and family discouraged her from seeking him out, suggesting that such a prominent sought-after master would have no time for her. Leen pressed on and eventually made her way to Mumbai. She contacted Zakirji at Simla House by phone. He told her to come over at a certain time to talk. When she finally contacted Zakirji and they eventually met face-to-face, he smiled and said, "What took you so long?"

As we talked further, I mentioned to Leen that I thought Zakirji was an extremely affecting person. "Yeah," she said, "He is a master; he is a spiritual master, too." "Does he guide you in your life?" I asked. "He's an example, yes. When I saw him for the first time, I laughed. I said, wow, here's my brother, the elder brother I always wanted." Leen continued:

> I felt that he was the same, in a way, the same as me. The energy! You can feel how he thinks and feels, how he plays the music. He transmits something and that is the thing that I want to do as well in my own way. Music is a channel to transmit something else, higher values in life, beauty, and love. And I just see him in a stage much further on than me. In terms of practical decisions, I'm in full control of my own life. It's my decision to do one thing or another. However, part of him attracts me.
>
> He opens up barriers that I don't see. It's like he can just push buttons. It's all in the plane of energy. He does things to you—that is a fact. It's like he holds this big mirror in front of you and you just have to look. So of course you grow, you learn, things change. Everything changes, and of course learning from him changes you. He's a powerful teacher. He becomes part of you, and this he has been from the very beginning.

Leen's description of her first encounter with Zakirji in a dream fascinated me. Later, after we had become closer friends, she told me that she dreams of him and of tabla all the time. I had first heard about tabla dreams years earlier from Satwantji. He told me that when he was in Mumbai studying with Abbaji, he was so intensely focused on learning the music that many nights he dreamt of compositions. I made a note about Satwantji's dreaming in my journal. It was not until I questioned Leen further that I realized dreaming of tabla was a much larger phenomenon affecting not only Leen and Satwantji's lives, but other students' lives as well. In fact, Leen said, "Peter, Dorothee and I all have these dreams." Tabla dreams can take the form of lessons in a house somewhere that Zakirji teaches a composition or part of a composition. Although there are many different kinds of dreams, the common denominator is the presence of the teacher. The dreaming times are usually, but not exclusively, connected to intense practice and class time with the master.

For Peter, the majority of tabla dreams that most resembled actual lessons occurred in the beginning years of studying the instrument. He did, however, recount a recent dream about his teacher. He had fallen asleep counting (or trying to count) a *chakradhar*, which he was to play that week at a performance with other advanced students. He was having a difficult time concentrating because of work pressures and deadlines, and he had not spent much time practicing the composition. Time was running out, and he had become frustrated with the task at hand. That night, Zakirji appeared at the foot of his bed as Peter sat counting out the composition. Zakirji was watching TV, sitting on the bed listening to Peter's continuous counting mistakes. He turned to Peter and said, "Why can't you get it? It's simple." Then he turned around and continued to watch the TV.

My interest in tabla dreams became more and more intense. Why were all these students dreaming of tabla? Why didn't I have these dreams? One of my first questions to students I met then became, "Have you had the dreams?" Inevitably, they all said, "Yes, I have had these dreams." Speaking with one of Zakirji's senior students, Michael, a member of the Rhythm Experience and an accomplished tabla player in the California scene, led me to the conclusion that the dreams were indeed a way of working out anxieties about tabla and about the relationship of student to teacher. Michael's dreams tended to revolve around the problems and pressures of playing in public with such a master. Although his dreams didn't usually include Zakirji teaching him compositions, Zakirji was always present.

The following year I met a young Indian tabla player, a Hindu, who told me about his dreams of Zakirji and of compositions. He had not only dreams of compositions but also spiritual dreams where Zakirji gave him guidance and comforted him. He always kept a picture of his teacher in his room, and he prayed to the icon before going to sleep. If he was having difficulty studying for an exam, he would pray to his teacher, and in the night, Zakirji would be there encouraging him, telling him that things would turn out well.

I went back to the transcriptions of the first interview I had conducted with an older female student of Zakirji's. Although she had taken up other Hindustani instruments and left tabla many years before, she remembered her dreams of Zakirji and tabla quite vividly. She would have dreams of compositions at night, go into class the next day, and find Zakirji playing it *bol* by *bol*. Certainly, the connection these students had to their teacher was an intense and intimate one.

Experiencing the Spiritual Side of Tabla

In my second year studying with Zakirji, I also experienced the dreaming. I had, by and large, given up on the idea, thinking that perhaps I was too inexperienced as a tabla student or that I just could not connect with my teachers in the same way others could. It happened one day after a very energetic class with Zakirji in Seattle. During the day, I had practiced for nearly five hours, carefully playing the new compositions over and over again. That night I suddenly awoke feeling tired and scared. My body felt heavy—it was as if I were going to fall through my bed onto the floor. I knew I was beside my husband, and so I tried to call out to him to help me. I was paralyzed. I could not move or speak. Just then, Zakirji whispered in my right ear, "Just relax, you have to go through this." My tension dissolved, knowing that Zakirji was with me.

I could not see him—but I could hear him. He played *bols* so loudly and so fast that I thought my ears would explode. He played to the right of me, then to the left, as if moving me through space to some kind of a destination. The *bols* were crystal clear but he played so frantically that as soon as I heard them, new ones came flooding out. This happened over and over again for what seemed like hours. He played well over fifteen compositions, none of which I could remember. We traveled to India, to Thailand, to China, and to the Berkeley campus, where he was, as I was told later, teaching that evening. I kept thinking, "Where is Zakirji?" At that moment, he appeared in front of me, dressed in a white *kurta*, waggling his head from side to side. "You must touch my feet," he said to me. Touch his feet? I thought this was strange. Usually, he did not ask anyone to touch his feet; people just did it. So I touched his feet and we continued on the journey. When I awoke the next morning, I had remembered much about the dream, but I could not remember any of the compositions Zakirji had played.

Since then, I have had many dreams of tabla lessons. Always, Zakirji is teaching us about life and tabla. These dreams have become for me another way of knowing, an ultimate kind of embodiment of Zakirji's teachings. It is a way of knowing and understanding that is deeply embedded in its Indian origins. I asked a colleague from India, an anthropologist, whether, if I were Indian, I would question the fact that I have these dreams of my teacher. "No", he replied, "Everyone knows that the guru gives you the third eye, the pathway to knowledge" (Bokhare 1997).

This pathway to knowledge in the world of tabla translates into something more than "play." Here, the role of apprentice is not one to be taken lightly but rather is one that is ongoing, ever changing, and adapting in new and different contexts over time. The more time an apprentice spends playing the music, the more in-depth and textured his or her knowledge becomes. This also holds true for my role as an anthropologist because I did not come to an understanding of the importance and frequency of dreaming tabla until I had been practicing and learning the instrument for at least two years. Like other students, I started to experience a deeper connection to our teacher in both my waking and unconscious moments. Dreaming tabla did not necessarily make me perform tabla *bols* more clearly or more precisely, but it did open up new ways of establishing intimacy with other students and teachers. Experiencing dreams or visions served to further my understanding of Indian cultural ways of being, so very important to the cultivation of the guru–disciple relationship. I am not a better tabla player or a worse anthropologist because I experienced the spiritual side of tabla. Rather, these acts of embodied learning deepened my connection to those with whom I lived and studied. These acts also led me to an avenue of investigation that I could not have examined otherwise.

Conclusion

Apprenticeship, as a method, can indeed transform the fieldworker into an apprentice. In the past, anthropologists spoke of such activities as highly undesirable or as making one liable to "go native." Despite his deep fear of going native, Evans-Pritchard stressed that a good anthropologist can't help but be affected by experiences lived during and after "the field" (Evans-Pritchard 1976, 245). Recently, other anthropologists have spoken of the necessity of documenting and exploring their own transformations in the process of doing fieldwork (Goulet 1994, 1998; Guédon 1994; Mills 1994; Jackson 1989; Stoller 1987; B. Tedlock 1991; E. Turner 1994a). Rather than marginalizing their extraordinary experiences in the process of collecting data to casual conversations within mainstream academic circles, they have brought discussions of their field encounters such as dreams, visions, sorcery, etc., to the center of anthropological investigation. In all these cases, the acquisition of cultural knowledge through experiential engagements with others has created an effective technique for furthering the anthropologist's understanding of other ways of knowing, seeing, and doing. As such, focusing on extraordinary exchanges among indigenous communities has become an additional instrument in the anthropologist's methodological toolkit and has also provided a new theoretical ground (Goulet and Young 1994) for analyzing and documenting other ways of knowing.

Following in the recent critique of the anthropology of the body and the emerging anthropology of the senses (Jackson 1989; Stoller 1989a, 1995; Howes 1991; Connerton 1989, and others), I suggest a movement away from the perception of cultural bodies as primarily language- or linguistic-based, where the body translates into symbols and signs only.[7] Learning to be a tabla player requires concentration on sound and image, and on feeling "correct" movements in the body. As Stoller (1995) advocates in his recent work on embodiment and spirit possession among the Hauka in West Africa, we need to return to our senses as anthropologists rather than continue to create disembodied accounts that are disconnected from the lives of the people we study. Sensing ethnography, or, in this case, sensing tabla, necessitates an exploration of the highly prized anthropological method of participant observation.

Clearly, the question of going native must be set aside in ethnographic encounters and experiences where phenomena like dreaming tabla and visions are commonplace. My intent was never to become "Indian"; instead, my objective was simply to become a tabla player and further my knowledge of Hindustani music in India and the global community. And as Tedlock reminds us, "Fieldwork is not simply a union card but the center of our intellectual and emotional lives, we are, if not 'going native,' at least becoming bicultural" (B. Tedlock 1991, 82).

Notes

1. Ustad Allah Rakha Khan's status in the world of *Hindustani* music rose in North America in the 1960s when he was the tabla accompanist for Pandit Ravi Shankar (sitar maestro). Prior to this, Ustad Allah Rakha Khan's popularity as a musician, both as a tabla soloist and accompanist, was rising substantially in the Indian subcontinent. Ustad Allah Rakha Khan as a master of the Punjab gharana is credited with many developments in the world of tabla music. There are six school or styles of tabla, each originating under a specific guru or master echoing the place or region in which the masters lived and taught. The Punjab gharana, originally located in the Punjab region of India and Pakistan and under the guidance of Ustad Kader Bux, was passed on to Ustad Allah Rakha Khan and then on to his son Ustad Zakir Hussain and others.

2. I am deeply grateful to the Shastri Indo-Canadian Institute for their financial support and assistance in India during my doctoral research.

3. All those who know him in the music industry commonly refer to Ustad Allah Rakha Khan as Abbaji, a Muslim kin term that means "father." The suffix, *-ji*, indicates respect. In this article, *-ji* is added to the names of my teachers. It is not uncommon among musicians and respectful audience members to refer to the masters as guruji or ustadji, or to say the master's name with *-ji* appended.

4. The various masters of tabla mentioned here represent a variety of schools. This list of masters does not include all whom were or are significant in the music industry in Ustad Allah Rakha's generation or in the current generation. For a more complete history of the various schools of tabla and their history and lineages, please see Aban Mistry's *Pakhawaj and Tabla: History, Schools and Traditions* (1984).

5. I have traveled back and forth from Canada to India every year for the past ten years living in Mumbai in the summers to learn and research tabla and visiting briefly in the winters for the annual music season. Foreign students who travel to India in the winter spend time with their teachers in music class, attending concerts together, and generally traveling with their teacher throughout the country.

6. Traditionally, most tabla players in the public sphere in India have been male. Although as tabla moves around the globe and the number of women learning classical *Hindustani* tabla increases, in India, it is still difficult for many women to take up the life of a tabla artist the way men can and do. There are many complex issues surrounding this problem, not the least of which is control over and access to patronage and performing-arts dollars. In Ustad Allah Rakha's school, there were only a handful of Indian female students when I began my research in 1995, and today the number remains the same. One female student of the Punjab *gharana*, Anuradha Pal, is an exception to the rule that only male tabla players can succeed. Recently, another young woman, Rimpa Shiva (Farukhabad *gharana*), from Kolkata (formerly Calcutta) has been mesmerizing audiences around the globe. Outside of India, female tabla percussionists seem to be on the increase. Various women from all over the world travel to California to learn from Zakir Hussain. One of Zakirji's students, Dana Pandey, has also climbed up through the ranks in the California school and performs alongside Zakirji in the percussive-based ensemble the Rhythm Experience.

7. Much of the research prior to the early 1990s treated the body as a sign, symbol, or linguistic metaphor for culture itself. It is this very idea of the body that pervades anthropological analyses and descriptions of everyday life. These past theories of the body in anthropology have almost exclusively focused on the social and cultural construction of an embodied self (Mauss 1973; Douglas 1966, 1970, 1975), following the Durkheimian model of the social body as essentially a moral one. Both Mauss and Douglas emphasized the connection between the physical and social bodies in relation to the individual, culture, and society. Whereas Mauss attended to the cultural construction of "body techniques" such as walking, sitting, or standing (Mauss 1973), Douglas treated the body as a classificatory schema, or as a metaphor for society at large. They firmly established in anthropology the idea of body as a sign or as a representation of culture. In contrast, Fabian (2000, 8) stresses that we get to "that which is real when we allow ourselves to be touched by lived experiences."

Glossary

The musical and dance definitions do not encompass all possible meanings or current usages in Hindustani and Karnatic practices. The ethnomusicological definitions are adopted from Gottlieb (1993), Ranade (1990), and Nuttall (1991).

Abbaji   Muslim address for father.
Bansuri   (Hindi) *Bans* (Sanskrit) *Vamsha*. Hindustani flute made of bamboo.

Bayan	(Hindi) "Left." The left-hand drum of the tabla pair. I have also heard the *bayan* referred to as *duggi* or *dugga*.
Bol	(Hindi) "Word." The Hindi verb *bolna* means "to speak." *Bols* are strokes on the tabla that correspond to a sound made by the voice. The *bols* are onomatopoeic syllables, used by tabla players as an aid in memorizing compositions. *Bols* are units that are then strung together to create phrases.
Chakradhar	(Hindi) "Wheel." A type of tabla composition that builds on fixed *bols* ending in a three-fold pattern, a *tihai*. A *chakradhar* itself is played three times.
Chilla	A ritual retreat of forty days and forty nights. Usually a disciple is instructed by his or her guru on the time and place of the event.
Dayan	(Hindi) "Right." Refers to the right-hand tabla drum, also known simply as "tabla."
Gab	(Bengali) The middle circle of the tabla and *bayan*, which is constructed from rice paste and iron fillings. Usually, it is referred to as *shyahi*; however, I have also heard tabla players in Delhi, Mumbai, Toronto, Seattle, and elsewhere use the word "gab."
Gharana	(Hindi) "Household." Implying of the same house or family. Typically translates into "school" or "style" in the performing arts.
Guru	(Sanskrit and Hindi) "Destroyer of ignorance." A teacher; a master. A form of address for a learned master.
Hindustani	Northern Indian music system.
Kaida	also *Qayada* (Hindi/Urdu) Lit. "law." A type of composition in tabla repertories that has a fixed structure. The kaida pattern always has a theme of fixed *bols* that is then followed by a number of variations based on those fixed bols, ending with a tihai.
Karnatic	Southern Indian music system.
Kathak	A Hindustani classical dance form that is accompanied by tabla.
Kurta-pajama	(Hindi) North Indian form of male dress. A long shirt with pockets is usually worn over loose-fitting pants or pajamas.
Lahra also *Lehra*	(Hindi) Lit. "a wave." It is a melodic pattern used in the accompaniment for solo tabla playing and performances. Whereas *sarangi* (Hindustani. Similar to a bowed fiddle that is played upright) and other melodic instruments are used as the accompaniment for concert performances, most tabla teachers use the harmonium (a keyboard with bellows) for in-class accompaniment.
Laya (or *Lay*)	"Tempo/rhythm." There are three: slow (*vilambit*), medium (*madhya*), and fast (*drut*).
Riaz	(Persian) "Practice." *Riaz* for tabla players includes both playing the actual *bols* and signing the *bols* in time, in *tal*.
Shagird	(Urdu/Persian) "Disciple" or "student."
Shishya	(Sanskrit) "Disciple."
Tala	(Sanskrit) "Palm of the hand." Also, *tal*. (Hindi) Rhythmic cycle in both Hindustani and Karnatic music systems. Gottlieb (1990, 140) notes that the word *tal* comes from the practice of counting time by clapping hands.

There are many different *tals*, each having a certain number of beats or *matras*. For example, one of the most widely used and popular *tals* in Hindustani music is *tin tal,* which has sixteen beats.

Tihai   (Hindi) "A third part." A *bol* phrase that is repeated three times.

Tihais   These standard cadential patterns are used to conclude various types of compositions such as the *rela* (a type of composition played very fast) and the *kaida.* They are also found at the end of *tukras* (short compositions), *chakradhars*, and others.

Theka   (Hindi) "Prop," "support," "mainstay." A rhythmic outline or structure used by tabla players to keep time within the *tal* cycle. It outlines the structural form and also the divisions of the *tal.* Each *tal* has a different *theka.* Each *theka* consists of a specified number and arrangement of *bols*; however, the structure of the *theka* can and is elaborated on in performance. *Theka* is played prior to and after a composition.

Ustad   (Persian) "Master," "expert." Used as a form of address for Muslim teachers.

15. Field of Dreams; Fields of Reality:
Growing with and in Anthropology

JEANNE SIMONELLI, ERIN MCCULLEY, AND RACHEL SIMONELLI

"Well, just don't wind up in jail, Ma," said my daughter Elanor, with laughter in her voice. She'd just asked me to fill in my itinerary for my next few months in the field, and this time the trajectory included both Chiapas, Mexico, and Northern Ireland.

At thirty-five, El was now a mother and she carried the six-month-old Fiona in a Maya Wrap, the forty-dollar version of a Latin American *rebozo*, and the legacy of a childhood in the field in Mexico. A month before, I'd come to visit with my friend Josefa from Chiapas, a real live Maya, who'd demonstrated three or four different ways to carry a baby in a shawl, using Dress-Me-Up Ernie to illustrate. She and Elanor talked about the experience of having a baby in the supportive cradle of Maya family life and compared it to the loneliness of the American nuclear family. It was a real cross-cultural moment.

Elanor was seven the first time I brought her to the field, and her sister Rachel, ten years younger, was a true child of fieldwork. Though I am now officially an applied cultural anthropologist, I began my wanderings doing archaeology in the northwest Mexican deserts. I was a thirty-year-old, single mom undergrad when Rich Pailes, my archaeology mentor at the University of Oklahoma was fool enough to allow me to bring my precocious daughter with me to do archaeological research. Years later, as I guided my own field programs, I thought kindly of the professor who'd let me have this opportunity, and modeled my programs after his. Over the years, there'd been "conventional" students, diabetics, mid-life non-traditionals and their youngsters, wanna-be hippies, affluent conservatives, and my own kids. For many of these apprentice anthropologists, the programs were formative experiences (R. Simonelli 2002).

Learning and teaching anthropology in the field requires a special set of skills and insights, some of which can be gleaned from books, and others, as yet another mentor said, "you'll figure . . . out when you get there." This chapter provides a narrative journey through one instance of the living apprenticeship of anthropological fieldwork, through a qualitative look at a program taught in Chiapas, Mexico, in 1999. Field programs have always been work-intensive, requiring arduous planning, but with the potential for unparalleled growth for *all* involved. They are life-changing experiences for those who participate, a chance to link classroom with the global and local community, to make teaching an interaction between the teacher, the learner, and what is being learned, an intricate quadrille where the dancers change places as the set progresses. Beyond this, they are also the seeds that our students can sow when they return, as subtle teachers among an American public that needs to see beyond its own borders (J. Simonelli 2000).

Learning from the Field

Intensive field-based learning has a long history in anthropology, but like the qualitative research model, it has been adopted by many other disciplines as part of a push to give students a taste of the "real world." In these diverse experiences, project directors use a wide range of models in designing and carrying out their off-campus experiential learning programs. They differ in the amount of pre-travel preparation, and in the focus of the program. Some are primarily to teach research methods, others to teach students how to engage with the global community. They also differ in the way students are housed and monitored during the actual field stay. On one end of the continuum, the "drag and drop" model involves minimal amounts of on-campus training, instructors meet many of the students for the first time at the airport, and students are housed in individual homestays. Students and directors come together daily or periodically to cover academic content and to consult on independent student projects. While the homestay model has obvious advantages for language learning and cultural exchange, students are on their own for a good part of the time, and the potential for illness and accidents, and the related liability, escalates.

Even with the best of planning and with intensive student oversight, we can't prepare for everything. Regardless of the study site, we fit our programs into national and international settings beset by their unique political, economic, and social problems. We also bring with us students with their own life-stage cultural agendas. In the mid-1990s this became even trickier as more and more women undertook field programs, a phenomenon experienced throughout the country. Male students were electing not to participate. Women felt safer traveling this way and were particularly interested in programs with a service component. Yet when a service focus is added to more traditional experiential learning, liability concerns multiply, since student and faculty enthusiasm about wanting to "help" the "needy" sometimes loses sight of whose needs are actually being met.

The model and focus of the programs I teach have evolved continuously since 1987, when I began teaching my first field school, the Southwest Summer Program. In retrospect, I realize it remains a work in progress. Labor- and contact-intensive, the Southwest Program is a multi-week, on-the-road learning experience that forces students to learn about not just academic course content during hours of on-site lecture each day but also other people and themselves. The group covers 1,500 miles of territory and 10,000 years of history, with participants camping and cooking the entire time. As always, I work with a codirector, and in the Southwest we attempt to teach about Native American, Hispanic, and Latino cultures, while at the same time meat eaters and hardcore vegetarians learn to coexist and to eat each other's foods. To survive the program, one must have an appetite for learning, and be flexible and adaptable.

The Chiapas Project, begun in 1997, demanded another brand of flexibility. Chiapas, the southernmost Mexican state, has one of the richest resource bases in that country, with the highest levels of poverty, among a population that is largely Maya Indian (J. Simonelli 1986). Since 1994, the people of the region have been actively struggling to put an end to injustice and resource inequity, resulting in a situation of continued conflict between the official organs of the Mexican government and the Zapatista rebels (Earle and J. Simonelli 2005; Simonelli and Earle 2003).

Begun by Kate O'Donnell of Hartwick College in Oneonta, New York, the Chiapas Project was built on her years of inquiry into rural poverty, years of activism in sociology and women's studies, and semesters of taking students out of the classroom and into the community (O'Donnell 1993). I joined her, first as a consultant and then as faculty representing the State University of New York at Oneonta, bringing to the new program the lessons learned in the Southwest. Preliminary trips to Chiapas laid the groundwork, allowing us to make program connections and begin to ask questions about Maya struggle and continuity that linked back to our own work and the goals for the project (J. Simonelli and Earle 2003; Earle and Simonelli 2005).

We used a full semester preparation course to help our students gain an understanding of what they would see and experience, and place the Chiapas conflict into a global perspective. Our months together before departure helped us know and judge each other's strengths and weaknesses; in fact, a full day's Challenge Workshop culminated in a contract for cooperation. As program directors we had a good sense of what group interactions would be like even before we arrived in Mexico. Upon arrival, the class combined on-site lectures by visiting local scholars and experts with the chance to witness and/or apply what we were learning in the field.

The first year's program, in January 1998, was a study in flexibility and caution. Following the fall preparation course at Hartwick, the group left for Chiapas, just three weeks following the massacre of forty-five Mayas in the highland village of Acteal. Because of the tenuous and often dangerous political situation, a trip to the Lacandón rainforest village of Nahá was not possible until the January 1999 field season. That year, as in others, we learned and did far more than we could ever have covered in classroom preparation. Some things are predictable; others are not. Whether they occur in the actual classroom, during guest lectures, or in the field, it is the unpredictable experiences, presented below, that are the so-called teachable moments of experiential learning.

Field of Dreams: Chiapas 1999

It's January 1999 and our merry band of nine women are two hours into the drive toward Naja in the Chiapas jungle when the two-way radio breaks into Tzotzil Maya. Roberto Mendez Mendez, driver of one of our two combis, answers the call, laughter in his clipped words. He pulls the combi over into the muddy verge and turns to the women, eyes twinkling.

"No tienes ir al baño?"

Pained expressions grade quickly into relief, then dissolve into concern. Of course we have to go to the bathroom, but the weeds are tall; the trees are distant. Roberto and Pepe have already walked ahead; they stand facing away from the combis—you can see their backs, hands reaching forward at waist level.

I make a sweeping gesture, indicating the field. "This is it, ladies." The women of the Chiapas Project step out gingerly, one by one, shedding a few inhibitions as they go. Had we forgotten to practice peeing in the woods while still in Oneonta?

Back into the combis. We round the crest of a hill, and the *milpas* move in to swallow us, tall fields of summer-green grasses and sunflowers reaching into the open windows. In the distance, the color changes subtly, becoming a clump of rumbling avocado, moving and groaning just ahead. *El Ejército Mexicano*, the Mexican army, stuck in the mud, at a place without a bridge.

Here we go, search time, just as we expected. I grab my pouch, taking out my visa, my smile, and my explanation. The combis come to a stop in front of three open humvees filled with military. The first is on our side of the cut, stopped, men spilling out to run back toward the muddy gash that is the bridge to be. The second is mired in undulating red ochre ooze, up to its monster truck wheels, going nowhere. The mass of green men head down to put their weight behind it, the motor groans, and it lumbers slowly over wide boards. It's difficult for the men to push and still keep the barrels of their automatics out of the muck. They shift the guns from side to shoulder and over the back and then Roberto is out of the combi, taking in the situation. I wonder if our drivers should even be here on a road into the *selva*. They are two *choferes* from San Andres Larrainzar, a place high in the Altos, where the 1996 peace accords were negotiated. They are two drivers with indigenous combis and a bunch of American women traveling through what we realize is officially part of the Conflict Zone.

Three companies of soldiers, three sets of commanders, torn between the problem of moving the Humvees and checking out the foreigners. I'm out of the combi; Kate, too. I can see her reminding the women "no pictures," and wondering when they'll want our papers. The army guys are young and curious; when was the last time they saw nine American women passing through an autonomous zone in Chiapas? Looking at the men, I think about how safe I'd feel if we armed our high school boys with automatics and set them about the business of protecting the country. Finally, they remember us, all three *jefes* carrying notebooks and pencils; they move to Roberto and begin the questioning: what is your name? Kate and I are smiling, hand them a document with more seals than the San Diego Zoo. Check papers, visas, bags, destinations, and days of departure, and our litany begins:

> *Roberto Mendez Mendez.*
> We come from dos colegios
> Somos Profesores; Son estudiantes
> Tenemos pasaportes, tenemos una lista
> No tenemos armas, no tenemos drogas
> No veimos nada, no oimos nada
> Tonina, Palenque,
> Chincultic y Tenem
> Este es un clase,
> Rumbo a la selva
> Programa de turismo
> Iremos a Nahá.
> Hart-week, Nueva York,
> Amen.

As we stand, surrounded by military giving contradictory orders, I wonder how the students are fitting this into what they have learned in their reading on Chiapas. The narrative moves to Erin McCulley, then a junior from SUNY–Oneonta.

Our miniature caravan was making its way through the *selva*, traveling at a pace that was persistent but moderate enough to keep the bodies inside the Volkswagen buses from being catapulted from their seats as yet another of the jungle's natural speed bumps was discovered. After various stops, some anticipated and others not, it seemed as if we might actually get there, get to Nahá. I was anticipating our arrival there with a large amount of delight and a small degree of anxiety, both of which had been keeping me awake while the other students in the van slept. Every time I began to drift away into slumber, I would begin to recreate the photographer Trudi Blom's black-and-white images in my mind, the aging faces of Lacandón Maya, adorned in their white tunics and so picturesque and prominent among the dense leaves of the selva. I was still suspended in a mystic dreamlike abstraction when I felt the van slow and come to a stop. Upon opening my eyes, I saw the sleepy faces of other students, Jeanne telling us to relax and keep calm, and then I finally saw the soldiers in the road: our very first military checkpoint.

Peering out through the tinted glass, I realized that there were more than a dozen of them—clustered around a large military humvee, and also some plainly dressed men. It appeared that where there once was a bridge there was now a mudpit, one that they were struggling to bypass with the construction of a new bridge. The soldiers approached the vans with very somber faces, initially at a pace that was extremely intimidating and that was transformed into a lingering movement, circumambulating around the vans. Occasionally, one of them would press his face against the windows, blocking the glare of the sun with his muddy hands and surveying the cargo with piercing eyes. Finally, Jeanne was called upon to exit the vehicle and join Roberto, our driver outside. Kate and her driver joined them at the rear of our van and began sputtering off their diplomatic terminology, flashing any and all documents supporting their proposed intentions.

Finally, Roberto returned to the van and we began to roll toward the muck and rushing water ahead. It would seem that we were attempting to gain enough momentum to drive through the chaos of the washout and onward to the other side. Roberto floored it and the rest of us just held on and prayed that we would not tip over or be sucked down into the mud. The van made it through approximately half way when the thick slop took hold of the tires and sucked us down into the sludge, making us stagnant among the workers and soldiers looking on.

We stopped, and then the soldiers surrounded us and were bending down, examining underneath our van, undoubtedly trying to access a way to get us out of the mud and out of their way. Momentarily, they surrounded the superior officer present, obtaining what appeared to be a variety of orders, and then dispersed to their tasks. After slinging their semiautomatic rifles over their shoulders and manipulating their machetes to a position that would not impede their movement, some began digging rocks out of the mud and tossing them to the side; others began digging at the tires.

We turned around to notice that some of the soldiers were inside of and on top of a Humvee that was making its way toward us. The vehicle began to swerve to the left, attempting to go around us through the mud, from which the rocks had recently been cleared. It appeared to be about to hit us dead on but then suddenly stopped. Because my seat was behind the driver, I had only to look out my window to realize that a rock was now wedged behind the tire and had caused the vehicle to stop. To put it more simply, now the Humvee was stuck, too.

It is at this point that Nicole, one of the Hartwick students in the seat in front of me, begins to analyze our situation and give it a little perspective. She says:

> Okay, dude, we are four students from New York in the middle of nowhere in Mexico. We are in a van by ourselves with no idea of what the hell is going on or any way to find out because all of the people who speak Spanish were smart enough to stay on the road. Our driver is now outside with about fifteen military guys who almost just hit us with a hummer and now they are all standing around us, staring at this van while we all sit here stuck in the mud—together.

I instantly burst into laughter, and by this point everyone in the van had so much nervous energy that they had been storing over the last twenty minutes that they too could no longer contain themselves.

The movement outside is ludicrous; some of the men are pushing us to one side while the others are trying to rock the army vehicle out of its muddy trap. Eventually, they move their vehicle out of the way and decide that there is only one way to get this god-forsaken Volkswagen out of here and that is to push it. Suddenly, there are camouflaged men surrounding our van, pushing it and trying to rock us back and forth.

When I looked outside my window now, I am face to face with a soldier who is desperately trying his hardest to push us out of the way. We can now no longer stand not laughing and do so openly at how funny this whole performance has become. I notice that the beginnings of a weak smile have surfaced on his face, and gradually it develops into a large grin and finally he begins to laugh. All these soldiers are giggling and laughing out loud, which makes us laugh and thus increases their laughter even more.

After a last effort, all the men managed to push us far enough out of the mud—and out of the way—to let them now move the Humvee in front of us and pull the van the remainder of the way. Before doing so, these dirty, gasping men helped us out of the van and over the muck.

"*Lodo*," they said, pointing to the slop oozing all around us.

"*Lodo*," we said, having learned a brand-new Spanish word.

As I stood outside, I looked across the chaos to our point of departure and at the faces of my professors. Although there was some relief in them, there was still absolute horror in their brows and anxiety in their stiffened lips. We hadn't covered this in class.

Later that night, it occurred to me that the soldiers were so much more cooperative than I had anticipated their being. I questioned their motives, and I questioned their humor. Today, sitting safely behind my desk and reviewing this event, I still have to ponder: Were they laughing with us, or at us? What ever they were up to on their military patrol, I hoped we provided them with a diversion that kept them from harassing the Zapatista community down the road. You never know how or when you might be called upon to serve!

Kate and I returned to our vans, chugged some water, and ate some cookies. We are out of the mud, sucked out of the dream and into the real Chiapas. How green the jungle is this year! Even in the dull drizzle, the blossoms are heavy and sumptuous, weighing down tropical branches. Last spring, a heated El Niño pulled in the rain waters. *Campesinos* burned their milpas, turned dry earth, waited for the storms, the rhythm of centuries, through a too-long spring. The milpa fires became wild fires, questionable fires, burning into the selva heart. Thirty percent of Lacandón land burned, mahoganies and cedars, and in the Maya village of Nahá the children of *Chan K'in Viejo*, the departed patriarch, waited for the rain, and old Antonio the shaman stood silent, dreaming under cloudless skies.

"Just a little bit longer now," Roberto says, bringing the combi around a long curve down into Nahá.

To the right, the tranquil silver waters of a lake are merging into the steady drizzle. On the left, blackened and burned tree stumps dot the hillside, legacy of last spring's wild fires. The leaves of trees still left standing are dry and brittle, as though a giant can of Round-up had been sprayed over the selva, starting a slow death among all living things. Given the conflict, it is not out of the realm of possibility. In the distance, I can see the houses of Nahá, rough-hewn boards, metal roofs, a few satellite dishes. My heart sinks into a nostalgic vision of the fabled ethnographic present, the "unchanging" setting of indigenous life. I've been looking at too many of Trudi Blom's photographs, shot with satin lenses over the last forty years.

Roberto turns down a narrow lane at the edge of the village, bringing the combi to a halt. I smile weakly, glad to be stopped. Glad we are all safe. There'd been two more military checkpoints after the last washout. Two more recitations of the litany of justification and destination, making it three checkpoints on seventy-five kilometers of barely traveled road. Opening the door of the combi, I groan, stiff from hours of vigilance. I turn to Kate. She's looking at the back wheel of the other combi, her eyes wide with adrenaline. The tire is flat. To the rim. Kate reads my obvious question.

"Been like that for the last hour." The driver had chosen not to stop. We grab our packs, bundles, leftover Maria cookies and trudge through the mud toward the campsite. Victor, a young guide who organizes and runs ecotourism programs for *Na Bolom*, the research institute, museum, and guesthouse started by Trudi and Franz Blom, is there to greet us. He leads us into a field in which a forest of meticulously placed flowerpots are standing like tombstones. There are ten thousand of them, line after line after line, filled with dirt, empty. Nothing green showing. The students are curious.

"It's a reforestation project," Victor says. "They haven't sent the seed. We've been waiting . . . months."

I look at the rows and see basketball courts, vacant clinics, speed bumps, empty flowerpots, the legacy of pre-election governmental patronage that excludes anything living.

Victor is the current incarnation of Trudi Blom's commitment to "help" the Lacandón. Trudi died in 1996 at the age of 94, just a week before the Zapatistas marched out of the jungle; a year to the day before her friend, Lacandón wisdom holder Chan K'in Viejo, stopped dreaming at 105.

Our camp is located at the outskirts of Nahá, away from the cluster of houses that is the tiny village. There is nothing else out this way except the house of Chan K'in Quinto, one of the twenty-five remaining children of the elder Chan K'in. Deformed, suffering from hard-to-control epilepsy, he lives with his sister Koh Juanita in an old and crowded cut-board house, exiled to the edges, just as we anthropologists are.

In the *campamiento*, lunch has been simmering over an open fire for three hours; but it is almost time for supper. We are exhausted, in need of intense reflection concerning our day, happy to be beneath the thick canopy of dripping jungle, caressed by mist. That night, I crawl into my quetzal-colored hammock, tuck the blankets around me, pull the bridal veil mosquito netting over my head, fold my arms across my breast and sleep a peace-filled sleep, unbroken till morning. There are no images, no vestiges of threat or fear or hidden struggle in the lands around us, no dreams or nightmares, just the gentle tapping of steady rain on a metal roof, unfettered slumber in the cradle of creation. Most of the students sleep equally well. The field remains a dream.

We wake early; it's still raining. We reschedule a hike that was to teach us about flora and fauna and look for alternative programming.

Dressed in layers and sweaters and raingear, we march into Nahá, another line of visitors on the ecotourism trail. Before coming, Kate asked Victor to set up a service project that the group could do while in Nahá. We had collected money for supplies and explored the meanings of community and service in our pre-departure study. Victor met with the Nahá elders: old Antonio, inheritor of Chan K'in's cosmic legacy; and K'ayum Ma'ax, worldly, traveled, holder of a different type of knowledge. They'd decided we should help with the school—a clean-up project, and provide whatever assistance we could for two other women named Koh—the last remaining widows of Chan K'in Viejo.

The students grumbled a little as we squished into the village. Nahá is growing and shrinking at the same time. The road from Ocosingo, the good road, is too good, and is both a catheter and a garbage truck. Nahá is the dump, absorbing all the paraphernalia we anthros want to "protect" the people from, with our well-intentioned information. We walk past the skeletal shape of an unfinished two-story dwelling, slide in the pudding soil to the door of Chan K'in's house. Flashes to Trudi's photos again, Discovery Channel videos, Chan K'in's enigmatic and glowing face, bent shape, smiling up at the towering Trudi. They called Trudi the queen of the jungle, celebrating her devoted, paternalistic relationship with the Lacandón and their selva.

The house is large, simple, dirt-floored, but with none of the smoky, cramped poverty of the banished Chan K'in Quinto's. Here, at different times, Chan K'in lived with four wives and thirty-five children, some dead, some moved to their own houses, some gone to sit on stones selling bows and arrows to the tourists in Palenque. A young, pale-skinned, red-haired boy comes in; smiles shyly. Still another son of Chan K'in; he is one of the Lacandón albinos, an anthropological lesson in endogamous marriage and genetics. Is this a de-colorized version of indigenous culture, a snapshot of the great white hope of total assimilation?

The widows are poor, thin, tiny. Left without the labor of their husband, they have taken over the milpa. Koh-the-elder makes ceramic animal and god pots for sale to the tourists. Koh-the-younger bore the last children of Chan K'in Viejo: a boy, preteen (do the arithmetic here), and a daughter, who was then given as a gift to the older wife, who was no longer fertile.

We crowd around, watch Koh make a toucan, stare at Chan K'in's hammock, where a century's dreaming tried to discern the Lacandón fortunes. The Koh-daughter shows me a tiny ceramic mouse that she's made. I offer to buy it, suspecting that mouse is one of my *naguals*, guardian spirits: we can't all be jaguars. She refuses money, tells me it's a gift. Pleased, I give her two barrettes to hold back her long black hair.

Then the sun is out, breaking through the low-lying cloud blanket in an instant, and we follow the Kohs up and down a long, narrow mud chute out to their distant milpa. We would learn later that the younger Koh was not well, so our simple gift of nine pairs of bleeding and bruised *gringa* hands really was a help. We learned to distinguish food plants and medicinal plants from those with no real purpose in the Lacandón schema. We pulled these, and the dead, dry stalks of last year's maize, finally clearing about two hectares. The sun was warm, healing, melting away unsettling images left over from the day before. We were a group of *compañeras*, sharing in that moment an ageless weave of work and silent companionship. Side by side, hand over hand, we worked with the two Kohs, whose proud, slow giggles commented on our haphazard labors.

We returned to camp, walking in a daze, wearing shit-eating smiles of pleased exhaustion, and looked up to see a Humvee and six soldiers waiting for us. We pass them, round the bend toward the cemetery of empty flowerpots, and there are three more. The closest extends his hand in effervescent greeting.

"Good af-ter-noon." In English. Switch to Spanish. "This is how you say it, no?"

Kate and I nod in unison. She turns to Victor, who is with us.

"Tourists," he whispers in English.

In unison, Kate and I begin the litany once again. We shift uneasily, all of us. I'm sore, my hands are blistered and bleeding, the students have to piss. We look at each other, maintaining the pleasantries.

At last, the soldier stretches out his hand in farewell and I bleed into his firm grip. They have tracked us down here, and though in 1999 our program had no overt political intent, the dream is fading. The soldier turns, ambling slowly back toward the Hummer, trailing his troops. A final wave. Kate and I breathe another sigh of relief.

Chayote for dinner, white cheese, chicken, and tortillas. By 9:00, gringa caterpillars crawl back into swaying cocoons, Nahá dozes; a solitary monkey climbs down a philodendron rope, curious. Midnight. A mechanical shriek cuts through the night. I open one eye, pull myself out of stuporous slumber, hear motor rumbling, wonder if it's the army once again, but there are no lights coming toward us. Air brakes, another shriek, night bus to Ocosingo. Fall back toward morning.

We're up, more tortillas, and there are nine gringas with machetes limply chopping at the high grass around the primary school. We're in hiking boots, long pants, long sleeves, doused in deet, warding off the jungle. We are joined by fourteen Lacandón men, white tunicked, sandled, keeping a steady work pace for three hours. One of them is Chan K'in Quinto. Exiled again, he works away from the others, with a few of the students, digging a trench around the school. He never falters, never takes a break, chops dirt all morning, deep in concentration. The ditch circles the entire building. In the wet season, it will keep the water from accumulating, keep the mosquitoes from propagating; keep the waves of malaria from infecting the children.

The head flies off an ancient hoe we are using, and the women stand there dumbly, looking at the two pieces. Quinto considers it solemnly, picks up a stick, and cuts a small shim.

"*Necesito una piedra,*" he says to no one in particular.

One of the students wanders off in search of the rock he is requesting, bringing it back to Quinto. He takes the rock, his crumpled face breaking into a broad smile.

"*Muy buena piedra,*" he tells her, praising the selection. A couple of hard blows and the hoe is ready for another few years of service. Lesson 18: nothing is disposable.

It's a hot, clear afternoon, bluer than the stucco on a Maya temple, and the women turn the weeds into a New England lawn. They line up, as K'ayum Ma'ax sharpens their machete blades, then try to imitate the kind of swing that takes the grass down to the ground.

Exhausted, we reflect together on yet another day in the field then crawl back into our hammocks. I'm awake early and throw back the netting that is swaying quietly in the flaxen dawn. The forest is barely an arm's length away, an entanglement of mutant houseplants searching for the sky. To me, the selva seems disturbingly empty. I'm used to herds of deer and flocks of turkey competing for lilies and lupines outside my window, screeching blue jays, chattering finches. In Nahá we have seen nothing. Heard nothing. Perhaps they come in the night, like wary Zapatistas; perhaps they are encircling the shaman Antonio in his millennial God's house, called to conference. But all I've seen are gaunt dogs and one small, speckled frog. Have all the howlers and long-tailed quetzals gone, the Lacandón rainforest just the ancestral memory of both humans and animals?

Three days later, we load up, back into the combis, a little anxious about the drive. We leave Nahá with a deep sigh. In the trees, there is an elusive black-and-orange flash, a toucan calling after us: *como estas en tu corazon?* Days later, we find ourselves invaded by a pervasive case of burrowing chiggers. They produce a relentless itch, like the poor of Chiapas under the protective coat of Mexican neoliberalism. Returning to San Cristóbal, we slather alcohol and Vick's *Vapo Roob* over our tormented bodies, killing most of the microscopic visitors. Weeks later, some seem to remain, a nighttime irritation, which is how Chiapas works its way into your soul.

It's chilly in the highlands, three weeks into the program, and the women are wearing contradictions, ethical dilemmas, stark reality beneath their thick Maya sweaters. Some nights are pain-filled. We sit in long reflections, reviewing past lectures and field travels, making connections into and out of our own lives, into and out of a global abyss that now seems bottomless. The students are consumed by issues as old as the Spanish colonial *entrada*, and issues more recent, fruit of this particular conflict. They want to fix everything. Kate reminds them: you have to pick your battles. The same message comes to us in the surreal backdrop of Internet cafés and stereo plaza music, the sound of Kenny Rogers's "You gotta know when to hold 'em, know when to fold 'em. . . ."

One morning, we hurry down to the *zocalo* for an audience with

Bishop Samuel Ruiz. We are astounded that he will see us. Don Samuel, as he is known, took over as Bishop in San Cristóbal in 1960, gradually "awakening" into social consciousness through his interaction with the Maya people. We'd heard him in prep-course videos, responding to accusations of preaching Marxist liberation ideology, as he took on the role as negotiator and intermediary in the attempt to forge and implement peace accords between the Zapatistas and the government in Chiapas. He countered the accusations against him by saying that hunger is not ideology. Hunger is hunger. Desperation is desperation. This we are learning.

In the *curia* next to the cathedral, we wait for Bishop Ruiz, sitting in a circle of chairs, saving the big bench for him. Paintings of past bishops look out above us, Bartolome de las Casas, others. Kate pokes me in the ribs. There's a familiar face staring down from a portrait next to the door.

"Isn't that Raul Julia?" she asks. I think of the final scene in a movie about El Salvador where actor Raul Julia played the role of the archbishop of that country, torn by brutal civil war in the 1980s. Bishop Romero, too, "awakened" through his interactions with the poor, and for this he was murdered in front of the altar, larger than life. We are thinking of this when the door opens and in walks a little old Mediterranean man, well-worn jacket buttoned against San Cristóbal mornings, flat wool worker's cap covering his head. We shift nervously and I begin in Spanish, introducing the group, saying that we've been traveling and that we studied Chiapas for a full semester before we came and he answers in English that perhaps we can teach him something and I swallow and keep my mouth shut after that.

Comfortable laughter, and a question from Erin,

"Can you tell us a little about the situation in Chiapas?"

Don Samuel smiles. "Ah," he begins.

The government is optimistic, without reason. In the last four years, life has gotten worse in Chiapas. Yet we have darkness with light inside, and that light is the hope. They build a fortification of intimidation around the people, intensifying the divisions within the community to create the impression that it is the people who are fighting each other. There is injustice, with impunity, in the midst of poverty and starvation. At the same time awareness is increasing. The conscience of the people is stronger. European groups, the UN, put pressure on the government and demand that Mexico recognize violations of human rights; Canada offers support for peace, and even the United States is admitting complicity.

The social justice issue in Latin American and Chiapas cannot be silenced. But we must ask, can solidarity produce change? Forty percent of the Mexican army is here in Chiapas to control a small group. But it is a group that has learned to use the media, and to control the mass media is to control knowledge. The government wants to clean up San Cristóbal and Chiapas for tourism, but as tourists you are expected to be blind and mute while you are traveling in Chiapas.

We are nodding our heads vigorously. Erin has stopped taking notes and has begun to sketch. Samuel continues.

We have begun to solve our problems from within. In Bachejon, the killers have come together with the victims in mediation, to discuss situations that are community problems. They chose from the community those who are to be representatives to the diocese. Dignity and respect are the laws guiding the future of the church. We are making agreements, performing pastoral activities that go beyond San Andrés.

He pauses. Since we are a group of women, someone poses the obvious question—how is the Church addressing the role and rights of women? The bishop crosses his legs, and smiles, settling into storytelling mode.

Sometimes, I am visiting in the pueblos. We sit in a circle, the men and the women, and I look around and say,

"How come it is that all of you men are wearing shoes, and all of the women are barefoot?" And the men look uncomfortable, but they answer,

"Well, Padre, *es que* shoes are very expensive and we men have to walk long distances to the milpas, through the *bosques*. . . ."

"Oh . . . then . . . perhaps the streams have moved closer to the houses, the wood is falling right into the center of the village??? . . . That's a nice watch you have there on your wrist; did it cost you a lot?"

"Well, Padré, you see, the Guatemalteco, he came last week, it was a very good price. . . ."

We all laughed. Samuel continued.

We try, in these ways, to connect the population with the larger world. It was the women who first came together to form cooperatives, and in the beginning they had no resources in common, so they put their debts in common. This has given them a way to come together; women can express themselves in reflections led by women catechists, link scripture to everyday life.

You know, we believe in the Catholic Church that there is holy succession reaching back to the apostles. When priests and deacons are ordained, they are ordained in a line reaching back to Jesus Christ. Now, all of the apostles were men. . . .

Don Samuel gives a little shrug. "But Mary, she was the mother of Jesus, she was almost an apostle. . . ." Into another story. "When we ordain deacons these days, we commission the couple, husband and wife." He pauses on the word commission, a canon-safe word.

They serve together in the communities, and then the husband dies. We try to appoint a new deacon to replace him, but the people say, "Padré, we already have a good deacon." So we said to ourselves, "Yes, this works," and so ministry is given to both men and women.

The group is dying to ask the big question, ask about abortion, but they already know the answer. Like the students, this diocese has had to pick its battles, and the first deals with basic human dignity.

The government is learning that its policies are having repercussions outside the country. They have not counted on the strength and hope of the people. There is a convergence of problems on the Earth. Working for peace in one place is working for peace everywhere. And you are everywhere, praying for us in Chiapas, and prayers are an unknown weapon in this war.

We all sigh. We are members of an unseen army, whether stuck in the mud or telling our stories back at home. Don Samuel's eyes twinkle. "*No traen cameras?*" Of course we have cameras. Troop outside for a group picture in the garden, autographed copies of the last pastoral letter, all of us grinning. In the end, we forgot to ask for a blessing, but it didn't matter. Don Samuel gave us absolution, walked us out of hopeless materialism and do-gooder desperation. He told us we can tag along on the coattails of the *esperanza*, the hope of the indigenous. We have permission to companion them in the kingdom of God; our salvation is that they are willing to include us.

A few days later, the Maya of Zinacantan celebrate the feast of San Sebastiano, a plucky convert who was murdered twice in early Christianity. Wanting to be part of the action, we arrange for Roberto Mendez Mendez to pick us up and drive us to Zinacantan for the festival. He parks the combi next to a market area resembling a giant Tzotzil-neighborhood garage sale. We all get out, listening to the din of fireworks that herald a new festival event.

We walk along the road, past the flamboyant sea of Zinacantecos, women dressed in red and pink and purple. This year's special fashion statement is bigger-than-ever satin hair bows, chartreuse, turquoise, magenta. Seated together, the women are more colorful than the fields of carnations and chrysanthemums that the pueblo raises for export. The women mingle quietly, talking, keeping track of the children. The men, equally vibrant, walk proudly, fulfilling official offices. A new round of fireworks is lit off from in front of the church. I jump, grabbing one of the students.

In front of us, the Jaguar reenactment is just beginning. Men dressed as monkeys, men dressed in moss, men in black face, men in jungle spots, parade by in procession. They move forward and backward, dancing and chanting, figures from the Maya past. They are headed toward Jaguar Rock, a little beyond the pueblo center, where they will play out another scene in Mayan cosmology, celebrating the birth of the world into its present configuration.

We follow slowly, pausing for peanuts and *refrescos*, down a path between Zinacanteco greenhouses, to the field where people gather.

The sun is penetrating, golden. Our group forms a shy line around the huge boulder where the Jaguar twins are attempting a difficult ascent. Their slapstick antics arise as much from the shape of the rocks as from the *pox*, the local cane alcohol that saturates many festivals. The jaguars are dressed in mustard cotton jumpsuits, spotted, topped off with ratty aviator helmet headdresses of real jaguar skin. A running commentary in Tzotzil accompanies their actions, and they reach the top of the rock in time to see the entire surface set ablaze.

Now they are in real trouble. A quick gust of wind spreads the fire from the mound of cornstalks at one corner, starting a steady burn on top of the rock. I think briefly of last spring's wildfires, easily envisioning another round. As we watch the play unfold, men pass through the crowd pouring jiggers of *pox* from unmarked bottles.

"I already had one," I tell them.

"You must have two."

I take the *pox*, stare at it for an instant, and chug it. It is nasty. The students do the same. For today, everybody is over twenty-one.

On the rock, the jaguars are trying to orchestrate their rescue. Our host for the day, a once blond, Jesus-looking, expatriate–scholar, translates. The Tzotzil language is jumping up and down with the jaguars, a wonderful sound, each clipped syllable more animated than the one before. We watch and listen, concentrating on a long, questioning passage that surrounds the word "gringas." Eyes drop, turn to slyly look at us. Everybody howls. We howl. Our host offers a quick translation:

"Is nobody going to help us? Surely someone will help us, or we will be burned up in these fires? Perhaps all those *gringas* have come here to help us?"

So there we are, uninvited guests, included and kidded at the same time. The anthropological field dilemma. The *pox* man comes by again.

"I already had two."

"You must have three."

The action is continuing. The bouncing *bolomes* fix their glance on our six-foot host. Rapid-fire Tzotzil. I turn for translation:

"Still no one helps us. Perhaps that albino over there will help us. Perhaps he'll come back with an airplane and take us off this rock."

The *pox* man makes another pass.

"I already had three."

"You must have four."

This time I shake my head, hoping the students will do the same. You can drink *pox* or you can refuse it, as long as you don't throw it away.

The fire smolders, and the play continues. In the end, the world is saved in a flawless game of catch, where stuffed squirrels are juggled back and forth between the jaguar twins and the rest of creation. The squirrel piece is incomprehensible to me, an observer, just as the got-it-right-in-seven-days creation by a perfect Christian God might not make sense to a Maya.

The performance, the celebration, the story is fantastic. It's good street theater, a set of beliefs that is dynamic, elastic, inclusive, changing. Perhaps this is what's wrong with the contemporary Catholic Church outside of Chiapas. No flexibility, a problem inherent in written history and social-scientific research. Blame it on scripture, blame it on the pope; but maybe there's a chance for change. The pope's preoccupied, dancing through TV commercials prior to a Mexican tour, waving, making speeches, and in Chiapas, Mary might have been an apostle.

The month is almost over, our line-listed itinerary has come to life. In between the lines are stories mounded on stories, lives mounded on lives. Chiapas has taught us her own tale. Our students are a little disappointed that we haven't really seen the Revolution. They've been dreaming of Subcommandante Marcos, maybe doing a cooking show, live, at the Zapatista kiosk close to the Zocalo. Still wearing his ski mask, with Julia Child apron, they see him extolling the virtue of chicken cutlets for the revolutionary on the run. "Fry 'em up; wrap 'em up, in-between meals or as a main dish—*pollo* in the pocket when there's just no time to cook." They wish they'd met the revolution face to face.

We want to point out the places they've just been, people they have heard, soldiers they've been searched by, but we don't fault them. In

the beginning we, too, looked for the reality of Chiapas in faxed com-
muniqués, Xeroxed publications, tiny black-masked dolls clustered in
the back of a child's wooden truck. It must be time to leave the field.
You won't find a formula for it in books about ethnographic research,
but you always know when it is time to go.

We swirl down the mountain to the airport, get into a plane, and
are disgorged hours and universes later into frigid New York. We ride
home, one by one walking back into our separate lives. As I drive the
final student up to the campus, we stop at a red light. Coming in the
other direction are two blond college guys, baseball caps turned backward, driving a brand new Subaru Outback. We are home. The young
woman straightens, suddenly frightened, suddenly aware of what she
has seen in her weeks in the field. I can read the story in her eyes.

"Does it always feel like *this* when you get back, Jeanne?"

I nod, overwhelmed by alternating joy and sadness. She was learning. She would never be the same.

Field of Reality: After the Trip

"I am different, not physically, but mentally, in my heart and eyes. I
have seen so many wonderful, devastating and upsetting situations in
a four-week period," wrote a Hartwick junior after the trip. Erin Mc-
Culley had similar reflections in her journal: "What can I say about
today, besides reinforcing the fact that this trip is getting better by
the minute," she reflected. "Each day I wake up feeling slightly more
accustomed to this strange place, a little more comfortable with not
knowing where I am a lot of the time. Then, by the end of the day,
I've gone through military checkpoints, through a stampede of men,
and into a rainforest hours from a phone among the most traditional
culture left in this entire country, and I am back to square one. But it
was so worth it."

Do our students' growth and learning experiences justify taking
them out of the protected environments of on-campus education and
bringing them to work with and learn from people in locations where
there may be risks to all involved? Many faculty would respond with
a resounding yes! So would many students. In Southwest Programs

from 1987 through 2004 and Chiapas Programs from 1998 through the present, the learning experience has thus far eclipsed the risks and the problems. As my daughter Rachel Simonelli, an "anthro brat" who later became an anthropology minor, completing not just the Southwest Program but also three months in Chiapas, points out:

> Though anthropology classes provide the basics and background of what students should be looking at when learning about other people's lives, the real world isn't structured by a course outline. A wide variety of experiential learning situations provide the opportunity to learn how things actually work. A good undergraduate curriculum equips students with an anthropological lens and the ability to make comparisons, then provides the space to be active in the communities the classes teach about. And, during field-based experiences, seeing other people make a difference can stimulate the desire to make a socially active contribution through your own education and to teach others because you were provided the freedom to learn through experience. These field programs have raised questions that I still try to answer: Can objectivity and activism coexist? Should anthropology as a field of study be an end in itself, or is our true contribution to take what we learn into other areas like law, social service, or education?

To my knowledge, no one has polled the communities we work in about their perception of the experiential exchange. The Chiapas Project has evolved since 1999, with Kate and me following our own separate goals and taking students to communities related to these interests. The extent of our involvement with the communities has also evolved, from tentative service projects, as requested by the communities, to actual faculty and student research, as designed in collaboration with our hosts, and approved after lengthy community meetings. But the overall goals of the project still reflect the original guidelines, as summarized by Kate:

1. To clarify values by examining the choices we make individually, locally, and globally

2. To help students grow through action on projects that are designed

and implemented in conjunction with community groups and
facilitators

3. To encourage team building through these cooperative-learning
projects

4. To foster interaction between individuals from all parts of the
community who share concern for, and commitment to, working on
major social issues

5. To strengthen the sharing of resources between the colleges and
related communities

6. To empower students and community members to be informed,
involved, and compassionate creators of humane communities both
locally and globally

In 1999 I began co-teaching programs in both the Southwest and
Chiapas with Dr. Duncan Earle (Earle, Simonelli, and Story 2004).
Working with a male co-director was not new to me, but working with
a male codirector in largely female programs did create a certain new
dynamic. Female–male co-directorship in Maya country fit within the
cultural logic, where notions of complementary duality dictate that
leadership roles be shared.

After a number of student programs within Zapatista communities, we have learned that activism and objectivity are not mutually
exclusive, that research and/or service projects can and must be designed in collaboration with our community partners, that our service is research and that research can inform our service. We are active
partners in a shared future, yet at the same time, as anthropologists
we are scribes of that experience, using our training to step back and
document a process of social change. But we have also been taught
by our Zapatista hosts that there is long-term educational benefit in
the simple cross-cultural exchanges that our visits bring. It is not always what we expect it to be.

In our programs in the Zapatista communities our most important
learning experience has been to value the visit itself. For our hosts, to
see a group of students coming to understand their struggle and perspective was a cultural learning experience for them as well, especially

in the midst of a sea of opponents, neighbors, paramilitaries, soldiers, hostile officials, and an enemy government. Our hosts define service-based learning as the visit itself. We lose sight of the fact that they know our culture only by reputation. Our service is to bring students, who show by their own behaviors that there is hope across the border. In turn, the students provide the service of internalizing what they are doing, socializing within the community, playing with the children and the elderly, eating their foods with them, participating in their expressive activities, and generally giving their isolated lives the temporary feel of an international festival. In a note sent to our students in August 2003, Ramón, a young Zapatista, reminded us of this:

> We wish to give you a thousand thanks for the school supplies you donated, which will help us a lot and are serving to help us move forward with autonomous education. All the children are very grateful for the help you gave us, but also they really miss your games and jokes...for us this is a gift, because the children need to enjoy themselves, because for them, the work, the problems, the obstructions that their parents suffer, they feel, and they become desperate, up to becoming sick. For this, your presence is very important, and at the same time, very festive.

The sight of nine American women limply swinging machetes and wielding pickaxes was a source of amusement to the fifteen Lacandón men who worked beside us in 1999, just as teaching Americans to plant a milpa amused the Zapatistas in 2001. But humor allows us to tell our stories with a gentle voice, while making serious connections that can affect the lives of more than just those involved. As Rachel continues:

> Part of the point of our education is to enable us to beat the stereotypes and to understand that each environment we enter is a separate but equal entity from the next. This is important if we remain anthropologists, but it is even more important if we go on into law, social service, and education. In fact, maybe that's what many of us ought to do! In fieldwork, it is a privilege to have a chance to give back in exchange for a look at the lives of others, to render service where help is needed. This not only gives one

the obvious sense of self-worth, it lets others see we are willing to learn what it is to be a part of their communities, both physically and mentally. Just as the people and cultures we observe have gifts to give us, we have gifts to give them in one way or another. The only way to know what gifts we can give is to have involvement outside the normal classroom world, to learn and observe, to both teach and be taught. With what we learn outside the classroom we can better teach our own peers; even our professors can learn from the knowledge and experience that we gain. The classroom is the manual, the guideline to what you will see and feel. The actual experience outside the classroom is when you learn firsthand how to operate your own mind and adapt to the world as a young adult. It is only with these skills that we can be scholar–activists, having the courage to use our anthropology to make a difference.

Our students may someday go on to be anthropologists, using their experiential learning as part of further research. But more than likely, like the veterans of both the Southwest and Chiapas Projects, they will be lawyers and social workers, teachers and nurses and doctors. Or they will have learned, like Elanor, to take pride in being stay-at-home mothers; the Maya wrap the baby rides in is not just a fancy *rebozo* but a wrap of learned cultural values that put hope into our own sometimes dismal American future.

Our presence in fieldwork settings remains positive only if it does not create more problems than our activities are worth. Though the 1999 Chiapas program only nibbled at the edges of Zapatista Chiapas, all that we learned in those initial experiences made what followed with Zapatista communities possible. Trust, like the information gleaned from anthropological fieldwork, is cumulative, and it is expressed in many ways, as when the Zapatistas approved our proposal to write a book about them after six months' considering our proposal. The Chiapas project has opened doors to other exchanges with Zapatista communities, a shared learning process in which each finds out more about the other. We receive formal commentary on the value of the exchange: "We appreciate your valiant cooperation for the resistance of our pueblos and for having considered autonomous education as one of the priorities of our communities. We send a warm greeting and thanks to those who have come and have collaborated in gathering the funds you have brought." But equally important to all is the memory of laughter and song.

We teach our students that we have an informed responsibility to other members of our human family. As faculty, part of our responsibility is to use the experience of experience, as outlined below, to carefully design experiential programs.

- Plan projects well in advance.

- Screen students carefully, but don't rule out the ones who seem unlikely.

- Keep talking and reflecting while traveling.

- Be reliable and gain the trust of informed field contacts, but expect to build trust slowly.

- Be flexible and open to program changes.

- Be aware of power relationships.

- Understand the way your initiative, whether research or service or both, fits into the political ecology of the area.

- Keep the relationship symmetrical.

Anthropology begins with dreaming and wondering, and then moves to seeing and trying to make sense of what you have seen. We describe our fieldwork in many ways: in statistics and comparisons, through life histories and ethnographies, in stories and in poems. For the most part, what we do and what we know remains inside the anthropological community.

Our students go to the field for numerous reasons. Some go to just have fun, others for credit, others as a prelude to anthropological careers, and others as an opportunity to see beyond themselves. Most could recite a list of what they learned if you asked them at the end of the trip, but I don't expect my students to show the results of the experience while on the road.

The true test of the efficacy of field-based learning is that they are living the experience years after the memories have begun to fade, that the dream of experiential learning informs the reality of their daily lives. Through our writing, teaching, and public speaking, we give what we have learned to others, so they may use it. Through our involvement with aid agencies and NGOs we give something back to those who teach us in the field. But to the general public, we can give only our stories, so these must be readable and humorous, yet packed with subtle insights into this complex and changing world. This chapter, then, is not just to bring a smile to the faces of those who have gone to the field, or evoke longing from those who wish they had, but it is for the American public out there who will never get to go.

Note

This chapter is dedicated to long-term Chiapas colleagues Natalia Arias Leal and Eduardo Serrano, who died unexpectedly on August 16, 2006.

16. Dancing Lessons from God

To Be the Good Ethnographer or the Good Bad Ethnographer

MILLIE CREIGHTON

Now, what I want is Facts. Teach these boys and girls nothing but Facts. Facts alone are wanted in life. Plant nothing else, and root out everything else. You can only form the minds of reasoning animals upon Facts: nothing else will ever be of any service to them. This is the principle on which I bring up my own children, and this is the principle on which I bring up these children. Stick to Facts, sir!

Charles Dickens, *Hard Times*

Thus, under the chapter heading, "The One Thing Needful," does Thomas Gradgrind pronounce his pedagogical philosophy, to begin Dickens's novel, *Hard Times*. Gradgrind, described as a person who himself "seemed a kind of canon loaded to the muzzle with facts" (Dickens 1958, 5), concludes his pontifications to his colleague, education Head and school "warden," McChoakumchild, by emphasizing, "In this life, we want nothing but Facts, sir; nothing but Facts!" (Dickens 1958, 4).

Dickens's satirical portrayal shows how an overemphasis on facts warps personalities, diminishes enthusiasm, and crushes the soul out of human life. I begin with Dickens's beginning to *Hard Times* because I believe it helps shed light on a contemporary problem in the anthropological engagement with a particular strain of anthropology emphasizing the discipline should be only about the collection of facts. Of course, Dickens's *Hard Times* is a novel, which makes it literature, which places it in the humanities. Anthropologists, who emphasize fact collection, might also dismiss a reference to a work in the humanities from a discussion of anthropology, believing that anthropology should be "science" and that science is removed from the humanities (and perhaps humanity) and its field methods. However, as I argue in this essay, anthropology and its engagement as a human science in search of the meanings people find and make in life is one that intersects with many fields, and thus Dickens's literary denouncement of a "facts only" approach to life or to an understanding of it can help expose possible fault lines in some methodological approaches of contemporary anthropology.

Often there are difficulties doing research in the field because there are inevitable contradictions between what happens, and what the models of good ethnography suggest is supposed to happen. After many years of doing ethnography, one comes to expect this and to develop a high level of ambiguity tolerance. One realizes that fieldwork about human life, like human life itself, does not always flow in a straight and linear fashion. Some anthropologists have attempted to document this disjunction between the realities of fieldwork, and what the models suggest will or is supposed to happen. This was a major theme of Rabinow's (1977), *Reflections on Fieldwork in Morocco*, and Rosaldo once dared to re-label the anthropological research method of participant observation as "deep hanging out" (Renato Rosaldo quoted in Clifford 1997, 188). The extent to which this disjunction between what actually happens and the models' projections of what should happen is problematic at any given time and is tied to shifts in an understanding of what anthropology is, or should be, within academic research. One of those periodic shifts, rendering it more problematic, urges us—after a long period of reflexivity—to return to a more positivistic, systematic, and scientific understanding of ethnographic research.

This renewed call to abide by the canons of good science is often obvious when reading revised specifications for research grant applications. When doing so, I often feel disheartened. In recent years, there seems to be a tightening of this trend, with increasing emphasis on things such as the following: that the research must involve a clearly specified plan; that it must stick only to that plan; that the researcher must do only what is stated in the plan; and that monies can be spent only as specified in the plan. The last is in part validly intended to prevent the abuse of funding by researchers veering too far afield of specified intentions. Carried to extremes, however, such guidelines rule out much of field research embedded in communities or in people's lives. This is what happens when anthropologists claim that since anthropology is (or should be) a science, every ethnographer should follow the same procedures. This, it seems, is a prevalent view in many recent methods textbooks. Fortunately, there is also a countertrend evident. Some of the recent methods texts or works on methodological philosophy that I reviewed and discuss here include *Using Methods in the Field: A Practical Introduction and Casebook* (deMunck and Sobo 1998), *Essential Ethnographic Methods: Observations, Interviews, and Questionnaires* (Schensul, Schensul, and LeCompte 1999), *Ethnography: A Way of Seeing* (Wolcott 1999), *The Ethnographer's Eye: Ways of Seeing in Modern Anthropology* (Grimshaw 2001), *Expressions of Ethnography: Novel Approaches to Qualitative Methods* (Claire 2003), *Narratives in Social Science Research* (Czarniawska 2004), and *Reflexive Ethnographic Science* (Aunger 2004).

Scientism, Interpretivism, Reflexivism

Here are some tidbits that I found in the first two texts listed above emphasizing a strictly fact-oriented data-collection approach. The two works present clearly specified, but severely limited, definitions of what ethnography is, and what ethnographers do. What (according to these texts) is ethnography? According to Schensul, Schensul, and LeCompte (1999), "Ethnography is a scientific approach to discovering and investigating social and cultural patterns and meaning in communities" (1). "Ethnographic Research is Guided By and Generates Theory" (1; this is a section heading, repeated on page 2). "Theory is important because it helps us to determine what to consider and what to *leave out of our observation*" (12, my emphasis). "The first job of an ethnographer is the organization of questions . . . into . . . formative theory that will guide the collection and, later, the analysis of data" (10). The ethnographer is cautioned to be "explicit and systematic" (deMunck and Sobo 1998, 20) or "systematic" and "efficient" (Schensul, Schensul, and LeCompte 1999, 71). Under specific guidelines for interacting with or interviewing informants, ethnographers are told to keep in mind how the topic relates to the established goal and "determine whether the person being interviewed is staying on topic, and if not, how to reintroduce the topic" (Schensul, Schensul, and LeCompte 1999, 122). Finally, an overall statement of the goal of ethnography is found under the subheading, "What Can Ethnography Tell Us? Just the Facts" (deMunck and Sobo 1998, 16). Here the goal of ethnographic research is defined as follows: "The purpose of ethnographic research is to pin down the facts about people" (deMunck and Sobo 1998, 16).

As I read through these texts, I could not help but think that anthropology seemed to have truly fallen on *Hard Times*, in the Dickensian sense. The rhythms of an old Geertzian blues tune nonetheless kept running through my mind. In *Interpretation of Cultures*, Clifford Geertz, drawing on Thoreau, provided anthropologists with a contrary conceptualization, reflected in the statement, "it's not worth it . . . to go all the way 'round the world to count the cats in Zanzibar" (1973, 16). He might have added, "even if it gives us a fact!"

The methods texts mentioned above also tell us what ethnography is not. "Ethnographic research is never autobiographical" (Schensul, Schensul, and LeCompte 1946, 72). The implication is that we can all go home, or stay home, because stories from the field are intrinsically autobiographical. Such stories inevitably derive from the life of the ethnographer enmeshed in the lives of other people who become hosts in their society and culture. Of course, it is valid to caution against some extreme forms of postmodernist or reflexive writings that seem to descend into "me studies," leaving the ethnographic subject completely out of focus. As Robert Smith notes, "The subjects of ethnographies, it should never be forgotten, are always more interesting than their authors" (1990, 369). Often, the designation of "anecdotal" has been used to devalue knowledge gained from personal experience that might provide profound insights into the motives and understandings of individual social actors. However, it is also increasingly acknowledged that ethnography stems from the ethnographer's particular experiences of and interactions with the culture being studied. Hence, some anthropologists embrace, rather than downplay, the consciousness of the self-aware ethnographer. Plath writes, "Our most important instrument of understanding continues to be our human sensibility, searching for "the cruel radiance of what is" (James Agee's phrase, Agee and Evans 1941, 11) *and* struggling for ways to communicate it" (Plath 1990, 379, his emphasis). To fully understand in context what the ethnographer does communicate after that struggle, it would be relevant to understand his or her reflections on his or her own positioning within the fieldwork. Another suggestion is inherent in these field methods texts decrying autobiographical inclusions: all researchers should maintain standard research practices that can be replicated by others. The possibility of different forms of anthropological research is therefore precluded. Where does this leave prospects for the Weberian view that, in order to be meaningful, social inquiry must be related "to 'understandable' action, that is without exception, to the actions of participating [individuals], because "the individual is the upper limit and sole carrier of meaningful conduct" (Weber 1946, 55)?

In fairness to these texts and those who wrote or edited them, they do recognize that some ethnographers believe linear research models cannot encompass all that we really do in ethnographic research. So alternatives are also presented. For example, they refer to Martin's model of ethnography, which she labeled the Garbage Can Model (Martin 1982). By using the phrase "garbage can model," Martin is emphasizing that ethnographic research does not conform to strict classical linear research models, and perhaps we should not try to coerce into such paradigms the kind of interpretive research that focuses on the experiences and meanings of people's lives. I think there is much truth to what Martin was attempting to suggest—not just for ethnography but pretty much for every other aspect of life and human endeavors in it. In discussing Martin's proposed idea of a garbage can model, de-Munck and Sobo (1998, 14) write: "The garbage can metaphor suggests that research is actually a messy, ad hoc affair only tidied up when put on display." Most researchers would recognize that this is true to some extent; Martin made a point of acknowledging it and bringing this aspect into the realm of possible discussion, much as Rabinow's

(1977) already cited book is largely a confession that the actual ethnographic experience often deviates from what is strictly proposed. However, although Martin's work is mentioned, her own intentionally exaggerated label of Garbage Can Model seems to be used to refute, rather than to recognize, other ways of going about research. DeMunck and Sobo (1998, 14) continue, "But in reacting against the immaculate structure of the classical linear model, the garbage-can model may have swung too far to the antistructural extreme."

What is also troubling is that this "garbage-can model of research, used for an explicit emphasis by Martin, seems to be applied to other ethnographic researchers who have argued for less strictly defined research-model objectives, hypotheses, and data-gathering techniques. For example, Becker (1986), a qualitative researcher in education, is cited discussing why his group's research did not fit the conventional expectations of linear research, and proposes that research is, and should be, an ongoing, interactive, and shared process of development between researchers and subjects. In suggesting that Becker and Martin hold "a similar view of research" the very label of "garbage can model" (not used by Becker) seems extended to other interpretations of research in a way that tends to devalue them or delegitimize them.

Maxwell's (1996) interactive model is also discussed in these texts. Maxwell suggests that we need a compromise between classical linear models of research and those at the other extreme. DeMunck and Sobo (1998, 14) recognize that "Maxwell's model allows for interactive feedback between the different parts of a research design while still maintaining a research structure." They acknowledge that "the choice and use of methods are embedded in and interact with other major components of a research design" (deMunck and Sobo 1998, 15). In the end, they nonetheless privilege a structured research format based on "scientific methods" (deMunck and Sobo 1998, 15). The emphasis is on keeping the ethnographer and informants "on topic" (deMunck and Sobo 1998, 122) and on track, in the pursuit of a strictly specified research agenda.

Where do these models, and particularly an insistence on scientific approaches, leave us as researchers? After more than twenty years of experience in the field, I believe that ethnographic research cannot always be approached only as science, nor should it solely embrace ideas of "scientific rigor." Nor do I feel comfortable with the suggestion that our interactions and experiences with people, usually from another culture, and in a sense from another world, should be approached or thought of as "natural experiments" (Bernard 1994, 52, 56–58, 60). However, I also would find it problematic to try to convince granting agencies of the legitimacy of encouraging other ways of doing ethnography by referencing these as the "garbage can" approach to research. I would certainly not encourage my students to think of their methods of study in such a way.

Since I am espousing a recognition of the validity of more fluid and interactive forms of research orientation, I should mention that I have received training in the types of methods emphasized by those upholding models of scientific rigor. Russell Bernard, a proponent of similar methodological approaches, provides a preface (1998) to deMunck and Sobo's *Essential Ethnographic Methods*. In this preface Bernard refers to the National Science Foundation Summer Institute on Research Methods in Cultural Anthropology, where he taught for several years with Pertti Pelto (co-author of *Anthropological Research: The Structure of Inquiry* (1978), and Stephen Borgatti, designer of the Anthropac computer software for cataloguing and analyzing ethnographic data (1992). I was one of those who trained through this "methods camp" (Bernard 1998, 7) and I have included in the anthropological methods courses I teach the more structured methods taught at the institute, along with materials on either Anthropac or other emerging software-analysis programs.[1] Thus, this paper is not a rejection of the use of such methods or applications. It is, however, the expression of a concern that these highly structured approaches, which can provide a lot of data and can be very valuable for certain forms of research, can also take on lives of their own, becoming methods in search of research. Research should not become a series of projects designed to fit methods that have been defined as acceptable within a narrow scientific paradigm. Rather, method ought to be chosen according to its fit to the context of research.

In this context, Wolcott describes the effects the espoused scientific rigor of the New Ethnography had on projects coming out at that time. An ethnographer studying the lives of firefighters directed her inquiries at topics that fit safely within the scientific model, such as "What is done at a fire?" She did not explore the ethos of firefighters or how they saw meaning in their lives. This, Wolcott argues, would have had much greater ethnographic value. He concludes that the "systemic approach of the New Ethnography was so seductive that many failed to recognize how very narrow it was" (Wolcott 1999, 38).

Having struggled with these sometimes seemingly contradictory convictions, and still having concerns about the emphasis on scientific paradigms that seemed to underlie some of these methods texts, I picked up Wolcott's *Ethnography: A Way of Seeing* (1999). Rays of hope immediately began to beam. It is not that I would agree with his suggestions entirely. It is unusual for anthropologists, including those with an interest in methods, to agree on things entirely. This text clearly emphasized that ethnography is, and should be, about something other than getting the facts. Ethnography is about life, human life, and it is not the case that "In this life, we want nothing but Facts" (Dickens 1958, 4). Rather than assert a particular scientific paradigm for ethnography, Wolcott discusses the history of the debate among anthropologists over this issue. Some assert that anthropology is a "science," in a purer sense; others that it is a "social science"; and still others that it falls in or overlaps with the "humanities." Wolcott writes that there has been "a context of insider argumentation about virtually every aspect of the discipline" and asks, "What is anthropology's proper place among the social sciences? Or should that read 'among the humanities' instead?" (Wolcott 1999, 10). The recognition that anthropology bridges all these fields, humanities included, perhaps renders my references to Dickens's literary work for insights as permissible for entry into these reflections of our work. I cannot agree with the assertion that anthropology and the "artistic lens," including that of "fiction writers," should be recognized as stuff of two differentiated worlds (deMunck and Sobo 1998, 22–23).

The ethnographic emphasis presented by Wolcott draws in part on John Berger's television series, *Ways of Seeing*. Importantly, "seeing" takes precedence over "looking," and definitely over "counting."

Accordingly, Wolcott's definition of ethnography differs from those of the other two books presented above. Rather than emerging from pinning down the facts about people, "ethnographic accounts arise not from the facts accumulated during fieldwork but from ruminating about the meanings to be derived from the experience" (Wolcott 1999, 12). This understanding of ethnography echoes Geertz's belief that the analysis of culture is "not an experimental science in search of law but an interpretive one in search of meaning" (Geertz 1973,5).

Wolcott recognizes that "we are accustomed to hearing about research framed in terms of purposes, goals, objectives, theories, issues to be investigated, or problems to be addressed" (1999, 19). He also explains, however, that while ethnographic research may often be thought of that way, "it is not necessarily *practiced* that way" (1999, 19, his emphasis). For good measure, Wolcott adds: "Any advice one might receive is almost certain to be accompanied by the well-worn caveat for *all* aspects of fieldwork: 'It depends.' Be prepared as well for the too frequently heard reply, 'Who knows?'" (1999, 5, his emphasis). Wolcott also notes, without apology, that he brings into his work his own experiences in the field. As a graduate student, I sought firmer grounds on which to conduct research or build a career. Years of research led me to welcome such statements as openly realistic.

Three Stories from the Field or "Not According to Plan"

My ethnographic field of research is Japan, about which I have specialized over many years. Each story shared in this paper occurred in the context of a detailed and well-specified research plan. In all three cases, however, something happened that led me to unexpected places, in one case geographical places, and in all cases, places of inquiry or reflection where I had not foreseen going. These stories demonstrate that the pursuit of emerging issues not specifically "on topic" with one's research plan leads to crucial insights and information that enriches rather than diminishes one's research projects and overall understanding of human beings, cultures, and the ongoing process of social life. These stories further illustrate that to insist that anthropology is or must be a science is to miss the realization that it is actually about life, typically about other people's lives as we in our lives interact with them and theirs. In other words, to some extent, John Lennon's commentary on life applies to ethnographic research findings: they are sometimes (perhaps often) something that happens to one while one is busy making or pursuing other plans.

In the three cases discussed below I verged from the initial research plan, if only for a while, when a new avenue of action or thought was somehow—unexpectedly—introduced by the person with whom I was interacting. I allowed myself to accept this change of focus, rather than believe my job was to get them back "on topic." Becoming the "bad ethnographer" I probably got a few less specific facts about the specific objectives I had set at the beginning. If I had insisted on being the "good ethnographer," however, it would have meant my missing the opportunity to gain much larger insights in my cultural area of study. In each case, the insights received related to issues of groups that might be designated as "minorities" in Japan, which was not the specific object of the specific research being pursued at that specific point. However, the findings contributed greatly to my own understandings of these issues and would later fit into a larger body of work on these topics and future writings. Perhaps there is a place and time for being not only the good ethnographer but also the good bad ethnographer.

Story #1: Research Interviews or "Bring Extra Notebooks" Advice

I begin my stories from the field, with echoes of advice from Radcliffe-Brown, now elevated to ancestral status in the founding of anthropological inquiry. He is reported to have given his students this advice on doing fieldwork: "Get a large notebook and start in the middle because you never know which ways things will develop" (quoted in Rubenstein 1991, 14, and Wolcott 1999, 33). When I first ran across this statement, I was surprised because I had actually been doing something of this nature as a practice that came from lengthy research experience. A caveat I would add to this advice is always take extra notebooks along for when you think things are over, they are not. This practice might have been born after the following incident.

At the time, back in the mid-1980s, I was conducting research in Japan on department stores as the subject of my PhD. Over the years of my tenure in Japan I have been actively pursuing this and other topics, all while pursuing a life, as everyone else does. When I heard that a civic center in the Tokyo ward I was living in was offering a free Korean conversation class to interested ward dwellers, I decided to take the course and registered with my partner, who was Japanese. A variety of people had signed up for the class, but I turned out to be the only acknowledged *gaijin* or "non-Japanese" citizen. For most of the others, learning Korean meant going from their native Japanese to a grammatically similar language. I often felt like my progress, as a native English speaker, was much slower. Some of the students in the classes had actually had previous exposure to Korean (two I would discover as the story unfolds much more than I would have imagined or they would have admitted). For the others, the similarities between Korean and Japanese meant it was easier for them to master the Korean language (or so it seemed to me).

As the class continued, we got to know each other better and started to do things together socially, in particular going out for refreshments after class, usually to a Japanese *kissaten* (coffee/tea shop), ubiquitous in Japan's urban settings. Among those who would go on these outings were two women with whom I became acquainted and who will become important elements of the story to follow. At the time, I thought of them as totally independent of each other. One woman was slender, with long swinging black hair. She was quite tall by Japanese standards then. The other, about seven or eight years older, was short, slightly plump, with very short hair and glasses. This woman was often the envy of everyone in the class in terms of Korean language acquisition. She always did better than everyone else and seemed to pick up everything quickly. These two women had (different) Japanese family names. There was no indication of any sort of prior relationship between the two of them, nor did they ever present or suggest they might have had a prior relationship. As classes progressed, they did seem to get to know each other, but in the same context in which we all seemed to get to know each other better as we began associating with each other in and out of the classes.

On one occasion when several of us went to a *kissaten*, I had a chance to ask the older of these two women how she had gotten involved in the class. She said she happened to turn the television on to an NHK (*Nihon Hōsō Kyōkai*, Japan Broadcasting Corporation) program on Korean language one day and thought it seemed interesting. As Japan's national educational television station, NHK offers several such language classes, and the books that coincide with these courses are stocked by bookstores throughout Japan, so viewers may purchase them easily. She therefore took the television version of a Korean language course offered by the station. After that initial involvement, she said, she heard about the city's free conversation course and thought it might be kind of interesting. She decided to try it. Listening to her, I felt a bit envious about the ease with which her language ability apparently progressed after this initial seemingly haphazard interest in learning Korean.

At some point in the evening, I began explaining my research on department stores. The younger of these two women then mentioned that she had once worked for a large Tokyo department store as a regular employee after she graduated from junior college. Always eager for more data, I asked if I could interview her about the time she spent as a department store employee. She thought for a bit and then agreed to do it. We immediately set a time and place to have the interview.

So far, I was behaving like the good ethnographer. I did not confuse a group social outing, based on specific criteria of group formation, with a one-on-one interview about my research topic. I explicitly asked if she would be willing to do this, and systematically set up an interview for a separate time and place (during which I would ask her many of the same questions I asked other department store employees I interviewed). This meant another time, another coffee shop, more questions and answers over yet another glass of colored drinkable stuff, this time while taking copious notes in one of those field notebooks. When this interview did occur, I directed its focus toward this woman's time as a department store employee, keeping the informant "on topic." I asked about and gathered facts regarding the conditions of her work, her status, what precisely she did. I also went beyond this to ask about the feelings and meanings it held for her, journeyed cautiously into areas of discontent and disillusion, and finally asked why she quit her job. I was being the good ethnographer as described by Spradley in *The Ethnographic Interview* (1979) and by Gordon in *Basic Interviewing Skills* (1992). I was so happy. It was a great interview. The facts collected eventually informed several publications related to work communities, female employment, and department store organizational culture (Creighton 1989, 1990, 1993, 1995a, 1995b, 1997a).

The interview lasted about an hour, the intended time length, and it was just right. I then did what the good ethnographer is supposed to do in exiting from the interview. One provides a transition from the interview back to usual forms of social exchange. In other words, typical textbook advice on interviewing suggests that one starts with lighter, social conversation before getting into the core business of the interview. Likewise, one does not just bluntly leave the informant after the facts have been drained from his or her mind like blood from his or her body. One exhibits a real or feigned interest in the person. One provides a transition back to usual forms of social communication and exchange by transitional conversation often unrelated to (or less related to) the specific purposes of the interview. One then completely ends the interview and leaves one's informant. Since the way I knew her socially was through the Korean language class, I got ready to put my notebooks away and said to her, transitionally, "So how did you happen to get interested in taking the Korean class?"

In making this inquiring comment, I was doing just what I had done socially at the coffee shop outings we both had gone to. I was doing what one is supposed to do. We ought to have been going home happy, with a sense that a cycle of engagement had been fulfilled, including, transitional entry into the interview, core of the interview, and transitional exit out of the interview back to usual concerns and interests. With a sense of closure, the ethnographic task is normally completed. However, something happened. Being the good ethnographer is one thing. Being the good informant, I learned, is another. The informant had apparently neither read the methods texts nor the books on how interviews should go. She did not then act as a good informant should. On the contrary, when I made the exiting interview comments about the Korean class, I received a reaction that seemed strange to me, one that I still recall well.

The woman seemed visibly upset. She started to fidget then shook her head. I became aware of her breathing. She finally said something, not to me but as if to herself, the air in the room, or the universe at large: "My sister told me I should not have come." Her consternation continued, as did her mumblings. There were several more muffled references to "her sister" and how her sister had reprimanded her and frequently warned her about things. Until that point, I had seen myself as the good ethnographer following protocol well. This came as a difficulty I could not quite remember being discussed in methods texts. At some point, I was nearly tempted to look under the table for this sister she suddenly kept mentioning, more to herself than to me. No mention of a sister or any other family members had ever come up in the interview or in any of my other interactions with her.

Far from marking the end of the interview, the informant seemed to be getting all geared up for something I did not yet understand. There were signs of agitation. Several textbooks or methods books suggest taking note of such responses to questions as clues to things not easily verbalized. I somehow knew not to put the notebook away yet and really wish I had left the first half blank. This reaction to a question outside the research topic did not seem to fit in to the flow of the rest of the interview at all. Things were indeed developing in ways I had not foreseen. Finally, the young woman looked at me. A decision seemed to have been made between herself and her understanding of her life and her relationship with her sister (who at this point remained a mysterious character to me). The floodgates were about to open. She was about to give a narrative of her life to the ethnographer. A new stage in note taking was beginning, not ending.

Again, if I had been the good ethnographer, I would have probably gotten her back "on topic." However, in *Basic Interviewing Skills*, Gordon cautions against "using too much topic control" (Gordon 1992, 147). He writes, "The art of interviewing involves skill in observing when the respondent should be given complete freedom from topic control and when strong topic control is needed" (Gordon 1992, 147). What the informant was on the verge of discussing was not on

track with the specified research agenda. She was not going to provide me with any more facts about being a Japanese department store
employee. However, as the good bad ethnographer, I noticed how important the new development was for her, and I allowed the narrative to come forth. Instead of ethnographic facts about department
stores, she was about to show me the experiential reality of a member
of a minority group in Japan. She was to tell me how she had spent
her, still as yet young, lifetime trying to pass as mainstream Japanese.
I did not coerce her story and had not even anticipated it. I had been
ready to go home, filled to the brim with facts; it had already been a
late evening. I had a choice: to continue to be the good ethnographer
by interrupting the flow of what was happening and getting the informant back on track and on topic as soon as possible, or to be the
good bad ethnographer and allow her to tell the story that was important to her.

She did tell her story, and as that story came forth, as a flood, it was
the story of a young woman who was what is called in Japan, *Zainichi
Kankokujin*, or "resident Korean." There are many "resident Koreans" in Japan, many third- or fourth-generation descendants of Koreans brought to Japan when Korea was a colonial attachment to Japan
(1910–1945). Even if born and raised in Japan, these Korean descendants are not granted Japanese citizenship at birth. Conversely, they
are legally defined as resident foreigners. In this case, the woman had
Japanese citizenship through her mother.[2] Her father was Korean, from
Korea (not a "resident Korean" from Japan), and her mother was Japanese, originally from Japan. There were two girls in the family, sisters. The older one was born in Korea, where the parents had moved
and were living until she was about eight or nine. She, the speaker,
who was seven or eight years younger than her older sister, was also
born in Korea but had little memory of this part of her life because she
left as a very young child. She was not quite two when her father died
and her mother took her two young daughters back to Japan to live.
They then took the mother's Japanese family name and got listed on
the Japanese registry system. Unlike the younger sister, the older sister
had strong and clear memories of the land of their birth. The older sister later married and took on the Japanese name of her husband, thus
having a different Japanese surname from the younger sister.

Given the manner in which this story just flooded forth from the informant, it took some time to begin to make sense of it to present it as I have just done. It became apparent that although quite attached to each other in their lives, during the Korean class, and in other contexts, the two sisters strove to appear as if they barely knew each other. I realized that the older sister's interest in the Korean language had not simply been sparked by happening to tune in to an NHK television program. This was the language she had learned first as a child, and to a much later age than her younger sister, such that it was well established by the time they left Korea. Knowing this did make me feel somewhat better in terms of understanding why her Korean could progress so much faster than mine.

For both women, taking the class had been very important and an intrinsic part of a desire to connect with who they were. For the older of the two this was her first language and she wanted to speak it again, and re-gain her competency in it. The younger of the two wanted some knowledge of it. She talked about having gone back at some point to Korea after her father's death and how she felt about not being able to talk to her relatives there at the time, although her sister and mother could. She hoped someday to go back again, and she wanted to be able to communicate with those same relatives in Korean when she went back again. Their desire to better their Korean language skills, even taking the free class offered by the Tokyo city ward office, had presented a dilemma for them. Her sister had expressed serious qualms about enrolling in the course. They discussed taking the course for some time, and although the older sister very much wanted to, she was reluctant to do so. The upcoming Seoul Olympics in 1988 had provided them with what seemed a window of opportunity to pursue their desire, because there was a "Korean-language boom" going on in Japan, generally as a response to the upcoming Olympic games. According to the informant, her older sister nonetheless repeatedly warned that it was not a good idea to appear to be able to speak Korean too well. It might be better not to be able to do so, or at least not to let people know one could speak Korean. She felt that if one knew Korean, people might suspect one were Korean, even if one were supposedly a Japanese person who had studied it as a foreign language, just as Japanese study many other foreign languages.

This young woman's story, like that of her older sister, was the story of the pressures to "pass" as Japanese and of the continuing discrimination against resident Koreans in Japan. Their desire to "pass" was so strong that the two women, older and younger sister, would hide in public their Koreanness, their language ability, and even their relationship to each other. The story seemed to have no place in my research, from the viewpoint of ethnography as objective experimental science. The story did make sense from the vantage point of ethnography as experience in the field, and the viewpoint that ethnography is an interpretive engagement in search of meaning. It could be seen to fit in with Malinowski's idea of the "complete ethnographer" (Wolcott 1999, 28) or with Mead's espoused belief in "grasping as much of the whole as possible" (quoted in Sanjek 1990, 225). These concepts, Wolcott points out, are best understood as advice to "study and report *in context*" (Wolcott 1999, 28, his emphasis). Although most of the "data" from this unanticipated second part of the interview with this young woman was not written about in publications on work cultures, consumerism, and department stores, it has served to inform my understandings of what it means to be a member of a minority in a self-proclaimed homogeneous society. The insights were incorporated into later publications dealing with issues of minorities (Creighton 1997b, 1998). As Radcliffe-Brown advised: "Get a large notebook, and start in the middle because you never know which ways things will develop." Bring extra notebooks—just in case, I would add.

Story #2 Flexibility in the Research Plan or "Get on the Bus" Advice

While telling these stories from the field, which intersect with my own autobiographical experiences of "being there" (Bradburd 1998), I am not rejecting the importance of set research methods, techniques, or tools, questions, and objectives. We should have them built into the research plan. We should also be prepared, in the name of larger understandings, to abandon them when in the field, according to changing circumstances. One of the characteristics attributed to human intelligence to recognize its potentially profound nature is the quality of flexibility, involving the capacity to shift from set patterns or guide-lines, depending on circumstances. This quality has been designated the "flexible intelligence" of human beings. Using one's intelligence, in-cluding this profound human capacity for flexible intelligence, should not be seen as a challenge to notions of responsible research practice. I am reminded of a posting on individual responsibility and account-ability I once encountered in a very different context, while on a ski-ing outing. Posted signs communicated a two-part mandate for re-sponsible skiing. One tenet stated: "Be prepared by having a plan." The next tenet stated: "Be prepared to abandon or change your plans as circumstances develop or change." Similar advice, often given for how we should live our lives, is apparently ruled out in research about how other people live their lives. Some would bind us hard and fast to empirical methods as a necessary condition of good ethnography. An axiom for good government is that one should govern by reason and not by rule. Good ethnography is generated when we have re-search objectives and plans but allow ourselves (and are allowed) to change them depending on contingencies and on the researcher's shift-ing sense of opportunities in the field.

This second story unfolds in the mid 1990s, when I was in Japan to conduct research as part of a Japan Foundation project. My part of the group project was to look at contemporary Ainu activities, par-ticularly those framed around Ainu identity constructions. Much of the work was done in Nibutani, Japan, on the island of Hokkaidō, where the largest remaining Ainu community in Japan (and the world) resided. I had already been to Nibutani and other areas of Hokkaidō researching the effects of dam-construction projects on Ainu life and cultural-revival attempts (see Creighton 1995c, 2003). In 1994, I made return visits to some of these communities, notably in Nibutani, to gather additional information (and possibly collect further facts). Al-together, the time spent in Nibutani was quite productive. I felt that I had exhausted what I could in relationship to the project there.

Prior to leaving for one's fieldwork, it is not always clear exactly how long data collection will take, and often we find ourselves frus-trated when time seems to run out. In this case, I felt I had some time in my schedule before flying out of Sapporo (the closest large city to

Nibutani) to another area for other commitments. Although there was much I could have pursued if I had had a great deal more time, I was faced with too much time to "waste" but not that much more I could accomplish regarding the set of objectives for the project on the Ainu in that location within the remaining time frame. The research plan allowed for such a possibility by including an optional trip to Abishiri, also located in Hokkaidō, where there is a museum on the Ainu; however, I had been there years earlier.

In Nibutani, I was staying at an inn run by an Ainu family. The last night I was there, they invited me to an extended dinner they were hosting outside in the back area of the inn compound. This led to the somewhat common ethnographic experience of drinking with the informant–host, in this case, the Ainu owner of the inn. Sensing a possible need to legitimize this, I draw on Malinowski's prescription for healthy ethnographic fieldwork. He writes: "It is good for the Ethnographer sometimes to put aside camera, note book and pencil, and to join in [oneself] in what is going on" (Malinowski 1922, 21). There was also a group of people having dinner with us. One of these, a bus driver, seemed to be good friends with the Ainu innkeeper. The innkeeper, who knew I was planning on leaving Nibutani the next day, introduced me to the bus driver and got me engaged in conversation with him. At one point, the innkeeper put his arm around my shoulder, and asked, "Where are you going tomorrow?" (A question that now strikes me as bearing similarity to Wolcott's (1999, 38) ethnographic question "where do you think you are going?" that shows how place intersects with purpose.) I really must have turned into the bad ethnographer, because the informants were now not only asking me the question but, as we shall see, also told me what the answer to this question was. In effect, I was being asked: "Where do you think you are going?"

I explained that I had decided to go to Abishiri, to the museum. "No," said the innkeeper, "you are going on the bus with my friend." Then he laid out what they had constructed as my travel plan. His bus driver friend was driving a group on a trip around the outer reaches of Hokkaidō. Places, he told me, that were very difficult to get to and that I would have to pay a great deal to get to by public transportation (which was true, independent of the difficulties of even getting to them by public transportation). These were indeed important and valuable places for a Japan specialist to visit. One was a noted northern port site, another the place from which one could see the marine border between Japan and Russia. Although the border was a distant marker on the water, it was one of the very few places from which one can see any kind of international border from the insular country of Japan. This was also a very important place in this context because it allowed one to view the contested islands between Japan and Russia. In the end, I was told that since I was his friend, I could travel along on the bus for free, as far as transportation was concerned. I would, of course, have to pay for any of my own expenses for accommodations or meals at the places we would be stopping.

The bus driver put his confirmation into the conversation and said that he, too, thought it would be a good idea for me to get on the bus with them. Sitting next to the driver was the woman who worked with him on the bus as the travel guide and bus hostess. The four of us were now discussing seriously this new shift in plan. The proposed bus routing was to go through these outer areas of Hokkaidō and end up at Sapporo, the largest city on the northern island of Hokkaidō, so the group could fly out from the Sapporo airport. In the course of the conversation, this sudden proposal began to shift from sounding incredibly unreasonable, to making a lot of sense. The voice of the purely good ethnographer in me, however, kept saying, "You cannot do that; it was not on the proposed research plan!" The voice of the purely bad ethnographer expressed excitement about the possibility of traveling in comfort on one of those swanky tourism buses (for a change), complete with the cushioned seats, pretty curtains on the windows and chandeliers on the ceilings, along with the nice maternally comforting bus guide and a driver wearing white gloves. Finally, the good bad ethnographer entered the mental debate to point out that, although unanticipated, there was much to be gained on such a trip in terms of one's overall development as a Japan specialist. I had, after all, already been to the museum in Abishiri. Moreover, the trip was close to free. It might even be fun. I decided that I should allow myself to go on this bus tour, believing that it might be more productive overall, in terms of understandings of Japan, than sticking to a narrowly defined alternative research option would be. So, I, together with the three of them, decided that I would be getting on the bus.

Later, at approximately two in the morning, I went to visit the restrooms located in a series of connected outhouses behind the inn buildings. When I came out of a restroom stall, I passed a man going in (a time and place when many significant but unrecorded ethnographic interactions possibly occur). He said: "I understand you are going with us in the morning." I mumbled that I was and went back to bed. Although I fell immediately to sleep, my subconscious mind must have been alerted to this communication exchange. When I woke up, I realized I should try to find out who this man was. He turned out to be the leader of the group that had chartered the bus trip. The innkeeper, the bus driver, and the nice maternal lady who passes out refreshments and gives information on the bus had all invited me along on this trip. The bus driver was an independent bus driver, who owned his bus. The tour, however, had been chartered by the man I met at the toilets. I realized that in some sense, he, and not the bus driver, owned "the trip," if not the bus. He was the one who really should have been deciding who could go along.

I therefore went to talk to him and apologized for any possible impertinence. He assured me he was quite happy I would be going along. The bus was actually quite empty and he was traveling with a group of young adults as part of Japan's *Kokusaika* or "Internationalization" projects. He knew I was a professor from a foreign country and thus felt it would be a bonus if I joined them. It would make it even more *Kokusai-teki* ("international-like") if I were willing to go along. They would like me to come along and also take part in their activities and discussions. If I had any doubts left, a line from a Kurt Vonnegut novel, *Cat's Cradle*, that I had read long ago as an undergraduate student, and that had particularly impressed me, rang through my mind: "Peculiar traveling suggestions, are dancing lessons from god" (Vonnegut 1963 [1998], 63). Ever since I first read the line, I have allowed it to enter in as a factor in pursuit of my path in life. Here was a chance to allow the same invocation to enter into the research plan.

I would learn on this journey that everyone in the group (excluding the leader, the bus driver and bus guide) was *Burakumin. Burakumin* are a discriminated-against minority group in Japan descended from people so categorized in Japan's historic Edo era (1600–1868). They were discriminated against because they were itinerant, rather than belonging to a place, or because their occupations dealt with the dead—considered a source of pollution. Although the discriminatory status has supposedly been "erased" in modern Japan, in actuality, it remains. *Burakumin* are identifiable through residency affiliation or masked information on family registries. For the group on the bus, this trip involved an exploration of identity in relationship to issues they were struggling with as *Burakumin* in Japanese society. I had allowed myself to be influenced by the suggestions, and indeed enthusiasm, of my informants. I had boarded the bus with a general plan and purpose but without a truly "clear idea of exactly where [I was] headed" (Wolcott 1999, 38).[3] In hindsight, it became clear that I learned much more accompanying this group of young *Burakumin* on their identity travels through Hokkaidō than I could have doing anything else with those few remaining days.

Among the discussions I recall best were those that they wanted to teach me, as a foreigner who was also a professor of Japanese studies, about the reality of being *Burakumin*. One young man discussed the yearnings of his existential quest for identity in terms of his objections to the imperial symbols of the Japanese state. He explained that as a *Burakumin* he was opposed to symbols of the emperor standing as symbols of Japan. Symbols of the emperor tend to be used in Japan to reinforce the cultural assertion of Japan as a homogenous, or one-people, nation (*tanitsu minzoku*) (see Weiner 1997). Minority objections to the symbols were one aspect of protest against the song long used by Japan as the "national anthem," *Kimigayo*, a song of tribute to the emperor, and the flag long used as the "national flag," *Hinomaru*, or the "circle of the sun" flag with a red circle on a white background. The symbols have also long been regarded as questionable by many in Japan because of their associations with pre–world war II colonialism and military atrocities conducted under symbols of the emperor.[4] Befu (1992) points out that given the questionable nature of these symbols, for decades after the war, Japanese searched for other identity symbols. The issue would again take center stage in Japan at the closing of the twentieth century, when in 1999, after decades of protests and resistance, the government passed the *Kokikok-kaho* (flag and anthem act) legislating *Kimigayo*, song of reverence to the emperor, and the *Hinomaru* flag as Japan's official national anthem and flag despite the decades of protest and resistance over these symbols. Since Japan was already using these symbols in international events, many outside Japan would not be aware of these internal debates over them. The process of legislating the symbols to official status also again involved the figurative erasure of minorities and minority issues in Japan, and a reassertion of a one-people nation under the father figurehead of the emperor.

The young *Burakumin* man talked about the concept of *kegare*, or "pollution." The reason, he believed, that *Burakumin* did not like imperial symbols was that they reinforced ideas of pollution as being in the blood and in the descent line. The emperor, he explained, is supposed to be pure, but purity cannot exist in society unless there is something else. For the emperor to be perceived as pure, there has to be something in society to take on the impurity, and hence something must exist as impure. This young man saw *Burakumin* as having been used as the residual reservoir of impurity to construct the contrasting purity of the emperor and others in Japanese society. Thus, he felt the construction of Japanese identity in terms of symbols of the emperor was a source of prejudice against *Burakumin* because it maintained the need for them to fill the role of sacrificial scapegoat of contrasting impurity. This is why he was opposed to imperial symbols as symbols of the state, or of Japanese culture. He went on to describe how this projection of inherited impurity left some *Burakumin* to wonder why they were born at all, if it meant they had to live under this conceptualization.

As I listened, I thought that this young man, who had probably not read, or maybe even heard of, major anthropological figures who dealt with the opposing structural contrast of purity and pollution, such as Mary Douglas in *Purity and Danger* (1969), or Claude Lévi-Strauss in *Structural Anthropology* (1973a, 1973b), was able, nonetheless, to set up clearly the oppositional contrasts of purity and pollution and also to put a reality to how they affected people's lives. Devos and Wagatsuma had done early research on *Burakumin* when this was still a topic kept hidden and not easily worked on in Japan (Devos and Wagatsuma 1966, Devos 1971). It took quite a bit of courage to even address the issues at that time and may have been even more difficult for Wagatsuma as a Japanese insider. Only recently are more researchers taking up the challenge of researching Japan's hidden minority. With these profound interactions, I could not help but feel that being flexible enough to allow an alteration in research plans, by getting on the bus, had added immensely to my own ethnographic understandings.

This said, as mentioned earlier, I do not wish to seem "flip" about the importance of research agendas and having a research plan but instead wish to argue for flexibility in deciding when to veer from it as circumstances develop in the field. Before getting on the bus, I had done as much as I felt I could reasonably accomplish in Nibutani. I did not expect to gain that much out of a repeated museum visit to Abishiri. There, thus, was a rational calculation of overall costs and benefits to going on the bus tour. However, there turned out to be an additional angle to this bus trip, one that I had not expected, and one that would also immensely facilitate the specific research objective on Ainu attempts at contemporary identity constructions.

While traveling, the members of the bus group were also engaged in discussing issues of minority identities with Ainu throughout Hokkaidō. This explained why they were visiting the Ainu inn in Nibutani in the first place. Thus, in addition to going to sites somehow associated with "internationalization," they were also planning to stop to allow visits with local Ainu. Hence, all along the journey, there were involvements in Ainu presentations, Ainu gatherings, Ainu exchanges of life stories. Sometimes these were in very remote locations that I would have had difficulty getting to on my own.

One of the Ainu we met on one of these stops was a contemporary Ainu crafts artist. He informed us that he, along with other Ainu, would be in Sapporo with an Ainu art exhibit at the airport at the time when the group's bus was expected to arrive there. This is where we were all supposed to get off the bus and where the journey was to end for the planned bus tour, as they would fly out from the Sapporo airport. The plan was that I would get off with them at the airport to carry on, on my own, after that. The Ainu exhibit was happening just that week at the Sapporo airport, with presentations, exhibits, artists, artisans, musicians, and performances. While viewing this exhibit, an Ainu gentleman there noticed how avidly I was taking notes. He asked me about this, and I gave him a name card, explaining who I was, what I was doing, and why the exhibit was of particular interest to me. He said he lived in Sapporo and would give me a ride there if I waited until he was ready to leave at the end of the day. I accepted the invitation and was pleased to learn that he was an officer in the Sapporo branch (the main branch) of the *Utari Kyōkai*, otherwise known as the Ainu association.[5]

I ended up spending the next few days associating with this man and his family. I was able to attend the Ainu language classes, part of the revival movement, offered at the Sapporo headquarters. I was taken to visit a small bar run by an Ainu woman, interacting with the mostly Ainu guests there. I spent a couple of days at a series of Ainu shops run for tourists, one of which was run by his wife. There, I was taught how to do Ainu embroidery, play the Ainu mouth harp, and help out at the shops run by the local Ainu artisans and merchants.

On this particular occasion, I was willing to set out without a precisely clear idea of exactly where I was going, and it seemed to make all the difference. How much I would have lost in experience gained, if I had not gotten on a bus whose exact route I did not know. The wealth of this experience even allowed me to wonder if perhaps there is a god of fieldwork out there. Are peculiar traveling suggestions not dancing lessons from god? Sometimes it is good advice to get on the bus.

Yarn #3 Ethnographic Unquestions of Participant Observation or "Listen Carefully to Answers to Questions Never Asked" Advice

Everybody does it. Asks questions, that is. Journalists do it; detectives do it; researchers do it. Why then do ethnographers feel so guilty about doing it when they might be asking questions on sensitive topics, or when a discussion might lead to their asking questions they had not anticipated? Wolcott (1999, 56–57) discusses the contradictions involved in our question asking. He notes that we may be unduly limited by cultural beliefs in our own backgrounds regarding what is and is not appropriate to ask questions about. In the following story, I discuss questions that I refrained from asking, even if they pressed fully in my mind while listening to someone's story. This woman's story can be seen as a yarn, in this case a silk yarn that unraveled over time, in the course of a long engagement in the field. I switch to the word "yarn," with its double meaning of "story" and "thread" intentionally, because the narrative thread of this woman's life was truly a silk yarn. Like the previous stories, this yarn emerged in the midst of a set research project with a set research purpose—however, one directed at something else.

In this particular research, my purpose was to collect ethnographic "facts" about weaving workshops conducted as leisure hobby pursuits for women in today's Japan. This research was about identity issues in terms of reclaiming the lost Japan and the place of pursuits traditionally done by women, but not necessarily controlled by them, such as silkworm raising (sericulture) and silk weaving. The research was about the intersections of the modern economy with gender roles, women's lives, consumerism, and the tourism industry. It focused on the repackaging of "fun" (travel to the Japanese Alps of Nagano Prefecture) into commodified forms of edutainment (a combination of education and entertainment, see Creighton 1994), cloaked in the guise of education (learning about silk weaving and Japanese cultural identity) as a co-optation of persisting Confucian social values emphasizing work and education, including self-development. Nothing in the research proposal I wrote prepared me for what I was to learn about surviving the atomic bombing of Hiroshima, or the need for a woman to find meaning in life as the surviving child of another woman who, as a *hibakusha* (atom-bomb survivor), resulting single mother, and convert to Christianity had also struggled to find meaning in her own life. All three of these definitions (*hibakusha*, single mother, and Christian) were atypical things to be in postwar Japanese society, one that then, even more than now, exerted pressures for individuals and families to conform to "normal" expectations.[6]

I had been involved in this research project over a number of years, starting while a graduate student living in Japan. I joined weaving sessions held in Nagano Prefecture, historically a major area of the silk-weaving industry in the Meiji area that had helped propel Japan economically into the modern world arena. The area of Nagano is known for the Tsumugi Pass through the mountains—one means that young Meiji women under contract had to escape onerous labor under bad conditions in silk mills. Even if they managed to leave, they did not always escape tuberculosis, highly correlated with the conditions of the mills (see Tsurumi 1990). This information I gathered during the archival-research stage of the project. In Nagano, during participant observation, I lived with, wove with, and conducted interviews with participants in weaving sessions. After several sessions over several years, I had a good knowledge of the social life and structured patterning that constituted a large part of my research plan objectives (Creighton 1998b). There was always a dinner party at the end of each week's session during which the participants could ask the teachers (a married couple who ran the sessions) any questions they wished. Although different groups of women took part in these workshops, certain questions were inevitably posed each time, directed more at their personal lives than at their interest in weaving. "How did you meet? How did you get married?" When asked such questions, the male teacher would first feign reluctance to speak, saying: "Oh no, I can't say, really." Then he would go on to say: "Well, OK, let me see, now. Oh yes, I was walking down the Ginza one day (a well-known trendy shopping and commercial district in Tokyo) and I saw this woman walking along. Something in my mind said, '*Ah, are da*'—that's her, and so it was." Everyone would laugh at what seemed to be a clearly fabricated story that did not really provide anyone any information about how the couple had met and decided to marry.

The wife's yarn was unwound for me over several workshops. I learned, one year, that she had grown up in Hiroshima. On another occasion, I learned her mother had been a Christian (a rarity in Japan), and so on, until one day she and I ended a session sitting for a long time by ourselves winding silk yarns together into usable balls. This gave us a special opportunity to talk to each other at length. As one of the two main instructors, she was generally busy transmitting knowledge of silk and weaving to all the students. The conversation started with my asking her about my mistaken understanding of her Christian background. "Oh no, I'm not Christian," she immediately responded. I explained I thought I had heard that her family was Christian in a previous session when she had also mentioned growing up in Hiroshima. "Oh no," she clarified, "my mother. My mother was a Christian, not me."

The yarn begins in this way. It is the story of this instructor as a young girl, growing up as the child of a woman who became a devoted Christian in a place where Christians were unusual, and a place where being unusual was not valued. As she grew into her teens, she developed a rebellious resentment toward the mother because of the mother's "difference," a difference she focused on as her mother's being Christian. As she tells the story, she remembers—regretfully now—being embarrassed by her mother. This typical identity story of adolescent and youth conflict toward one's parent is resolved in the typical way. The daughter goes on to mentally explore more and more the mother's life reality. As she does so, she recognizes the mother's strengths, given the situations and circumstances of life with which she had to deal. Coming to a new understanding of her, the daughter replaces the resentment toward the mother with a new sense of appreciation, based on her better understanding of the context of life in which the mother was caught. Instead of rejection, she ends up satisfied, and even proud to have had this mother, to have been her daughter. Although a typical story of a youthful identity crisis, resolved in a typical way, the details were not so typical.

As the story continues, it begins to shift away a bit. The story of the mother, rather than of the woman (my teacher) telling it, now becomes the focus of the story. She became a Christian after the atomic bombing. For a long time, the daughter could only think of such a conversion as a desperate attempt to grasp something that offered meaning, and cling to it, after an incredibly destructive event. Perhaps it was so, the response to a desperate need by a woman for whom meaning had been shattered. As the story continues, I notice that another shift has occurred in the telling of it. It is no longer even the story of the teller's mother, but is now the story of "a woman." What started as the instructor's story had become a story about her mother and had now turned into the story about a woman who went through a very profound experience in life, that deeply touched—too deeply—herself and those she loved.

The mythic epic, Gilgamesh, tells a similar story. Mason's verse narrative of the epic Gilgamesh begins with the following:

> It is an old story
> But one that can still be told
> About a man who loved
> And lost a friend to death
> And learned he lacked the power
> To bring him back to life. (1970, 11)

The story from the field became the story about a woman who lost most of those she loved to death, the grandfather of her family, and her own two young sons. Just like Gilgamesh, the woman was forced to learn that she did not have the power to bring them back to life. The woman's conversion to Christianity grew out of her associations with the nuns that looked after her during her lengthy recovery from her own atomic wounds in the hospital. In a search for meaning amid numerous deaths, that of loved ones, of a lifestyle, of a future, not to mention the near death of hope, the woman responded to those who were caring for her by converting to their faith.

The initial blast and its destruction was certainly extremely traumatic for *the woman*. The woman was severely injured, but she herself did not die. The woman's father, who lived with the family, was killed instantly. The woman's two little boys were not killed instantly. However, this perhaps only made the woman's pain of losing them even worse. One small boy died first, and as the child died before her eyes, she was helpless to do anything about it. For the baby, though, she believed there was a chance. The baby was alive but screamed in agony. He wanted to suck, wanted the breast, wanted to drink. Among those who initially survived the blast and died from radiation exposure in the following days or weeks, there was also reported an acute yearning for water to quench the sense of an incredible thirst. A tribute to this is represented in the architecture and art of the Hiroshima Peace Park, memorializing the blast, through the use of fountains or structures that perpetually provide water.

The positioning of their home, and of the woman that morning when the blast occurred, meant that physically she had been affected from the back, and her back was completely burnt. In appearance at least, the front of her body did not seem much affected. Her chest area and breasts were normal, or appeared normal, despite the sense of intense burning and soon-to-be scar tissue that would cover the back of her body. So, when the child screamed for the breast, she tried to give it to him. She felt like she could give it to him and could have him drink. If he had, if he could have just done that, perhaps he would have, could have lived. This was the feeling the woman had to suffer with as her own life continued, for the child did not suck. Although he wanted the breast and cried to suck her breasts, which were fine and which had milk that could have nourished him, the child did not suck. Despite his pleas and efforts at the woman's breast, he could not suck because the inside of his mouth was too burned to allow for this. So the agony for the woman was intensified by the sense that she should have, could have been able to do something; she should have, could have saved him, but at the same time she could not. This child of hers also died in front of her eyes.

Now, as the good ethnographer, what was I to do with this story from the field? It did not seem to fit into my research on silk weaving and the commoditization of leisure-travel tourism packages for contemporary Japanese women at all. Should I have decided that it did not fit the research agenda, and therefore that there were no relevant collectible facts to be gathered from it? Should I have stopped the informant's narrative and gotten her back "on topic." Should I have tried to determine if the new "facts" were replicable? From a literary-analysis perspective, I could note a step-by-step displacement of the teller of the tale from the tale itself. It started out as a story about herself and her relationship with her mother, then turned into the mother's story—from which the storyteller already seemed absent, and then into the story of some woman. In the end, it was the story of a woman who lost her children to death in the atomic bombing, as many did, as many continue to do in other forms of bombing around the world. At some point, as I listened to this story, I thought of one of the statues at the Hiroshima Peace Park of a mother, bent over, with her two children clinging to her back, as she is engaged in the post-bombing struggle of helping them all survive.

It was difficult to forget this story, buried somewhere in my notes. What had happened seemed an important ethnographic moment in participant observation. The story was not told to all who participated in the workshops. It seemed to emerge as an unexpected gift of narrative from person to person. What then should I, as good, or good bad ethnographer, do about or with the story?

In *Alice in Wonderland* (1957 [1986]) the characters of Lewis Carroll celebrate "unbirthdays." They espouse this as a recommended policy, since people have many more unbirthdays than they do birthdays. As ethnographers, we always have questions we never ask, because we do not have the time, or do not have the opportunity, or because we feel we just cannot. It is likely that we have many more unquestions that remain unasked than we have questions. During her telling of this story, I became aware of the unquestions I was not asking, even though perhaps the solely good ethnographer might have asked them. As the good bad ethnographer, I simply did not feel I could ask them. (What does the face of an infant look like if the inside of its mouth is burnt out, and does this matter to its mother?) Some of these unquestions that I never asked were related to the growing absence of the storyteller from the story itself. *Unasked Unquestion #1:* Where were you when all this was going on? Presumably she would have been there as well, along with her mother and grandfather, a witness to the scene, and thus possibly definable as a *hibakusha* herself, and not just the daughter of a *hibakusha*. *Unasked Unquestion #2 (a corollary to #1):* Was it really the uniqueness of being the daughter of a Christian, or being the daughter of a hibakusha, or some combination of both, that made her being different so difficult in a society in which pressure to conform to norms is so great?

And so on, and so on, with many other unqueries. *Unasked Unquestions grouping #3* (a missed opportunity to bring in standard ethnographic questions related to anthropological kinship concerns): So, what happened to father (your own, not your mother's or father's)? Was he there with the rest of the family? Was he off to the war as was commonly the case with men his age at the time? Did he have a war related death, or did he survive and not remain with the family after the war? *Unasked Unquestions grouping #4:* Why the growing absence of the storyteller from the story? And what about that little white line "do-hickey" that runs across your eye? Is that from age, is it genetic, or did it have anything to do with . . . ? (It would be a few years later, while doing work in conjunction with the fiftieth anniversary of the atomic bombings for a special symposium organized by Alan Wolfe at the University of Oregon, that I would read about the "classic cataract" effect experienced by many bomb survivors. I think it likely that this explained the eye, but cannot confirm this, because I was being the good bad ethnographer, and thus did not ask this question that the solely good ethnographer likely would have, and thus did not pin down the facts on this one.)

At the beginning of this story–yarn, I mentioned Wolcott's discussion of our difficulties with questions. Wolcott points out that sometimes we bring our own cultural "baggage" about what can and cannot properly be brought up in conversation. Wolcott writes, "Question-asking is culturally-specific; we follow our own implicit rules in the absence of anything better to guide us" (1999, 56). Sometimes, Wolcott argues, this is based on restrictions in our own culture, and it might be possible to discover that more can be asked than we imagined (Wolcott 1999, 56). I think something a little different was happening in the interaction described above. It can also be valid sometimes to allow oneself not to ask certain questions even if one knows one can.

Finally, there was *Unasked Unquestion #5*. Although never asked, at least orally, this one seemed clearly present during the telling of the tale. It was related to the unquestion of the distancing of storyteller from the story. It was not just the unquestion mentioned above, "where were you?" but the unquestion "where are you?" At the end of the story about the woman who lost her two little boys to death and learned she did not have the power to keep them in life, this unquestion was there as a presence. It was in me, in the air, in the inbetweenness of us, storyteller and story receiver. As the unquestion hung between us, so likely did a look, and to that look the storyteller answered the unquestion, without actually answering it. In her final mention of the woman who had to accept that her two sons had died, her look met mine, and her response to my unasked unquestion brought her back to the story and back into a direct relationship to the time, to the scene, and to the two little boys themselves. She said suddenly, *watakushi no otōto-tachi*, "my little brothers." Maybe being the good bad ethnographer was OK after all, since informants were still answering questions, sometimes even those never asked.

Conclusions

In the end, I argue for recognition of the possible art of being the good and the good bad ethnographer, allowing for possible alternations between applying careful and explicit methods and pursuing another sort of understanding through insights born out of the unexpected encounters that emerge in the field context, and out of evolving relationships. Doing so can allow us to perform appropriate ethnography in ordinary and extraordinary circumstances. Clearly, there are good reasons for set research objectives. However, we should also remain open to experiences and insights that come from outside their parameters. Otherwise, we relinquish too much in our search for the full range of knowing about human cultures and experience. For this reason, I cannot so easily embrace the assertion that anthropology is, and must only be, a science in the strict sense. Like Wolcott (1999, 10), I think that we are continually constructing the "proper place" of anthropology among, as he says "the social sciences," wondering if perhaps that should not read instead "among the humanities"?[7]

Finding anthropology's "proper place" among the disciplines, and the "proper approaches" to good ethnography are issues potentially much more complicated than some of the models discussed earlier in this essay would suggest. In addition to those methodological approaches that are explicit and systematic, there is also a place for those that build upon more reflexive engagements of ethnographers and hosts. Wolcott writes, "As you will discover, I lean heavily on the integrity of the ethnographer to figure what he or she is up to rather than admonishing everyone to work at devising grand theories or themes" (1999, 14). In other words, for some, anthropology is more of a science in search of law; for others, it is an interpretive exploration of meaning or of stories, the stories of other people's lives and how we come to know them. Like Geertz, I lean toward the latter paradigm.

Although a renewed call for scientism in anthropology may be more and more often heard, as reflected in the orientations of some of the texts reviewed earlier, other methods' texts indicate that Wolcott's view is not unique. Also drawing on John Berger's work in *Ways of Seeing*, Anna Grimshaw focuses on the idea of vision and seeing as an anthropological metaphor. She contends that there is not one view of what anthropology is (or should be) but contrasting ways of seeing the discipline and seeing within the discipline. She writes:

> There are a number of kinds of anthropological visuality or ways of seeing making up the modern project. . . . Indeed, anthropology is characterized by what I call its distinctive ways of seeing. . . . For, as we will discover, the modern project has different visions contained within it. It is sometimes conceived to be about the cumulation of scientific knowledge, a process by which the world is rendered knowable; but in other cases it may be concerned with ethnographic understanding as a process of interrogation, a means of disrupting conventional ways of knowing the world; or, modern anthropology might be considered to involve transformations, intense moments of personal revelation. (Grimshaw 2001, 7)

Other approaches to methods likewise argue for multiple possibilities of interpreting the anthropological project. Claire (2003) provides insights to novel approaches to methods, defining them as "expressions of ethnography" rather than as tools of fact collecting. Czarniawska's (2004) work places renewed emphasis on the role of narratives as a method of social science research. Then there are others, such as Aunger (2004) who argues for a return to anthropology as science, but, in doing so, attempts to bring together reflexive analysis to combine empirical forms of data collecting with postmodern objectives through reflexive realism.

Through a "more and more scientistic" orientation (Grimshaw 2001, 7) we have managed to demystify anthropology. Perhaps it is time to allow some of the mystery and some of the magic back into the art of managing meaningful fieldwork in the pursuit of knowledge. I am not suggesting that we revert to the "fieldwork is like childbirth" analogy that says "you can't really figure out what it is like until you've done it, and then you can't possibly explain it." Those who emphasize scientific rigor in their research justly react against such a stance. We do not need that kind of mystification. We can explain childbirth and teach techniques to help prepare people for it, and we can explain and provide tools and techniques to help researchers with fieldwork. I refer to putting back the mystery and the magic in another sense. It is the human mystery, in the sense that Gomes (1996), a theological scholar, posits as being at the basis of the existence of life, and of relationships. If one is ever to truly understand experience, life, and relationships, these are things that must at some point be seen not just as facts (to be collected around their peripheries) but as forms of a mystery that one must enter into. Since anthropology is, at heart, trying to understand the meanings humans have come to have about life and experience, perhaps we can also recognize the validity of field experiences that arise from a willingness to move out of our minds, and instead to enter into that mystery.

Some scientific views of anthropology assert that ethnography is not about the ethnographer. I would agree that there can be a problem when *ways of telling* shift overly emphatically from the *ethnographic eye* to the *ethnographic I*. However, ethnography is also about the reflective understandings gained through the experiences of the ethnographer, and therefore, in some sense, the ethnographer is not only the teller but an aspect of the telling, and, in the end, of what is told. This is true even for specific data-collection methods such as interviews. Despite arguing for scientific cultural anthropology, Aunger recognizes: "In the case of interviewing, the data collection situation involves recognition that there are two active participants, the interviewer and the informant (each of which has a number of relevant characteristics)" (2004, 42). Some anthropologists, such as Bernard, argue for the importance of specific systematic method use, claiming that "anthropology has always been about methods" (1998, 9). In contrast, Wolcott makes the case that, at its historic beginnings, there was little emphasis on methods in anthropology, and that shifts in the concepts of methods and the nature of methods used have long been part of the anthropological engagement (1999, 41–42). He prefers an understanding of ethnography as process, and even argues for the use of phrases such as ethnographic techniques, or ethnographic research, rather than references to ethnographic methods.

Anthropology has been the discipline long teaching that different human beings have different valid ways of understanding what it means to be human. Perhaps the time has come to accept the possibility that anthropologists might validly have different ways of understanding what the anthropological project means and how it should be carried out. If so, it should be possible to embrace an anthropology that admits to different ways of seeing and allows different ways of telling. Anthropology is somewhere among and between the sciences, the social sciences, and, yes, the humanities. If there is an alternate identity by which the discipline might be known, let it not be the natural experiments discipline, the garbage can discipline, or the leftovers discipline.[8] Perhaps there are new ways we could think of anthropology's central emphases on people and on place, whether the field is geographically far away, or increasingly close to home (remembering that sometimes places closer to home can be more difficult to get to than places far away).[9] Perhaps, as anthropologists have long argued is the case within cultures, it is possible to have engagements in magic and science at the same time. Perhaps it might even be possible to recognize that anthropology is sometimes a discipline of "Peculiar Traveling Suggestions," otherwise known as "Dancing Lessons from God."

Notes

In completing this article, I ran up against the process of uprooting my usual life and academic work in Vancouver to take up a year's work as a visiting professor at Ritsumeikan University in Kyoto, Japan. Since I could not finalize the essay before departure, I was left with the difficulties of securing the materials I needed to finish from my bookshelves in Vancouver, or by struggling through Japanese academic bureaucracy to get the English texts on ethnographic field methods that indeed were available somewhere in Japan, but not always easily accessible. I am grateful to my colleague Patrick Moore for our e-mail exchanges identifying newly emerging methods texts, and to Masa Kagami and Eirin Kagami for shipping me materials that I needed while in Japan.

1. I was a student of the three-week National Science Foundation "methods camp" in Gainesville, Florida, in the summer of 1993. At that time, participants were chosen through a competitive application process and were expected to be post-doctoral anthropologists with teaching appointments at major universities. The year I participated, Steve Borgatti

and Russ Bernard were the instructors. Bert Pelto was also to have been an instructor, but circumstances did not allow his participation in that particular year.

2. In Japan, citizenship is tied to being entered on a family-line registration system, so one either has to be added to an existing family registration, or be the initiator of a new one (a much rarer occurrence). With the assumption that women marry out of their natal families, where they are "crossed out" and written into the husband's family (true in the overwhelming majority of cases), Japanese law recognized citizenship only through a Japanese father in most cases. A woman was not allowed to pass citizenship to her children until changes in the Japanese family act in 1983. At that time, those with a Japanese mother could apply and receive citizenship but had to assume a Japanese name. There were many contradictions to this earlier system in terms of children of mixed parentage. For example, children of Japanese men who had moved and taken permanent residence abroad were granted Japanese citizenship at birth even though they were born and raised elsewhere, whereas children born and raised in Japan to a Japanese mother but not a Japanese father did not receive Japanese citizenship.

3. In including this quotation from Wolcott, I believe it should be made clear that he is not criticizing those who are willing to set off with no "clear idea of exactly where they are headed" but, conversely, seems to be poking fun at those who cannot set out without a plan. For context, I include more of the quotation here: "Place and purpose have to intersect. For the ethnographer I think there is no necessary order as to which must come first. Here I put emphasis on *place* because I think it somewhat peculiar to ethnography that *where* one conducts research plays such an important role. . . . When the question comes first—a seemingly more logical way to begin for those who can't set out until they have a clear idea of exactly where they are headed—recognition must still be given to the fact that place will impose constraints anyway, so one's guiding question(s) must still be fine-tuned and adjusted to the situation" (Wolcott 1999, 39–40).

4. I follow the convention of not capitalizing designations such as world war II as a means of questioning whether such a practice grants greater value to wars, potentially reifies them, and thus enters into their repetition.

5. Prejudice against Ainu in Japan has been so strong that, when this organization was initiated, there was even reluctance to use the word "Ainu" in the title of the organization. Hence, it was instead called *Utari Kyokai*. Utari is an Ainu word meaning "friend" and *kyokai* is a Japanese word meaning "association." At different times, there have been debates over changing the name. When the organization started in 1946 it was actually called the Hokkaidō Ainu Kyokai, but there was a decision to change the name at the organization's general meeting in 1960 because some members felt uncomfortable with the use of the term Ainu because it carried such strong discrimination in Japan; the constitution modified the name change in 1961 (Creighton 1995c, 78, note 7). Since that time, some Ainu have been encouraging re-embracing the name "Ainu" in the title, but at the time of my involvement here, the organization went by the name of *Utari Kyokai*.

6. In a recent book, Merry White suggests the pressures that have existed in Japan for people to conform to some kind of expectations of normalcy in social roles, in her chosen title, *Perfectly Japanese: Making Families in an Era of Upheaval*. The book deals with examples of "normal" Japanese today, showing that many individuals and families actually live lives—often like the women in this story that depend on circumstances rather

than choice—that are somehow at variance with continually recreated assertions of what is "normal" in Japan.

7. This theme also runs through talks and sermons presented by Gomez as the Plummer Professor of Theology at Harvard University.

8. Wolcott points out that some have posited anthropology as the "science of leftovers" (1999, 10).

9. Umberto Eco makes the analogy between art and cultural anthropology when he says that both efficiently take on the role of imperialism's guilty conscious: "And so the last beach ideology develops its thirst for preservation of art from an imperialistic efficiency, but at the same time it is the bad conscience of this imperialistic efficiency, just as cultural anthropology is the bad conscience of the white man who thus pays his debt to the destroyed primitive cultures" (Eco 1986, 39).

References

Abu Lughod, Lila. 1991. Writing against culture. In *Recapturing anthropology: Working in the present*, ed. Richard G. Fox, 191–210. Santa Fe NM: School of American Research Press.

Acedo, Edith. 2000. Le magnétisme, un lien entre le corps et l'esprit. In *Guérir l'âme et le corps: Au-delà des médecines habituelles*, ed. Philippe Wallon, 53–68. Paris: Albin Michel.

Adams, Vincanne. 1996. *Tigers of the snow and other virtual sherpas: An ethnography of Himalayan encounters*. Princeton: Princeton University Press.

Agee, James, and Walker Evans. 1941 [1980]. *Let us now praise famous men*. Boston: Houghton Mifflin.

American Anthropological Association. 1998. Code of ethics of the American Anthropological Association. http://www.aaanet.org/committees/ethics/ethcode.htm.

Amit, Vered. 2000. Constructing the Field: Ethnographic fieldwork. In *The contemporary world*. London: Routledge.

Anzaldúa, G. 1999 *Borderlands—La Frontera*. San Francisco: Aunt Lute Books.

Aubrée, Marion, and François Laplantine. 1990. *La table, le livre et les esprits: naissance, évolution et actualité du mouvement social spirite entre France et Brésil*. Paris: Éditions J. C. Lattes.

Augé, Marc. 2004. *Oblivion*. Trans. Marjolijn de Jager. London: University of Minnesota Press.

Aunger, Robert. 2004. *Reflexive ethnographic science*. Walnut Creek CA: AltaMira.

Austen, Jane. 1999. *Pride and prejudice*. Introduction by William Trever. Oxford: Oxford University Press.

Bakhtin, Mikhail M. 1981. *The dialogic imagination*. Trans. C. Emerson and M. Holquist. Austin: University of Texas Press.

Barbanell, Sylvie. 1940. *When your animal dies*. London: Psychic Press.

Barth, Frederik. 1992. Social/cultural anthropology. In *Wenner-Gren Foundation report for 1900–1991*, 62–70. Fiftieth anniversary issue. New York: Wenner-Gren Foundation.

———. 1995. Other knowledge and other ways of knowing. *Journal of Anthropological Research* 51 (1): 65–68.

———. 2002. Toward a richer description and analysis of cultural phenomena. In *Anthropology beyond Culture*, eds. Richard G. Fox and Barbara J. King, 23–36. Oxford: Berg.

Barz, Gregory F., and Timoth J. Cooley, eds. 1997. Shadows in the field: New perspectives for fieldwork. In *Ethnomusiology*. New York: Oxford University Press.

Basso, Keith H. 1990. "To give up on words": Silence in Western Apache culture. In *Western Apache language and culture: Essays in linguistic anthropology*, ed. K. Basso, 80–98. Tucson: University of Arizona Press.

———. 1996. *Wisdom sits in places*. Albuquerque: University of New Mexico Press.

Bateson, Gregory, and Mary Catherine Bateson. 1987. *Angels Fear: Towards an epistemology of the sacred*. New York: Macmillan.

Battiste, Marie, ed. [2000] 2002. *Reclaiming indigenous voice and vision*. Vancouver: University of British Columbia Press.

Becker, Howard S. 1986. *Writing for social scientists: How to start and finish your thesis, a book or article*. Chicago: University of Chicago Press.

Befu, Harumi. 1992. Symbols of nationalism and nihonjinron. In *Ideology and practice in modern Japan*, ed. Roger Goodman and Kirsten Refsing, 26–46. London: Routledge.

Behar, Ruth. 1993. *Translated woman: Crossing the border with Esperanza's story*. Boston: Beacon.

———. 1996. *The Vulnerable observer: Anthropology that breaks your heart*. Boston: Beacon.

Berger, John. 1973. *Ways of seeing*. New York: Viking.

Bernard, Russell H. 1994. *Research methods in anthropology: Qualitative and quantitative approaches*. Walnut Creek CA: AltaMira.

———. 1998. Foreword. In *Using methods in the field: A practical introduction and casebook*. Ed. Victor C. de Munck and Elisa J. Sobo, 7–9. Walnut Creek CA: AltaMira.

Bierwurt, Crisca. 1999. *Brushed by cedar, living by the river: Coast Salish figures of power*. Tucson: University of Arizona Press.

Bibby, Reginald. 1990. La religion à la carte au Québec: une analyse de tendances. *Sociologie et sociétés* 21:133–45.

Bokhare Narendra. 1997. Interviews with author, Pune, India.

Borgatti, Stephen P. 1992. *ANTHROPAC*. Columbia SC: Analytic Industries.

Bourdieu, Pierre. 1970. *The logic of practice*. Trans. Richard Nice. Cambridge: Polity.

———. 1977. *Outline of a theory of practice*. Trans. Richard Nice. Cambridge: Cambridge University Press.

———. 1984. *Distinction: A social critique of the judgment of taste*. Cambridge: Harvard University Press.

———. 1985. The forms of capital. In *Handbook of theory and research for the sociology of education*. Ed. J. G. Richardson, 41–58. New York: Greenwood.

Bousquet, Marie-Pierre. 2002. Quand nous vivions dans le Bois, le changement spatial et sa dimension générationnelle: L'exemples des Algonquins du Canada. PhD diss., Dept. of Anthropology, Université Laval, Quebec.

Bradburd, Daniel. 1998. *Being there: The necessity of fieldwork*. Washington: Smithsonian Institution Press.

Braude, Ann D. 1989. *Radical spirits, spiritualism and women's rights in 19th century America*. Boston: Beacon.

Breidenbach, Paul S. 1979. *Sunsum Edwuma*: The limits of classification and the significance of events. *Social research* 46 (1):63–87.

Brettell, Caroline, ed. 1993. *When they read what we write: The politics of ethnography*. Westport CT: Bergin and Garvey.

Bricker, Victoria Reifler. 1981. *The Indian Christ, the Indian king: The historical substrate of Maya myth and ritual*. Austin: University of Texas Press.

Briggs, Jean. 1998. *Inuit morality play: The emotional education of a three-year-old*. New Haven: Yale University Press.

———. 1991. Expecting the unexpected: Canadian Inuit training for an experimental lifestyle. *Ethos* 19:259–87.

Brinton, Daniel G. 1894. Nagualism. A Study. In *Native American folklore and history*. Philadelphia: MacCalla.

Bruner, Edward M. 1993. Introduction: The ethnographic self and the personal self. In *Anthropology and literature*, ed. Paul Benson, 1–26. Urbana: University of Illinois Press.

Buber, Martin. 1965. *The knowledge of man*. Ed. and with an introductory essay by Maurice Freedman. London: George Allen Unwin.

Buckley, Thomas. 2002. *Standing ground. Yurok Indian spirituality, 1850–1990*. Berkeley: University of California Press.

Burridge, K. 1960. *Mambu: A study of Melanesian cargo movements and their ideological background*. New York: Harper and Rose.

———. 1969. *New heaven, new earth*. Oxford: Basil Blackwell.

Canada. 2001. 2001 Census of Canada. http://www12.statcan.ca/english/census 01/home/Index.cfm.

Carlson, Keith Thor, ed. 1997. *You are asked to witness: The Stó:lō in Canada's Pacific Coast history*. Chilliwack BC: Stó:lō Heritage Trust.

Carlson, Thomas A. 2003. Locating the mystical subject. In *Mystics: Presence and aporia*. Ed. Michael Kessler and Christian Sheppard, 207–38. Chicago: University of Chicago Press.

Carrera, Florencio, and Geert Bastiaan Van Doesburg. 1992. Chan chaon yoma: el calendario agricola mazateco. Unpublished manuscript. Huautla, Mexico.

Carroll, Lewis. 1957 [1986]. *Alice in Wonderland*. New York: Grosset and Dunlop.

Castells, Manuel. 1997. *The power of identity. The information age: Economy, society and culture. Volume II*. Malden MA: Blackwell.

Cataldi, Sue L. 1993. *Emotion, depth, and flesh: A study of sensitive space reflections on Merleau-Ponty's philosophy of embodiment*. New York: State University of New York Press.

Chernoff, John Miller. 1993. A fieldworker's initiation: African rhythm and African sensibility. In *Art in small-scale societies: Contemporary readings*, ed. Richard L. Anderson and Karen L. Field, 9–27. Inglewood Cliffs NJ: Prentice Hall.

———. 1979. *African rhythm and African sensibility: Aesthetics and social action in African musical idioms*. Chicago: University of Chicago Press.

Chouinard, Jeffrey. 1995. *Mouths of stone: Stories of the ancient Maya from newly deciphered inscriptions and recent archeological discoveries*. Durham NC: Carolina Academic Press.

Christian, Jane, and Peter M. Gardner. 1977. *The individual in Northern Dene thought and communication: A study in sharing and diversity*. Ottawa: National Museums of Canada.

Claire, Robin Patric. 2003. *Expressions of ethnography: Novel approaches to qualitative methods*. Albany NY: State University of New York Press.

Clammer, John, Sylvie Poirier, and Eric Schwimmer. 2004. Introduction: The relevance of ontologies in anthropolgy—Reflections on a new anthropological field. In *Figured worlds: Ontological obstacles in intercultural relations*, ed. John Clammer, Sylvie Poirier, and Eric Schwimmer, 3–22. Toronto: University of Toronto Press.

Clark, Katerina. 1981. *The Soviet novel: History as ritual*. Chicago: University of Chicago Press.

Clifford, James. 1988. *The predicament of culture. Twentieth-century ethnography, literature, and art*. Cambridge MA: Harvard University.

———. 1997. Spatial practices: Fieldwork, travel and the disciplining of anthropology. In *Anthropological locations: Boundaries and grounds of a field science*, ed. Akhil Gupta and James Ferguson, 185–222. Berkeley: University of California Press.

Clifford, James, and George E. Marcus, eds. 1986. *Writing culture: The poetics and politics of ethnography*. Berkeley: University of California Press.

Coe, Michael D., and Gordon Whittaker. 1982. *Aztec sorcerers in seventeenth century Mexico: The treatise on superstitions by Hernando Ruiz de Alar-*

cón. New York: Institute for Mesoamerican Studies, State University of New York Publication No. 7.

Coffey, Amanda. 1999. *The ethnographic self. Fieldwork and the representation of identity.* London: Sage.

Cohen, Patrice. 2002. Le chercheur et son double. À propos d'une recherche sur le vécu des jeunes de la Réunion face au sida. In *De l'ethnographie à l'anthropologie réflexive: nouveaux terrains, nouvelles pratiques, nouveaux enjeux,* ed. Christian Ghasarian, 73–90. Paris: Armand Colin.

Cole, Peter. 2004. Trick(ster)s of aboriginal research: or how to use ethical review strategies to perpetuate cultural genocide. *Native Studies Review* 15 (2): 7–30.

Connerton, Paul. 1989. *How societies remember.* Cambridge: Cambridge University Press.

Cooley, Timothy J. 1997. Casting shadows in the field: An introduction. In *Shadows in the field: New perspectives for fieldwork in ethnomusicology,* ed. Gregory F. Barz and Timothy J. Cooley, 3–19. New York: Oxford University Press.

Cooper, Eugene. 1989. Apprenticeship as a field method: Lessons from Hong Kong. In *Apprenticeship: From theory to method and back again.* Ed. Michael W. Coy, 137–48. Albany: State University of New York Press.

Cove, John. 1999. Cultural relativism in the Americist tradition: From anthropological method to indigenous emancipation. In *Theorizing the Americanist tradition,* ed. Lisa Philips Valentine and Regna Darnell, 108–20. Toronto: University of Toronto Press.

Cowan, Florence Hausen. 1946. Notas etnograficas sobre los Mazatecos de Oaxaca, Mexico. *America Indigena* 3:27–39.

Coy, Michael W., ed. 1989. *Apprenticeship: From theory to method and back again.* Albany: State University of New York Press.

———. 1989. Being what we pretend to be: The usefulness of apprenticeship as a field method. In *Apprenticeship: From theory to method and back again,* ed. M. Coy. Albany: State University of New York Press.

Crapanzano, Vincent. 1980. *Tuhami. Portrait of a Moroccan.* Chicago: University of Chicago Press.

———. 1986. Hermes' dilemma: The masking of subversion in ethnographic description. In *Writing culture. The poetics and politics of ethnography,* ed. James Clifford and George E. Marcus, 51–76. Berkeley: University of California Press.

———. 1977. On the writing of ethnography. *Dialectical Anthropology* 2(1):69–73.

Creighton, Millie. 1989. *Women in the Japanese department store industry: Capturing the momentum of the equal employment opportunity law.* Women in International Development series #185. East Lansing MI: Michigan State University Press.

———. 1990. Contemporary Japanese women: Employment and consumer roles. In *Canadian perspectives on modern Japan*, ed. T. G. McGee, Kate Eliot, and Bev Lee, 56–88. Vancouver: Institute of Asian Research, University of British Columbia.

———. 1993. Sweet love and women's place: Valentine's Day, Japan style. *Journal of Popular Culture* 27 (3): 1–19.

———. 1994. Educating children: Consumer and gender socialization in Japanese marketing. *Ethnology* 33 (1): 35–52.

———. 1995a. Creating connected identities among Japanese company employees: Learning to be members of department store work communities. *Culture* 15 (2): 47–64.

———. 1995b. Socialization into a Japanese corporate community: The case of department stores. In *Japan Studies 91*, ed. Claus Pringsheim, 31–43. Ottawa: Japan Studies Assn. of Canada.

———. 1995c. The non-vanishing Ainu: A damming development project, internationalization and Japan's indigenous other. *American Asian Review* 13 (2): 69–96.

———. 1997a. Marriage, motherhood, and career management in a Japanese "counter culture." In *Re-imaging Japanese women*, ed. Anne Imamura, 192–220. Berkeley: University of California Press.

———. 1997b. Soto others and Uchi others: Imaging racial diversity, imagining homogeneous Japan. In *Japan's minorities: The illusion of homogeneity*, ed. Michael Weiner, 211–38. London: Routledge.

———. 1998. Was Japan post-modern when post-modern wasn't cool?: "New" and "old" anthropological lenses on Japanese self, other and identity. *Reviews in Anthropology* 27:33–55.

———. 2003. May the Saru River flow: The Nibutani Dam and the resurging tide of the Ainu identity movement. In *Joining past and future: Japan at the millennium*, ed. David Edgington, 120–43.

Cruikshank, Julie. 1998. *The social life of stories. Narrative and knowledge in the Yukon Territory*. Vancouver: University of British Columbia Press.

Csordas, Thomas. 1997. *The sacred self: A cultural phenomenology of charismatic healing*. Berkeley: University of California Press.

———. 2001. *Language, charisma and creativity: Ritual life in the Catholic charismatic renewal*. New York: Palgrave.

Czarniawska, Barbara. 2004. *Narratives in social science research*. Thousand Oaks CA: Sage.

Davis, Wade. 1985. *The serpent and the rainbow*. New York: Simon and Schuster.

Davis, Lynne, Bonnie Jane Maracle, John Phillips, and Tessa Reed. 2002. *Con-*

sultation on Policy Directions Related to Aboriginal Peoples. A Discussion Paper for the Roundtable Consultation, Social Sciences and Humanities Research Council (SSHRC), PhD Program in Native Studies, Trent Univ., Peterborough ON, *November 29, 2002.*

De Boeck, Filip. 1998. The rootedness of trees: Place as cultural and natural texture in rural southwest Congo. In *Locality and belonging*, ed. Nadia Lovell, 25–52. New York: Routledge.

DeMunck, Victor C., and Elisa J. Sobo, eds. 1998. *Using methods in the field: A practical introduction and casebook.* Walnut Creek CA: AltaMira.

Denniston, Glenda. 1981. Sekani, in *Handbook of North American Indians, vol. 6: The Subarctic*, ed. J. Helm. Washington DC: Smithsonian Institution.

Denzin, Norman K. 1989. *Interpretive biography. Qualitative research methods series 17.* London: Sage.

———. 1999. Interpretive ethnography. Ethnographic practices for the 21st century. *Journal of Contemporary Ethnography* 28 (5): 510–19.

Desgent, Jean-Marc, and G. Lanoue. 2005. *Errances. Comment se pensent le Nous et le Moi dans l'espace mythique des nomades septentrionaux sekani.* Gatineau, Quebec: Musée Canadien des Civilisations.

Desjarlais, Robert. 1992. *Body and emotion: The aesthetics of illness and healing in the Nepal Himalayas.* Philadelphia: University of Pennsylvania Press.

De Vita, Philip R. 2000. *Stumbling toward truth. Anthropologists at work.* Prospect Heights IL: Waveland.

DeVos, George. 1971. *Japan's outcastes: The problem of the Burakumin.* London: Minority Rights Group, Report #3.

DeVos, George, and Hiroshi Wagatsuma, eds. 1966. *Japan's invisible race: Caste in culture and personality.* Berkeley: University of California Press.

Dewalt, Kathleen M., and Billie R. Dewalt. 2002. Participant observation. *A guide for fieldworkers.* Walnut Creek CA: AltaMira.

Diaz De Rada, Angel, and Francisco Cruces. 1994. The incarnated field: Some problems of analytical language. In *Social experience and anthropological knowledge*, ed. K. Hastrup and P. Hervik. London: Routledge.

Dickens, Charles. 1958. *Hard times.* New York: Harper and Row.

Douglas, Mary. 1969. *Purity and danger: An analysis of concepts of pollution and taboo.* London: Routledge and K. Paul.

———. 1970. *Natural symbols.* Middlesex: Penguin.

———. 1975. *Implicit meanings: Essays in anthropology.* London: Routledge.

Dow, James. 1981. The image of limited production: Envy and the domestic mode of production in peasant society. *Human Organization* 40:360–63.

———. 1989. Apprentice shaman. In *Apprenticeship: From theory to method and back again*, ed. Michael W. Coy, 199–210. Albany: State University of New York Press.

Dunning, J. 1997. When folkways point the way to innovation. Ethnic dance in New York City. *New York Times.* June 1, sec. 2, p. 10, late edition.

Duran, Bonnie, and Eduardo Duran. 2000. Applied postcolonial clinical and research strategies. In *Proclaiming indigenous voice and vision,* ed. Marie Batiste, 86–100. Vancouver: University of British Columbia Press.

Durán, Diego. 1964. *The Aztecs: The history of the Indies of New Spain.* New York: Orion.

Durkheim, Émile. 1912. *Les formes élémentaires de la vie religieuse.* Paris: Alcan.

Earle, Duncan, and Jeanne Simonelli. 2005. *Uprising of hope: Sharing the Zapatista journey to alternative development.* Walnut Creek CA: AltaMira.

Earle, Duncan, Jeanne Simonelli, and Elizabeth Story. 2004. *Acompañar obediciendo:* Learning how to help in collaboration with Zapatista communities. *Michigan Journal of Service Learning* 10 (3): 43–56.

Eco, Umberto. 1986. *Travels in hyper reality.* Trans. from the Italian by William Weaver. San Diego: Harcourt Brace.

Engelke, Matthew. 2000. An interview with Edith Turner. *Current Anthropology* 41 (5): 843–52.

Eunshill, Kim. 1998. Studying my own culture as feminist practice. *Asian Journal of Women's Studies* 4 (4): 60.

Evans-Pritchard, E. E. 1976. *Witchcraft, oracles and magic among the Azande.* Oxford: Clarendon.

Fabian, Johannes, guest ed. 1979. Beyond charisma: religious movements as discourse. *Social Research: An International Quarterly of the Social Sciences* 46 (1): 1–203.

———. 1979. The anthropology of religious movements: From explanation to interpretation. *Social Research: An International Quarterly of the Social Sciences* 46 (1): 4–35.

———. 1983. *Time and the other: How anthropology makes its object.* New York: Columbia University Press.

———. 1991. Ethnographic objectivity revisited: From rigor to vigor. *Annals of Scholarship: International Quarterly in the Humanities and Social Sciences* 8 (3–4): 381–408.

———. 2000. *Out of our minds. Reason and madness in the exploration of Central Africa.* Berkeley: University of California Press.

———. 2001. *Anthropology with an attitude: Critical essays.* Stanford: Stanford University Press.

Fackenheim, Emil L. 1982 [1994]. *To mend the world, foundations of post-Holocaust Jewish thought.* Bloomington: Indiana University Press.

Faris, James C. 1994. *The nightway: A history and documentation of a Navajo ceremonial.* Albuquerque: University of New Mexico Press.

Favret-Saada, Jeanne. 1977. *Les mots, la mort, les sorts: la sorcellerie dans le Bocage*. Paris: Gallimard.

———. 1980. *Deadly words: Witchcraft in the Bocage*. Trans. Catherine Cullen. New York: Cambridge University Press.

Feinberg, Benjamin. 1997. Three Mazatec wise ones and their books. *Critique of Anthropology* 17:411–37.

Feld, Steven, and Keith Basso. 1996. Introduction. In *Senses of place*, ed. Seven Feld and Keith Basso, 3–11. Santa Fe: School of American Research Press.

Fernandez, James. 1979. On the notion of religious movement. *Social Research* 46 (1): 36–62.

Fernández, Kelly, M. P. 1995. Social and cultural capital in the urban ghetto: Implications for the economic sociology of immigration. In *The economic sociology of immigration. Essays on networks, ethnicity and entrepreneurship*, ed. A. Portes, 213–47. New York: Russell Sage Foundation.

Ferrara, Nadia, and Guy Lanoue. 2004. The Self in Northern Canadian Hunting Societies: "Cannibals" and Other "Monsters" as Agents of Healing. *Anthropologica* 46 (1).

Few, Martha B. 1997. Mujeres de mal vivir: Gender, religion and the politics of power in colonial Guatemala, 1650–1750. PhD diss., University of Arizona.

Fienup-Riordan, Ann, with William Tyson, Paul John, Marie Meade, and John Active. 2000. *Hunting tradition in a changing world*. New Brunswick: Rutgers University Press.

Fogelson, Ray. 1999. Nationalism and the Americanist tradition. In *Theorizing the Americanist tradition*, ed. Lisa Philips Valentine and Regna Darnell, 75–83. Toronto: University of Toronto Press.

Fonseca, Claudia. 1991. La religion dans la vie quotidienne d'un groupe populaire brésilien. *Archives de sciences sociales des religions* 73:125–39.

Foster, George. 1965. Peasant society and the image of limited good. *American Anthropologist* 67:293–315.

———. 1966. Reply to Kaplan, Seler, and Bennet [on *Image of Limited Good*]. *American Anthropologist* 68:210–14.

———. 1972. The anatomy of envy: A study in symbolic behavior. *Current Anthropology* 13:165–86.

Foucault, Michel. 1976. *The archaeology of knowledge*. New York: Harper and Row.

———. 1984. *The Foucault reader*, ed. P. Rabinow. New York: Pantheon.

Fox, Christopher. 1995. How to prepare a noble savage: The spectacle of human science. In *Inventing human science: Eighteenth-century domains*, ed. C. Fox, R. Porter, and R. Wokler, 1–30. Berkeley: University of California Press.

Frederiksen, Sven. 1968. Some preliminaries on the soul complex in Eskimo shamanistic beliefs. In *Eskimo of the Canadian Arctic*, ed. V. F. Valentine and F. G. Vallee, 49–54. Toronto: McClelland and Stewart.

Frigault, Louis-Robert. 1999. Entre la raison et l'expérience: Une rencontre avec les esprits des morts au Brésil. *Frontières* 11:42–47.

Fuller, Robert C. Wonder. 2006. *From emotion to spirituality*. Chapel Hill: University of North Carolina Press.

Ganguly, Debjani. 2002. History's implosions: A Benjaminian reading of Ambedkar. *Journal of Narrative Theory* 32 (3): 326–47.

Gardner, Peter M. 1966. Symmetric respect and memorate knowledge: The structure and ecology of individualistic culture. *Southwestern Journal of Anthropology* 22:389–415.

———. 1976. Birds, words, and a requiem for the omniscient informant. *American Ethnologist* 3:446–68.

———. 2000. *Bicultural versatility as a frontier adaptation among Paliyan foragers of South India*. Lewiston NY: Edwin Mellen Press.

———. 2006. *Journeys to the edge: In the footsteps of an anthropologist* Columbia: University of Missouri Press.

Garroutte, Eva Marie. 2003. *Real Indians. Identity and the survival of Native America*. Berkeley: University of California Press.

Geertz, Clifford. 1971. *Islam observed: Religious development in Morocco and Indonesia*. Chicago: University of Chicago Press.

———. 1973. *The interpretation of cultures*. New York: Basic Books.

———. 1977. *The interpretation of cultures. Selected essays*. New York: Basic Books.

———. 1983. *Local knowledge: Further essays in interpretive anthropology*. New York: Basic Books.

———. 1986. Making experiences, authoring selves: Epilogue. In *The anthropology of experience*, ed. Victor Turner and Edward M. Bruner, 373–80. Urbana: University of Illinois Press.

———. 1988. *Works and lives*. Stanford: Stanford University Press.

———. 1996. Afterword. In *Senses of place*, ed. S. Feld and K. Basso, 259–62. Santa Fe: School of American Research Press.

———. 2000. *Available light. Anthropological reflections on philosophical topics*. Princeton: Princeton University Press.

———. 2005. Shifting aims, moving targets: On the anthropology of religion. *Journal of the Royal Anthropological Institute* 11:1–15.

———. 2006a. Religion and modernity: Some revisionary views. Paper presented at Social Sciences in Mutuation, an international colloquium organized by the Center for Sociological Analysis and Intervention (CADIS), Paris, May.

———. 2006b. *La religion, sujet d'avenir*. Paper presented at Social Sciences in Mutuation, an international colloquium organized by the Center for Sociological Analysis and Intervention (CADIS), Paris, May. http://www.voem-vzw.be/modules.php?op=modload&name=News&file=article&sid=354&mode-thread&order-o&hold=o.

Glaskin, Katie. 2005. Innovation and ancestral revelation: The case of dreams. *Journal of the Royal Anthropological Institute* 11:297–314.

Glassie, Henry H. 1982. *Irish folk history: Texts from the North.* Philadelphia: University of Pennsylvania Press.

Goertzen, C., and M. S. Azzi. 1999. Globalization and the tango. *Yearbook for Traditional Music* 31: 67–76.

Goffman, Erving. 1959. *The presentation of self in everyday life.* Garden City NY: Doubleday.

Golde, Peggy. 1970. *Women in the field: Anthropological experiences.* Chicago: Aldine.

Gomes, Peter J. 1996. *The Good Book: Reading the Bible with mind and heart.* New York: William Morrow.

Goodale, Jane Carter. 1994 [1971]. *Tiwi wives: A study of the women of Melville Island, North Australia.* Prospect Heights IL: Waveland.

Goodman, Felicita D. 1972. *Speaking in tongues: A cross-cultural study of glossolalia.* Chicago: University of Chicago Press.

———. 1988. Spiritualism. In *How about demons,* ed. Felicitas Goodman, 25–41. Bloomington: Indiana University Press.

———. 1990. *Where the spirits ride the wind: Trance journeys and other ecstatic experiences.* Bloomington: Indiana University Press.

Goody, Esther N. 1989. Learning apprenticeship and the division of labour. In *Apprenticeship: From theory to method and back again,* ed. Michael W. Coy, 233–56. Albany: State University of New York Press.

Gordon, Raymond L. 1992. *Basic interviewing skills.* Itasca IL: Peacock.

Gossen, Gary H., and Richard M. Leventhal. 1993. The topography of ancient Maya religious pluralism: A dialogue with the present. In *Lowland Maya civilization in the eighth century AD,* ed. Jeremy A. Sabloff and John S. Henderson, 185–218. Washington DC: Dumbarton Oaks Research Institute.

Gotlib, Lesley. 2005. Doctors with borders. In *Auto-ethnographies. The Anthropology of academic practices,* ed. Anne Meneley and Donna J. Young, 39–50. Peterborough ON: Broadview.

Gottlieb, Robert S. 1993. *Solo tabla drumming of North India: Its repertoire, styles, and performance practices.* Vol. 1, *Text and commentary.* Delhi: Motilal Banarsidass.

Goulet, Jean-Guy. 1982. Religious dualism among Athapaskan Catholics. *Canadian Journal of Anthropology/Revue Canadienne d'Anthropologie* 3 (1): 1–18.

———. 1994a. Dreams and visions in other lifeworlds. In *Being changed by cross-cultural encounters. The anthropology of extraordinary experiences,* ed. David Young and Jean-Guy Goulet, 16–38. Peterborough ON: Broadview.

———. 1994b. Ways of knowing. Towards a narrative ethnography of experiences among the Dene Tha. *Journal of Anthropological Research* 50 (2): 113–39.

———. 1998. *Ways of knowing. Experience, knowledge and power among the Dene Tha.* Lincoln: Nebraska University Press.

———. 2004a. Une question éthique venue de l'autre monde. Au-delà du Grand Partage entre nous les autres. *Anthropologie et Sociétés* 28 (1): 109–126.

———. 2004b. The Dene Tha of Chateh: Continuities and transformations. In *Native peoples. The Canadian experience*, ed. R. Bruce Morrison and C. Roderick Wilson, 157–77. Don Mills: Oxford University Press.

Goulet, Jean-Guy, and Kim Harvey-Trigoso. 2005. L'espérance passe de la forêt au milieu scolaire: clivage et continuité dans les valeurs entre générations de Dènès Tha. *Recherches amérindiennes au Québec* 35 (3): 71–84.

Goulet, Jean-Guy, and David Young. 1994. Theoretical and methodological issues. In being changed by cross-cultural encounters. The anthropology of extraordinary experiences, ed. David Young and Jean-Guy Goulet, 298–335. Peterborough ON: Broadview.

Green, Jesse, ed. 1979. *Selected writings of Frank Hamilton Cushing.* Lincoln: University of Nebraska Press.

Gregory, Jane R. 1975. Image of limited good, or expectation of reciprocity? *Current Anthropology* 16:73–92.

Grimshaw, Anna. 2001. *The ethnographer's eye: Ways of seeing in modern anthropology.* Cambridge: Cambridge University Press.

Guédon, Marie-Françoise. 1994. Dene ways and the ethnographer's culture. In *Being changed by cross-cultural encounters. The anthropology of extraordinary experiences*, ed. David Young and Jean-Guy Goulet, 39–70. Peterborough ON: Broadview.

Guemple, Lee. 1994. Born-again pagans: The Inuit cycle of spirits. In *Amerindian rebirth: Reincarnation beliefs among the North American Indians and Inuit*, ed. A. Mills and R. Slobodin, 107–22. Toronto: University of Toronto Press.

Gupta, M. G. 1994. *The guru in Indian mysticism.* Agra, India: MG Publishers.

Haraway, Donna. 1989. *Primate visions: Gender, race, and nature in the world of modern science.* New York: Routledge.

Harries-Jones, P. 1995. *A recursive vision: Ecological understanding and Gregory Bateson.* University of Toronto Press, Toronto.

Hart, Mickey. 1990. *Drumming at the edge of magic: A journey into the spirit of percussion.* San Francisco: Harper.

He, M., and F. J. Phillion. 2001. Trapped in-between: A narrative exploration of race, gender, and class. *Race, gender and class* 8 (1): 47.

Helm, June. 1994. *Prophecy and power among the Dogrib Indians.* Lincoln: University of Nebraska Press.

Hendrickson, Carol. 1995. *Weaving identities: Construction of dress and self in a Highland Guatemala town.* Austin: University of Texas Press.

———. 1996. Women, weaving and education in Maya revitalization. In *Maya cultural activism in Guatemala*, eds. Edward F. Fischer, R. McKenna Brown, 156–62. Austin: University of Texas Press.

Hermitte, M. Esther. 1970. *Poder sobrenatural y control social en un pueblo Maya contemporáneo.* Mexico, D.F.: Instituto Indigenista Interamericano.

Hervieu-Léger, Danièle. 1993. *La religion pour mémoire.* Paris: Cerf.

———. 2001. *La religion en miettes ou la question des sectes.* Paris: Calmann-Lévy.

Hilbert, Vi. 1985. *Haboo: Native American stories from Puget Sound.* Seattle: University of Washington Press.

Hood, L. 1994. Warming up to Latin rhythms. *Américas.* 46:14–19.

Hornborg, A. 2001. Ecological embeddedness and personhood: Have we always been capitalists? In *Ecology and the sacred: Engaging the anthropology of Roy A. Rappaport*, ed. E. Messer and M. Lambek, 88–98. Ann Arbor: University of Michigan Press.

Houston, Stephen, and David Stuart. 1989. *The way glyph: Evidence for co-essences among the Classic Maya.* Research reports on Ancient Maya Writing 30. Barnardsville NC: Center for Maya Research.

Howard, Jane. 1984. *Margaret Mead, a life.* New York: Simon and Schuster.

Howes, David, ed. 1991. *The varieties of sensory experience: A source book in the anthropology of the senses.* Toronto: University of Toronto.

Hussain, Zakir Ustad. 1996. Interview on CKUA Radio Station Network. Edmonton, Alberta. April.

———. 1995. Interviews with Denise Nuttall, July–August. Seattle, Washington.

Ingold, Tom. 1996. Hunting and gathering as ways of perceiving the environment. In *Redefining nature: Ecology, culture and domestication*, ed. R. Ellen and K. Fukui, 117–55. Oxford: Berg.

Jackson, Bruce, and Edward D. Ives, ed. 1996a. *The world observed. Reflections on the fieldwork process.* Chicago: University of Chicago Press.

Jackson, Bruce, and Edward D. Ives. 1996b. From entertainment to realization in Navajo fieldwork. In *Reflections on the fieldwork process.* Ed. Bruce Jackson and Edward D. Ives, 1–17. Urbana: University of Illinois Press.

Jackson, Michael. 1989. *Paths toward a clearing: Radical empiricism and ethnographic inquiry.* Bloomington: Indiana University Press.

———. 1996. *Things as they are: New directions in phenomenological anthropology.* Bloomington: Indiana University Press.

———. 1998. *Minima ethnographica: Intersubjectivity and the anthropological project.* Chicago: University of Chicago Press.

James, William. 1922. *Essays in radical empiricism.* New York: Longmans, Green.

———. 1997. *The varieties of religious experience.* New York: Simon and Schuster.

Janzen, John M. 1979. Deep thought: Structure and intention in Kongo prophetism, 1910–1920. *Social Research* 46 (1): 106–39.

Jenness, Diamond. 1937. *The Sekani Indians of British Columbia.* National Museum of Canada, Bulletin no. 84, Ottawa: Department of Mines and Resources.

Jochelson [Iokhelíson], Waldemar [Vladimir] Ilíich. 1908. *The Koryak. Jesup North Pacific Expedition, memoirs of the American Museum of Natural History, New York* 6, ed. Franz Boas. Leiden, The Netherlands: E. J. Brill & G. E. Stechart.

Johnson, Michelle C. 2000. Becoming a Muslim, becoming a person: Female "circumcision," religious identity, and personhood in Guinea-Bissau. In *Female "circumcision" in Africa: Culture, controversy and change,* ed. Bettina Shell-Duncan and Ylva Hernlund, 215–33. Boulder: Lynne Riener.

———. 2002. Being Mandinga, being Muslim: Transnational debates on personhood and religious identity in Guinea-Bissau and Portugal. PhD diss., Dept. of Anthropology, University of Illinois, Urbana-Champaign.

Joyce, Rosemary A. 2000. *Gender and power in pre-Hispanic America.* Austin: University of Texas Press.

Jung, Carl J. 1960. The psychological foundation of belief in spirits. In *The collected works of C. G. Jung.* Vol. 8, *The structure and dynamics of the psyche,* 301–18. London: Routledge.

Kahane, David. 2004. What is culture? Generalizing about aboriginal and newcomer perspectives. In *Intercultural dispute resolution in aboriginal contexts,* ed. Catherine Bell and David Kahane, 28–56. Vancouver: University of British Columbia Press.

Kan, Sergei. 1989. *Symbolic immortality: The Tlingit potlatch of the nineteenth century.* Washington DC: Smithsonian Institution Press.

Kaplan, David, and Benson Saler. 1966. Foster's image of limited good: An example of anthropological explanation. *American Anthropologist* 68:202–6.

Kawano, Satsuki. 2005. *Ritual practice in modern Japan. Ordering place, people and action.* Honolulu: University of Hawaii Press.

Kippen, James. 1988. *The tabla of Lucknow: A cultural analysis of a musical tradition.* Cambridge: Cambridge University Press.

———. 1991. Changes in the social status of tabla players. *Bansuri* 8:16–29.

Kisliuk, Michelle. 1997. (Un)doing fieldwork: Sharing songs, sharing lives. In *Shadows in the field: New perspectives for fieldwork in ethnomusiology,* ed. Gregory F. Barz and Timothy J. Cooley, 23–43. New York: Oxford University Press.

Klein, Cecilia F., Eulogia Guzmun, Elisa C. Mandell, and Maya Stanfield-Mazzi. 2002. The role of shamanism in Mesoamerican art: A reassessment. *Current Anthropology* 43 (3): 383–419.

Kublu, A., and J. Oosten. 1999. Changing perspectives of name and identity among the Inuit of Northeast Canada. In *Arctic identities: Continuity and change in*

Inuit and Saami societies, ed. J. Oosten and C. Remie, 56–78. Leiden, The Netherlands: Research School CNWS, Leiden University.

Kulik, Don, and Margaret Wilson, ed. 1995. *Taboo: Sex, identity, and erotic subjectivity in anthropological fieldwork*. London: Routledge.

Lambeck, Michael. 2005. Our subjects/ourselves: A view from the back seat. In *Auto-ethnographies. The anthropology of academic practices*, ed. Anne Meneley and Donna J. Young, 229–40. Peterborough ON: Broadview.

Lambert, Elizabeth Y., ed. 1990. *The collection and interpretation of data from hidden populations*. Research Monograph Series, 98. Rockville MD: National Institute on Drug Abuse.

Lanoue, Guy. 1990. *Beyond values and ideology: Tales from six North American Indian peoples*. Rome: Nuova Arnica Editrice.

———. 1992. *Brothers: The politics of violence among the Sekani of northern British Columbia*. Oxford: Berg Publishers.

———. 2000. *The poetics of myth by Meletinsky*. Trans. Guy Lanoue. New York: Routledge.

Laplantine, François. 1985. *Un voyant dans la ville. Le cabinet de consultation d'un voyant contemporain: Georges de Bellerive*. Paris: Payot.

Laughlin, Robert M. 1976. *Of wonders wild and new: Dreams from Zinacantan*. Washington DC: Smithsonian Institution Press.

Laugrand, Frédéric. 2002. Les onze "apotres" du révérand E. J. Peck. *Recherches Amérindiennes au Québec* 32 (2): 83–98.

Laugrand, Frédéric, Jarich Oosten, and François Trudel. 2002. Hunters, owners, and givers of light: The Tuurngait of South Baffin Island. *Arctic Anthropology* 39 (1–2): 27–50.

Lave, Jean, and Etienne Wenger. 1991. *Situated learning: Legitimate peripheral participation*. New York: Cambridge University Press.

Leavitt, John. 1996. Meaning and feeling in the anthropology of emotions. *American Ethnologist* 23:514–39.

Legros, Dominique. 1999. *Tommy McGinty's Northern Tutchone story of Crow. A First Nation elder recounts the creation of the world*. Mercury Series, Canadian Ethnology Services, Paper 132. Ottawa: Canadian Museum of Civilization.

Levinas, Emmanuel. 1996. *Outside the subject*. Trans. M. Smith. Stanford: Stanford University Press.

Lévi-Strauss, Claude. 1973a. *Anthropologie structurale*. Paris: Plon.

———. 1973b. *Structural anthropology*. Trans. from the French by Claire Jacobson and Brooke Grundfest Schoepf. London: Penguin.

Lex, Barbara W. 1974. Voodoo death: New thoughts on an old explanation. *American Anthropologist* 76:818–23.

Linteau, Paul-André, René Durocher, Jean-Claude Robert, and François Ricard.

1989. *Histoire du Québec contemporain, tome III: Le Québec depuis 1930.* Montréal: Éditions Boréal.

Lishke, Ute, and David T. McNab, eds. 2005. *Walking a tightrope: Aborginal people and their representations.* Aboriginal Studies Series. Waterloo ON: Wilfrid Laurier University Press.

Little Bear, Leroy. 2000 Jagged worldviews colliding. In *Proclaiming indigenous voice and vision,* ed. Marie Batiste, 77–85. Vancouver: University of British Columbia Press.

Lock, Margaret, and Nancy Scheper-Hugues. 1997. The mindful body. *Medical Anthropology Quarterly* 1 (1): 6–41.

Long, David, and Brenda LaFrance. 2004. Speaking the truth with care: Introduction to a dialogue on aboriginal research issues. *Native Studies Review* 15 (2): 1–5.

Looper, Matthew G. 2002. Women-men (and Men-women): Classic Maya rulers and the third gender. In *Ancient Maya women,* ed. Traci Arden. Walnut Creek CA: AltaMira .

López, Austin. 1988. *The human body and ideology concepts of the ancient Nahuas.* Vols. 1 and 2. Trans. Thelma Ortiz de Montellano and Bernard Ortiz de Montellano. Salt Lake City: University of Utah Press.

Lovell, Nadia. 1998. Introduction. In *Locality and belonging,* ed. Nadia Lovell, 1–24. New York: Routledge.

Lovelace, Robert. 2004. A review of Peter Cole's Trick(ster)s of aboriginal research. *Native Studies Review* 15 (2): 31–36.

Low, Setha, and Denise Lawrence-Zuniga. 2003. Locating culture. In *The anthropology of space and time: Locating culture,* ed. Setha Low and Lawrence-Zuniga, 3–50. Oxford: Blackwell.

Lowie, Robert. 1966. Dream, idle dreams. *Current Anthropology* 7 (3): 378–82.

Madison, D. Soyini. 2005. *Critical ethnography. Method, ethics, and performance.* Thousand Oaks CA: Sage.

Maher, Vanessa. 1998. Mistaken identities: A journey through prejudice. *Mediterranean Review* 5–6:9.

Malinowski, Bronislaw. 1916. Baloma; the spirits of the dead in the Trobriand Islands. *Journal of the Royal Anthropological Institute of Great Britain and Ireland* 46:353–430.

———. 1922. *Argonauts of the Western Pacific.* London: Routledge.

———. 1953. Argonauts of the Western Pacific. An account of native enterprise and adventures in the archipelagoes of Melanesian New Guinea. New York: Dutton.

Marcus, George E. 1986. Contemporary problems of ethnography in the modern world system. In *Writing culture,* ed. James Clifford and George E. Marcus, 165–93. Berkeley: University of California Press.

———. 1994. What comes (just) after "post"? The case of ethnography. In *The handbook of qualitative research*, ed. Norman Denzin and Y. Lincoln, 565–82. Newbury Park CA: Sage.

———. 1998. *Ethnography through thick and thin*. Princeton: Princeton University Press.

Marion, Jean-Luc. 2003. Introduction: What do we mean by "mystic"? In *Mystics: presence and aporia*, ed. Michael Kessler and Christian Sheppard, 1–7. Chicago: University of Chicago Press.

Martin, Joanne. 1982. A garbage can model of the research process. In *Judgment calls in research*, ed. Joseph E. McGrath, Joanne Martin, and Richard A. Kulka. Beverly Hills: Sage.

Mason, Herbert. 1970. *Gilgamesh: A verse narrative*. New York: New American Library.

Maturana, H., and F. Varela. 1998. *The tree of knowledge: The biological roots of human understanding*. Rev. ed. Boston: Shambala.

Mauss, Marcel. 1973. The techniques of the body. Trans. Ben Brewster. *Economy and Society* 2 (1): 70–88.

Maxwell, Joseph A. 1996. *Qualitative research design: An interactive approach*. Thousand Oaks CA: Sage.

McGuire, Meredith B. 1988. *Ritual healing in suburban America*. New Brunswick: Rutgers University Press.

———. 1996. Religion and healing the mind/body/self. *Social Compass* 43:101–16.

Mcilwraith, Thomas. 1996. The problem of imported culture: The construction of contemporary Stó:lō identity. *American Indian Culture and Research Journal* 20 (4): 41–70.

McLuhan, T. C. 1971. *Touch the earth: A self-portrait of Indian existence*. Photographs by Edward S. Curtis. New York: Promontory.

McNaughton, Craig, and Daryl Rock. 2004. Opportunities in aboriginal research. Results of SSHRC's dialogue on research and aboriginal peoples. *Native Studies Review* 15 (2): 37–60.

Meintel, Deirdre. 1984. *Race, culture, and Portuguese colonialism in Cabo Verde*. Syracuse: Maxwell School of Citizenship and Public Affairs Syracuse University.

———. 2002. Transmitting pluralism: Mixed urban unions in Montreal. *Canadian Ethnic Studies* 34:99–120.

———. 2003. La stabilité dans le flou: parcours religieux et identités de spiritualistes. *Anthropologie et sociétés* 27 (1): 35–64.

Menchú, Rigoberta. 1984. *I, Rigoberta Menchú: An Indian woman in Guatemala*, ed. Elisabeth Burgos-Debray. London: Verso.

Meneley, Anne, and Donna J. Young, eds. 2005. *Auto-ethnographies. The anthropology of academic practices*. Peterborough ON: Broadview.

Miller, Bruce. 1998. Ceremonial ties that bind. Paper presented to the American Anthropological Association Annual Meetings, Philadelphia, December 2.

———. 2000. Ecstatic research: Where does it take you? Paper presented in session entitled "Ethnographic objectivity revisited: From rigor to vigor," organized by Jean-Guy A. Goulet and Bruce Miller, at the 27th Congress of the Casca (Canadian Anthropological Society/Société canadienne d'anthropologie), Vancouver, May 4–7.

———. 2002. Salish. In *Aboriginal peoples of Canada: A short introduction*, ed. Paul Robert Magosci, 237–50. Toronto: University of Toronto Press.

Miller, Jay. 1991. A kinship of spirits. In *America in 1492: The world of the Indian people before the arrival of Columbus*, ed. Alvin Josephy, Jr., 305–8. New York: Vintage.

Mills, Antonia. 1994. Making a scientific investigation of ethnographic cases suggestive of reincarnation. In *Being changed by cross-cultural encounters. The anthropology of extraordinary experiences*, ed. David Young and Jean-Guy Goulet, 237–69. Peterborough ON: Broadview.

Mills, Antonia, and Richard Slobodin, eds. 1994. *Amerindian rebirth: Reincarnation beliefs among North American Indians and Inuit*. Toronto: University of Toronto Press.

Minton, Leen. 1995. Interviews. Mumbai, India (March), and Oakland, California (September/October).

Mistry, Aban E. 1984. *Pakhawaj and Tabla: History, schools and traditions*. Trans. Smt. Yasmin E. Tarapore. Mumbai: Pt. Keki S. Jijina Swar Sadhna Samiti.

Mlecko, Joel. 1982. The guru in Hindu tradition. *Numen* 29 (1): 33–61.

Monaghan, John. 1995. *The covenants with earth and rain: Exchange, sacrifice, and revelation in Mixtec sociality*. Norman: University of Oklahoma Press.

Montejo, Victor. 1999. *Voices from exile: Violence and survival in modern Maya history*. Norman: University of Oklahoma Press.

———. 2001. *El Q'anil: Man of lightning a legend of Jacaltenango, Guatemala. In English, Spanish and Popb'al Ti (Jakaltek Maya)*. Tucson: University of Arizona Press.

Morrison, Kenneth. 1994. They act as though they have no relatives: A reply to Geertz. In *On reciprocity and mutual reflection in the study of Native American religions*, ed. Armin W. Geertz. *Religion* 24:1–22.

Naimpally, Anuradha. 1988. The teaching of Bharata Natyam in Canada: Modifications within the Canadian context. MFA thesis in Dance, York University, Toronto.

Nasr, Wren. 2001. Empathy, interpretation, and embodiment: Methodology in Three ethnographies of Nepalese shamanism. Honors thesis, McGill University, Montreal.

Neitz, Mary Jo. 2002. Walking between the worlds: Permeable boundaries, ambiguous identities. In *Personal knowledge and beyond: Reshaping the eth-*

nography of religion, ed. James V. Spickard, J. Shawn Landres, and Meredith B. McGuire, 33–46. New York: New York University Press.

Nelson, Diane M. 1999. *A finger in the wound: Body politics in quincentennial Guatemala*. Berkeley: University of California Press.

Neuman, Daniel. 1974. The cultural structure and social organization of musicians in India: The perspective from Delhi. PhD diss., University of Illinois at Urbana-Champaign.

———. 1980. *The life of music in North India: The organisation of an artistic tradition*. Detroit: Wayne State Univ.

Nuttall, Denise. 1997. The anthropology of apprenticeship: Studying Hindustani musicians in Vancouver. In *Perspectives on South Asia at the threshold of the 21st century. Selected articles from the annual conferences of the South Asia Council 1994–1996*, ed. Reeta Chowdhari Tremblay, 51–58. Montreal: Canadian Asian Studies Association.

———. 1998. Embodying culture: Gurus, disciples and tabla players. PhD diss., Dept. of Anthropology, University of British Columbia, Vancouver.

Nuttall, Mark. 1991. Privileging the body: Indo-Canadian performance in Ontario. MA thesis, Dept. of Anthropology, University of Western Ontario.

———. 1994. The name never dies: Greenland Inuit ideas of the person. In *Amerindian rebirth: Reincarnation beliefs among the North American Indians and Inuit*, ed. A. Mills and R. Slobodin, 123–35. Toronto: University of Toronto Press.

Oberoi, Harjot. 1995. Mapping Indic fundamentalisms through nationalism and modernity. In *Fundamentalisms comprehended*, ed. Martin E. Marty and R. Scott Appleby, 96–114. Chicago: University of Chicago Press.

Obeyesekere, Gananath. 1984. *Medusa's hair: An essay on personal symbols and experience*. Chicago: University of Chicago Press.

———. 1990. *The work of culture: Symbolic transformation in psychoanalysis and anthropology*. Chicago: University of Chicago Press.

Obregon, Luiz Gonzales, ed. 1912. *Procesos de Indios idolatras y hechiceros. Publicaciones del Archivo General de la Nación III*. Mexico: Tip Guerroro Hnos.

O'Donnell, Katherine. 1993. Vision, community, action. *January Term Bulletin*, Hartwick College, Oneonta NY.

Okely, Judith. 1984. Fieldwork in home countries. *Royal Anthropological Institute Newsletter* (61): 4–5.

Okely, Judith, and Helen Callaway, eds. 1992. *Anthropology and autobiography*. London: Routledge.

Orsi, Robert A. 2005. *Between heaven and earth*. In *The religious worlds people make and the scholars who study them*. Princeton: Princeton University Press.

Ortiz, Alphonso. 1969. *The Tewa world: Space, time, being and becoming in a Pueblo society*. Chicago: University of Chicago Press.

Ortner, Sherry B. 1995. Resistance and the problem of ethnographic refusal. *Comparative Studies in Society and History* 37 (1): 173–93.

Otzoy, Irma. 1996a. Maya clothing and identity. In *Maya cultural activism in Guatemala*, ed. Edward F. Fischer and R. McKenna Brown, 141–55. Austin: University of Texas Press.

———. 1996b. *Maya' B'anikil Maya' Tzyaqb'äl (Identidad y Vestuario Maya)*. Guatemala City: Cholsamaj Centro Educativo y Cultural Maya.

Overing, Joanna, and Alan Passes. 2000. Conviviality and the opening up of Amazonian anthropology. In *The anthropology of love and anger. The Aesthetics of conviviality in Native Amazonia*, ed. Joanna Overing and Alan Passes, 1–30. London: Routledge.

Paper, Jordan. 1989. *Offering smoke. The sacred pipe and Native North American religion*. Edmonton: University of Alberta Press.

Pelinski, Ramon. 2000. *El tango nómade: Ensayos sobre la diáspora del tango*. Buenos Aires: Corregidor.

Pelto, Pertti, and Gretel Pelto. 1978. *Anthropological research: The structure of inquiry*. New York: Harper and Row.

Peters, Larry. 1981. *Ecstasy and healing in Nepal: An ethnopsychiatric study of Tamang shamanism*. Malibu CA: Undena.

Petrich, Perla, ed. 1996. *Vida de las mujeres del Lago de Atitlán. Coleccion Palabras del venado*. Serie Memoria de mi pueblo, no. 3. Guatemala: IRIPAZ.

———. 1997. *Pueblos y santos del Lago Atitlán*. Guatemala: Cholsamaj Ediciones, IRIPAZ.

———. 1999. *Historias de la noche en el Lago Atitlán*. Coleccion Xokomil, no. 11. Quetzaltenango, Guatemala: CAEL/MUNI-KAT .

Petterson, Carmen L. 1976. *The Maya of Guatemala: Their life and dress*. Guatemala City: Ixchel Museum.

Pelto, Pertti, and Gretel Pelto. 1978. *Anthropological research: The structure of inquiry*. New York: Harper and Row.

Plath, David. 1990. Fieldnotes, filed Notes, and the conferring of note. In *Fieldnotes: The makings of anthropology*, ed. Roger Sanjek, 371–84. Ithaca: Cornell University Press.

Poirier, Sylvie. 2001. Les politiques du savior rituel: Réflexions sur les relations de genre chez les Kukatja (désert occidental australien). In *Sexe relatif ou sexe absolu? De la distinction de sexe dans les sociétés*, ed. Catherine Alès and Cécile Barraud, 111–34. Paris: Éditions de la Maison des sciences de l'homme.

———. 2003. "This is a good country. We are good dreamers." Dreams and dreaming in the Australian Western Desert. In Dream travelers: Sleep experiences and culture in the Western Pacific, ed. R. Lohmann, 107–25. New York: Palgrave Macmillan.

———. 2004. Ontology, ancestral order, and agencies among the Kukatja of Australian Western Desert. In *Figured worlds. Ontological obstacles in intercultural relations*, ed. John Clammer, Sylvie Poirier, and Eric Schwimmer, 58–82. Toronto: University of Toronto Press.

———. 2005. *A world of relationships. Itineraries, dreams, and events in the Australian Western Desert*. Toronto: University of Toronto Press.

Polo, Anne-Lise. 2001. Appropriation de l'espace et pratiques municipales de gestion de la diversité ethnoculturelle: Le cas des lieux de culte pentecôtistes. Research report, INRS—Urbanisation, Culture et Société; Programme de recherche sur les pratiques municipales de la diversité dans la ville pluriethnique Montréal.

Povinelli, Elizabeth A. 1995. Do rocks listen? The cultural politics of apprehending Australian Aboriginal labor. *American Anthropologist* 97 (3): 505–18.

Rabinow, Paul. 1977. *Reflections on fieldwork in Morocco*. Berkeley: University of California Press.

Radin, Paul. 1963. *The autobiography of a Winnebago Indian*. New York: Dover Publications.

Ranade, Ashok D. 1984. *On music and musicians of Hindoostan*. New Delhi: Promilla.

———. 1990. *Keywords and concepts: Hindustani classical music*. New Delhi: Promilla.

Read, Peter. 1997. Eleven o'clock on the last night of the conference. *The UTS Review* 3 (1): 142–59.

Reed-Danahay, Deborah E. 1997. *Auto/ethnography. Rewriting the self and the social*. New York: Oxford University Press.

Rethmann, Petra. 2000. Skins of desire: Poetry and identity in Koriak women's gift exchange. *American Ethnologist* 1:52–72.

———. 2001. *Tundra passages: History and gender in the Russian Far East*. University Park: Pennsylvania State University Press.

———. 2004. A dream of democracy in the Russian Far East. In *In the way of development: Indigenous peoples, life projects, and globalization*, ed. Mario Blaser, Harvey A. Feit, and Glenn McRae, 256–79. London: Zed.

———. (n.d.) *The moral imagination of the land*. Manuscript.

Richter, Curt P. 1957. On the phenomenon of sudden death in animals and man. *Psychosomatic Medicine* 19:191–98.

Ridington, Robin. 1988a. *Trail to heaven: Knowledge and narrative in a northern community*. Iowa City: University of Iowa Press.

———. 1988b. Knowledge, power, and the individual in Subarctic hunting societies. *American Anthropologist* 90 (1): 98–110.

———. 1990. *Little bit know something: Stories in a language of anthropology*. Vancouver: Douglas and McIntyre.

Robbins, J., and S. Bamford, eds. 1997. Fieldwork revisited: Changing contexts of ethnographic practice in the era of globalizaton. *Anthropology and Humanism* 22:6–30.

Rogers, Mary F. 1983. *Sociology, ethnomethodology, and experience. A phenomenological critique.* ASA Rose Monograph Series of the American Sociological Association. Cambridge: Cambridge University Press.

Rosaldo, Renato. 1989. *Culture and truth: The remaking of social analysis.* Boston: Beacon.

Rose, Deborah. 1999. Taking notice. *Ecological Worldviews, Australian Perspectives,* special edition of *Worldviews: Environment, culture, religion* 3:97–103.

———. 2000 [1992]. *Dingo makes us human: Life and land in an Australian Aboriginal culture.* Cambridge: Cambridge University Press.

———. 2002. *Country of the heart: An indigenous Australian homeland.* Canberra: Aboriginal Studies Press.

———. 2004. *Reports from a wild country: Ethics for decolonisation.* Sydney: University of New South Wales Press.

Rubel, Arthur J. 1977. Limited good and social comparison. *Ethos* 5:224–38.

Rubenstein, Robert A., ed. 1991. *Fieldwork: The correspondence of Robert Redfield and Sol Tax.* Boulder: Westview.

Rushforth, Scott. 1992. The legitimation of beliefs in a hunter–gatherer society: Bearlake Athapaskan knowledge and authority. *American Ethnologist* 19 (3): 483–500.

Ryan, Joan. 1995. *Doing things the right way. Dene traditional justice in Lac La Martre, N.W.T.* Calgary: University of Calgary Press and the Arctic Institute of North America.

Sahagún, Fray Barnardino de. 1979. *Florentine Codex: General history of the things of New Spain.* Books 4 and 5. Trans. Arthur J. O. Anderson and Charles E. Dibble. Salt Lake City: University of Utah Press.

Said, Edward. 1978. *Orientalism.* New York: Pantheon.

———. 1989. Representing the colonized: Anthropology's interlocutors. *Critical Inquiry* 15:205–25.

Salamon, Hagar. 2003. Between conscious and subconscious: Depth-to-depth communication in ethnographic space. *Ethos* 30 (3): 249–72.

Samarin, William J. 1979. Making sense of glossolalic nonsense. *Social Research* 46 (1) 88–105.

Samsi, Yogesh. 1996–98. Interviews with author. Mumbai, India.

Sanjek, Roger. 1990. The secret life of fieldnotes. In *Fieldnotes: The making of anthropology,* ed. Roger Sanjek, 187–270. Ithaca: Cornell University Press.

Savigliano, Marta Elena. 1995. *Tango and the political economy of passion.* Boulder: Westview.

———. 2003. *Angora Matta: Fatal acts of North–South translation.* Middletown CT: Wesleyan University Press.

Scheper-Hughes, Nancy. 2002. Bodies for sale—Whole or in parts. In *Commo-*

difying bodies, ed. Nancy Scheper-Hughes and Loïc Wacquant, 1–8. London: Sage.

Schensul, Stephen L., Jean J. Schensul, and Margaret D. LeCompte. [1946] 1999. *Essential ethnographic methods: Observations, interviews and questionnaires.* Walnut Creek CA: AltaMira.

Shevill, Margot Blum. 1985. *Evolution in textile designs from the Highlands of Guatemala.* Berkeley: Lowie Museum of Anthropology.

Schutz, Alfred. 1964. Making music together: A study in social relationship. In *Collected papers II; Studies in social theory,* ed. Arvid Broderson, 159–79. The Hague: Martinus Nijhoff.

———. 1967. *Collected papers I: The problem of social reality.* The Hague: Martinus Nijhoff.

Schutz, Alfred, and Thomas Luckmann. 1967. *Collected papers I: The problem of social reality.* The Hague: Martinus Nijhoff.

———. 1973. *The structures of the life-world.* Evanston IL: Northwestern University Press.

Schwartz, Regina M. 2003. From ritual to poetry: Herbert's mystical eucharist. In *Mystics: presence and aporia,* ed. Michael Kessler and Christian Sheppard, 138–60. Chicago: University of Chicago Press.

Scott, Joan W. 1992. Experience. In *Feminists theorize the political,* ed. Judith Butler and Joan Scott, 22–40. New York: Routledge.

Searles, Edmund. 1998. From town to outpost camp: Symbolism and social action in the Eastern Canadian Arctic, PhD diss., Dept. of Anthropology, University of Washington, Seattle.

———. 2001a. Interpersonal politics, social science research and the construction of Inuit identity. *Etudes/Inuit/Studies* 25 (1–2): 101–20.

———. 2001b. Fashioning selves and tradition: Case studies on personhood and experience in Nunavut. *American Review of Canadian Studies* 31 (1–2): 121–36.

———. 2002. Food and the making of modern Inuit identities. *Food and Foodways* 10 (1–2): 55–78.

Sharp, Henry S. 1987. Giant fish, giant otters and dinosaurs, apparently irrational beliefs in a Chipewyan community. *American Ethnologist* 14 (2): 226–35.

———. 1988. *The transformation of Big Foot: Maleness, power and belief among the Chipewyan.* Washington DC: Smithsonian Institution Press.

Shweder, Richard A. 1991. *Thinking through cultures: Expeditions in cultural psychology.* Cambridge MA: Harvard University Press.

Shestov, Lev. 1970. Children and stepchildren of time: Spinoza in history. In *Speculation and revelation. A Shestov anthology.* Trans. B. Martin. Athens OH: Ohio University Press.

———. 1982. *Speculation and revelation. A Shestov anthology.* Trans. B. Martin. Athens OH: Ohio University Press.

Shore, Bradd. 1999. Strange fate of holism. *Anthropology News*. December.

Simonelli, Jeanne. 1986. *Two boys, a girl, and enough!: Reproductive and economic decision-making on the Mexican periphery*. Boulder: Westview.

———. 2000. Service learning abroad: Lessons about liability and learning. *Metropolitan Universities* 11 (1): 35–44.

Simonelli, Jeanne, and Duncan Earle. 2003. Meeting resistance: Autonomy, development, and "informed permission" in Chiapas, Mexico. *Qualitative Inquiry* 9 (February): 74–89.

Simonelli, Rachel. 2002. The patience to see; the courage to act: Anthropology beyond the classroom. Paper presented at the annual meeting of the American Anthropological Association, New Orleans LA, November.

Smith, Carol A. 1991. Maya nationalism. NACLA *Report on the Americas* 23 (3): 29–33.

Smith, Carolyn D., and Wiliam Kornblum. 1996. *Readings on the field research experience*. 2nd ed. London: Praeger.

Smith, Robert. 1990. Hearing voices, joining the chorus: Appropriating someone else's fieldnotes. In *Fieldnotes: The makings of anthropology*, ed. Roger Sanjek, 356–70. Ithaca: Cornell University Press.

Smith, Tuhiwai Linda. 1999. *Decolonizing methodologies: Research and indigenous people*. New York: Zed.

Spagna, Francesco, and Guy Lanoue, curatori. 2001. Introduzione a "La forza nelle parole." I percorsi narrativi degli indigeni canadesi da Jacques Cartier a oggi. *Rivista Di Studi Canadesi / Canadian Studies Review / Revue d'études canadiennes* 13 supp.: 11–16.

Spiro, Melford. 1987a. Collective representations and mental representations in religious symbol systems. In *Culture and nature: Theoretical papers of Melford Spiro*, ed. Benjamin Kilborne and L. L. Langness, 161–84. Chicago: University of Chicago Press.

———. 1987b. Is the Oedipus complex universal? In *Culture and nature: theoretical papers of Melford Spiro*, ed. Benjamin Kilborne and L. L. Langness, 72–103. Chicago: University of Chicago Press.

Spivak, G. C. 1988. Can the subaltern speak? In *Marxism and the interpretation of culture*, ed. Cary Nelson and Lawrence Grossberg, 271–313. Chicago: University of Illinois Press.

Spradley, James P. 1979. *The ethnographic interview*. New York: Holt, Rinehart and Winston.

Ssorin-Chaikov, Nikolai V. 2003. *The social life of the state in Subarctic Siberia*. Stanford: Stanford University Press.

Stoller, Paul, and Cheryl Olkes. 1987. *In sorcery's shadow: A memoir of apprenticeship among the Songhay of Niger*. Chicago: University of Chicago Press.

Stoller, Paul. 1989a. *The taste of ethnographic things: The senses in anthropology*. Philadelphia: University of Philadelphia Press.

————. 1989b. Speaking in the name of the real. *Cahiers d'études africaines* 113:113–25.

————. 1995. *Embodying colonial memories: Spirit possession, power and the Hauka in West Africa.* New York: Routledge.

————. 2004. *Stranger in the village of the sick: A memoir of cancer, sorcery and healing.* Boston: Beacon.

Sudnow, David. 1978. *Ways of the hand, the organization of improvised conduct.* Cambridge MA: Harvard University Press.

Taussig, Michael. 1987. *Shamanism, colonialism, and the wild man: A study in terror and healing.* Chicago: University of Chicago Press.

————. 1993. *Mimesis and alterity.* New York: Routledge.

————. 2004. *My cocaine museum.* Chicago: University of Chicago Press.

TCPS. 1998. *The Tri-Council policy statement: Ethical conduct for research involving humans.* Rev. 2002 and 2003. Ottawa: Medical Research Council (MRC), Natural Sciences and Engineering Research Council (NSERC), and Social Sciences and Humanities Research Council (SSHRC). http://www.ncehr-cnersh.org/english/code_2.

Tedlock, Barbara. 1991. From participant observation to observation of participation. *Journal of Anthropological Research* 47:69–94.

————. 1992. Dreaming and dream research. In *Dreaming: Anthropological and psychological interpretations,* ed. Barbara Tedlock, 1–30. Santa Fe: School of American Research Press.

Tedlock, Dennis. 1995. Interpretation, participation, and the role of narrative in dialogical anthropology. In *The dialogic emergence of culture,* ed. Dennis Tedlock and Bruce Mannheim, 253–87. Urbana: University of Illinois Press.

————. 1997. The poetics of time in Mayan divination. In *Poetry and prophecy: The anthropology of inspiration,* ed. John Leavitt, 77–92. Ann Arbor: University of Michigan Press.

Thom, Brian. 2004. Review of *At home with the Bella Coola Indians: T. F. McIlwraith's field letters, 1922–4,* ed. John Barker and Douglas Cole. *Anthropologica* 46 (1): 116–17.

Toelken, Barre. 1996. From entertainment to realization in Navajo fieldwork. In *The world observed. Reflections on the fieldwork process,* ed. Bruce Jackson and Edward D. Ives, 1–16. Chicago: University of Illinois Press.

Trigger, Bruce. 1995. Conflicts and blind spots: Can non-native scholars write a history of the native peoples of North America? Paper presented at the McGill Institute for the Study of Canada, Sixth Seminar, Montreal, March 28.

Tsurumi, E. Patricia. 1990. *Factory girls: Women in the thread of Meiji Japan.* Princeton: Princeton University Press.

Tungilik, Victor, and Rachel Uyarasuk. 1999. The transition to Christianity, Volume 1. In *Inuit perspectives on the 20th century,* ed. Jarich Oosten and Frédéric Laugrand. Iqaluit: Nunavut Arctic College.

Turnbull, Colin. 1972. *The mountain people.* New York: Simon and Schuster.
———. 1990. Liminality: A synthesis of subjective and objective experience. In *By means of performance: Intercultural studies of theatre and ritual,* ed. R. Schechner and W. Appel, 50–81. Cambridge: Cambridge University Press.
Turner, David H. 2002. *The spirit lives. A personal journey from loss to understanding through religious experience.* New York: Peter Lang.
———. 1999. *Genesis regained: Aboriginal forms of renunciation in Judeo-Christian scriptures and other major traditions.* New York: Peter Lang.
———. 1989. *Return to Eden: Journey through the promised landscape of Amagalyuagba.* New York: Peter Lang.
———. 1987. *Life before Genesis, a conclusion: An understanding of the significance of Australian Aboriginal culture.* New York: Peter Lang.
Turner, David H., and P. Wertman. 1977. *Shamattawa: The structure of social relations in a Northern Algonkian band.* Ottawa: National Museum of Canada, Canadian Ethnology Service Paper No. 36.
Turner, Edith, with William Blodgett, Singleton Kahona, and Benwa Fideli. 1992. *Experiencing ritual: A new interpretation of African healing.* Philadelphia: University of Pennsylvania Press.
Turner, Edith. 1994a. A visible spirit form in Zambia. In *Being changed by cross-cultural encounters. The anthropology of extraordinary experiences,* ed. David Young and Jean-Guy Goulet, 71–95. Peterborough ON: Broadview.
———. 1994b. The effect of contact on religion of Inupiat hunters. In *Circumpolar religion and ecology: An anthropology of the North,* ed. Takashi Irimoto and Takako Yamada, 143–62. Tokyo: University of Tokyo Press.
———. 1996. *The hands feel it: Healing and spirit presence among a Northern Alaskan people.* DeKalb IL: Northern Illinois University Press.
Turner, Victor, and Edith Turner. 1978. *Image and pilgrimage in Christian culture: Anthropological perspectives.* New York: Columbia University Press.
Turner, Victor. 1968. *The drums of affliction: A study of religious process among the Ndembu of Zambia.* Oxford: Clarendon.
———. 1975. *Revelation and divination.* Ithaca: Cornell University Press.
———. 1985. *On the edge of the bush: Anthropology as experience,* ed. Edith L. B. Turner. Tuscon: University of Arizona Press.
Underhill, Evelyn. 1995. *Concerning the inner life.* Oxford: One World.
Valentine, Lisa Phillips, and Regna Darnell, eds. 1999. *Theorizing the Americanist tradition.* Toronto: University of Toronto Press.
van den Hoonaard, Will C. 2002. Introduction: Ethical norming and qualitative research. In *Walking the tightrope. Ethical issues for qualitative researchers,* ed. Will C. Van denHoonaard, 3–16. Toronto: Toronto of University Press.
Van Maanen, John. 1988. *Tales of the field: On writing ethnography.* Chicago: University of Chicago Press.
———. 1995. An end to innocence: The ethnography of ethnography. In *Representation in ethnography,* ed. John Van Maanen, 1–35. London: Sage.

Vdovin, Innokentii St. 1973. *Ocherki etnicheskoi istorii Koriakov (Essays on the ethnic history of the Koriaks)*. Leningrad: Nauka.

Viladrich, Anahí. 2003. Social careers, social capital, and immigrants' access barriers to health care: The case of the Argentine minority in New York City. PhD diss., Graduate School of Arts and Sciences, Columbia University, New York.

———. 2004a. From the brothel to the salon: The tango's social history as an evolving artistic trend. *The Lost Notebook* 2 (January). http://www.wallis knot.org.

———. 2004b. Tango immigrants in New York City. *Journal of Contemporary Ethnography*. Submitted for publication.

Vonnegut, Kurt. 1963 [1998]. *Cat's cradle*. New York: Dell.

Wagner, Roy. 1979. The talk of Koriki: A Daribi contact cult. *Social Research* 46 (10): 140–65.

Waldram, James B. 1997. *The way of the pipe. Aboriginal spirituality and symbolic healing in Canadian prisons*. Peterborough ON: Broadview.

Warren, Kay B. 1998. *Indigenous movements and their critics. Pan Maya activism in Guatemala*. Princeton: Princeton University Press.

Watanabe, John M. 1990. From saints to shibboleths: Images, structure and identity. *American Ethnologist* 17 (1): 131–50.

Watson, Graham, and Jean-Guy A. Goulet. 1992. Gold in, gold out: The objectivation of Dene Tha dreams and visions. *Journal of Anthropological Research* 48 (3): 215–30.

Watson, Graham, and Ann Irwin. 1996. The mundane miracle of social order. *Ethnos* 61 (1–2): 85–102.

Webb, Eugene J. 1966. *Unobtrusive measures. Nonreactive research in the social sciences*. Chicago: Rand McNally.

Weber, Max. 1946. Science as a vocation. In *From Max Weber: Essays in sociology*, ed. H. H. Gerth and C. Wright Mills, 129–56. New York: Oxford University Press.

Weber-Pillwax, Cora. 2004. Indigenous researchers and indigenous research methods: Cultural influences or cultural determinants of research methods. *Pimatisiwin* (Spring): 77–90.

Weiner, Michael, ed. 1997. *Japan's minorities: The illusion of homogeneity*. London: Routledge.

Wernitznig, Dagmar. 2003. *Going native or going naive? White shamanism and the neo-noble savage*. Boston: University Press of America.

Weitlaner, Roberto, and Irmgard Weitlaner. 1946. The Mazatec calendar. *American Antiquity* 11:194–97.

White, Jerry P. 2003. Introduction: The focus of aboriginal conditions. In *Aboriginal conditions: Research as a foundation for public policy*, ed. Jerry P. White, Paul S. Maxim, and Dan Beavon, xxiii–xxvii. Vancouver: University of British Columbia Press.

White, Merry. 2001. *Perfectly Japanese: Making families in an era of upheaval.* Berkeley: University of California Press.

Whitehead, Tony, and Mary Ellen Conaway, eds. 1986. Self, sex, and gender. In *Cross-cultural fieldwork.* Urbana: University of Illinois Press.

Wierzbicka, Anna. 1989. Soul and mind: Linguistic evidence for ethnopsychology and cultural history. *American Anthropologist* 91 (1): 41–58.

Wikan, Unni. 1991. Toward an experience-near anthropology. *Cultural Anthropology* 6 (3): 285–305.

Williams, Rowan. 2002. *Ponder these things: Praying with icons of the Virgin.* Franklin WI: Sheed and Ward.

Williamson, R. G. 1988. Some aspects of the history of Eskimo naming system. *Folk* 30:245–63.

Wilson, C. Roderick. 1994. Seeing they see not. In *Being changed by cross-cultural encounters: The anthropology of extraordinary experiences,* ed. David E. Young and Jean-Guy A. Goulet, 197–208. Petersborough ON: Broadview.

Windhausen, R. A. 2001. El fenómeno del tango en Nueva York. *La Gaceta* (Tucumán, Argentina), February 28, sección literaria.

Wolcott, Harry F. 1999. *Ethnography: A way of seeing.* Walnut Creek CA: AltaMira.

Wolf, Erik. 1982. *Europe and the people without history.* Berkeley: University of California Press.

Young, David E., and Jean-Guy A. Goulet, eds. 1994 [1998]. *Being changed by cross-cultural encounters. The anthropology of extraordinary experience.* Peterborough ON: Broadview.

Young, David E. 1994. Visitors in the night: A creative energy model of spontaneous visions. In *Being changed by cross-cultural encounters. The anthropology of extraordinary experience,* ed. David E. Young and Jean-Guy Goulet, 166–94. Peterborough ON: Broadview.

Zammito, John H. 2002. *Kant. Herder. The birth of anthropology.* Chicago: University of Chicago Press.

Zaretsky, Irving I. 1974. In the beginning was the word: The relationship of language to social organization in Spiritualist churches. In *Religious movements in contemporary America,* ed. Irving I. Zaretsky and Mark P. Leone, 166–222. Princeton: Princeton University Press.

Zarrilli, Phillip. 1984. Doing the exercise: The in-body transmission of performance knowledge in a traditional martial art. *Asian Theatre Journal* 1 (Fall): 191–206.

———. 1987. Where the hand [is] . . . *Asian Theatre Journal* 4 (1): 205–15.

———. 1990. What does it mean to 'Become the character': Power, presence, transcendence in Asian in-body discipline of practice. In *By means of performance,* ed. Richard Schechner and Willa Appel, 131–49.

List of Contributors

Edward Abse, University of Richmond, has conducted research on Mexico, with an emphasis on indigenous cultures of Oaxaca, social and religious change, shamanism and sorcery (witchcraft), ritual and cosmology, ecstatic and visionary experience and culture, and ethnographic methods and fieldwork ethics. He is the translator with notes and annotations of the first bilingual edition of Alejandro Mendez Aquino's classic *Noche e Rabanos: An Ethnohistory of Oaxacan Wintertime Customs and Celebrations* (Oaxaca: Instituto Oaxaqueno de la Culturas, 1997), and the author of "Maria Sabina," a biographical article about the renowned Mazatec shamaness in the *Oxford Encyclopedia of Mesoamerican Cultures: the Civilizations of Mexico and Central America* (2001).

Millie Creighton, University of British Columbia, specializes in the study of East Asia and serves on the Executive Management Boards of both the Centre for Japanese Research and the Centre for Korean Research at the University of British Columbia. In 1998 she received the international Canon Foundation Prize for her article "Pre-Industrial Dreaming in Post-Industrial Japan: Department Stores and the Commoditization of Community Traditions." Her extensive research on popular culture, and representational images in Japan, includes work on the imaging of children and the imaging of foreigners, particularly Canada and Canadians.

Duncan Earle, Clark University, Massachusetts, has research interests in the social and cultural anthropology of Mesoamerica, with a particular focus on comparative efforts at development in Guatemala and Chiapas, Mexico. A published poet and performance artist, he lives in the borderlands when not away in the Northeast teaching community development from an anthropological perspective. He most recently finished, with Jeanne Simonelli, *Uprising of Hope: Zapatistas and Alternative Development in Chiapas* (AltaMira Press, Walnut Creek CA) (2005).

Peter M. Gardner, professor emeritus from the University of Missouri, has specialized in the study of hunters and gatherers in Southern India and in the Canadian Subarctic. His extensive body of work deals with culture contact and ecological adaptation, the so-called individualism of hunter–gatherers, the anthropology of knowledge, and the structure of classical Hindu civilization. His more recent publications include: "Respect and Nonviolence among Recently Sedentary Foragers," *Journal of the Royal Anthropological Institute* 6 (2000):215–36; *Bicultural Versatility as a Frontier Adaptation among Paliyan Foragers of South India* (2000), and "Respect for All: The Paliyans of South India," in *Keeping the Peace: Conflict Resolution and Peaceful Societies around the World* (2004).

Jean-Guy A. Goulet, Saint Paul University (Ottawa), investigates the many dimensions of the social life of the Wayu of Venezuela and Columbia and of the Dene Tha of northwestern Alberta. He is the co-editor of *Being Changed by Cross-Cultural Encounters: The Anthropology of Extraordinary Experiences* (1994), and is author of *Ways of Knowing: Experience, Knowledge and Power among the Dene Tha* (1998), and of numerous book chapters and journal articles on Dene Tha religious, political, and social life.

Guy Lanoue, Université de Montréal, carried out fieldwork between 1978 and 1979 among the Sekani, nomadic hunters in north-central British Columbia, Canada, and in 1999 and 2000 among the Roman bourgeoisie. His publications include *Brothers: The Politics of Violence among the Sekani of Northern British Columbia* (1992) and *Beyond Values and Ideology: Tales from Six North American Indian Peoples* (1990). He is the translator of Eleazar Meletinsky's *The Poetics of Myth* published by Routledge in 2000.

Deirdre Meintel, Université de Montréal, is director of the Groupe de Recherche Ethnicité et Société. Her research interests focus on migration; urban anthropology, religion, and modernity; transnationalism; ethnicity; plural identities; and globalization. She was co-editor, with Sylvie Fortin, of a special issue of *Canadian Ethnic Studies* entitled *The New French Fact in Montreal: Francization, Diversity, Globalization* (2002) and the guest editor for a special issue of *Anthropologie et Sociétés* on religion in movement (2003).

Bruce Granville Miller, University of British Columbia, is involved in the comparative study of political and legal issues facing indigenous peoples and the problems in the production of knowledge in anthropology. He has served as an expert witness in indigenous litigation in the United States and Canada and is co-director of the UBC graduate ethnographic field school. He has recently published *The Problem of Justice: Tradition and Law in the Coast Salish World* (2001) and *Invisible Indigenes: The Politics of Nonrecognition* (2003). *"Be of Good Mind": Essays on the Coast Salish* (University of British Columbia Press) will appear in 2007.

Denise Nuttall, York University, has as research interests embodiment and cultural theory; anthropology of the body and performance; apprenticeship as a method in the social sciences; South Asia, India, and the South Asian diaspora; indigenous knowledge systems; postcolonial anthropology; transnational, transcultural, and intercultural studies; and ethnomusicology. She is currently researching a book entitled *A Biography of Tabla: Following the Masters*.

Petra Rethmann, McMaster University, has specialized in issues of indigenous and political culture in the Chukotka and Kamchatka peninsulas in the Russian Far East, with particular attention to issues of gender, history, and the politics of cultural imaginations. The recipient of awards from the Social Sciences and Research Council of Canada, the DAAD (German Academic Exchange Service), and the Woodrow Wilson Center in Washington DC, she has taught as a visiting professor at the University of Chicago. She is the author of *Tundra Passages: Gender and History in the Russian Far East* (2001), and numerous articles in edited volumes and journals.

Deborah Bird Rose, Centre for Research and Environmental Studies, Institute of Advanced Studies, The Australian National University. Her work with Aboriginal people is focused on social and ecological justice. She is the author of *Country of the Heart: An Indigenous Australian Homeland* (2002), *Nourishing Terrains: Australian Aboriginal Views of Landscape and Wilderness, Dingo Makes Us Human* (winner of the 1992/1993 Stanner Prize), and *Hidden Histories* (winner of the 1991 Jessie Litchfield Award). Her most recent book is with University of New South Wales Press: *Reports from a Wild Country: Ethics for Decolonisation*.

Edmund Searles, Bucknell University, specializes in the study of personal and cultural identity among the Inuit of Nunavut, Canada, and in the investigation of the changing nature of social and human–environment relations in the circumpolar North. He is currently researching Anglican Inuit spirituality in the Canadian Arctic. He has published the results of his investigations in *Anthropologie et Sociétés*, *Études/Inuit/Studies*, and the *Annual Review of Canadian Studies*.

Jeanne Simonelli, Wake Forest University, is the new editor of *Practicing Anthropology* and is co-director of the Maya Study Program, which teaches undergraduate students in anthropology to conduct field research. She has received the 2000 prize for poetry from the Society for Humanistic Anthropology for her poetry and short stories based on field experiences. Among her publications, one notes *Two Boys, A Girl, and Enough!* (1986), *Too Wet to Plow: The Family Farm in Transition* (1992), and *Crossing between Worlds: The Navajos of Canyon de Chelly* (1997). From Alta Mira Press, and co-authored with Duncan Earle, is her latest book: *Uprising of Hope: Sharing the Zapatista Journey to Alternative Development*.

Janferie Stone, PhD candidate at the University of California, Davis. She studies practices of the everyday, such as the narration of tales, especially among Maya women, to create degrees of consciousness, intentionality, and the will to work against violence to create worlds within which they can themselves be authentic and free. She has presented results of her investigations at recent meetings of the American Anthropological Association, including an earlier version of the paper published in this book first presented at the AAA Chicago meetings in 2004.

Anahí Viladrich, Hunter College, City University of New York. Director of the "Immigration and Health Initiative" funded by the School of Health Sciences, she has research interests in immigrant health and unequal access to health resources, social networks, and ethnic enclaves and niches (including the tango world), and ethnographic approaches to the study of ethnomedical systems. She is the recipient of the Marisa De Castro Benton Prize at Columbia University for her dissertation on Argentine immigrants in New York City, which is soon to appear as a book.

Barbara Wilkes, University of Alberta School of Native Studies, has directed her recent research on the social construction and lived experience of disability (spinal-cord injury) among the Kanai (Blood Tribe) of Southern Alberta. She has presented several papers at conferences regarding the Native experience of disability and her own experiences as a Sundancer. The title of her PhD dissertation is *Máátsikómatapíikssis "Broken People": The Lived Experience of Spinal Cord Injury among the Kainai.*

Index

DATE DUE

Demco, Inc. 38-293